THIS IS
VOCA

VOCABULARY

For Advanced Learners

THIS IS VOCABULARY 고급

지은이 권기하
펴낸이 임상진
펴낸곳 (주)넥서스

출판신고 1992년 4월 3일 제311-2002-2호 2-13
10880 경기도 파주시 지목로 5
Tel (02)330-5500 Fax (02)330-5555

ISBN 979-11-6165-206-1 54740
      979-11-6165-203-0 (SET)

www.nexusbook.com

어휘의
달인이 되는

THIS IS

VOCA

VOCABULARY

권기하 지음

고급
For Advanced
Learners

NEXUS Edu

Preface

영어에서 어휘는 듣기·말하기·읽기·쓰기의 기초를 이루는 핵심적인 요소입니다. 그리고 학습자들의 영어 실력이 높아질수록 어휘가 차지하는 비중이 높아집니다. 즉, 독해지문 읽기와 대화에서 발음이나 문법을 몰라서라기보다는 어휘의 정확한 의미나 쓰임을 알지 못해 문맥을 이해하는 데 어려움을 느끼거나 제대로 활용할 수 없는 경우가 많습니다. 더군다나 초등학교의 영어 노출 시기가 앞당겨지면서 중학교와 고등학교 과정에서 요구하는 어휘의 수준은 점점 높아지고 있습니다. 실제 각종 시험이나 수능에서 느끼는 체감 난이도도 평상시보다 높다는 것을 알 수 있습니다. 이것은 교과서나 한 권의 어휘 교재만으로는 해결할 수 없음을 의미합니다.

그렇다면 어떻게 어휘를 효과적으로 학습할 수 있을까요? 무조건 많은 양의 어휘를 기계적으로 외우기만 하면 될까요? 단순히 많은 양의 영단어를 암기하는 것도 어휘 학습의 한 방법이긴 합니다. 하지만 이러한 방법으로는 무수히 많은 어휘를 학습하기는 불가능하며, 암기하더라도 금방 잊어버리거나 외운 단어를 실제 생활이나 시험에서는 활용할 수 없게 됩니다. 따라서 단순히 어휘의 정의만이 아니라, 연어 또는 회화나 독해를 통해 문맥 속에서 어휘의 의미를 유추하고, 중심 개념, 어원의 이해 등을 통해 체계적으로 학습하는 것이 중요합니다.

〈This Is Vocabulary 최신개정판〉 시리즈는 어휘를 주제별로 정리해 의미의 연계성을 통해 학습자들이 각각의 어휘를 자연스럽게 학습하고 기억할 수 있도록 했습니다. 그리고 어휘 수준에 따라 초급, 중급, 고급, 어원편 등으로 구성, 다양한 어휘 활동을 추가하였으며, 학습 효과를 극대화하기 위해 빈도가 높은 연어, 파생어, 예문 등을 제시했습니다.

〈This Is Vocabulary 최신개정판〉 시리즈를 통해 언어의 기본 단위인 어휘를 효과적으로 학습하고 더 나아가 이 책의 다양한 어휘 학습 장치를 통해 영어의 4가지 skill을 모두 향상시킬 수 있었으면 합니다.

권기하

이것이 더 강력해진
"THIS IS VOCA" 시리즈다!

✏️ 효과적인 주제별 어휘 학습

〈This Is Vocabulary 최신개정판〉 시리즈는 어휘를 주제별로 분류하여, 학습자들이 각각의 어휘를 연상 작용을 통해 효과적으로 암기하고 쉽게 기억할 수 있도록 구성하였습니다.

✏️ 문맥을 통한 어휘 학습

어휘는 단독으로 사용되지 않으므로 예문이나 어구의 형태에서 확인하는 과정이 필요합니다. 따라서 단순히 주제와 관련된 어휘만을 나열한 것이 아니라, 연어, 파생어, 주제와 관련된 예문을 함께 제시하여 가능한 한 다양한 표현을 반영, 문맥을 통해 학습할 수 있도록 구성하였습니다.

✏️ 입문(주니어)부터 수능완성, 고급 단계까지의 연계성

어휘 학습이 체계적이고 단계적으로 이루어질 수 있도록 입문(주니어)부터 초급, 중급, 수능 완성, 어원편, 고급, 그리고 뉴텝스까지 시리즈로 구성했습니다. 각 단계에 맞는 표제어를 선정하고 적절한 예문, 수능 기출 예문, 그리고 추가 어휘를 제시하여 보다 효과적으로 학습할 수 있도록 구성하였습니다.

✏️ 다양한 학습 방법

레벨에 따라 Word Search, Word Bubbles, Crossword Puzzles, Word Mapping 등 다양한 활동을 추가함으로써 앞서 배운 어휘를 복습하는 과정을 자연스럽게 즐길 수 있도록 구성하였습니다. 또한 언제 어디서나 학습이 가능하도록 모바일로 영/미 발음을 확인하고, 모바일 VOCA TEST를 통해 자기주도학습을 할 수 있는 최적화된 학습 시스템을 제공합니다.

Features

Thematic Grouping

시험에 자주 등장하는 주요 고급 어휘를 9개의 chapter, 48개의 unit으로 정리하고, 각각의 unit에는 엄선된 40개의 고급 표제어(약 2,000개)를 소개합니다. 각 unit은 테마별로 분류되어 있어서 단어가 쓰이는 상황, 장소, 분야에 따라 해당 단어를 함께 학습할 수 있습니다.

품사 표시

n 명사 **v** 동사 **a** 형용사 **ad** 부사
conj 접속사 **prep** 전치사 **ant** 반의어
syn 동의어 **c.f.** 비교

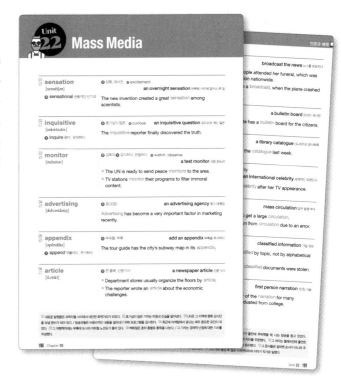

Collocation

두세 단어의 짧은 collocation(연어)을 통해서 표제어가 어떤 어휘와 주로 같이 쓰이고 의미가 어떻게 확장되는지 배울 수 있습니다.

01 **sensation**
[senséiʃən]
n 감동, 대사건 **⊝** excitement
an overnight sensation 하룻밤 사이에 일어난 큰 일
a sensational 선풍적인 인기의
The new invention created a great sensation among scientists.

Word Family

파생어 및 유의어/반의어까지 정리되어 있어 표제어의 의미를 더 정확히 알 수 있고 어휘의 배경지식을 향상시키는 데 큰 도움이 됩니다.

★ The news was dispatched throughout the nation very quickly yesterday.

ⓥ (주의를) 딴 데로 돌리다 **distract one's attention** ~의 관심을 딴 곳으로 돌리다

Some people argue that the press distracts people from certain issues.

ⓝ 취재, 적용 범위　　　　　　**in-depth news coverage** 심층 취재

★ Every major newspaper gave front-page coverage about

Sample Sentence

교과서, 시험 문제에 자주 나오는 문장 유형을 반영한 예문을 통해서 해당 어휘가 실제로 어떻게 쓰이는지 파악할 수 있으며 독해 실력의 기본을 탄탄하게 쌓을 수 있습니다.

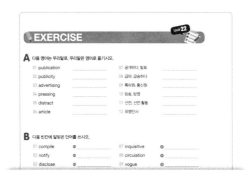

Exercise

어휘의 기본기를 확인하는 마무리 문제를 통해서 배운 단어를 복습, 점검할 수 있습니다.

Crossword Puzzle

Unit마다 앞에서 배운 단어를 영영풀이 퍼즐을 통해 사전적 의미를 정확히 확인할 수 있습니다.

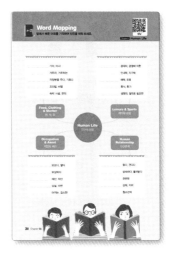

Word Mapping

Chapter에서 배운 단어를 테마별로 나누어 정리하며 복습할 수 있습니다. 주제별 어휘를 함께 묶어봄으로써 단어들을 효과적으로 더 오래 암기할 수 있습니다.

언제 어디서든
THIS IS VOCA를
모바일로 학습하자!

MP3 듣기
VOCA TEST
정답 확인

QR코드를 찍으면 아래의 모든 것이 가능합니다!

어휘/뜻/예문 듣기
영/미 발음 MP3 제공

모바일 VOCA TEST로
게임을 통해 복습하기

Crossword Puzzle
정답 확인하기

Word Mapping
정답 확인하기

추가 제공 자료   www.nexusbook.com

❶ 어휘리스트/테스트   ❸ MP3 음원
❷ 테스트 도우미   ❹ 혼동 어휘 단어장

Contents

"THIS IS VOCA 고급"을
얼마나 알고 있는지 VOCA?

☑ 자신이 아는 단어를 체크하고 그 의미를 제대로 알고 있는지 확인해 보세요!

□ abandon	□ assignment	□ atmosphere	□ biological	□ cognitive
□ confirm	□ considerate	□ cooperate	□ countless	□ criminal
□ demolish	□ enhance	□ essential	□ expenditure	□ extinct
□ fiction	□ flammable	□ forbid	□ harsh	□ intersection
□ jealous	□ reluctant	□ revoke	□ sorrow	□ substance
□ symptom	□ tolerate	□ transmit	□ urge	□ vivid

맞은 개수	권장 학습 방법
0~15	음원을 여러 번 듣고 따라 말하며, 직접 어휘도 써 보면서 반복 학습을 통해 공부해 보세요! 모바일 VOCA TEST로 학습한 내용을 수시로 점검해 보는 것이 어휘 암기에 큰 도움이 됩니다!
16~25	단어의 의미를 좀 더 깊게 파고들기 위해서는 표제어의 파생어도 함께 암기하는 것이 좋습니다. 또한 Exercise 문제도 빠짐없이 풀어 본다면 더욱 더 향상된 어휘력을 갖출 수 있습니다.
26~30	상당한 어휘 실력을 갖고 있네요! 단어와 뜻 그 자체도 중요하지만, 문장에서 해당 단어가 어떻게 쓰이는지 주어진 예문을 통해서 공부한다면 상당한 양의 어휘를 단숨에 마스터할 수 있습니다.

어휘 뜻 확인하기

☑ ____ / 30

□ 포기하다	□ 과제, 숙제	□ 대기, 분위기	□ 생물학적인	□ 인식의
□ 확실히 하다	□ 사려 깊은	□ 협력하다	□ 수많은	□ 범인; 범죄의
□ 파괴하다	□ 향상시키다	□ 필수의	□ 지출, 소비	□ 멸종한
□ 소설, 허구	□ 가연성의	□ 금지하다	□ 거친	□ 교차로
□ 질투심이 많은	□ 마지못해 하는	□ 취소하다	□ 슬픔	□ 물질, 재료
□ 증상, 징후	□ 참다, 견디다	□ 전하다	□ 재촉하다	□ 생생한

Chapter
01

Language and Knowledge

Unit 01 Speech & Expression

---

01 ☑ **bilingual**
[bailíŋgwəl]

ⓝ **bilingualism** 2개 국어 병용

ⓐ 2개 국어를 쓰는, 두 나라 말을 하는　　　**bilingual broadcast** 음성 다중 방송

Her bilingual ability helped her to get a job quickly.

---

02 ☑ **boastful**
[bóustfəl]

ⓥ **boast** 자랑하다

ⓐ 자랑하는, 허풍 떠는　　　**boastful look** 자랑스러운 표정

His boastful speech made us more confused about the purpose of the seminar.

---

03 ☑ **censure**
[sénʃər]

ⓝ 비난, 책망 ⓥ 비난하다, 나무라다　⊜ blame

censure a person for a fault ~의 잘못을 나무라다

★ Despite international censure, North Korea conducted its second nuclear test.

★ I censured him when I heard that he stole my book.

---

04 ☑ **chuckle**
[tʃʌ́kl]

ⓐⓓ **chucklingly** 웃으면서

ⓥ 낄낄 웃다, (혼자서) 기뻐하다　　　**chuckle out loud** 크게 소리 내어 웃다

I chuckled while watching a movie and dropped my popcorn.

---

05 ☑ **proposition**
[pràpəzíʃən]

ⓥ **propose** 제안하다

ⓝ 제의, 제안, 진술　⊜ proposal 제의, 제안

accept a proposition 제의를 받아들이다

Your proposition will be accepted by the committee.

---

06 ☑ **consent**
[kənsént]

ⓝ 동의, 승낙 ⓥ 동의하다, 찬성하다　⊜ assent 동의하다

written consent 서면 동의

★ She sent me a letter of consent to work with her company.

★ She will consent to participate in his experiment.

---

01 그녀의 2개 국어를 쓰는 능력이 그녀가 빨리 취업할 수 있게 했다.　02 그의 허풍스러운 발표는 우리를 그 세미나의 목적에 대해 더 헷갈리게 했다. 03 국제적인 비난에도, 북한은 두 번째 핵실험을 감행했다. / 나는 그가 내 책을 훔쳤다는 말을 들었을 때 그를 비난했다.　04 나는 영화를 보면서 낄낄 웃다가 팝콘을 떨어뜨렸다.　05 너의 제안은 위원회에서 받아들여질 것이다.　06 그녀는 자신의 동료와 같이 일하겠다는 동의서를 보냈다. / 그녀는 그의 실험에 참여하는 것에 동의할 것이다.

---

07 **consult**
[kənsʌ́lt]
ⓝ consultant 상담자

Ⓥ 참고하다, 상담하다, 진찰 받다 · · · · · · · **consult the plans** 계획을 참고하다

Before starting an exercise program, you should consult your doctor.

---

08 **contradiction**
[kɑ̀ntrədíkʃən]
Ⓥ contradict 부정하다, 반박하다

ⓝ 부인, 부정, 모순 · Ⓔ denial · · · · · · **a direct contradiction** 직접적인 반박

The result of the vote count was in contradiction to the predictions suggested by him.

---

09 **convincing**
[kənvínsiŋ]
Ⓥ convince ~에게 납득시키다

ⓐ 설득력 있는, 납득이 가게 하는 · Ⓔ persuasive

a convincing answer 설득력 있는 답변

They ordered me to give a convincing argument.

---

10 **demonstrate**
[démənstrèit]

Ⓥ 증명하다, 설명하다, 시위하다 · Ⓔ prove 증명하다, protest 시위하다

demonstrate flexibility 유연성(융통성)을 보이다

★ This paper needs to be demonstrated by the principal of your school.
★ Thousands of people demonstrated against the war.

---

11 **deny**
[dinái]
ⓝ denial 부정, 부인

Ⓥ 부정하다, 부인하다 · Ⓔ admit 인정하다 · · · · · **deny permission** 허가를 거부하다

I denied the news because I didn't want to believe it.

---

12 **dictation**
[diktéiʃən]
Ⓥ dictate 받아쓰게 하다, 명령하다

ⓝ 받아쓰기, 명령 · · · · · · · · · · · · · · · · **a dictation test** 받아쓰기 시험

★ Kindergarten students are taking a dictation test.
★ The dictation could not be withdrawn as it came from a higher authority.

---

13 **oath**
[ouθ]

ⓝ 법정의 선서, 맹세 · · · · · · · · · · · · · · · **take an oath** (법정) 선서하다

The oath of telling the truth isn't always good.

---

07 운동 프로그램을 시작하기 전에 의사와 상담해야 한다. 08 투표 결과는 그의 예측과 반대였다. 09 그들은 내게 설득력 있는 논지를 말하라고 명령했다. 10 이 서류는 네 학교의 교장선생님이 증명해야 한다. / 수천 명의 사람이 전쟁에 반대하는 시위를 벌였다. 11 나는 믿고 싶지 않았기 때문에 그 소식을 부정했다. 12 유치원 아이들이 받아쓰기 시험을 보고 있다. / 그 명령은 최고의 권위자가 했기 때문에 철회할 수 없었다. 13 진실을 말할 것을 맹세하는 것이 항상 좋은 것은 아니다.

14 evaluate
[ivǽljuèit]

ⓝ evaluation 평가

ⓥ 평가하다

evaluate outcomes 결과를 평가하다

University professors should be free to evaluate students without interference.

15 exaggerate
[igzǽdʒərèit]

ⓝ exaggeration 과장

ⓥ 과장하다 ⊜ overstate ⊜ understate 줄여 말하다

exaggerate the difficulty 어려움을 과장하다

She always exaggerated, so no one believed her.

16 emphasis
[émfəsis]

ⓥ emphasize 강조하다

ⓝ 강조, 강세 ⊜ stress, accent

lay emphasis on ~에 중점을 두다

The emphasis of the highlighted lines shows the importance of the schedule.

17 glorify
[glɔ́ːrəfài]

ⓝ glorification 찬미

ⓥ 찬미하다, 칭찬하다

glorify the past 과거를 찬양하다

He glorifies her fashion taste and adores her.

18 implore
[implɔ́ːr]

ⓝ imploration 애원, 탄원
ⓐ imploratory
애원하는, 탄원하는

ⓥ 애원하다, 탄원하다 ⊜ appeal, plead

implore forgiveness 용서해 주기를 애원하다

She implored senior officials to improve conditions for orphans.

19 interactive
[ìntərǽktiv]

ⓥ interact 상호 교류하다
ⓝ interaction 상호작용

ⓐ 상호 작용하는, 대화식의

interactive teaching 대화식 수업

Law professors like interactive teaching in classes.

20 interpretation
[intə̀ːrprətéiʃən]

ⓥ interpret 해석[통역]하다
ⓝ interpreter 통역가

ⓝ 해석, 통역

an accurate interpretation 정확한 해석

After the 2002 World Cup, many taxies provide free interpretation service.

---

14 대학교수는 방해받지 않고 자유롭게 학생들을 평가해야 한다. 15 그녀는 항상 과장했기 때문에 아무도 그녀를 믿지 않았다. 16 형광색으로 줄이 그어진 강조 표시는 일정이 중요하다는 것을 보여준다. 17 그는 그녀의 패션 감각을 칭찬하고 그녀를 존경한다. 18 그녀는 고위 관리들에게 고아들의 처우를 개선해달라고 애원했다. 19 법대 교수들은 수업 중 대화식 교육을 좋아한다. 20 2002년 월드컵 이후로, 많은 택시가 무료 통역 서비스를 제공한다.

21 ☑ **whisper** [hwíspər] **ⓝ whisperer** 밀고자	ⓥ 속삭이다 ⓝ 속삭임, 소문 **in a whisper** 귓속말로 ★ She whispered to him to follow her after the class. ★ No one has listened to the whispers for the last 90 years.
22 ☑ **moan** [moun]	ⓥ 신음하다, 끙끙대다 ⊜ groan **moan in a distress** 고통으로 신음하다 I moaned when I felt the pain in my stomach.
23 ☑ **monologue** [mάnəlɔ̀ːg]	ⓝ 독백, 1인 극 **dramatic monologue** 극적 독백 The young students fell asleep while listening to his long monologue. c.f.) dialogue 대화
24 ☑ **mumble** [mʌ́mbəl]	ⓥ 중얼거리다 **mumble to oneself** 혼잣말로 중얼거리다 Jane mumbles to herself when she is scolded by her mother.
25 ☑ **mutter** [mʌ́tər]	ⓥ 중얼거리다, 불평하다 ⊜ mumble 중얼거리다, complain 불평하다 **mutter about working** 일에 대해 투덜대다 ★ "I don't want to come here again," he muttered to himself. ★ He kept on muttering and complaining about the loud music.
26 ☑ **nag** [næg]	ⓥ 잔소리하다 **a nagging person** 잔소리가 심한 사람 ★ My mother never nagged me to study. ★ The child will not stop nagging his mother until she buys him the toy.
27 ☑ **nonverbal** [nɑnvə́ːrbəl]	ⓐ 비언어적인, 말을 사용하지 않는 ⊜ verbal 구두의, 말의 **nonverbal communication** 비언어적인 의사소통 Babies use nonverbal communication to show their feelings.

21 그녀는 그에게 수업이 끝나면 따라오라고 속삭였다. / 지난 90년간 누구도 그 소문에 귀를 기울이지 않았다. 22 배에서 통증이 느껴졌을 때 나는 끙끙댔다. 23 어린 학생들은 그의 긴 독백을 듣는 동안 잠이 들었다. 24 Jane은 엄마에게 혼날 때 혼잣말로 중얼거린다. 25 그는 "나는 다시는 여기 오고 싶지 않아."라고 혼자 중얼거렸다. / 그는 시끄러운 음악에 대해 계속 투덜거렸다. 26 어머니는 나에게 공부하라는 잔소리를 한 적이 없다. / 아이는 장난감을 사줄 때까지 엄마를 조르는 것을 멈추지 않을 것이다. 27 아기들은 자신의 감정을 비언어적인 의사소통으로 표현한다.

28 omit
[oumít]

n omission 생략

v 빼다, 생략하다 **=** eliminate

omit one's name from the list 목록에서 ~의 이름을 생략하다

You need to omit several lines from your speech for the seminar.

29 oral
[ɔ́:rəl]

ad orally 구두로, 말로

a 구술의, 구두의

an oral agreement 구두 합의

They added an oral examination to the TOEFL test.

30 orator
[ɔ́(:)rətər]

v orate 연설하다

n 연설자, 강연자

a political orator 정치 연설가

She especially liked the orator who talked funny.

31 grumble
[grʌ́mbəl]

v 불평하다 **=** complain

grumble about meals 밥투정하다

He grumbled that the decision was not fair.

32 whimper
[hwímpər]

v 울다, 훌쩍이다 **=** cry, weep

a whimpering dog 낑낑대는 개

He should get over it, stop whimpering, and start defending himself.

33 plead
[pli:d]

n plea 청원, 변명

v 간청하다, 변명하다, 변호하다 **=** appeal 간청하다

plead one's ignorance ~의 무지를 변호하다

★ Civil rights groups pleaded for government help.

★ She kept pleading for forgiveness when she was late for the class.

34 prediction
[pridíkʃən]

v predict 예언하다

n 예언, 예보 **=** forecast

an accurate prediction 정확한 예측

My mother's dreams are always predictions.

---

28 세미나에서 네가 할 연설에서 몇 줄을 생략할 필요가 있다. 29 그들은 토플 시험에 구술시험을 추가했다. 30 그녀는 특히 독특하게 말했던 그 강연자를 좋아했다. 31 그는 그 결정이 공평하지 않다고 불평했다. 32 그는 그것을 극복하고, 투덜거리지 말고, 자신의 변호를 시작해야 해. 33 민권 단체들은 정부의 도움을 간청했다. / 그녀는 수업에 늦었을 때 계속해서 용서를 구했다. 34 어머니의 꿈은 항상 예언이다.

35 prophecy
[práfəsi]

v prophesy [práfəsài]
예언하다

n 예언, 예언서   **make a prophecy** 예언하다

The prophecy of the Earth being destroyed in 1999 wasn't true.

36 questionnaire
[kwéstʃənɛ́ər]

n 질문서, 설문지   **hand in a questionnaire** 설문지를 제출하다

Fill in the blanks on the questionnaire.

37 tease
[tiːz]

v 놀리다, 괴롭히다   **e** harass

tease a person about one's defect ~의 결점을 놀리다

The boy teased the girl to try to show her that he liked her.

38 reprimand
[réprəmænd]

v 꾸짖다, 질책하다   **e** reproach 비난하다

reprimand the student 학생을 꾸짖다

She reprimands her son whenever he comes home with dirty clothes.

39 seduce
[sidʒúːs]

n seduction 유혹, 매력

v 부추기다, 속이다, 유혹하다   **e** lure

seduce a person into error ~을 속여 실수하게 하다

He seduced me to see the movie with him on a rainy day.

40 proficiency
[prəfíʃənsi]

a proficient 숙달된, 능숙한

n 능숙, 숙달   **e** ability   **a test of proficiency in English** 영어 실력 테스트

Matthew's proficiency in Japanese is known to all his classmates.

---

35 1999년에 지구가 멸망한다는 예언은 사실이 아니었다.   36 이 설문지의 빈칸을 채워라.   37 남자아이는 여자아이를 좋아한다는 것을 표현하려고 괴롭혔다.   38 그녀는 자신의 아들이 더러운 옷을 입고 집에 올 때마다 꾸짖는다.   39 그는 비 오는 날 자기와 함께 영화 보러 가자고 나를 부추겼다. 40 Matthew가 일본어에 능숙한 것은 모든 학급 친구들에게 알려졌다.

EXERCISE

A 다음 영어는 우리말로, 우리말은 영어로 옮기시오.

01 monologue _____

02 consent _____

03 whimper _____

04 oral _____

05 interactive _____

06 interpretation _____

07 설명하다, 시위하다 _____

08 중얼거리다, 불평하다 _____

09 꾸짖다, 질책하다 _____

10 자랑하는, 허풍 떠는 _____

11 간청하다, 변명하다 _____

12 2개 국어를 쓰는 _____

B 다음 빈칸에 알맞은 단어를 쓰시오.

01 moan ⊜ _____

02 convincing ⊜ _____

03 omit ⊜ _____

04 exaggerate ⇔ _____

05 deny ⇔ _____

06 nonverbal ⇔ _____

07 glorify ⓝ _____

08 seduce ⓝ _____

09 proficiency ⓐ _____

10 prophecy ⓥ _____

11 proposition ⓥ _____

12 dictation ⓥ _____

C 다음 빈칸에 들어갈 알맞은 말을 고르시오. (필요하면 형태를 바꾸시오.)

contradiction	chuckle	implore	prediction	evaluate

01 The grandfather _____ quietly as he watched his grandchildren play together.

02 Now the government faces a problem of how to _____ a teacher's proficiency.

03 The new proposed policy is quite a(n) _____ to the minister's previous declarations.

04 The criminal's family _____ the judge for a lighter sentence than the life sentence he was given.

05 Based on the weather forecaster's _____, we will enjoy a full week of good weather.

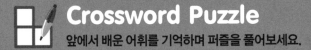

Crossword Puzzle

앞에서 배운 어휘를 기억하며 퍼즐을 풀어보세요.

Across

1 to say something too quietly or not clearly enough, so that other people cannot understand you

8 a difference between two statements, beliefs, or ideas about something that means they cannot both be true

9 to laugh at someone and make jokes in order to have fun by embarrassing them, either in a friendly way or in an unkind way

10 to judge how good, useful, or successful something is

Down

2 special attention or importance

3 a good standard of ability and skill

4 to show or prove something clearly

5 to ask for something that you want very much in a sincere and emotional way

6 a formal and very serious promise

7 not using words

Literature & Story

---

01 ☑ **aesthetic**
[esθétik]

ⓝ aestheticism 예술 지상주의

ⓐ 미적 감각이 있는, 미의　　　　　　　　**aesthetic sense** 미적 감각

Your story is so aesthetic that I can picture the scene.

---

02 ☑ **anecdote**
[ǽnikdòut]

ⓝ anecdotage 일화집

ⓝ 일화, 이야기　　⊜ story, tale　　**an entertaining anecdote** 재미있는 일화

Her latest book is full of amusing anecdotes about her life.

---

03 ☑ **genre**
[ʒɑ́:nrə]

ⓝ 장르, 유형　　　　　　　　**a literary genre** 문학 장르

The genre of her books is almost always romance.

---

04 ☑ **cite**
[sait]

ⓥ 인용하다　　⊜ quote　　**cite data** 자료를 인용하다

This essay isn't originally yours because you cited Shakespeare more than necessary.

---

05 ☑ **commentary**
[káməntèri]

ⓝ 논평, 해설　　⊜ comment 논평　　**a political commentary** 정치적 논평

His commentary about the book was not as good as his assistant's.

---

06 ☑ **complement**
[kámpləmənt]

ⓐ complementary 보완적인

ⓝ 보충, 보어　ⓥ 보충하다　　　　**subject complement** 주격 보어

★ This sentence is a perfect complement for your story.
★ Mary needs a scarf that complements her simple white dress.

---

01 네 이야기는 매우 미학적이어서 나는 그 장면을 그려볼 수 있다. 02 그녀의 최신작은 자신의 인생에 관한 재미있는 이야기로 가득하다. 03 그녀의 책의 장르는 거의 언제나 로맨스다. 04 너는 필요 이상으로 셰익스피어를 인용했기 때문에 이 수필은 순전히 너의 것이 아니다. 05 그 책에 대한 그의 논평은 그의 조수가 쓴 것만큼 훌륭하지 않다. 06 이 문장은 네 이야기의 완벽한 보충이다. / Mary는 단순한 흰 드레스를 보완해 줄 스카프가 필요하다.

07 compliment
[kámpləmənt]
ⓐ complimentary 칭찬의

ⓝ 칭찬, 찬사　　　　a heartfelt compliment 마음에 우러나오는 칭찬

After the concert, we all gave the show compliments.

08 composition
[kàmpəzíʃən]
ⓥ compose 작문하다, 구성하다

ⓝ 작문, 구성, 성분　ⓢ essay 작문　　a composition book 작문 연습장

★ It was the most perfect composition I had ever read.
★ The color of a star depends on its chemical composition.

09 conclusion
[kənklú:ʒən]
ⓥ conclude 결론짓다

ⓝ 결말, 결론　　　　a hasty conclusion 성급한 결론

I believe your book won't have a foregone conclusion.

10 context
[kántekst]

ⓝ 문맥　　　　out of context 문맥을 벗어나, 전후 관계없이

The context of his script was confusing for me to understand.

11 convey
[kənvéi]

ⓥ 전달하다, 전하다　ⓢ carry　　convey an impression 인상[느낌]을 주다

Her expression conveys the feelings of her pain like we can feel it.

12 critical
[krítikəl]
ⓥ criticize 비판하다
ⓝ criticism 비평

ⓐ 비평의, 비판적인, 중요한　　a critical remarks 비판적인 말

★ He is a critical journalist who always criticizes celebrities.
★ It is absolutely critical for us to know the truth.

13 dialect
[dáiəlèkt]
ⓐ dialectal 방언의, 방언 특유의

ⓝ 방언　　　　a standard dialect 표준어

The Jeju dialect is extremely hard to understand.

---

07 공연이 끝나고 우리는 모두 그 쇼에 찬사를 보냈다. 08 그것은 내가 읽어 본 작문 중에 최고였다. / 별의 색깔은 화학적 구성에 따라 다르다. 09 나는 네 책의 결말이 뻔하지 않을 거라 믿어. 10 그의 원고의 문맥은 내가 이해하기에 혼란스러웠다. 11 그녀의 표현은 우리가 느낄 수 있을 정도로 그녀의 고통을 전달한다. 12 그는 항상 유명인들을 비판하는 비평적인 기자다. / 우리가 진실을 아는 것은 절대적으로 중요하다. 13 제주도 방언은 매우 알아듣기 어렵다.

14 ☑ discourse
[dískɔːrs]

ⓝ 이야기, 담화　**⊜** essay

a tedious discourse 따분한 이야기

The discourse the teacher gave us that morning gave us the energy to study.

15 ☑ eloquence
[éləkwəns]

ⓐ eloquent 웅변의

ⓝ 웅변, 설득력

fiery eloquence 열변

Her eloquence made him sign the document right away.

16 ☑ epic
[épik]

ⓝ 서사시 **ⓐ** 서사시의, 장대한

an epic poet 서사시인

★ My friend tried to tell me an epic but I actually abhor it.

★ The movie was an epic accomplishment.

17 ☑ fable
[féibəl]

ⓝ fabler 거짓말쟁이, 우화 작가

ⓝ 우화, 전설, 설화

Aesop's Fables 이솝 이야기

The best-known of Aesop's fables is *The Tortoise and the Hare*.

18 ☑ fiction
[fíkʃən]

ⓝ 소설, 지어낸 이야기, 허구　**⊜** nonfiction 수기, 실화

science fiction 공상과학 소설

★ His fiction has been a best seller for the past five weeks.

★ It can sometimes be difficult to tell fact from fiction.

19 ☑ refer
[rifə́ːr]

ⓝ reference 참조, 언급

ⓥ 언급하다, 참조하다

refer to A as B A를 B라고 부르다

★ Students referred to their opponents as liars.

★ He gave the speech without referring to his notes.

20 ☑ paradox
[pǽrədɑ̀ks]

ⓝ 역설, 모순된 말

a well-known paradox 유명한 역설

He likes to use paradox when he maintains his point.

---

14 그날 아침 선생님이 이야기해 준 담화는 우리에게 공부할 힘을 주었다. 15 그녀의 설득력은 그가 바로 서류에 사인하게 하였다. 16 내 친구는 나에게 서사시를 들려주려고 했지만, 나는 사실 그것을 정말 싫어한다. / 그 영화는 큰 업적이었다. 17 이솝 우화 중 가장 잘 알려진 것은 '토끼와 거북이'다. 18 그의 소설은 지난 5주 동안 베스트셀러였다. / 때때로 사실과 허구를 구분하는 것은 어렵다. 19 학생들은 그들의 상대방을 거짓말쟁이라고 말했다. / 그는 메모를 참고하지 않고 연설을 했다. 20 그는 자신의 의견을 주장할 때 역설을 이용하기를 좋아한다.

21 irony
[áirəni]

ⓐ ironic 빈정대는

ⓝ 반어, 뜻밖의 결과

bitter irony 신랄한 반어법

dramatic irony 극적 아이러니(전혀 뜻밖의 결과)

The irony is that the poorest country has the richest natural resources.

---

22 legend
[lédʒənd]

ⓐ legendary 전설의, 전설적인

ⓝ 전설, 설화

a living legend 살아있는 전설

There are lots of scary stories in the legends of Korea.

---

23 legible
[lédʒəbəl]

ⓐⓓ legibly 읽기 쉽게

ⓐ 읽기 쉬운, 명료한 ⓔ illegible 읽기 어려운

legible handwriting 읽기 쉬운 필체

His writing is far from legible, so it looks more like scribbling.

---

24 literacy
[lítərəsi]

ⓝ 읽고 쓰는 능력 ⓔ illiteracy 문맹

computer literacy 컴퓨터 사용 능력

Max doesn't have literacy because he has never been taught.

---

25 literal
[lítərəl]

ⓐⓓ literally 글자 뜻 그대로

ⓐ 문자의, 글자 그대로의

a literal error 오자

a literal translation 직역, 글자 그대로의 번역

My answer, in the literal sense of the word, is no.

---

26 lyric
[lírik]

ⓐ lyrical 서정적인, 낭만적인

ⓝ 서정시, 가사

a lyric poem 서정시

★ The lyrics are very melodious and soothing to listen to.

★ His personality is calm, so his writings are all lyrical.

---

27 manuscript
[mǽnjəskrìpt]

ⓝ 원고

edit a manuscript 원고를 편집하다

The manuscript of the book is supposed to be finished by today.

---

21 가장 가난한 나라가 가장 풍부한 천연자원을 가지고 있다는 것은 뜻밖이다. 22 한국의 전설 중에는 무서운 이야기가 많다. 23 그의 필적은 알아보기 쉽지 않아서 낙서 같다. 24 Max는 배운 적이 없어서 읽고 쓰는 능력이 없다. 25 나의 대답은 글자 그대로의 의미로 거절이다. 26 그 서정시는 듣기 좋고 마음을 가라앉혀 준다. / 그는 성격이 차분해서 그의 글은 다 서정적이다. 27 그 책의 원고는 오늘까지 완성되어야 한다.

28 mediate
[míːdièit]

ⓝ mediation 중재, 화해

ⓥ 중재하다, 조정하다 **mediate both sides** 양쪽을 중재하다

The U.N. officials were asked to mediate in the dispute.

29 memoir
[mémwɑːr]

ⓝ 회고록, 자서전 ⓔ biography 전기, autobiography 자서전

personal memoirs 개인 비망록

Bradley is the author of memoirs entitled *My Miserable Life*.

30 metaphor
[métəfɔːr]

ⓐ metaphorical 은유적인

ⓝ 은유, 상징 **a metaphor for capitalism** 자본주의의 상징

I comprehended the metaphor he used at the sermon.

31 fluency
[flúːənsi]

ⓐ fluent 유창한

ⓝ 유창함, 달변 **fluency in English** 영어의 유창함

Fluency in English is a requirement for admission to the college that I want to go to.

32 compress
[kəmprés]

ⓝ compression 압축, 응축

ⓥ 압축하다, 요약하다 ⓔ condense **compress the file** 파일을 압축하다

She told me to compress the sentences and give it to her to check.

33 parody
[pǽrədi]

ⓝ 모방, 풍자, 패러디 **a parody of the president** 대통령 패러디

★ Although her comment was a parody of the truth, he was upset by it.

★ The comedy show performed a parody based on the government officials.

34 plot
[plɑt]

ⓝ 줄거리, 음모 ⓔ conspiracy 음모 **the plot of a film** 영화의 줄거리

★ The plot of this story is very creative and interesting.

★ The plot was quickly discovered, and five men were arrested.

---

28 그 유엔 임원들이 그 분쟁을 중재하도록 요청받았다. 29 Bradley는 '내 비참한 인생'이라는 제목의 회고록 저자다. 30 나는 그가 설교할 때 사용했던 은유를 이해했다. 31 능숙한 영어 구사가 내가 가고 싶어 하는 대학의 입학 조건이다. 32 그녀는 나에게 그 문장들을 요약하여 자신이 확인할 수 있게 다시 달라고 말했다. 33 그녀의 말은 사실에 대한 풍자였지만, 그는 그 말에 언짢았다. / 그 코미디 쇼는 정부 공무원들을 토대로 한 패러디를 공연했다. 34 이 이야기의 줄거리는 매우 독창적이고 흥미롭다. / 음모는 곧 발각되었으며, 다섯 명의 남성이 체포되었다.

35 ☑ **postscript**
[póustskrìpt]

ⓝ (편지의) 추신, (책의) 발문, 후기　　　**affix a postscript** 추신을 덧붙이다

The postscript to the novel contains some surprising details about the main character.

---

36 ☑ **preach**
[priːtʃ]

ⓝ **preacher** 설교자

ⓥ 설교하다, 전도하다　　　**preach the gospel** 복음을 전하다

He preached at churches in America and Bangladesh.

---

37 ☑ **theory**
[θíəri]

ⓐ **theoretical** 이론적인

ⓝ 학설, 이론, 추측　　　**theory and practice** 이론과 실제

It's only a theory that many people argue about.

---

38 ☑ **synopsis**
[sinápsis]

ⓝ 개요, 대강의 줄거리　⊜ summary

a synopsis of the film 영화의 간단한 줄거리

Your essay is fine, so just write a brief synopsis for tomorrow.

---

39 ☑ **verse**
[vəːrs]

ⓝ 운문, 시　⊜ poetry　　　**recite verse** 시를 낭송하다

Read me a few verses from the book, and then I should be able to sleep.

---

40 ☑ **term**
[təːrm]

ⓝ 말, 용어, 조건, 기간, 기한

in the scientific [medical] terms 과학적[의학적] 용어로

the terms of payment 지불 조건

the first term 1학기

Many legal terms have more than one meaning.

---

35 그 소설의 후기는 주인공에 대한 놀라운 세부 사항을 담고 있다.　36 그는 미국과 방글라데시에 있는 교회에서 설교했다.　37 이건 그냥 많은 사람이 논쟁하는 학설일 뿐이다.　38 너의 수필은 괜찮으니, 내일 간략한 개요를 써와라.　39 네가 그 책에서 시 몇 구절을 읽어주면 나는 잠들 수 있을 것이다. 40 많은 법률 용어들은 한 가지 이상의 의미가 있다.

✎ EXERCISE

A 다음 영어는 우리말로, 우리말은 영어로 옮기시오.

01 fable _____ 07 장르, 유형 _____

02 metaphor _____ 08 줄거리, 음모 _____

03 legible _____ 09 추신, 후기 _____

04 aesthetic _____ 10 원고 _____

05 verse _____ 11 역설, 모순된 말 _____

06 commentary _____ 12 문맥 _____

B 다음 빈칸에 알맞은 단어를 쓰시오.

01 compress ⊜ _____ 07 composition Ⓥ _____

02 anecdote ⊜ _____ 08 critical Ⓥ _____

03 cite ⊜ _____ 09 compliment ⓐ _____

04 synopsis ⊜ _____ 10 eloquence ⓐ _____

05 literacy ⇔ _____ 11 theory ⓐ _____

06 fiction ⇔ _____ 12 refer Ⓝ _____

C 다음 빈칸에 들어갈 알맞은 말을 고르시오. (필요하면 형태를 바꾸시오.)

complement	literal	mediate	convey	dialect

01 A new project will be launched to _____ ongoing research.

02 Through songwriting, the singer was able to _____ his deepest emotions.

03 There are several words whose _____ meanings are different from their contextual meanings.

04 In China there are many _____ of the Chinese language.

05 The ambassador was sent overseas in an attempt to _____ the international problems.

Crossword Puzzle

앞에서 배운 어휘를 기억하며 퍼즐을 풀어보세요.

1 a _ _ | 2 c _ _ _ _ _ _

3 f _ _ _ _ _ _

4 c

5 c _ _ _ _ _ _ _ _ _

6 m

7 l

8 p

9 a _ _ _ _ _ _ _

10 c _ _ _ _ _ _ _

Across

1 a short story based on your personal experience

3 the ability to speak or write easily and accurately

5 to make a good combination with someone or something else

9 connected with beauty and the study of beauty

10 expressing adverse or disapproving comments or judgements

Down

2 to communicate or express something, with or without using words

4 to press something or make it smaller so that it takes up less space, or to become smaller

6 a way of describing something by referring to it as something different and suggesting that it has similar qualities to that thing

7 written or printed clearly enough for you to read

8 to talk about a religious subject in a public place, especially in a church during a service

Thought & Judgment

01 ☑ abstract
[æbstrǽkt]

n abstraction 추상

ⓐ 추상적인 **↔** concrete 구체적인   **abstract noun** 추상명사

When I saw the abstract painting, I began to wonder if even the artist knew what the painting represented.

02 ☑ acknowledge
[əknάlidʒ]

n acknowledgement
인정, 승인

ⓥ 인정하다, 승인하다 **≒** recognize 인정하다

acknowledge one's defeat 패배를 인정하다

She couldn't help acknowledging the fault of her choices.

03 ☑ alter
[ɔ́:ltər]

ⓥ 바꾸다, 변경하다 **≒** change   **alter the design** 디자인을 바꾸다

Alter your mind, and then you will understand why we are all here.

04 ☑ alternative
[ɔːltə́:rnətiv]

ⓥ alternate 번갈아 일어나다

ⓐ 대체의 **n** 대안   **alternative medicine** 대체의학

★ Alternative energy includes natural energies such as the sun and the earth's heat.

★ He had no alternative but to give it up.

05 ☑ ambiguous
[æmbígjuəs]

n ambiguity 애매함

ⓐ 애매한, 확실치 않은   **ambiguous decision** 모호한 결정

The ambiguous decision made him more confused.

06 ☑ analysis
[ənǽləsis]

ⓥ analyze 분석하다

n 분석, 분해   **chemical analysis** 화학 분석

Analysis showed that it contained a lot of vitamin C.

---

01 그 추상화를 보고 있으려니 나는 화가조차 그 그림이 무엇을 나타내는지 알고 있을까 궁금해지기 시작했다. 02 그녀는 자신의 선택에 잘못이 있다는 걸 인정할 수밖에 없었다. 03 너의 마음을 바꾼다면, 우리가 여기 왜 모여 있는지 이해할 수 있을 것이다. 04 대체 에너지는 태양과 지열 같은 자연 에너지를 포함한다. / 그는 그 일을 포기하는 것 외에는 대안이 없었다.(= 그는 마지못해 단념했다.) 05 애매한 결정은 그를 더욱 혼란스럽게 만들었다. 06 분석 결과 비타민 C가 많이 함유되어 있음이 밝혀졌다.

07 approving
[əprúːviŋ]

v approve 승인하다, 찬성하다

a 찬성하는, 승인하는 **e** disapproving 반대하는

an approving vote 찬성투표

The directors and shareholders in the company are unanimous in approving the change of ownership.

08 assert
[əsə́ːrt]

n assertion 주장

v 단언하다, 주장하다 **e** declare

assert one's innocence ~의 무죄를 주장하다

He asserted that he didn't think about the result.

09 assess
[əsés]

n assessment 감정, 평가

v 평가하다 **e** evaluate **assess the quality** 품질을 평가하다

This test is for assessing the students' progress.

10 clarify
[klǽrəfài]

n clarification
깨끗이 하기, 해명

v (의미를) 분명히 설명하다 **clarify the situation** 상황을 분명히 하다

She clarified that she never went out of her room.

11 complex
[kəmpléks / káːmpleks]

a 복잡한, 어려운 **n** 복합단지 **e** complicated 복잡한

a complex problem 복잡한 문제

★ His complex idea wouldn't help us to figure out this problem.

★ We drove up to the height of the dam and stopped at a leisure complex.

12 comprehend
[kàmprihénd]

n comprehension 이해

v 이해하다, 파악하다, 깨닫다 **e** understand

how to read and comprehend 읽고 이해하는 법

I comprehended the situation right away when I got there.

13 confirm
[kənfə́ːrm]

a confirmed 확인된
n confirmation 확인, 확정

v 확실히 하다, 확인하다 **confirm a reservation** 예약을 확인하다

It is important to confirm your schedule before you leave.

---

07 그 회사의 이사들과 주주들은 소유권 변동을 만장일치로 찬성했다. 08 그는 자신이 결과에 대해서 생각하지 않았다고 주장했다. 09 이 시험은 학생들의 학습 진행 상태를 평가하기 위한 것이다. 10 그녀는 자신의 방 밖으로 나온 적이 없다고 분명히 말했다. 11 그의 복잡한 생각은 우리가 이 문제를 해결하는 데 도움이 되지 않을 것이다. / 우리는 댐의 높은 곳까지 차를 몰고 가서 종합위락시설에서 멈추었다. 12 나는 그곳에 도착했을 때 바로 그 상황을 파악했다. 13 떠나기 전에 일정을 확인하는 것이 중요하다.

14 ☑ contemplate
[kántəmplèit]

ⓝ contemplation 심사숙고

ⓥ 잘 생각하다, 심사숙고하다　**≡** consider

contemplate quitting one's job 사직을 고려하다

It's frightening to contemplate the possibility of another war.

15 ☑ conviction
[kənvíkʃən]

ⓥ convince 확신시키다

ⓝ 신념, 확신

a religious conviction 종교적 신념

His conviction gave me the courage to stand up again.

16 ☑ criterion
[kraitíəriən]

ⓝ criteria 〈복수형〉 표준

ⓝ 기준, 표준　**≡** standard

criterion of success 성공의 기준

She thinks the criterion of success is money.

17 ☑ deduce
[didʤúːs]

ⓝ deduction 추론

ⓥ 추론하다　**≡** infer

deduce from figures 그림을 보고 추론하다

She deduced how the accident occurred at that time.

18 ☑ depict
[dipíkt]

ⓝ depiction 묘사

ⓥ 묘사하다, 그리다　**≡** describe

depict a story 이야기를 묘사하다

He depicted you as a little, but smart girl.

19 ☑ determination
[ditə̀ːrmənéiʃən]

ⓥ determine 결심하다, 결정하다

ⓝ 결정, 결심

a man of great determination 결심이 굳은 사람

The president has been steady in his determination to protect freedom and democracy.

20 ☑ fallacy
[fǽləsi]

ⓝ 잘못된 생각

a popular fallacy 흔한 오류

It was a fallacy that he liked her as more than a friend.

---

14 또 다른 전쟁이 발발할 수 있다는 가능성을 생각하는 것은 두렵다.　15 그의 신념은 내가 다시 일어설 용기를 주었다.　16 그녀는 성공의 기준이 돈이라고 생각한다.　17 그녀는 그때 어떻게 그 사건이 일어났는지를 추론했다.　18 그는 너를 작지만, 영리한 여자아이로 묘사했다.　19 대통령은 자유와 민주주의 수호를 위한 확고한 의지를 보였다.　20 그가 그녀를 친구 이상으로 좋아한다는 것은 잘못된 생각이었다.

---

21 ☑ **meditation**
[mèdətéiʃən]
v meditate 명상하다

n 명상, 심사숙고 **≡** reflection 숙고   **a meditation room** 명상실

I love meditation with soft music and gentle rain.

---

22 ☑ **hypothesis**
[haipáθəsis]
a hypothetic(al)
가설의, 가정의

n 가설(假說), 가정   **a hypothesis testing** 가설 검증

Less snow here supports the hypothesis that the Earth is getting warmer and warmer.

---

23 ☑ **illogical**
[ilάdʒikəl]

a 불합리한, 비논리적인 **≡** logical 논리적인

an illogical conclusion 불합리한 결론

No one can understand you because you are illogical.

---

24 ☑ **imaginative**
[imǽdʒənətiv]
v imagine 상상하다
n imagination 상상력

a 상상력이 풍부한   **an imaginative poet** 상상력 풍부한 시인

My imaginative friend told me exaggerated stories of his dream.

---

25 ☑ **imply**
[implái]
n implication 함축, 내포

v 의미하다, 함축하다   **implied consent** 암묵적 동의

She implied happiness in that bright smile.

---

26 ☑ **inconsistent**
[ìnkənsístənt]
n inconsistency 모순, 불일치

a 모순된, 일치하지 않는 **≡** consistent 일관된, 모순이 없는

an inconsistent statement 모순된 진술

His kind of attitude is inconsistent with what we expected.

---

27 ☑ **indecisive**
[ìndisáisiv]
n indecision 우유부단

a 우유부단한, 결정적이지 않은 **≡** decisive 단호한, 결정적인

an indecisive character 우유부단한 성격

Her indecisive acts look like laziness to me.

---

21 나는 부드러운 음악과 잔잔히 내리는 비와 함께하는 명상을 좋아한다. 22 이곳에 눈이 더 적게 내리는 것은 지구가 점점 더 따뜻해지고 있다는 가설을 뒷받침한다. 23 너는 비논리적이기 때문에 아무도 너를 이해할 수 없다. 24 상상력이 풍부한 나의 친구는 자신의 꿈을 과장해서 이야기해주었다. 25 그녀는 환한 미소로 행복함을 함축했다. 26 그의 그런 행동은 우리가 기대한 것과 일치하지 않는다. 27 그녀의 우유부단한 행동이 내게는 게을러 보인다.

28 insight
[ínsàit]
ⓐ insightful 통찰력이 있는

ⓝ 통찰, 통찰력　　　　　　　　a person of insight 통찰력이 있는 사람

He has an insight to choose the work he can handle.

29 intuition
[ìntʃuíʃən]
ⓐ intuitive 직관적인, 직감적인

ⓝ 직관, 직감　　ⓔ instinct　　　　know by intuition 직감적으로 알다

I can't trust your intuition because you were wrong last time.

30 notion
[nóuʃən]

ⓝ 관념, 개념, 이해력　　ⓔ concept 개념, 생각

a widespread notion 널리 퍼져있는 생각

An odd notion hit me so I wrote it down and read it again.

31 objection
[əbdʒékʃən]
ⓥ object 반대하다

ⓝ 반대, 반감　　　　　　　　a valid objection 타당한 반대 의견

My objection to your proposal has a reason.

32 positive
[pázətiv]

ⓐ 확신하는, 긍정적인　　ⓔ negative 부정적인

positive thinking 긍정[적극]적인 사고

★ She was positive that she saw him on 5th Street.

★ The report has both positive and negative consequences.

33 prejudice
[prédʒədis]
ⓐ prejudiced 선입관을 가진

ⓝ 편견, 선입관　　ⓔ bias　　racial [sexual] prejudice 인종[성별]에 대한 편견

Many Koreans have color prejudice even though they are of color themselves.

34 reject
[ridʒékt]
ⓝ rejection 거절

ⓥ 거절하다, 사절하다　　ⓔ refuse　　reject a manuscript 원고를 퇴짜 놓다

I'm sorry to reject your proposal, but I have no choice.

---

28 그는 자신이 처리할 수 있는 일을 고를 수 있는 통찰력을 가졌다. 29 네가 저번에 틀렸기 때문에 너의 직감을 믿을 수 없다. 30 특이한 생각이 갑자기 떠올라 적어보고 다시 읽었다. 31 너의 제안에 대한 나의 반대에는 이유가 있다. 32 그녀는 5번가에서 그를 보았다고 확신했다. / 그 보고서는 긍정적인 측면과 부정적인 측면을 모두 갖고 있다. 33 많은 한국인은 자신도 유색 인종이면서 유색 인종에 대한 편견이 있다. 34 너의 제안을 거절하는 것이 미안하지만, 다른 방법이 없다.

35 resolve
[rizálv]

ⓐ resolute 굳게 결심한
ⓝ resolution 결의, 각오

ⓥ 해결하다, 결심하다 ⊜ decide 결심하다
resolve the problem 문제를 해결하다
She resolved to go abroad when this semester ends.

36 speculate
[spékjəlèit]

ⓝ speculation 심사숙고

ⓥ 숙고하다, 사색하다 ⊜ consider 숙고하다
speculate on the issue 이슈에 대해 생각하다
I speculated when to tell him to stop calling me.

37 standpoint
[stǽndpɔ̀int]

ⓝ 입장, 관점   **from a political standpoint** 정치적 관점에서
The standpoint of seniors is different from ours.

38 stereotype
[stériətàip]

ⓐ stereotypic 흔히 있는, 진부한

ⓝ 고정관념   **racial stereotype** 인종적 고정관념
I have a stereotype that sweet foods make me fat.

39 withhold
[wiðhóuld]

ⓥ 억제하다, 보류하다   **withhold information** 정보를 비밀로 해주다
I'll withhold judgment until the experiment is completed.

40 subliminal
[sʌblímənəl]

ⓐ 잠재의식의   **subliminal perception** 잠재의식
Every bird has a subliminal desire to spread its wings and fly to the sky.

35 그녀는 이번 학기가 끝나면 외국에 나가기로 했다. 36 나는 그에게 전화를 그만 걸라고 언제 말해야 할지 깊게 생각했다. 37 어른들의 관점은 우리와는 다르다. 38 나는 단 음식을 먹으면 살이 찔 거라는 고정관념이 있다. 39 나는 그 실험이 완료될 때까지 판단을 보류할 것이다. 40 모든 새는 날개를 펴고 하늘을 날아가는 잠재적 욕망이 있다.

EXERCISE

A 다음 영어는 우리말로, 우리말은 영어로 옮기시오.

01 depict _____

02 intuition _____

03 assert _____

04 speculate _____

05 analysis _____

06 inconsistent _____

07 인정하다, 승인하다 _____

08 잠재의식의 _____

09 대체의, 대안 _____

10 기준, 표준 _____

11 고정관념 _____

12 평가하다 _____

B 다음 빈칸에 알맞은 단어를 쓰시오.

01 deduce ⊜ _____

02 notion ⊜ _____

03 reject ⊜ _____

04 complex ⊜ _____

05 approving ⊜ _____

06 abstract ⊜ _____

07 conviction ⓥ _____

08 meditation ⓥ _____

09 hypothesis ⓐ _____

10 resolve ⓐ _____

11 clarify ⓝ _____

12 comprehend ⓝ _____

C 다음 빈칸에 들어갈 알맞은 말을 고르시오. (필요하면 형태를 바꾸시오.)

ambiguous	prejudice	indecisive	withhold	alter

01 We were all confused by the _____ message.

02 The boss threatened to _____ their payment or to sue them.

03 In order to wear her new pants, she brought them to the tailor to have the length _____ .

04 When shopping for bags, women tend to become _____ as all the bags are appealing.

05 Due to the media's attention, a judge had a hard time making a right decision without _____ .

Across

1 to suggest that something is true, without saying this directly

3 an unreasonable dislike and distrust of people who are different from you in some way, especially because of their race, gender, religion, etc.

8 not right according to a particular set of principles or standards

9 to evaluate or estimate the nature, ability, or quality of

10 to understand something that is complicated or difficult

Down

2 the practice of emptying your mind of thoughts and feelings, in order to relax completely or for religious reasons

4 open to more than one interpretation; not having one obvious meaning

5 to guess about the possible causes or effects of something, without knowing all the facts or details

6 to state firmly that something is true

7 to think about something that you might do in the future

Books & Arts

01 ☑ adapt
[ədǽpt]

ⓝ adaptation 각색, 적응

ⓥ 번안[각색]하다, 적응시키다

adapt a novel for the stage 소설을 극본으로 각색하다

The children are finding it hard to adapt to the new school.

02 ☑ adorn
[ədɔ́:rn]

ⓝ adornment 꾸미기, 장식

ⓥ 꾸미다, 장식하다　**⊜** decorate　　**adorn with jewels** 보석으로 치장하다

I was fascinated by the flowers that adorn the walls.

03 ☑ artful
[ɑ́:rtfəl]

ⓐⓓ artfully 교묘하게

ⓐ 교묘한, 솜씨 있는　　　　　　　　　**artful tricks** 교묘한 속임수

His story was so artful that I couldn't identify the criminal until the end.

04 ☑ award
[əwɔ́:rd]

ⓥ 주다, 수여하다 **ⓝ** 상, 수상　**⊜** prize 상　**award a scholarship** 장학금을 주다

★ She should be awarded for her magnificent sculpture.

★ The award ceremony will be held at the National Theater tonight.

05 ☑ biography
[baiágrəfi]

ⓝ autobiography 자서전

ⓝ 전기, 일대기　　　　　**biography of Oprah Winfrey** 오프라 윈프리의 전기

I don't usually read biographies because I think they're diaries.

06 ☑ booklet
[búklit]

ⓝ 소책자, 팸플릿　**⊜** pamphlet　**the booklet of the musical** 뮤지컬 팸플릿

Detailed information of the musical is in the booklet on the table.

---

01 아이들이 새로운 학교에 적응하는 것을 어려워한다. 02 나는 벽을 장식하는 꽃에 매료되었다. 03 그의 이야기는 매우 교묘해서 나는 책의 마지막까지 범인을 알지 못했다. 04 그녀는 훌륭한 조각상으로 상을 받을 만하다. / 시상식은 오늘 밤 국립극장에서 열릴 것이다. 05 나는 전기가 일기라고 생각하기 때문에 잘 읽지 않는다. 06 뮤지컬에 대한 자세한 정보는 테이블 위에 있는 소책자에 있다.

07 chronicle
[kránikl]

ⓝ 연대기, 역사 **ⓔ** history

the Chronicles of Narnia 〈책, 영화〉 나니아 연대기

We found the chronicles of the period at the exhibition.

08 chronology
[krənálədʒi]

ⓝ 연대학, 연대기

brief chronology 간략한 연대기

He wanted to go to the museum to see the chronology of that period.

09 rehearsal
[rihə́ːrsəl]

ⓥ rehearse 연습하다, 시연하다

ⓝ 예행연습, 리허설

a public rehearsal 공개 시연
a dress rehearsal 총 연습

The cast was in rehearsal when he called his mother.

10 draft
[dræft]

ⓝ 밑그림, 초안 **ⓔ** outline

draw a draft 밑그림을 그렸다

Let me take a look at your draft from the class.

11 elaborate
[ilǽbərèit]

ⓝ elaboration 공들여 함, 정교

ⓐ 공들인, 정교한 **ⓔ** exquisite, delicate   an elaborate work 공들인 작품

She wouldn't let us touch her elaborate art piece.

12 encyclopedia
[ensàikloupíːdiə]

ⓝ 백과사전

an online encyclopedia 온라인 백과사전

He is a walking encyclopedia of music.

13 entitle
[entáitl]

ⓝ entitlement 권리

ⓥ 제목을 붙이다, 권리를 부여하다 **ⓔ** name, label 제목[이름]을 붙이다

entitle a name 이름을 짓다

★ With my sadness the book was entitled *Gloomy Sky*.
★ Being a member entitles you to discounts on tickets.

---

07 우리는 전시회에서 그 시기의 연대기를 찾았다. 08 그는 그 시대의 연대기를 보러 박물관에 가고 싶어 했다. 09 그가 어머니에게 전화했을 때는 배우들이 리허설 중이었다. 10 수업을 들었을 때 네가 그린 초안을 한번 살펴볼게. 11 그녀는 우리에게 그녀의 정교한 예술 작품을 만지지 못하게 했다. 12 그는 살아있는 음악 백과사전이다. 13 내 슬픔을 담아 그 책에 '우울한 하늘'이라는 제목을 붙였다. / 회원이 되면 표를 할인해서 살 수 있다.

14 exhibition
[èksəbíʃən]

ⓥ exhibit 전시하다

ⓝ 전람, 전시회 **ⓢ** display

an exhibition game 시범경기

The exhibition of musical instruments has successfully ended.

15 fantasy
[fǽntəsi]

ⓝ 공상, 환상 **ⓢ** fancy 공상

fantasy fiction 공상 소설

Harry Potter is famous in the genre of fantasy fictions.

16 illustration
[ìləstréiʃən]

ⓥ illustrate
삽화를 넣다, 설명하다

ⓝ 삽화, 실례

a full-color illustration 총천연색 삽화

★ This illustration on the cover of his book was drawn by his sister.

★ He pointed up his remarks with suitable illustrations.

17 author
[ɔ́:θər]

ⓝ 저자, 작가 **ⓢ** writer

the author of ~의 저자

He is one of my favorite authors because he is good at expressing his feelings.

18 transcribe
[trænskráib]

ⓝ transcription 베낀 것, 사본

ⓥ 복사하다, 베끼다

transcribe a book 책을 복사하다

I hate that other students transcribe my notes for tests.

19 illiterate
[ilítərit]

ⓐ 글자를 모르는, 무식한 **ⓞ** literate 읽고 쓸 수 있는

technologically illiterate 기술적으로 무지한

He has to read the book for his grandmother because she is illiterate.

20 illuminate
[ilú:mənèit]

ⓝ illumination 조명, 계몽

ⓥ 조명하다, 밝게 하다 **ⓞ** darken 어둡게 하다

illuminate the subject 주제를 명확히 하다

His passage illuminated the whole book.

---

14 악기 전시회는 성공적으로 끝났다. 15 '해리 포터'는 공상 소설 장르에서 유명하다. 16 그의 책의 표지에 있는 삽화는 그의 여동생이 그린 것이다. / 그는 적절한 예를 들어 그의 소견을 강조했다. 17 그는 감정을 잘 표현하기 때문에 내가 가장 좋아하는 작가 중 한 명이다. 18 나는 다른 학생들이 시험을 위해 내 필기를 베끼는 것이 싫다. 19 그의 할머니가 글을 읽을 줄 모르기 때문에 그가 할머니 대신 책을 읽어 드려야 한다. 20 그의 구절은 책 전체를 밝게 해주었다.

21 footnote
[fútnòut]

n 각주　　　　　　　　　　　　　　　**add a footnote** 각주를 달다

The little numbers at the end of the sentences refer to the footnotes.

22 imitate
[ímitèit]

n imitation 모방

v 흉내 내다, 모조하다　**≐** copy, mimic　　**imitate an actor** 배우를 흉내 내다

A lot of writers have tried to imitate Shakespeare's style.

23 imprint
[ímprint]

n imprinting 각인

v 찍다, 인쇄하다 **n** 자국, 흔적　　　　　**the imprint of a foot** 발자국

At the ceramic workshop, the imprint of the child's hand was used as decoration.

24 index
[índeks]

n 색인, 찾아보기　　　　　　　　　　**a subject index** 주제별 색인

★ The index of this pamphlet shows that she is the third performer.

★ It's very easy to find the book if you use the index.

25 version
[və́:rʒən]

n 각색, 번역　**≐** edition

a movie version of the essay 수필을 영화화한 것

This book is the Korean version of *the Phantom of the Opera*.

26 marvel
[má:rvəl]

a marvelous 놀라운

n 경이, 놀라운 일　**≐** wonder　　　**marvels of nature** 자연의 경이

It is a marvel that her work is finally exhibited.

27 vulgar
[vʌ́lgər]

n vulgarian 속물

a 저속한, 선정적인　**≐** crude　　　　**a vulgar fellow** 야비한 사람

His words are so vulgar that I don't want to chat with him.

---

21 문장 끝에 작은 숫자들은 각주를 가리킨다. 22 많은 작가가 셰익스피어의 스타일을 모방하려고 시도했다. 23 도예 강습회에서는 아이의 손자국이 장식으로 사용되었다. 24 소책자에 적힌 색인은 그녀가 세 번째 공연자라는 것을 보여준다. / 색인을 이용하면 책을 찾기가 매우 쉽다. 25 이 책은 '오페라의 유령'의 한글 번역판이다. 26 그녀의 작품이 드디어 전시된다는 것은 놀라운 일이다. 27 그의 말은 너무 저속해서 나는 그와 대화하고 싶지 않다.

28 mold
[móuld]

ⓝ 모양, 주물 **ⓥ** 형성하다　**⊜** shape 모양　**mold the character** 성격을 형성하다

★ The sculptor's mold looked like a baby elephant.

★ The 4th grade students will learn how to mold clay into plates, bowls, and cups.

29 narrative
[nǽrətiv]

ⓥ narrate 이야기하다

ⓝ narration 서술, 화법

ⓐ 이야기체의　　　　　　　　　　**a narrative poem** 이야기 시, 설화시

★ A kind of psychotherapy using narration is called narrative therapy.

★ You can find narrative structure in some computer games, too.

30 paragraph
[pǽrəgræf]

ⓝ (문장의) 절, 단락　**⊜** passage, section

a short paragraph 짧은 한 문단

He left this paragraph out of the text for some reason.

31 refine
[rifáin]

ⓥ 세련되게 하다, 품위 있게 하다　　　**a refined method** 세련된 방법

She refines people with makeup and clothes backstage.

32 perspective
[pə:rspéktiv]

ⓝ 원근법, 견해, 관점　**from a historical perspective** 역사적인 관점에서

★ The artist showed a fine command of perspective.

★ His perspective of the book wasn't affirmative.

33 playwright
[pléiràit]

ⓝ 각본가, 극작가, 각색자

a successful Broadway playwright 성공한 브로드웨이 극작가

He loves the playwrights who are sentimental.

34 preface
[préfis]

ⓝ 서문, 머리말　**⊜** epilogue 후기, 발문

the preface to World War 세계 대전의 발단

When you want to buy a book, it's important to read the preface first.

---

28 그 조각가가 만든 틀은 마치 새끼 코끼리 같았다. / 4학년 학생들은 찰흙으로 접시, 그릇, 컵을 만드는 법을 배울 것입니다. 29 이야기를 사용하는 심리치료의 한 종류를 '이야기 치료'라고 한다. / 몇몇 컴퓨터 게임에서도 이야기 구조를 발견할 수 있다. 30 그는 어떤 이유에선지 이 단락을 본문에서 뺐다. 31 그녀는 무대 뒤에서 사람들을 화장과 옷으로 세련되게 만든다. 32 그 화가는 훌륭한 원근법 구사력을 보여주었다. / 그 책에 대한 그의 시각은 긍정적이지 않았다. 33 그는 감상적인 극작가를 매우 좋아한다. 34 책을 사고 싶을 때, 먼저 머리말을 읽어보는 것이 중요하다.

35 ☑ **preview**
[príːvjùː]

ⓝ (영화 등의) 예고편, 미리 보기 ● trailer 예고편 **a movie preview** 영화 시사회

After reading the preview of the book, I didn't buy it.

---

36 ☑ **punctuation**
[pʌ̀ŋktʃuéiʃən]
ⓥ punctuate 구두점을 찍다

ⓝ 구두점, 구두법 **a punctuation mark** 구두점

Punctuation is sometimes forgotten when writing a book.

---

37 ☑ **quote**
[kwout]
ⓝ quotation 인용

ⓥ 인용하다 ● cite **quote a passage from** ~의 구절을 인용하다

The following passage was quoted from a well-known fable.

---

38 ☑ **theatrical**
[θiǽtrikəl]
ⓝ theater 극장

ⓐ 연극의, 극장의 ● dramatic **theatrical genre** 연극 장르

★ He is soon to become a powerful force in the theatrical world.

★ The gestures of the actor are theatrical as he is a very expressive artist.

---

39 ☑ **recite**
[risáit]
ⓝ recitation 암송

ⓥ 암송하다, 낭송하다, 열거하다 **recite poetry** 시를 낭송하다

★ The children will recite the short story at the assembly today.

★ Let me recite some of the merits in his book.

---

40 ☑ **performance**
[pərfɔ́ːrməns]
ⓥ perform 실행하다, 연기하다

ⓝ 연주, 공연, 실행, 수행 **performance evaluation** 업무수행 평가

★ Anna's performance at the stage was unbelievably amazing.

★ The annual school performance report says 38 percent of the district's teachers have master's degrees.

---

35 나는 그 책의 미리 보기를 보고 나서 사지 않았다. 36 구두점은 책을 쓸 때 가끔 잊어버리게 된다. 37 다음 구절은 한 유명한 우화에서 인용되었다. 38 그는 곧 연극계의 강력한 세력이 될 것이다. / 그 배우는 매우 표현력이 풍부한 예술가로 그의 몸짓은 극적이다. 39 오늘 조회 시간에 아이들은 짧은 이야기를 암송할 것이다. / 그의 책의 장점을 몇 개 열거하겠습니다. 40 무대에서의 Anna의 연기는 믿기 어려울 정도로 놀라웠다. / 연간 학교 업무보고서를 보면, 이 학군 교사의 38%가 석사학위가 있다.

EXERCISE

A 다음 영어는 우리말로, 우리말은 영어로 옮기시오.

01 elaborate _____

02 transcribe _____

03 preview _____

04 imprint _____

05 artful _____

06 theatrical _____

07 삽화, 실례 _____

08 세련되게 하다 _____

09 번안[각색]하다 _____

10 각본가, 극작가 _____

11 공상, 환상 _____

12 연대기, 역사 _____

B 다음 빈칸에 알맞은 단어를 쓰시오.

01 draft ⊜ _____

02 imitate ⊜ _____

03 paragraph ⊜ _____

04 exhibition ⊜ _____

05 illuminate ⇔ _____

06 preface ⇔ _____

07 narrative ⓥ _____

08 performance ⓥ _____

09 marvel ⓐ _____

10 adorn ⓝ _____

11 theatrical ⓝ _____

12 entitle ⓝ _____

C 다음 빈칸에 들어갈 알맞은 말을 고르시오. (필요하면 형태를 바꾸시오.)

illiterate	perspective	quote	biography	vulgar

01 As one grows older and matures, her _____ on life changes.

02 In the poorest countries around the world, many of the adults are _____ .

03 Young college students majoring in English literature often _____ Shakespeare.

04 Some of my co-workers want to quit the job because they can't stand the boss's _____ jokes about women.

05 Before the movie star passed away, she made sure that her favorite author completed a(n) _____ on her life.

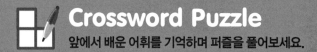

Crossword Puzzle

앞에서 배운 어휘를 기억하며 퍼즐을 풀어보세요.

Across

2 how well or badly a person, company, etc. does a particular job or activity

4 to copy the way someone behaves, speaks, moves, etc., especially in order to make people laugh

7 to give someone the official right to do or have something

8 a piece of writing or a plan that is not yet in its finished form

9 carefully planned and organized in great detail

Down

1 a written record of a series of events, especially historical events, written in the order in which they happened

3 to gradually change your behavior and attitudes in order to be successful in a new situation

4 unable to read or write

5 a show of paintings, photographs, or other objects that people can go to see

6 to improve a method, plan, system, etc. by gradually making slight changes to it

Unit 05

Education & Learning

01 ☑ **thesis**
[θíːsis]

   n 학위 논문, 논제   **a doctoral thesis** 박사 논문

   ★ I didn't choose the topic for my thesis yet.

   ★ The data supports the thesis that women aren't as aggressive as men.

---

02 ☑ **admission**
[ædmíʃən]

   n 입학 (허가), 승인, 입장(료)   **admission fee** 입장료

   He couldn't believe his admission to Harvard University was approved.

---

03 ☑ **anthropology**
[æ̀nθrəpálədʒ]

  n anthropologist 인류학자

   n 인류학   **cultural anthropology** 문화 인류학

   Anthropology is complicated and hard to study for me.

---

04 ☑ **assignment**
[əsáinmənt]

  v assign 배정하다, 할당하다

   n 과제, 숙제 **=** task   **carry out an assignment** 임무를 완수하다

   The assignment for tomorrow is reading Chapter 5.

---

05 ☑ **attendance**
[əténdəns]

  v attend 참석하다

   n 출석, 참석 **↔** absence 결석, 부재   **regular attendance** 개근

   The game had an attendance of over 50,000 people.

---

06 ☑ **certificate**
[sərtífikət]

  v certify 증명하다, 공인하다

   n 증명서 **=** licence   **birth certificate** 출생증명서

   She had to get a certificate to prove her degree.

---

01 나는 아직 학위 논문의 주제를 정하지 않았다. / 그 자료는 여성이 남성만큼 공격적이지 않다는 논제를 뒷받침한다. 02 그는 자신이 하버드 대학교 입학 허가를 받은 것을 믿을 수 없었다. 03 인류학은 내가 공부하기 복잡하고 어려운 과목이다. 04 내일 숙제는 5과를 읽는 것이다. 05 그 경기는 5만 명이 넘는 사람들이 관람했다. 06 그녀는 자신의 학위를 증명할 증명서를 떼어 와야 했다.

07 coeducation
[kòuedʒukéiʃən]

ⓥ coeducate
남녀공학을 실시하다

ⓝ 남녀 공학(= coed)　　　**the coeducational system** 남녀 공학 제도

He strongly supported coeducation and the education of African-Americans.

---

08 condense
[kəndéns]

ⓝ condensation 압축, 응축

ⓥ 요약하다, (표현을) 간결하게 하다　　　**condense a story** 이야기를 요약하다

He condensed a paragraph into a sentence.

---

09 correction
[kərékʃən]

ⓐ correct 옳은, 정확한

ⓝ 정정, 수정　　　**make corrections** 수정하다

The paper badly needs corrections before she turns it in.

---

10 curriculum
[kəríkjələm]

ⓐ curricular 교과[이수] 과정의

ⓝ 교육 과정, 이수 과정　　　**a school curriculum** 학교의 교과 과정

I don't like this year's summer school curriculum.

---

11 dean
[diːn]

ⓝ 학장　　　**the dean of the college** 대학 학장

The dean of the College of Education is a sophisticated woman.

---

12 degree
[digríː]

ⓝ 학위, 정도, 도　　　**master's[doctor's] degree** 석사[박사] 학위

★ I already have a bachelor's degree but I want to study more.

★ The temperature dropped to five degrees Centigrade.

---

13 diploma
[diplóumə]

ⓝ 졸업 증서, 학위증　　　**a college diploma** 대학 학위증

He cried when he finally got the diploma in his hand.

---

07 그는 남녀공학과 아프리카계 미국인의 교육을 강력히 지지했다. 08 그는 한 문단을 한 문장으로 요약하였다. 09 그녀가 그 과제를 제출하기 전에 수정이 시급하다. 10 나는 올해 여름학기의 교육 과정이 마음에 들지 않는다. 11 사범 대학의 학장은 세련된 여자다. 12 나는 이미 학사 학위가 있지만, 더 공부하고 싶다. / 온도가 섭씨 5도로 떨어졌다. 13 마침내 졸업 증서를 손에 쥐었을 때 그는 울었다.

14 disciple
[disáipəl]

n 제자, 문하생 **=** student, follower

the twelve Disciples (예수의) 12명의 제자

His disciples wouldn't let him alone, and always asked questions.

15 discipline
[dísəplin]

@ disciplinary 학과의, 규율상의

n 훈련, 학과, 규율

self-discipline 자기훈련, 자제

★ Disciplines such as yoga improve mental and physical fitness.
★ It was desirable for principals to enforce discipline.

16 economics
[ìːkənámiks]

@ economic 경제(학)의

n 경제학

an economics department 경제학과

Most of my friends are majoring in economics.

17 elementary
[èləméntəri]

n element 초보, 입문

@ 초등 교육의, 기본의 **=** basic 기본의

elementary education 초등 교육

★ I didn't like math when I was at elementary school.
★ The right to defend itself is an elementary right of every state.

18 enlighten
[enláitn]

@ enlightening 계몽적인
n enlightenment 교화, 개화

v 계몽하다, 가르치다 **=** instruct

enlighten the public 대중을 계몽하다

The book has enlightened me on many points.

19 enrollment
[enróulment]

v enroll 등록하다

n 입학, 등록

certificate of enrollment 재학 증명서

I received a letter of enrollment from a university last week.

20 ethics
[éθiks]

@ ethical 윤리적인

n 윤리학

professional ethics 직업 윤리학

Reading a book of ethics helps my mind to be calm and still.

---

14 그의 제자들은 그를 가만히 두지 않고 언제나 질문을 했다. 15 요가 같은 훈련은 정신적, 육체적 건강을 향상시킨다. / 교장선생님이 규율을 강요하는 것은 바람직했다. 16 내 친구들은 대부분 경제학을 전공하고 있다. 17 나는 초등학교에 다닐 때 수학을 싫어했다. / 자기를 방어하는 것은 모든 국가의 기본적 권리다. 18 그 책은 많은 점에서 나를 가르쳤다. 19 나는 저번 주에 대학 입학통지서를 받았다. 20 윤리학 책을 읽는 것은 내 마음을 진정시키고 가라앉히는 데 도움이 된다.

21 expertise
[èkspərtíːz]

n expert 전문가, 달인

n 전문 지식 **=** knowledge, know-how　**legal expertise** 법률적 전문 지식

We need expertise to solve this problem.

22 extracurricular
[èkstrəkəríkjələr]

n extracurriculum 과외

a 과외의, 정규 과목 이외의　　**extracurricular activities** 과외활동

She took an extracurricular class after her Spanish class.

23 flunk
[flʌŋk]

v 낙제하다 **=** fail　　**flunk the exams** 시험에서 낙제하다

★ I didn't even flunk the hardest class.

★ Without studying, the students will flunk the extremely difficult exam.

24 idealism
[aidíːəlìzəm]

n 이상주의, 관념론 **=** materialism 유물론　**green idealism** 환경보호 이상주의

His idealism makes him see the world in a different way from how I see it.

25 instructive
[instrʌ́ktiv]

v instruct 가르치다, 지시하다
n instruction 교수, 교훈

a 교육적인, 유익한　　**an instructive experience** 유익한 경험

★ Tommy's father spoke in a very instructive manner.

★ It would have been an instructive lecture if I hadn't fallen asleep.

26 tuition
[tjuːíʃən]

a tuitionary 수업료의

n 수업, 수업료 **=** education, teaching　　**a tuition fee** 수업료

The tuition for the next semester is going to be reduced.

27 learned
[lə́ːrnid]

n learning 배움, 학문

a 학식이 있는, 학문적인 **=** intellectual 지적인　**a learned society** 학회

I like to chat with a friend who is both learned and funny.

---

21 우리는 이 문제를 풀기 위한 전문 지식이 필요하다. 22 그녀는 스페인어 수업이 끝나고 과외 수업을 받았다. 23 나는 가장 어려운 수업조차 낙제하지 않았다. / 공부를 하지 않으면 학생들은 그 매우 어려운 시험에서 낙제하게 될 것이다. 24 그의 이상주의는 그가 내가 보는 것과는 다르게 세상을 보게 한다. 25 Tommy의 아버지는 매우 설교적인 어조로 말씀하셨다. / 내가 만약 졸지 않았다면 그것은 유익한 강의였을 것이다. 26 다음 학기의 등록금이 인하될 것이다. 27 나는 학식이 있으면서도 재미있는 친구와 대화하는 것을 좋아한다.

28 tutor
[tjúːtər]

ⓐ tutorial 개인 교사의

ⓝ 개인 교사   **ⓢ** teacher   **a private tutor** 과외 교사

Some Korean mothers think that all tutors are smart.

---

29 linguistics
[liŋgwístiks]

ⓐ linguistic 언어의, 언어학의

ⓝ 어학, 언어학   **computational linguistics** 컴퓨터 언어학

Studying linguistics can be more difficult than you expect.

---

30 logic
[ládʒik]

ⓐ logical 논리적인

ⓝ 논리학, 논리   **economic logic** 경제 논리

She is especially good at logic, which I don't get at all.

---

31 lore
[lɔːr]

ⓝ (전해 내려오는) 지식, 정보   **ancient lore** 고대의 지식

There has been a lot of history and lore in Korea.

---

32 syllabus
[síləbəs]

ⓝ (강의의) 계획   **draw up a syllabus** 강의 계획을 만들다

The syllabus of today's class was as important as I thought.

---

33 maxim
[mǽksim]

ⓝ 격언, 좌우명   **an unchangeable maxim** 변치 않는 격언

The teacher liked to tell us maxims when starting a class.

---

34 mentor
[méntər]

ⓝ 조언자, 스승   **a business mentor** 사업 조언자

He was the best mentor for me when I studied law at university.

---

28 몇몇 한국 엄마들은 개인 교사들이 모두 똑똑하다고 생각한다. 29 언어학을 공부하는 것은 네가 예상하는 것보다 더 어려울 수도 있다. 30 그녀는 내가 전혀 이해하지 못하는 논리학을 특히 잘한다. 31 한국에는 많은 역사와 전해 내려오는 지식이 있다. 32 오늘 강의 계획은 내가 생각한 대로 중요했다. 33 선생님은 수업을 시작할 때 격언을 말해 주는 것을 좋아했다. 34 내가 대학에서 법을 공부했을 때, 그는 최고의 조언자였다.

---

35 ☑ **motto**
[mátou]

ⓝ 좌우명, 표어

a lifelong motto 일생의 좌우명

My motto for this semester is "study like a monster."

---

36 ☑ **pedagogy**
[pédəgòudʒi]

ⓝ 교육학, 교수법

vocal pedagogy 성악 교육학

If you want to be a teacher, you have to study pedagogy.

---

37 ☑ **pupil**
[pjú:pəl]

ⓝ 학생, 제자

a private school pupil 사립학교 학생

She is such a hardworking pupil that I cannot help loving her.

---

38 ☑ **upbringing**
[ʌ́pbrìŋiŋ]

ⓝ (유년기의 가정에서의) 양육, 교육　**◉** breeding, raising

individual upbringing 개인 양육

The personality of a person is shaped by his or her upbringing.

*bring up : 아이를 양육하다, 가르치다

---

39 ☑ **sophomore**
[sáfəmɔ̀:r]

ⓝ (4년제 대학, 고등학교의) 2학년

a sophomore slump 2년차 증후군

I got A+s for all the classes when I was a sophomore at college.

---

40 ☑ **lowbrow**
[lóubráu]

ⓐ 이해가 쉬운, 저급한　**◉** highbrow 지적인

lowbrow art 저급한 예술

It was a bad decision to visit the museum, which was exhibiting lowbrow paintings.

---

35 이번 학기 나의 좌우명은 "괴물처럼 공부해라"이다. 36 네가 선생님이 되고 싶다면, 교육학을 공부해야 한다. 37 그녀는 매우 열심히 공부하는 학생이라 좋아하지 않을 수 없다. 38 사람의 성격은 가정교육에서 형성된다. 39 나는 대학교 2학년 때 모든 과목에서 A+를 받았다. 40 저급한 그림을 전시하는 박물관을 방문한 것은 잘못된 결정이었다.

EXERCISE

A 다음 영어는 우리말로, 우리말은 영어로 옮기시오.

01 dean _____

02 enrollment _____

03 anthropology _____

04 linguistics _____

05 syllabus _____

06 expertise _____

07 입학 (허가), 승인 _____

08 윤리학 _____

09 2학년 _____

10 양육, 교육 _____

11 학위 논문, 논제 _____

12 경제학 _____

B 다음 빈칸에 알맞은 단어를 쓰시오.

01 enlighten = _____

02 disciple = _____

03 learned = _____

04 lowbrow ⇔ _____

05 attendance ⇔ _____

06 idealism ⇔ _____

07 certificate ⓥ _____

08 coeducation ⓥ _____

09 discipline ⓐ _____

10 tuition ⓐ _____

11 elementary ⓝ _____

12 extracurricular ⓝ _____

C 다음 빈칸에 들어갈 알맞은 말을 고르시오. (필요하면 형태를 바꾸시오.)

| flunk | assignment | lowbrow | instructive | diploma |

01 The journalist's _____ was to cover the malaria outbreak in Africa.

02 Not only was the new television show educational, it was also _____.

03 Without studying for the exam, Joseph _____ the mathematics exam.

04 To interview for most jobs, one needs to have obtained his high school _____.

05 There are some TV channels specializing in _____ entertainment, online game, stock market, or travel information.

Crossword Puzzle

앞에서 배운 어휘를 기억하며 퍼즐을 풀어보세요.

Across

2 special skills or knowledge in a particular subject that you learn by experience or training

3 the scientific study of people, their societies, cultures, etc.

6 the money you pay for being taught

7 a document showing that a student has successfully completed their high school or university education

8 the process of arranging to join a school, university, course, etc.

9 to give someone greater knowledge and understanding about a subject or situation

Down

1 an official document that states that a fact or facts are true

4 moral rules or principles of behavior for deciding what is right and wrong

5 to make something that is spoken or written shorter, by not giving as much detail or using fewer words to give the same information

_____ 과장하다

_____ 증명하다, 설명하다

_____ 설득력 있는

_____ 통역

_____ 문자의, 글자 그대로의

_____ 전달하다

_____ 비평의, 비판적인

_____ 반어, 뜻밖의 결과

Speech & Expression
말과 표현

Literature & Story
문학과 이야기

Education & Learning
교육과 학문

Language and Knowledge
언어와 학문

Books & Arts
책과 예술

_____ 전문 지식

_____ 학위, 정도, 도

_____ 계몽하다

_____ 초등 교육의, 기본의

_____ 글자를 모르는

_____ 견해, 관점

_____ 전기, 일대기

_____ 흉내 내다, 모조하다

Thought & Judgment
생각과 판단

_____ 편견, 선입관

_____ 인정하다

_____ 확실히 하다

_____ 일치하지 않는

Chapter
02

Number, Time, and Space

Number & Quantity

01 abundant
[əbʌ́ndənt]

n abundance 풍부함

a 많은, 풍부한   **an abundant number of textbooks** 많은 교과서

We have an abundant amount of money to spend.

02 algebra
[ǽldʒəbrə]

a algebraic 대수(학)의

n 대수(학)   **do algebra** 대수를 공부하다

I had a hard time studying algebra in high school.

03 approximate
[əprάksəmət / əprάksəmèit]

ad approximately 대략

a 대략의, 대체의 **v** ~에 가까워지다   **the approximate cost** 대략의 비용

★ Give me the approximate number of people you need.

★ His statement approximates the truth, and we have no doubt about it.

04 arithmetic
[əríθmətik]

n 산수 **a** 셈의   **an arithmetic problem** 산수 문제

★ Korean children learn arithmetic earlier than American children.

★ The arithmetic element of problem solving is more difficult for the more verbal person.

05 countless
[káuntlis]

a 셀 수 없을 정도로 많은, 수많은 **⊜** innumerable

a countless number of businesses 수많은 기업들

Countless foreign businesses have established regional offices in Seoul.

06 calculate
[kǽlkjəlèit]

n calculation 계산

v 계산하다   **calculate an amount** 액수를 계산하다

I must have made an error when I calculated the average.

---

01 우리는 쓸 돈이 아주 많다. 02 나는 고등학교에서 대수학을 공부하는 것이 무척 어려웠다. 03 네가 필요한 사람이 대략 몇 명인지 알려줘. / 그의 진술은 사실에 가깝고, 우리는 그것을 의심치 않는다. 04 한국 아이들은 미국 아이들보다 산수를 일찍 배운다. / 문제를 푸는 산술의 원리는 언어적인 사람들에게 더 어렵다. 05 수많은 외국기업이 서울에 지사를 설립했다. 06 내가 평균을 계산할 때 실수를 했던 것이 분명하다.

07 triple
[trípəl]

ⓐ 3중의, 3배의　　　　　　　**a triple gold medallist** 금메달 삼관왕

He must have been traveling at triple the speed of any normal human.

08 equation
[i(:)kwéiʒən]

ⓥ equate 같게 하다, 등식화하다

ⓝ 방정식, 같게 함　　　　　　**solve the equation** 방정식을 풀다

They have to solve a crossword puzzle and mathematical equations.

09 equivalent
[ikwívələnt]

ⓝ equivalence 등가

ⓐ 동등한, ~에 상당하는 ⓝ 동등한 것　　**an equivalent sum** 같은 액수

★ The weight of the items on the scale is equivalent.

★ One piece of chocolate is equivalent to 30 calories.

10 estimate
[éstəmèit / éstəmət]

ⓝ estimation 의견, 판단, 추정

ⓥ 어림잡다 ⓝ 견적, 평가　　　　**an estimated sum** 추정액

★ I estimate the job will take about two hours to finish.

★ Financial analysts expect corporate profit for the year to be more than the original estimate.

11 even
[íːvən]

ⓐ (수가) 같은, 짝수의　⊜ equal 같은 ⊜ odd 홀수의　　**even numbers** 짝수

an even score 동점

★ We have an even chance of winning this game.

★ Please, make sure the even pages of a book are on the left.

12 quadruple
[kwɑdrúːpəl]

ⓥ 4배가 되다, 4배로 만들다 ⓐ 4배의　　**a quadruple pay raise** 4배의 임금인상

★ The market size has quadrupled compared to the past year.

★ With the birth of twins, the laundry has become quadruple overnight.

---

07 그는 보통 인간의 3배 속도로 움직였음에 틀림이 없었다. 08 그들은 십자말풀이와 수학 방정식을 풀어야 한다. 09 저울에 있는 물건의 무게는 서로 같다. / 초콜릿 한 조각은 30칼로리와 같은 것이다. 10 작업을 완료하는 데 두 시간 정도 걸릴 것으로 추정한다. / 재정 분석가들은 올해의 회사 이윤이 원래 견적보다 더 클 것으로 예상한다. 11 우리가 이 게임을 이길 확률은 반반이다. / 책의 짝수 페이지가 왼쪽에 있는지 확인해 주세요. 12 시장 규모가 작년과 비교하면 거의 4배 증가했다. / 쌍둥이가 태어나자, 빨래가 하룻밤 사이에 4배가 되었다.

13 formula
[fɔ́ːrmjələ]

v formulate
형식[공식]으로 나타내다

n (수학) 공식   **a chemical formula** 화학 공식

★ I'm not sure which mathematical formula I can use here.

★ We had endless conversations on how to formulate a peace agreement.

---

14 length
[leŋkθ]

a long 긴

n 길이   **the length and width of the hall** 강당의 길이와 너비

You had better shorten the manuscript to an acceptable length.

---

15 magnitude
[mǽgnətjùːd]

n 크기, 큼   **≒ immensity** 거대   **a considerable magnitude** 상당한 크기

The magnitude of the problem is greater than we can handle.

---

16 mass
[mæs]

a massive 부피가 큰

n 덩어리, 다량, 부피, 질량   **a huge mass of information** 많은 양의 정보   **the mass of the air** 공기의 질량

A mass of errors have been found in the report.

---

17 multiple
[mʌ́ltəpəl]

a 복합의, 다수의, 배수의   **≒ many** 많은, 다수의   **multiple choice testing** 선다형 시험

I have multiple reasons to protest against you.

---

18 multiply
[mʌ́ltəplài]

v 증가시키다, 곱하다   **≒ increase** 증가시키다 **multiply rapidly** 빠르게 증식하다

★ Three multiplied by five is fifteen.

★ Eating junk food often multiplies the risk of obesity and other health problems.

---

19 millennium
[miléniəm]

a 천 년간의, 천년기의   **the second millennium AD** 서기 2천년

That law was written more than a millennium before the Christians existed.

---

13 여기서 어떤 수학 공식을 쓸 수 있는지 확실히 모르겠다. / 우리는 평화조약을 공식화하는 방법에 관해 무한한 대화를 했다. 14 너는 원고를 적절한 길이로 줄이는 것이 낫겠다. 15 문제의 중대성은 우리가 처리할 수 있는 것보다 더 크다. 16 보고서에서 많은 오류가 발견되었다. 17 당신에게 반대할 이유가 여러 가지 있다. 18 3곱하기 5는 15다. / 정크 푸드를 자주 먹는 것은 비만과 다른 건강 문제의 위험을 증가시킨다. 19 그 법은 기독교도들이 존재하기 천 년이 넘는 세월 전에 글로 쓰였다.

20 plural
[plúərəl]

ⓐ 복수의, 다종교[다인종]의 ● singular 단수의   **a plural culture** 다문화

★ You add an '-s' to many nouns in order to make them the plural forms.

★ 'We', 'they' and 'you' are plural pronouns.

21 primary
[práimèri]

ad primarily 첫째로, 처음에는

ⓐ 첫째의, 제1의, 최초의   **the primary stage of civilization** 문명 초기 단계

His primary role as a host is to keep the audience from getting bored.

22 quota
[kwóutə]

ⓝ 몫, (수입품, 이민의) 할당 ● share 몫

import [export] quota 수입[수출] 할당량

Tom has to sell ten more cell phones to achieve this month's sales quota.

23 quotient
[kwóuʃənt]

ⓝ 지수, 몫   **intelligence quotient (IQ)** 지능 지수

Nothing but traveling abroad can increase Jennifer's happiness quotient.

24 rank
[ræŋk]

ⓥ ~로서 자리[지위]를 차지하다 ⓝ 열, 줄, 등급

rank low [high] in one's class 반에서 성적이 낮다[높다]

★ The Empire State Building was ranked number one on the List of America's Favorite Architecture in 2007.

★ The soldiers fell into rank very quickly.

25 rate
[reit]

ⓝ 속도, 비율, 등급 ● grade 등급   **illiteracy rate** 문맹률

The rate of production is increasing faster than ever.

26 reckon
[rékən]

ⓥ 세다, 생각하다 ● count, consider   **reckon up** 합계를 내다

The men came to reckon the size of the hole.

---

20 많은 단어에 '-s'를 추가하여 복수형으로 만들 수 있다. / 'we', 'they', 'you'는 복수대명사다. 21 사회자로서 그의 역할은 관중이 지루함을 느끼지 않게 만드는 것이다. 22 Tom은 자신의 이번 달 판매 몫을 달성하려면 휴대전화를 열 개 더 팔아야 한다. 23 외국여행 외에는 어떤 것도 Jennifer의 행복 지수를 올릴 수 없다. 24 엠파이어스테이트 빌딩은 2007년 미국인이 가장 좋아하는 건축물 순위에서 1위를 차지했다. / 병사들이 매우 신속하게 줄을 맞춰 섰다. 25 생산 속도가 그 어느 때보다 더 빠르게 증가하고 있다. 26 사람들이 구멍의 크기를 측정하러 왔다.

27 redundant
[ridʌ́ndənt]

ⓐ 여분의, 과다한 　ⓔ extra 여분의

get rid of redundant information 불필요한 정보를 없애다

We need to dispose of the redundant items in storage.

28 statistics
[stətístiks]

ⓐ statistical 통계적인

ⓝ 통계, 통계학 　　　**manipulate statistics** 통계를 조작하다

The statistics show that the population has recently grown in this area.

29 subtract
[səbtrǽkt]

ⓝ subtraction 뺄셈

ⓥ 빼다, 공제하다 　ⓔ add 더하다 　　**subtract a number** 숫자를 빼다

If you subtract the costs from the income, you get the profit.

30 twofold
[tú:fòuld]

ⓐ 이중의, 두 배의 　　　　**a twofold purpose** 이중의 목적

The benefits of this opportunity are twofold.

c.f.) threefold : 세 겹의, 세배의

31 dual
[djú:əl]

ⓐ 둘의, 이중의 　　　　　**a dual nationality** 이중 국적

The engineer used a dual-monitor system for his computer.

32 bulk
[bʌlk]

ⓝ 크기, 부피, 대부분 　ⓔ mass 덩어리, 다량, 부피 　　**bulk mail** 대량 우편

The thief committed the bulk of his crimes in big cities.

33 extent
[ikstént]

ⓝ 크기, 정도, 범위 　ⓔ size 크기, degree 정도 　**to a great extent** 대부분, 크게
a vast extent of land 광활한 토지

The judges discussed to what extent he should be punished.

---

27 우리는 창고에 있는 불필요한 물건들을 폐기해야 한다. 28 통계에 의하면 최근에 이 지역의 인구가 증가했다. 29 수입에서 비용을 빼면 이윤을 구할 수 있다. 30 이 기회를 통해 얻을 수 있는 이익은 두 가지다. 31 기술자는 컴퓨터에 이중 모니터 시스템을 사용했다. 32 도둑은 범죄 대부분을 대도시에서 벌였다. 33 재판관들은 그가 어느 정도의 처벌을 받아야 할지 논의했다.

---

34 **multitude**
[mʌ́ltitʲùːd]

🄽 군중, 다수

a noun of multitude 군집 명사

He looked up to the night sky, watching the multitude of stars.

---

35 **peak**
[piːk]

🄽 절정, 최고점

reach a peak 절정에 달하다

The investors waited until the stock market reached its peak.

---

36 **fraction**
[frǽkʃən]

🄰 fractional 분수의

🄽 분수, 파편, 일부

a decimal fraction 소수

a proper [an improper] fraction 진분수[가분수]

His pride was not damaged even by a fraction.

---

37 **quarter**
[kwɔ́ːrtər]

🄽 4분의 1 🄰 4분의 1의

the quarter finals 8강전

★ My mother cut the pizza into quarters.

★ Experts say the third quarter of the year will be the turning point.

---

38 **trillion**
[tríljən]

🄽 1조(兆), 무수(無數)

a trillion = a thousand billion 1조

Revenue reached 24.5 trillion won in 2009, up 1.5 percent from a year earlier.

---

39 **stockpile**
[stákpàil]

🅅 비축하다 🄽 비축량, 축적량

a stockpile of weapons 무기 비축량

Many locals have been stockpiling food as a precaution against shortages.

---

40 **notation**
[noutéiʃən]

🅅 notate 적어 두다

🄽 기호법, 표시법

decimal notation 10진법

musical notation 음표

The mathematical notation was created to record mathematical concepts.

---

34 그는 무수한 별을 보며, 밤하늘을 올려다보았다. 35 투자가들은 주식시장이 최고점에 이를 때까지 기다렸다. 36 그의 자존심은 조금도 상처입지 않았다. 37 어머니는 피자를 네 조각으로 잘랐다. / 전문가들은 올해 삼사분기가 전환점이 될 것이라고 이야기한다. 38 2009년도 매출액은 전년보다 1.5%가 늘어난 24조 5,000억 원에 달했다. 39 많은 지방에서 부족에 대한 예방책으로 식량을 비축하고 있었다. 40 수학적 기호법은 수학의 개념을 기록하기 위해서 만들어졌다.

✎ EXERCISE

A 다음 영어는 우리말로, 우리말은 영어로 옮기시오.

01 arithmetic _____

02 twofold _____

03 formula _____

04 millennium _____

05 multitude _____

06 quadruple _____

07 동등한, ~에 상당하는 _____

08 첫째의, 제1의 _____

09 비축하다, 비축량 _____

10 지수, 몫 _____

11 분수 _____

12 대략의, 대체의 _____

B 다음 빈칸에 알맞은 단어를 쓰시오.

01 magnitude ⊜ _____

02 countless ⊜ _____

03 quota ⊜ _____

04 even ⇔ _____

05 subtract ⇔ _____

06 plural ⇔ _____

07 equation ⓥ _____

08 notation ⓥ _____

09 statistics ⓐ _____

10 mass ⓐ _____

11 calculate ⓝ _____

12 abundant ⓝ _____

C 다음 빈칸에 들어갈 알맞은 말을 고르시오. (필요하면 형태를 바꾸시오.)

multiply	redundant	algebra	reckon	extent

01 _____ is taught to students when they are in junior high school.

02 When editing your essay, it is important to remove _____ opinions and ideas.

03 The _____ of the damage to the car amounted to three hundred dollars in repair costs.

04 With good gardening skills, Shelly was able to _____ the beautiful plants in her garden.

05 We would _____ that there are at least one hundred pumpkins growing in the pumpkin patch.

Crossword Puzzle

앞에서 배운 어휘를 기억하며 퍼즐을 풀어보세요.

1 p
2 c
3 a
4 e
5 r
6 s
7 c
8 m
9 a
10 e
11 e

Across

2 to find out how much something will cost, how long something will take, etc., by using numbers

3 close to the actual, but not completely accurate or exact

9 existing or available in large quantities

10 having the same value, purpose, job, etc. as a person or thing of a different kind

11 how large, important, or serious something is, especially something such as a problem or an injury

Down

1 denoting more than one

4 a calculation of the value, size, amount, etc. of something made using the information that you have, which may not be complete

5 not or no longer needed or useful

6 a set of numbers which represent facts or measurements

7 too many to be counted

8 the great size or importance of something

Chart & Figure

---

01 ☑ **analogy**
[ənǽlədʒi]

ⓐ analogous 비슷한

ⓝ 유사, 비슷함, 닮음 **⊜** similarity　　**a superficial analogy** 표면적 유사성

The two figures have some analogy with each other.

---

02 ☑ **aspect**
[ǽspekt]

ⓝ 양상, 모양, 점, 면　　　　　　　　　**in all aspects** 모든 면에서
an aspect of hair loss 탈모의 양상

This chart shows that we are facing a new aspect of the market.

---

03 ☑ **comparative**
[kəmpǽrətiv]

ⓥ compare 비교하다

ⓐ 비교의, 상대적인 **⊜** relative　　**a comparative analysis** 비교 분석

We need comparative data to define the characteristics.

---

04 ☑ **figurative**
[fígjərətiv]

ⓝ figure 숫자, 그림

ⓐ 비유적인, 조형의, 상징적인　　　　**a figurative expression** 비유적 표현

The picture has many figurative meanings that are hidden.

---

05 ☑ **resemblance**
[rizémbləns]

ⓥ resemble ~와 닮다

ⓝ 유사, 유사점　　　　　　　**a close resemblance** 매우 흡사함
bear a resemblance to ~을 닮다

That drawing bears no resemblance to me!

---

06 ☑ **similarity**
[sìməlǽrəti]

ⓐ similar 비슷한

ⓝ 유사, 비슷함 **⊜** difference 다름, 차이　　**close similarity** 근접한 유사성

The two drawings have a few similarities in style.

---

01 두 형태는 서로 비슷한 면이 있다. 02 이 도표는 우리가 시장의 새로운 국면을 맞이했음을 보여준다. 03 특성을 알기 위해서는 비교 자료가 필요하다. 04 그 그림에는 숨어 있는 여러 비유적인 의미들이 있다. 05 저 그림은 나와 전혀 닮지 않았어! 06 두 그림은 화풍에서 몇 가지 유사성이 있다.

07 row
[rou]

ⓝ 열, 줄, (극장 따위의) 좌석의 줄

sit in the front row 첫 번째 줄에 앉다
in a row 연속적으로

The first row of the chart shows our progress.

08 diminish
[dəmíniʃ]

ⓝ diminution 감소
ⓐ diminutive 소형의, 작은

ⓥ 줄이다 ⊖ decrease ⊕ increase 늘리다

diminish in efficiency 효율성이 감소하다

The graph visualized the diminished rate of growth.

09 linear
[líniər]

ⓝ line 선

ⓐ 선의, 직선의

a linear series 한 줄로 늘어선 것

This drawing used a linear perspective to make it look realistic.

10 counterpart
[káuntərpàːrt]

ⓝ 한 쌍의 한 쪽, 상대방

a counterpart of ~에 대응하는 사람[물건]

If two figures are in symmetry, they are each other's counterparts.

11 diagram
[dáiəgræm]

ⓝ 그림, 도형, 도식

a Venn diagram 벤 다이어그램

Diagrams make complex things easier to understand.

12 diameter
[daiǽmitər]

ⓝ 직경, 지름

the diameter of a circle 원의 지름

Draw a circle which is seven centimeters in diameter.

13 dimension
[dimén∫ən]

ⓐ dimensional ~ 차원의

ⓝ 넓이, 치수, 차원

dimensions of the room 방의 넓이
of three-dimensions 3차원의, 입체의

You should measure the dimensions of your room before you buy a desk.

---

07 도표의 첫 줄은 우리의 진행 상황을 보여준다. 08 그래프는 감소한 성장률을 시각화했다. 09 이 그림은 사실적으로 보이게 하기 위해서 직선 원근법을 사용했다. 10 두 도형이 대칭이면, 둘은 서로의 쌍이다. 11 도식은 복잡한 것들을 이해하기 쉽게 만든다. 12 지름이 7cm인 원을 그리시오. 13 너는 책상을 사기 전에 네 방의 치수를 재야 한다.

14 geometry
[dʒiːámətri]

ⓐ geometric(al) 기하학적인

ⓝ 기하학   **the concepts of geometry** 기하학의 개념

Geometry is the study of lines, angles, surfaces, and solids.

15 fluctuate
[flʌ́ktʃuèit]

ⓝ fluctuation 변동

ⓥ 변동하다, 오르내리다   ⊜ change

fluctuate hourly[widely] 시시각각[크게] 변하다

This graph fluctuates between zero and one.

16 phase
[feiz]

ⓝ 단계, 국면   **the last phase** 마지막 단계

The phase diagram shows the points with significant change.

17 horizontal
[hɔ̀ːrəzántl]

ⓝ horizon 지평선

ⓐ 수평의, 지평선상의   ⊜ vertical 수직의   **a horizontal line** 수평선

A square has two horizontal sides and two vertical sides.

18 lofty
[lɔ́ːfti]

ⓐ 높은, 고상한   ⊜ noble 고상한   **a lofty mountain** 높은 산

The lofty peaks are expressed as the white parts in the picture.

19 erect
[irékt]

ⓐⓓ erectly 똑바로

ⓐ 똑바로 선, 직립의   **stand erect** 똑바로 서다

What is the name of that erect art piece?

20 oval
[óuvəl]

ⓐ 달걀 모양의, 타원형의 **ⓝ** 달걀 모양, 타원   **an oval face** 갸름한 얼굴

★ A rugby ball can bounce randomly because of its oval shape.

★ Mix all the ingredients, and shape into ovals on a cookie sheet.

---

14 기하학은 선, 각도, 면, 입체에 대한 학문이다. 15 이 그래프는 0과 1 사이를 오르내린다. 16 상태도표에는 중요한 변화가 일어나는 지점을 보여준다.
17 사각형은 두 개의 수평면과 두 개의 수직면이 있다. 18 높은 산꼭대기는 그림에서 흰색으로 표현되었다. 19 저기 똑바로 서 있는 예술 작품의 이름이
뭔가요? 20 럭비공은 타원형이기 때문에 무작위로 튈 수도 있다. / 모든 재료를 섞고 쿠키 시트에 타원형으로 만드세요.

---

21 **semicircle**
[sémisə:rkəl]

ⓐ semicircular 반원(형)의

ⓝ 반원   **sit in a semicircle** 반원 모양으로 둘러앉다

You can make a semicircle if you cut a circle by its diameter.

---

22 **parallel**
[pǽrəlèl]

ⓐ 평행한 **ⓝ** 위도선, 평행선   **the 38th parallel** 38선

★ If two lines are parallel, it means that they can never meet.

★ Parallel parking is one of the most difficult driving skills.

---

23 **pentagon**
[péntəgàn]

ⓐ pentagonal 오각형의

ⓝ 오각형   **a regular pentagon** 정오각형

You can find two types of triangle within the pentagon.

---

24 **portion**
[pɔ́:rʃən]

ⓥ apportion 할당하다

ⓝ 한 조각, 일부 **ⓔ** part, piece   **a portion of land** 한 구획의 토지

The largest portion of the chart shows basic information.

---

25 **portrait**
[pɔ́:rtrit]

ⓥ portray 그리다, 묘사하다

ⓝ 초상, 초상화   **a self portrait** 자화상

One of the most well known portraits in the world is the *Mona Lisa*.

---

26 **proportion**
[prəpɔ́:rʃən]

ⓐ proportional
비례의, 비례하는

ⓝ 비율, 균형 **ⓔ** ratio   **direct[inverse] proportion** 정[반]비례

The proportion of the two figures is three to one.

---

27 **rectangular**
[rektǽŋgjələr]

ⓝ rectangle 직사각형

ⓐ 직사각형의, 직각의   **a rectangular box** 직사각형 상자

The four angles of a rectangular figure are all 90 degrees.

---

21 원을 지름으로 자르면 반원을 만들 수 있다. 22 두 선이 서로 평행하다는 것은 서로 절대 만날 수 없다는 것을 의미한다. / 평행 주차는 가장 어려운 운전 기술 중 하나이다. 23 오각형 안에서 두 종류의 삼각형을 찾을 수 있다. 24 도표의 가장 큰 부분은 기본 정보를 나타낸다. 25 전 세계에서 가장 유명한 초상화 중 하나는 '모나리자'다. 26 두 도형의 비율은 3:1이다. 27 직사각형의 네 각은 모두 90도이다.

28 ☐ scale
[skeil]

ⓝ 비율, 규모 **ⓢ** ratio, proportion 비율   **on a large scale** 대규모로

This map shows the city drawn on a scale of one to ten.

29 ☐ section
[sékʃən]

ⓐ sectional 부분적인

ⓝ 절단, 단면, 구분 **ⓢ** part   **a sports section** (신문의)스포츠란

The right section of the diagram represents group A.

30 ☐ segment
[ségmənt]

ⓐ segmental 부분의

ⓝ 단편, 조각 **ⓢ** section, part   **the segment of an orange** 오렌지 조각

We gathered small segments of information to make this chart.

31 ☐ shallow
[ʃǽlou]

ⓝ shallowness 얕음

ⓐ 얕은, 피상적인 **ⓢ** superficial 피상적인 **ⓐ** deep 깊은

shallow water 얕은 물

★ A shallow vessel can only hold shallow water.

★ Jerry is a shallow person who is not used to serious conversations.

32 ☐ share
[ʃɛər]

ⓝ 몫, 할당, 지분 **ⓥ** 나누다, 공유하다   **market share** 시장점유율

★ We can calculate each person's share with these statistics.

★ The parking lot is shared by all the tenants in the apartment complex.

33 ☐ sphere
[sfiər]

ⓐ spheral 구의, 구 모양의

ⓝ 구체, 둥근 모양   **a crystal sphere** 수정구

A long time ago, not many people believed that the Earth was a sphere.

34 ☐ spiral
[spáiərəl]

ⓐ 나선형의, 소용돌이 모양의   **a spiral staircase** 나선 계단
a spiral spring 나선형 용수철

The galaxy we live in has a spiral form.

---

28 이 지도는 도시를 1:10의 비율로 축소하여 보여준다. 29 도식의 오른쪽 부분은 A그룹을 나타낸다. 30 우리는 이 도표를 만들기 위해 단편적인 정보들을 모았다. 31 얕은 그릇은 얕은 물 밖에 담을 수 없다. / Jerry는 진지한 대화에 익숙하지 않은 가벼운 사람이다. 32 우리는 이 통계로 각자의 몫을 계산할 수 있다. / 주차장은 아파트 단지 모든 세입자들에 의해 공유된다. 33 오래전에는 지구가 구체라는 것을 믿는 사람들은 많지 않았다. 34 우리가 사는 은하계는 나선형이다.

35 □ vertical
[və́:rtikəl]

ⓐ 수직의 **⟷** horizontal 수평의   **vertical landing** 수직 착륙

If two lines meet and they are vertical, they make a 90 degree angle.

36 □ symmetry
[símətri]

ⓐ symmetrical 대칭적인

ⓝ 좌우 대칭, 균형   **perfect symmetry** 완전 대칭

★ All symmetry is based on an axis.

★ When designing a floral arrangement, symmetry is very important.

37 □ range
[reindʒ]

ⓝ 범위 **ⓥ** 범위가 ~이다, 정렬시키다

range between A and B 범위가 A와 B 사이에 있다

★ The range of the explosion will have a radius of five meters.

★ Our store has many luxurious bags ranging in price from $1,000 to more than $5,000.

38 □ square
[skwɛər]

ⓝ 정사각형, 제곱, 광장 **ⓐ** 정사각형의, 제곱의

four square meters of ground 4제곱미터의 땅

★ A square is a rectangle whose four sides have equal length.

★ I ordered a mushroom pizza, sliced in squares.

★ The new glasses I chose are square in shape.

39 □ height
[hait]

ⓐ ⓐⓓ high 높은; 높이, 높게

ⓝ 높이, 키, 고지   **the height above sea level** 해발

His height is much higher than you think.

40 □ cube
[kju:b]

ⓐ cubic 세제곱의

ⓝ 정육면체, 세제곱 **ⓥ** (음식 등을) 정육면체로 자르다

ice cube 정육면체 모양의 얼음조각

★ A dice is a cube which has numbers, between one and six, on each side.

★ To cook curry, first of all, cube carrots, potatoes and any other vegetables you like.

---

35 두 선이 만나고, 수직이면 90도의 각도를 이룬다. 36 모든 대칭은 하나의 축을 바탕으로 한다. / 꽃꽂이를 할 때, 균형이 매우 중요하다. 37 폭발의 범위의 반경은 5미터가 될 것이다. / 우리 가게는 천 달러에서 오천 달러 이상의 가격대인 호화로운 가방을 보유하고 있습니다. 38 정사각형은 네 변의 길이가 같은 직사각형이다. / 나는 네모 모양으로 자른 버섯 피자를 주문했다. / 내가 고른 새 안경은 모양이 사각이다. 39 그의 키는 네가 생각하는 것보다 훨씬 더 크다. 40 주사위는 1부터 6까지 숫자가 각 면에 있는 정육면체다. / 카레를 만들려면, 가장 먼저 당근, 감자와 여러분이 좋아하는 다른 모든 채소를 정육면체로 자릅니다.

EXERCISE

Unit 07

A 다음 영어는 우리말로, 우리말은 영어로 옮기시오.

01 aspect _____
02 semicircle _____
03 square _____
04 portion _____
05 diagram _____
06 spiral _____

07 똑바로 선, 직립의 _____
08 비유적인, 조형의 _____
09 단편, 조각 _____
10 비율, 규모 _____
11 좌우 대칭, 균형 _____
12 넓이, 치수, 차원 _____

B 다음 빈칸에 알맞은 단어를 쓰시오.

01 shallow ⊜ _____
02 lofty ⊜ _____
03 proportion ⊜ _____
04 horizontal ⇔ _____
05 similarity ⇔ _____
06 diminish ⇔ _____

07 resemblance ⓥ _____
08 portrait ⓥ _____
09 analogy ⓐ _____
10 geometry ⓐ _____
11 fluctuate ⓝ _____
12 rectangular ⓝ _____

C 다음 빈칸에 들어갈 알맞은 말을 고르시오. (필요하면 형태를 바꾸시오.)

| counterpart | phase | range | parallel | comparative |

01 The company is a _____ newcomer to the automobile industry.

02 Explain that when two lines are _____, the slopes are the same.

03 Puberty is a _____ when boys and girls undergo several physical changes.

04 At the community college there is a wide _____ of students, from the very young to the very old.

05 When working at the international company, Jim found that his _____ in Europe shared many of his thoughts and concerns about work.

Crossword Puzzle

앞에서 배운 어휘를 기억하며 퍼즐을 풀어보세요.

Across

2 a part, share, or number considered in comparative relation to a whole

5 a person or thing closely resembling another, especially in function

8 an aspect, trait, or feature like or resembling another or another's

9 (of lines, planes, or surfaces) side by side and having the same distance continuously between them

10 pointing up in a line that forms an angle of 90° with a flat surface

Down

1 departing from a literal use of words; metaphorical

3 to rise and fall irregularly in number or amount

4 measured or judged by estimating the similarity or dissimilarity between one thing and another

6 to become or make something become smaller or less

7 the quality of being made up of exactly similar parts facing each other or around an axis

Expression of Space

---

01 ☑ **counter**
[káuntər]

ⓐ 반대의, 한쪽의 ⓐⓓ 반대로, 거꾸로   ⊜ opposite to ~의 반대편인

run counter to ~에 반대하다

★ Being rude is counter to everything I believe in as a cultured lady.

★ That girl standing counter to the window is my sister.

---

02 ☑ **breadth**
[bredθ]

ⓐ broad 넓은

ⓝ 폭, 넓음   **the breadth of the stream** 시내의 폭

This building is 40 meters in height, and 70 meters in breadth.

---

03 ☑ **chamber**
[tʃéimbər]

ⓝ 방, 응접실   **chamber orchestra** 실내 관현악단

The council chamber is rectangular and made of black brick.

---

04 ☑ **compartment**
[kəmpáːrtmənt]

ⓝ (비행기, 열차 등의) 칸막이 방, 칸막이   **a smoking compartment** 흡연실

One of the reasons why I like a first-class compartment is that it's very quiet.

---

05 ☑ **converse**
[kənvə́ːrs]

ⓐⓓ conversely 거꾸로

ⓐ 정반대의, 거꾸로의 ⓝ 반대, 전환   **converse figure** 반대 모양

★ This figure completely matches its converse figure.

★ Sean thinks every woman likes him, but in fact the converse is the case.

---

06 ☑ **dense**
[dens]

ⓝ density 농도, 밀도

ⓐ 밀집한, 조밀한   ⊜ sparse 성긴, 희박한   **a dense population** 조밀한 인구

My dog can't stand still in a dense room with many people.

---

01 무례하게 구는 것은 교양 있는 여성으로서 내가 생각하는 모든 것에 반대된다. / 창문의 반대방향으로 서 있는 여자아이가 내 여동생이다. 02 이 빌딩은 높이가 40미터, 폭이 70미터이다. 03 시의회 회의실은 직사각형이며 검정 벽돌로 만들어져 있다. 04 내가 일등실을 좋아하는 이유 중 하나는 그것이 매우 조용해서다. 05 이 모양은 이것의 반대 모양과 완전히 조화된다. / Sean은 모든 여자가 그를 좋아한다고 생각하지만, 사실은 그 반대다. 06 나의 개는 많은 사람이 밀집한 방에서 가만히 있지를 못한다.

---

07 compact
[kəmpǽkt]

ⓐ 빽빽하게 찬, 밀집한, 아담한 ⓥ 압축하다 ⊜ dense 밀집한, compress 압축하다
compact disc (CD) 시디, 콤팩트디스크

★ The map was compact in size to make it easier to carry.

★ This crusher is used to compact aluminum cans or containers to reduce them to 40 percent of their size.

---

08 hollow
[hάlou]

ⓐ 속이 빈, 우묵한 ⊜ empty **a hollow tree** 속이 빈 나무

It could be said that a pipe is a hollow cylinder.

---

09 edge
[edʒ]

ⓝ 가장자리, 모서리 **a double-edged sword** 양날의 검

Don't put the mug on the edge of the table.

---

10 elevation
[èləvèiʃən]
ⓥ elevate 올리다, 높이다

ⓝ 높이, 고도, 해발 **a high elevation** 높은 고도

The highest elevation on the island is only 60 feet above sea level.

---

11 capacity
[kəpǽsəti]
ⓐ capacious 널찍한

ⓝ 용량, 수용능력 ⊜ volume, room **storage capacity** 저장 용량

The water capacity of a bowl is equal to its volume.

---

12 extension
[iksténʃən]
ⓥ extend 뻗다, 펴다

ⓝ 연장, 확대 **extension cord** 연장 코드

This house needs an extension to make three more rooms.

---

13 flat
[flæt]

ⓐ 납작한, 편평한, 단호한 **flat as a pancake** 팬케이크처럼 납작한

She folded the clothes flat and neat.

---

07 지도는 들고 다니기 편하도록 아담한 크기였다. / 이 분쇄기는 알루미늄 캔이나 용기를 압축시켜 크기를 40%로 줄이는 데 사용된다. 08 파이프는 일종의 속이 빈 원기둥이라고 할 수 있다. 09 테이블의 가장자리에 머그잔을 놓지 마라. 10 그 섬의 최고 높이는 겨우 해발 60피트에 불과하다. 11 그릇이 담을 수 있는 물의 용량은 그 부피와 같다. 12 이 집은 방을 세 개 더 만들기 위해 확장이 필요하다. 13 그녀는 옷들을 납작하고 깔끔하게 접었다.

14 fragment
[frǽgmənt]

ⓝ 부분, 조각 **ⓥ** 분해하다　　**fragments of a broken window** 깨진 유리 조각

The delicate china ornament fragmented when it was dropped.

15 expansion
[ikspǽnʃən]

ⓥ expand 확장하다, 확대하다

ⓝ 팽창, 확대　　　　　　　**volume expansion** 부피 확대

Most fish in this area suffered heavily due to the expansion of the red tide.

16 inverse
[invə́:rs]

ⓝ inversion 역, 정반대

ⓐ 역의, 반대의, 반비례의

Our sales volume is in inverse proportion to the price of the oil.

17 width
[widθ]

ⓐ wide 넓은
ⓥ widen 넓히다

ⓝ 폭, 너비　**ⓔ** breadth　　**fifty centimeters in width** 넓이가 50센티미터인

Measure the width of your room before you buy a bed.

18 layer
[léiər]

ⓝ 층 **ⓥ** 층을 내다, 층을 이루다　　　　　**ozone layer** 오존층

★ A layer of dust on the desk made my nose itchy.

★ To appear like I had less hair, my front hair was layered by the hairdresser.

19 location
[loukéiʃən]

ⓥ locate 위치를 정하다

ⓝ 장소, 위치, 지역　　　　　　　**a mining location** 탄광 지대

I hid my diary in an undisclosed location.

20 narrow
[nǽrou]

ⓝ narrowness 좁음, 궁핍

ⓐ 폭이 좁은, 부족한　　　　　　　**a narrow road** 좁은 도로

He got too fat to sit on the narrow chair.

---

14 정교한 도자기 장식품은 떨어지자 산산조각이 났다. 15 적조의 확산으로 이 지역 물고기 대부분이 큰 피해를 입었다. 16 우리의 판매량은 휘발유의 가격과 반비례한다. 17 침대를 사기 전에 네 방의 폭을 재라. 18 책상 위에 있는 먼지 층은 내 코를 가렵게 했다. / 머리숱이 적어 보이도록 미용사는 내 앞머리를 층을 냈다. 19 나는 내 일기를 비밀 장소에 숨겨두었다. 20 그는 살이 너무 쪄서 폭이 좁은 의자에 앉을 수 없었다.

---

21 □ **quantity**
[kwántəti]

n 양, 분량, 다량 **↔** quality 질, 재질   **a large quantity of books** 다수의 책

When it comes to work, he prefers quality to quantity.

---

22 □ **rear**
[riər]

n 뒤 **a** 뒤쪽의 **↔** front 앞, 앞쪽의   **a rear window** 뒤쪽 창문

★ The rear of my car was damaged by the big truck.

★ I didn't know a rear tire of my car had gone flat.

---

23 □ **remote**
[rimóut]

ad **remotely** 멀리 떨어져서

a 먼, 외딴   **a remote relative** 먼 친척

People sometimes think that they want to go somewhere remote.

---

24 □ **rotation**
[routéiʃən]

v **rotate** 회전하다, 교대하다

n 회전, 순환, 교대   **by rotation** 차례로

Crop rotation is practiced to keep the soil healthy.

---

25 □ **spatial**
[spéiʃəl]

n **space** 공간

a 공간의, 공간적인   **spatial relationships** 공간적 관계

This set of questions is to test spatial ability.

---

26 □ **spot**
[spɑt]

n 현장, 점, 얼룩   **on the spot** 현장에서

You should be careful to keep your clothes safe from spots and stains.

---

27 □ **summit**
[sʌ́mit]

n 꼭대기, 정상, 정상 회담   **summit talks** 정상 회담

I finally reached the summit of the mountain.

---

21 일에 관한 것이면, 그는 양보다는 질을 택한다. 22 큰 트럭이 내 차의 뒷부분을 망가뜨렸다. / 나는 내 자동차의 뒤 타이어 하나가 구멍 났었다는 것을 몰랐다. 23 사람들은 가끔 외딴곳으로 떠나고 싶다고 생각한다. 24 윤작은 흙을 건강하게 유지하기 위해 실행된다. 25 이 문제 세트는 공간 지각 능력을 측정하기 위한 것이다. 26 너는 옷에 얼룩이 지지 않도록 주의해야 한다. 27 나는 드디어 산 정상에 다다랐다.

28 sunken
[sʌ́ŋkən]

v sink 가라앉았다

ⓐ 가라앉은, 침몰한

a sunken ship 가라앉은 배

Sunken treasure is believed to be on the *Titanic*.

29 threshold
[θréʃhòuld]

ⓝ 입구, 발단

the threshold to the building 건물 입구

I had to cross the threshold to meet my boss.

30 medium
[míːdiəm]

ⓝ 중간, 매개(물) **ⓐ** 중간의

medium-sized 중간 크기의

★ The artist used a visual medium of images to express his artwork.

★ This cannon is used for medium range attacks.

31 magnify
[mǽgnəfài]

ⓝ magnification 확대, 과장

ⓥ 확대하다 **⊜** enlarge

a magnifying glass 돋보기

This model is a magnified version of the human DNA structure.

32 vacant
[véikənt]

ⓝ vacancy 공허, 공간

ⓐ 공허한, 비어있는

a vacant seat 비어있는 좌석

She looked at me with a vacant stare.

33 void
[vɔid]

ⓝ 빈 공간

a silent void 고요하고 텅 빈 공간

It will be difficult to fill the void left by his best friend who moved to Europe.

34 pit
[pit]

ⓝ 구멍, 패인 곳, 구덩이

dig a pit 구덩이를 파다

My dog is digging a pit to hide his food.

---

28 가라앉은 보물은 타이타닉 호에 있던 것으로 여겨진다. 29 나는 상사를 만나려고 입구를 지나가야 했다. 30 예술가는 자신의 예술 작품을 표현하고 자 시각을 매체로 하는 이미지를 사용했다. / 이 대포는 중거리 공격에 사용된다. 31 이 모형은 인간의 DNA 구조를 확대한 것이다. 32 그녀는 나를 무표 정한 눈빛으로 바라보았다. 33 유럽으로 떠난 그의 가장 친한 친구가 남긴 빈자리를 채우기 어려울 것이다. 34 나의 개는 마당을 파서 음식을 숨기고 있다.

35 central
[séntrəl]

ⓝ center 중심, 중앙

ⓐ 중앙의, 중심의　　　**central processing unit (CPU)** 중앙 처리 장치

Dwight is the central student in this class.

36 brink
[briŋk]

ⓝ (벼랑 따위의) 가장자리, 직전

on the brink of (멸망 죽음 등)에 임박하여, ~의 직전에

on [at] the brink of starvation 아사 직전에

★ Be careful not to be too close to the brink of the cliff.

★ Over two hundred species are currently on the brink of extinction.

37 empty
[émpti]

ⓐ 텅 빈, 공허한　**⊜** vacant　　　**an empty milk bottle** 빈 우유병

An empty bag has literally hundreds of uses — especially while traveling.

38 cubic
[kjú:bik]

ⓐ 입방의, 3제곱의　　　**cubic meter** 세제곱미터

The estimation of this room is thirty cubic meters.

39 pothole
[páthòul]

ⓝ 깊은 구멍, 둥근 웅덩이　　　**a pothole in the road** 도로의 깊은 구멍

This road has so many potholes, twists, and cracks.

40 heighten
[háitn]

ⓝ height 높이, 고도

ⓥ 높게 하다, 높이다　　　**heightening tension** 고조되는 긴장

She heightened the tension in the room, with her statement.

---

35 Dwight는 우리 반의 중심에 있는 학생이다. 36 절벽의 가장자리에 너무 다가가지 않도록 주의하세요. / 200개가 넘는 종이 현재 멸종 직전에 처해 있다. 37 빈 가방은 특히 여행하는 동안에 말 그대로 아주 많은 용도가 있다. 38 이 방의 견적은 30세제곱미터. 39 이 도로는 웅덩이, 뒤틀림, 갈라진 틈이 매우 많았다. 40 그녀는 자신의 말로 방 안의 긴장을 고조시켰다.

✏️ EXERCISE

A 다음 영어는 우리말로, 우리말은 영어로 옮기시오.

01 compact _____

02 medium _____

03 fragment _____

04 heighten _____

05 narrow _____

06 counter _____

07 정반대의, 반대, 전환 _____

08 장소, 위치, 지역 _____

09 입방체의, 3제곱의 _____

10 빈 공간 _____

11 가장자리, 모서리 _____

12 중앙의, 중심의 _____

B 다음 빈칸에 알맞은 단어를 쓰시오.

01 width ⊜ _____

02 magnify ⊜ _____

03 capacity ⊜ _____

04 rear ⇔ _____

05 quantity ⇔ _____

06 dense ⇔ _____

07 evaluation ⓥ _____

08 sunken ⓥ _____

09 rotation ⓥ _____

10 breadth ⓐ _____

11 vacant ⓝ _____

12 spatial ⓝ _____

C 다음 빈칸에 들어갈 알맞은 말을 고르시오. (필요하면 형태를 바꾸시오.)

| layer | summit | threshold | remote | converse |

01 _____ to what you may believe, Sharon and I are still the best of friends.

02 I asked the hair dresser to _____ my hair so it would not appear too full.

03 Since we live in a _____ part of the country, each trip to the city has to be planned carefully.

04 Most of the presidents of the developed countries attended the important economic _____.

05 The wedding day marked the _____ of a new life together for the young couple.

Crossword Puzzle

앞에서 배운 어휘를 기억하며 퍼즐을 풀어보세요.

1. r
2. q
3. c
4. v
5. t
6. c
7. s
8. c
9. m
10. s

Across

1. far from towns or other places where people live
2. an amount of something that can be counted or measured
6. small, but arranged so that everything fits neatly into the space available
8. having characteristics which are the reverse of something else already mentioned
9. to make something seem bigger or louder, especially using special equipment
10. relating to the position, size, shape, etc. of things

Down

1. the practice of regularly changing the thing that is being used or done, or the person who does a particular job
3. the total amount that can be contained or produced
4. not occupied
5. the level at which something starts to happen or have an effect
7. an important meeting or set of meetings between the leaders of several governments

Unit 09

Expression of Time

---

01 ☑ **bygone**
[báigɔ̀:n]

ⓐ 과거의, 지나간 ⓝ 〈복수형〉 과거의 일　　　　**bygone days** 지난날, 옛날

★ My bygone days of happiness will be remembered.
★ Let bygones be bygones.

---

02 ☑ **centennial**
[senténiəl]

ⓝ **century** 1세기, 100년

ⓐ 100년마다의, 100년(간)의 ⓝ 100주년
　　　　　　　　　a centennial anniversary 100주년 기념

★ His grandfather had a centennial birthday party.
★ The centennial of the museum was celebrated throughout the city.

---

03 ☑ **coincide**
[kòuinsáid]

ⓝ **coincidence** 동시발생, 일치

ⓥ 동시에 일어나다(with), 일치하다

My birthday coincides with a Korean holiday so I have never had a birthday party.

---

04 ☑ **consecutive**
[kənsékjətiv]

ⓐⓓ **consecutively** 연속적으로

ⓐ 연속적인, 잇따른　　　　**consecutive numbers** 일련 번호

They have ten consecutive wins.

---

05 ☑ **contemporary**
[kəntémpərèri]

ⓐⓓ **contemporarily** 현대적으로

ⓐ 동시대의, 현대의 ⓝ 동시대의 사람　　**contemporary literature** 현대 문학

★ Some people like contemporary jazz more than original jazz.
★ Mr. Smith was a contemporary of the famous actor James Dean.

---

06 ☑ **imminent**
[ímənənt]

ⓝ **imminence** 절박, 급박

ⓐ 절박한, 급박한　　　　**imminent danger** 임박한 위험

The deadline for my homework is imminent.

---

01 나의 행복했던 지난 시간은 기억될 것이다. / 〈속담〉 과거의 일은 잊어버려라.　02 그의 할아버지는 100주년 생일 파티를 했다. / 박물관의 100주년 기념일은 도시 전역에 걸쳐 기념되었다.　03 나의 생일은 한국의 공휴일과 겹쳐서 한 번도 생일 파티를 해본 적이 없다.　04 그들은 10연승을 했다.　05 어떤 사람들은 정통 재즈보다 현대 재즈를 좋아한다. / Smith 씨는 유명한 배우 제임스 딘과 동시대인이었다.　06 내 숙제의 마감일이 가깝다.

07 dawn
[dɔːn]

ⓝ 새벽, 처음, 시작 **ⓥ** 날이 새다, 밝아지다　　　　　**at dawn** 새벽녘에

★ I couldn't sleep till dawn thinking of the job interview.

★ When it dawns, the sunlight streams gently into my room.

08 decade
[dékeid]

ⓝ 10년　　　　　　　　　　　**for several decades** 수십 년간

★ His mother passed away a decade ago.

★ I am now three decades old.

09 epoch
[épək]

ⓐ epochal 신기원의, 획기적인

ⓝ 시대, 신기원　　　　　　　　　**the recent epoch** 현세

Now is the time to move into a new epoch.

10 foregone
[fɔːrgɔ́(ː)n]

ⓐ 이전의, 앞선, 미리 정해진, 불가피한　　**a foregone conclusion** 뻔한 결과

The outcome of the election was a foregone conclusion.

11 former
[fɔ́ːrmər]

ⓐ 전의, 앞의　**ⓔ** previous　　　　**a former student** 예전 학생

She missed a problem on the former test.

12 immediate
[imíːdiət]

ⓐd immediately 지금 당장, 즉시

ⓐ 인접한, 즉시의, 가까운　　　　　**an immediate cause** 직접적인 원인

If you don't have an immediate answer, you should go home.

13 initial
[iníʃəl]

ⓐd initially 초기에

ⓐ 최초의, 시작의　　　　　　　　**an initial letter** 머리글자

The initial shock didn't go away until he came home.

---

07 나는 구직 면접 생각으로 새벽까지 잠들지 못했다. / 날이 밝으면 햇빛이 부드럽게 내 방으로 흘러들어온다.　08 그의 어머니는 10년 전에 돌아가셨다.
/ 나는 이제 서른 살이다.　09 이제 새로운 시대로 들어갈 시간이다.　10 선거 결과는 너무 뻔했다.　11 그녀는 이전 시험에서 한 문제를 놓쳤다.　12 질문에
바로 답할 수 없으면, 집에 가는 것이 나을 것이다.　13 그가 집에 오기 전까지 초기의 충격이 가시지 않았다.

14 lapse
[læps]

ⓝ 시간의 경과, 추이　　　**a considerable lapse of time** 상당한 시간의 경과

After a lapse of two months, he replied to my letter.

15 long-term
[láŋtə̀ːrm]

ⓐ 장기(간)의　**ⓞ** short-term 단기(간)의　　　**a long-term loan** 장기 대출

We signed on the paper for a long-term lease for a car to travel.

16 medieval
[mìːdíːvəl]

ⓐ 중세풍의, 중고의, 낡은　　　**medieval history** 중세사

ⓐⓓ medievally 중세풍으로

The buildings of the medieval era are so fascinating.

17 momentary
[móuməntèri]

ⓐ 순간의, 시시각각의　　　**a momentary silence** 순간의 고요

ⓝ moment 순간

There was momentary silence in the room.

18 nocturnal
[nɑktə́ːrnl]

ⓐ 밤의, 야간의　**ⓞ** diurnal 낮의, 주간의　　　**nocturnal animals** 야행성 동물

ⓝ nocturne 녹턴, 야상곡

I think I am nocturnal because I go to bed in the morning.

19 occasional
[əkéiʒənəl]

ⓐ 때때로, 임시의, 우연의　　　**occasional decrees** 임시 법령

ⓝ occasion 때[경우], 행사

ⓐⓓ occasionally 가끔, 이따금씩

Seoul and Gyeonggi will be cloudy with occasional rain.

20 onset
[ánsèt]

ⓝ 시작, 개시, 공격　　　**onset of winter** 겨울의 시작

★ I am standing on the onset of my career in law.

★ With the onset of puberty, my younger brother is dealing with the problem of pimples.

★ The troops were not able to stand against the onset of the enemy.

---

14 두 달이 지난 후 그는 내 편지에 답장했다.　15 우리는 여행을 가기 위해 장기로 차를 빌리는 서류에 사인했다.　16 중세시대의 건물들은 참 매력적이다.　17 방 안에는 일시적인 침묵이 흘렀다.　18 나는 아침에 잠이 들기 때문에 야행성이라고 생각한다.　19 서울과 경기도는 흐리고 한때 비가 내릴 것이다.　20 나는 나의 법조계에서의 경력의 시작에 서 있다. / 내 남동생은 사춘기의 시작과 함께 여드름 문제를 겪고 있다. / 군대는 적의 습격을 이겨내지 못했다.

---

21 **perennial**
[pəréniəl]

n perenniality 여러 해 계속함

a 다년생의, 연중 끊이지 않는　**⊜** annual 1년생의

a perennial [annual] plant 다년생[일년생]식물

I want to see a perennial plant when I go to the flower shop.

---

22 **periodical**
[pìəriádikəl]

ad periodically 주기적으로

a 주기적인, 정기적인 **n** 정기간행물

bound periodicals (도서관에 비치되어 있는) 정기간행물

★ He wants periodical check on the project.

★ My favorite periodical discusses fashion in Europe.

---

23 **posterity**
[pɑstérəti]

a posterior 뒤의, 다음의

n 자손, 후세

hand down something to posterity ~을 자손에게 물려주다

He is the only posterity of the royal family.

---

24 **posthumous**
[pástʃuməs]

ad posthumously 사후에

a 죽은 뒤의

posthumous fame 사후의 명성

If I suddenly die, I want a posthumous publication of my book.

---

25 **precede**
[pri:sí:d]

v ~보다 먼저 일어나다, ~보다 앞서다　**⊜** antecede ~에 선행하다

the preceding year 그 전해

Do you think the cause precede the effect?

---

26 **predecessor**
[prédisèsər]

n 전임자　**⊜** successor 상속자, 후임자　**one's predecessor** ~의 전임자

His boss is the kindest of the predecessors.

---

27 **preliminary**
[prilímənèri]

a 준비의, 예비의

preliminary stages 준비 단계

This research is preliminary to a larger project.

---

21 꽃가게에 들르면 다년생 식물을 보고 싶다. 22 그는 프로젝트를 주기적으로 확인하길 원한다. / 내가 가장 좋아하는 정기간행물은 유럽의 패션에 대해 다룬다. 23 그는 왕족의 하나밖에 없는 자손이다. 24 내가 갑자기 죽는다면, 내 책의 사후 출판을 원한다. 25 너는 원인이 결과에 앞선다고 생각하니? 26 그의 상사는 전임자 중 가장 친절하다. 27 이 연구는 더 큰 프로젝트에 앞선 예비 단계이다.

28 primitive
[prímətiv]

ⓐ 원시의, 원시적인　**ⓞ** modern 현대의　　　**a primitive tribe** 원시 부족

The students visited the museum to learn about primitive culture.

29 prior
[práiər]

ⓝ priority 우선(중요) 사항

ⓐ 앞의, ~전의　**ⓐⓓ** ~보다 전에　　　**a prior engagement** 선약

★ You should know that this work is prior to your date.

★ It is best to book a room at least two weeks prior to your arriving there.

30 punctual
[pʌ́ŋktʃuəl]

ⓐ 시간을 엄수하는　　**punctual as the clock** 시계처럼 시간을 어기지 않는

I am very punctual so I don't like people who are late.

31 session
[séʃən]

ⓝ 회기, 개정 기간, 학기　**a question-and-answer session** 질의응답 시간

The training session for new teachers will last two weeks.

32 simultaneous
[sàiməltéiniəs]

ⓐⓓ simultaneously 동시에

ⓐ 동시의, 동시에 일어나는　**ⓞ** coincident

simultaneous translation 동시통역

The job interview was a simultaneous interview with four other rivals.

33 span
[spæn]

ⓝ 기간, 범위　　　　　　　　　　　　　**life span** 수명

During a brief span, he didn't speak a word.

34 spell
[spel]

ⓝ 한 동안의 계속, 잠시 동안　　　　　**a dry spell** 건기, 불황기

The current cold spell will be gone by next week.

---

28 학생들은 원시문화를 배우기 위해 박물관을 방문했다. 29 지금 이 일이 너의 데이트보다 먼저라는 것을 알아야 한다. / 당신이 그곳에 도착하기 적어도 2주 전에 방을 예약하는 것이 가장 좋다. 30 나는 시간을 지키기 때문에 늦는 사람들이 싫다. 31 새로 채용된 교사들을 위한 연수 과정은 2주일간 계속될 것이다. 32 그 면접은 다른 4명의 경쟁자와 동시에 하는 면접이었다. 33 짧은 기간 동안, 그는 한마디도 하지 않았다. 34 지금의 한파는 다음 주에는 풀릴 것이다.

---

35 ☑ **subsequent**
[sʌ́bsikwənt]

ⓝ subsequence 뒤이어 일어남

ⓐ 뒤의, 다음의   **a subsequent event** 후에 생긴 일

They didn't think about the subsequent happening.

---

36 ☑ **synchronize**
[síŋkrənàiz]

ⓥ 동시에 일어나게 하다   **synchronize watches** 시계들의 시간을 똑같이 맞추다

The book publisher always synchronizes publication with online marketing campaigns.

---

37 ☑ **temporary**
[témpərèri]

ad temporarily
일시적으로, 임시로

ⓐ 임시의, 순간의 ⊖ permanent 영구적인   **a temporary position** 임시직

It was only a temporary job to fill the vacant position.

---

38 ☑ **terminal**
[tə́ːrmənəl]

ⓥ terminate 끝내다, 종점이 되다

ⓐ 말기의, 말단의 ⓝ 끝, 종점   **terminal lung [liver] cancer** 폐[간]암 말기

★ They measured the terminal velocity of the rocket.

★ Baghdad was chosen to be the terminal station for the railroad line.

---

39 ☑ **transient**
[trǽnʃənt]

ⓐ 일시적인, 덧없는   **a transient fashion trend** 일시적인 패션 경향

She gave us a transient solution at the moment.

---

40 ☑ **foremost**
[fɔ́ːrmòust]

ⓐ 최초의, 일류의   **a foremost boxer** 최고의 복싱선수

★ Which animal is the foremost animal on the Earth?

★ She's one of the foremost experts on child psychology.

---

35 그들은 뒤에 생길 일은 생각하지 않았다. 36 그 출판사는 항상 출판과 온라인 마케팅 활동을 동시에 한다. 37 그것은 빈자리를 채우기 위한 임시적인 일에 불과했다. 38 그들은 로켓의 최종 속도를 측정했다. / 바그다드는 철도 노선의 종착역으로 선택되었다. 39 그녀는 바로 우리에게 일시적인 해결방법을 주었다. 40 어떤 동물이 지구의 최초의 동물일까? / 그녀는 아동 심리학 분야에서 최고의 전문가 중 한 사람이다.

EXERCISE

A 다음 영어는 우리말로, 우리말은 영어로 옮기시오.

01 immediate   _____

02 terminal   _____

03 periodical   _____

04 span   _____

05 onset   _____

06 coincide   _____

07 중세풍의, 중고의   _____

08 연속적인, 잇따른   _____

09 동시에 일어나게 하다   _____

10 시간을 엄수하는   _____

11 최초의, 시작의   _____

12 준비의, 예비의   _____

B 다음 빈칸에 알맞은 단어를 쓰시오.

01 former   ⊜ _____

02 precede   ⊜ _____

03 simultaneous   ⊜ _____

04 primitive   ⊜ _____

05 predecessor   ⊜ _____

06 nocturnal   ⊜ _____

07 posterity   ⓐ _____

08 occasion   ⓐ _____

09 perennial   ⓝ _____

10 centennial   ⓝ _____

11 imminent   ⓝ _____

12 prior   ⓝ _____

C 다음 빈칸에 들어갈 알맞은 말을 고르시오. (필요하면 형태를 바꾸시오.)

dawn	epoch	foremost	contemporary	posterity

01 The discovery of the DNA opened up a new _____ in biology.

02 Maintaining one's integrity is _____ when making a business deal.

03 The museum had many _____ pieces of artwork from the early 1800s.

04 The _____ brings with it new sounds and light that wakes up the soul.

05 The message we want to leave behind for _____ is to take good care of the earth.

Crossword Puzzle

앞에서 배운 어휘를 기억하며 퍼즐을 풀어보세요.

정답

Across

2 to happen at the same time as something else, especially by chance

3 the length of time over which someone's life, ability to pay attention to something, etc. continues

8 happening sometimes but not often or regularly

9 a period of time between two events

Down

1 occurring, operating, or done at the same time

2 following each other continuously

4 arriving, happening, or being done at exactly the time that has been arranged

5 belonging to a simple way of life that existed in the past and does not have modern industries

6 done, occurring, or active at night

7 happening at the beginning

_____ 동등한

_____ 대략의, 대체의

_____ 어림잡다

_____ 계산하다

_____ 많은, 풍부한

_____ 유사, 비슷함

_____ 비교의, 상대적인

_____ 변동하다

_____ 비율, 균형

_____ 수직의

Number & Quantity
수와 양

Chart & Figure
도표와 그림

Number, Time, and Space
수, 시간, 공간

Expression of Space
공간적 표현

Expression of Time
시간적 표현

_____ 회전, 순환

_____ 공간의, 공간적인

_____ 확대하다

_____ 용량, 수용능력

_____ 역의, 반비례의

_____ 연속적인, 잇따른

_____ 동시의

_____ 10년

_____ ~보다 먼저 일어나다

_____ 시간을 엄수하는

Chapter
03

Society and Culture

Unit 10 Economy & Finance

---

01 ☑ affordable
[əfɔ́ːrdəbəl]
ⓥ **afford** ~할 여유가 있다

ⓐ 값이 알맞은, 입수 가능한   **an affordable price** 적당한 가격

The price of the stock this week is affordable enough for me to buy.

---

02 ☑ application
[æpləkèiʃən]
ⓥ **apply** 신청하다, 적용하다

ⓝ 지원서, 신청서, 적용   **application form** 입사지원서

★ She sent an application to join an insurance company.
★ A computer has a wide range of applications for businesses.

---

03 ☑ asset
[ǽset]

ⓝ 자산, 재산   ⊜ property   **capital asset** 자본 자산

The assets of the corporation were not enough to buy more goods.

---

04 ☑ insurance
[inʃúərəns]
ⓥ **insure** 보증하다, 확신하다

ⓝ 보험, 보증   **life insurance** 생명 보험

The company bought insurance in case of bankruptcy.

---

05 ☑ peddle
[pédl]
ⓝ **peddler** 행상인

ⓥ 행상하다, 소매하다   ⊜ sell   **peddle drugs** 마약을 밀매하다

He makes a living by peddling corn dogs on the street.

---

06 ☑ bankrupt
[bǽŋkrʌpt]
ⓝ **bankruptcy** 파산, 파탄

ⓐ 파산한   **go bankrupt** 파산하다

The company was forced to declare that they went bankrupt.

---

01 이번 주 주식 가격은 내가 사기에 적당하다. 02 그녀는 보험사에 가입하기 위해 신청서를 보냈다. / 컴퓨터는 업무용으로 다양하게 적용된다. 03 그 회사의 자산은 상품을 더 살 정도로 충분하지 않았다. 04 그 회사는 파산에 대비하여 보험을 들었다. 05 그는 길거리에서 핫도그를 팔아서 생계를 유지한다. 06 회사는 어쩔 수 없이 파산했음을 선언했다.

07 bargain
[bá:rgən]

n 싼 물건 **v** 흥정하다   **a bargain day** 할인 판매일

★ The department store is starting a bargain sale today.

★ The ship owner bargained with traders about transport fees.

08 barter
[bá:rtər]

v 물물교환하다, 교역하다 ● trade   **barter goods** 상품을 물물교환하다

Merchants from different nations gather here to barter goods.

09 personnel
[pè:rsənél]

n 직원, 인사과 ● staff, employee

a personnel department 인사부, 인사과

Untrained personnel must not enter this area.

10 broker
[bróukər]

n brokerage 중개업

n 중개인, 증권 중개인 ● dealer   **a stock broker** 주식 중개인

I bought a large amount of stock through the broker.

11 deposit
[dipázit]

n 예금, 보증금 **v** 예금하다, 맡기다   **deposit rate** 예금 금리

★ If there is no damage in the room, the deposit is fully refunded when you move out.

★ I try to deposit as much money as possible.

★ You are advised to deposit your valuables in the hotel safe.

12 CEO

n 최고경영자(Chief Executive Officer)

the CEO of the company 회사의 최고경영자

She is the first female CEO since the foundation of our company.

13 client
[kláiənt]

n 의뢰인, 고객, 거래처   **a local client** 지방 거래처

He is one of the oldest clients of our insurance company.

---

07 백화점에서 오늘부터 할인 판매를 시작한다. / 배 주인은 상인과 운송비를 흥정했다. 08 다양한 나라의 상인들이 여기에 모여 물물교환을 한다. 09 훈련받지 않은 직원이 이 구역에 출입이 금지되어 있습니다. 10 나는 중개인을 통해서 많은 양의 주식을 사들였다. 11 방에 아무런 훼손이 없으면, 보증금은 이사 갈 때 모두 반환됩니다. / 나는 가능한 한 많은 돈을 예금하려고 한다. / 네 귀중품을 호텔 금고에 맡기도록 충고하는 바이다. 12 그녀는 회사 창립 이래 최초의 여성 최고경영자다. 13 그는 우리 보험회사의 가장 오래된 고객 중 한 명이다.

14 commercial
[kəmə́:rʃəl]

n commerce 상업

a 상업의 **n** 광고방송　　　　　　　　　**a commercial area** 상업지구

★ Unauthorized commercial activity in the park is prohibited.

★ TV shows more toy commercials just before Christmas.

---

15 commodity
[kəmádəti]

n 상품, 물자　　　　　　　　　　**prices of commodities** 물가

Experts argue that clean air should be regarded as a commodity.

---

16 commute
[kəmjú:t]

n commuter 통근자

v 통근하다 **n** 통근　　　　　　　　**a reverse commuter** 역방향 통근자

★ Some colleagues and I commute to work by bicycle.

★ I recently moved close to my work to avoid the long commute.

---

17 consumption
[kənsʌ́mpʃən]

v consume 소비하다
a consumptive 소비의

n 소비, 소비량　　　　　　　　　　**fuel consumption** 연료 소비

Domestic consumption is expected to rise in the next quarter.

---

18 receipt
[risí:t]

v receive 받다

n 영수증, 수령　　　　　　　　**receipt for goods** 제품에 대한 영수증

As you know, the receipt is your proof of purchase.

---

19 depose
[dipóuz]

n deposition 파면

v (왕위 등을) 파면하다, 찬탈하다　**●** dismiss

depose the president 대통령을 퇴위시키다

He was deposed because of his unforgivable mistakes.

---

20 budget
[bʌ́dʒit]

n 예산, 경비　　　　　　　　　**compile a budget** 예산을 편성하다

We had to lower our budget due to the recession.

---

14 공원에서의 무허가 상업 활동은 금지되어 있다. / TV에는 성탄절 직전에 장난감 광고를 더 많이 보여준다.　15 전문가들은 깨끗한 공기를 상품으로 간주해야 한다고 주장한다.　16 나는 동료 몇 명과 직장까지 자전거로 통근한다. / 나는 긴 통근시간을 피하기 위해 최근에 직장 근처로 이사했다.　17 다음 분기에 국내 소비량이 증가할 것으로 기대된다.　18 당신도 알듯이, 그 영수증은 당신의 구매 증거다.　19 그는 자기의 용서받을 수 없는 실수들 때문에 해임되었다.　20 우리는 불경기 때문에 예산을 낮춰야 했다.

---

21 ☑ **donation**
[dounéiʃən]
ⓥ donate 기부하다

ⓝ 기부, 기증　**㊀** contribution　　**a voluntary donation** 자발적 기부

Our company is willing to give a donation for the community.

---

22 ☑ **executive**
[igzékjətiv]

ⓝ 경영진, 행정부　　**a senior executive** 고위 임원

★ The executives had a meeting to discuss the problem.

★ Power is shared between three main branches of government: the executive, the legislative, and the judiciary.

---

23 ☑ **financial**
[finǽnʃəl]
ⓝ finance 재정

ⓐ 재정적인, 재무의　　**financial support** 재정적 지원

Our company's financial problems slowly became visible.

---

24 ☑ **firm**
[fəːrm]
ⓐⓓ firmly 굳게, 단단히

ⓝ 회사　**ⓐ** 굳은, 확고한　**㊀** corporation 회사　　**a firm price** 변동 없는 가격

★ Mary works for a law firm in Boston.

★ I am looking for a job that pays a firm salary.

---

25 ☑ **slump**
[slʌmp]

ⓝ 폭락, 경기 침체　**㊀** boom 급속한 발전, (가격의) 폭등
a worldwide slump 세계적인 불황

The economic slump began in the housing and financial markets of the United States.

---

26 ☑ **guarantee**
[gæ̀rəntíː]

ⓥ 보증하다, 보장하다　**㊀** promise, warrant
a money-back guarantee 환불 보증

He guaranteed that the plan was going to work.

---

21 우리 회사는 지역사회에 기부할 의향이 있다. 22 경영진은 그 문제를 의논하고자 회의를 열었다. / 권력은 정부의 세 주요 분야인 행정부, 입법부, 사법부로 나뉜다. 23 우리 회사의 재정 문제가 천천히 가시화되었다. 24 Mary는 보스턴에 있는 한 법률 회사에 근무한다. / 나는 안정된 월급을 주는 일자리를 찾고 있다. 25 경제 위기는 미국의 주택과 금융시장에서 시작되었다. 26 그는 계획이 성공할 것이라고 보장했다.

27 laborious
[ləbɔ́ːriəs]

ⓝ labor 노동

ⓐ 힘이 드는, 부지런한　　　　　**laborious work** 힘든 일

Although it was a laborious project, we successfully finished it.

---

28 lease
[liːs]

ⓝ leaser 임대인

ⓝ (집, 토지, 차 등의) 임대 계약　　**renew a lease** 임대 계약을 갱신하다

He had to come up with money before the lease expired.

---

29 retail
[ríːteil]

ⓝ retailer 소매업자

ⓝ 소매(小賣) **ⓐ** 소매의　**ↄ** wholesale 도매　　**a retail store** 소매점

★ All you have to do is buy wholesale and sell retail.

★ I went to the retail dealer to check out this month's new products.

---

30 merge
[mə́ːrdʒ]

ⓝ mergence 합병, 융합

ⓥ 합병하다, 합체(合體)시키다　**ↄ** combine

merge companies 회사를 합병하다

The small companies decided to merge into one big corporation.

---

31 merchant
[mə́ːrtʃənt]

ⓝ merchandise 상품

ⓝ 상인, 무역상인　　　　　　**a wine merchant** 포도주 상인

Several merchants crossed the ocean to find new markets.

---

32 monetary
[mánətəri]

ⓐⓓ monetarily
금전적으로, 재정적으로

ⓐ 화폐의, 재정의　**International Monetary Fund (IMF)** 국제 통화 기금

The monetary value of labor has changed greatly over the past few years.

---

33 monopoly
[mənápəli]

ⓥ monopolize 독점하다

ⓝ 독점, 전매　　　　　　**a government monopoly** 국가 독점

There is a law that prohibits monopoly in the market.

---

27 비록 매우 힘든 프로젝트였지만, 우리는 성공적으로 마쳤다.　28 그는 임대 계약이 만료되기 전에 돈을 구해야 했다.　29 여러분이 해야 할 일은 도매로 사고 소매로 파는 것이다. / 나는 이번 달의 신제품을 확인하려고 소매상을 찾았다.　30 작은 회사들이 하나의 큰 기업으로 합병하기로 했다.　31 여러 상인이 새로운 시장을 찾기 위해 바다를 건넜다.　32 지난 몇 년 동안 노동의 금전적 가치가 크게 변했다.　33 시장에서 독점을 금지하는 법이 있다.

34 dividend
[dívidènd]

ⓝ 배당금, 특별 수당   **ⓔ** bonus 보너스, 특별 수당

a dividend payment 배당금 지급

My father made a lot of money by share dividends.

---

35 premium
[prí:miəm]

ⓝ 할증금, 보험금   **pay a premium** 할증금을 내다

★ Top quality cigars are being sold at a premium.

★ The insurance company paid him a premium for the car accident.

---

36 recruitment
[rikrú:tmənt]

ⓥ recruit 고용하다

ⓝ 채용, 보충   **a recruitment agency** 직업소개소

Companies are planning an increase in recruitment.

---

37 stock
[stɑk]

ⓝ 재고, 주식   **ⓔ** supply 재고, shares 주식   **the stock market** 주식 시장

★ We need to dispose of the items that are kept in stock.

★ The Korean stock markets are where we have lost money already.

---

38 loan
[loun]

ⓝ 대출, 융자   **home mortgage loan** 주택 담보 대출

I got a loan from the bank to buy a house.

---

39 transaction
[trænsǽkʃən]

ⓥ transact 거래하다, 처리하다

ⓝ 거래, 처리   **ⓔ** deal   **cash transaction** 현금 거래

Commercial transactions through the Internet are greatly increasing.

---

40 e-commerce
[í:kɑ́mərs]

ⓝ commerce 교역, 상업

ⓝ 전자상거래   **ⓔ** e-business

e-commerce market 전자상거래 시장

The number of e-commerce users is increasing rapidly.

---

34 아버지는 주식 배당금으로 큰돈을 버셨다. 35 최고급 시가는 추가 금액을 받고 판매되고 있다. / 보험 회사는 자동차 사고 때문에 그에게 보험금을 지급했다. 36 기업들은 채용을 늘리기로 계획 중이다. 37 우리는 재고로 있는 물건들을 폐기해야 한다. / 한국 주식 시장은 우리가 이미 손해를 본 적이 있는 곳이다. 38 나는 집을 사려고 은행에서 대출을 받았다. 39 인터넷을 통한 상거래가 매우 증가하고 있다. 40 전자상거래 이용자 수가 급격하게 늘고 있다.

EXERCISE

A 다음 영어는 우리말로, 우리말은 영어로 옮기시오.

01 executive _____

02 recruitment _____

03 application _____

04 lease _____

05 deposit _____

06 commodity _____

07 싼 물건, 흥정하다 _____

08 기부, 기증 _____

09 힘이 드는, 부지런한 _____

10 보험, 보증 _____

11 통근하다, 통근 _____

12 거래, 처리 _____

B 다음 빈칸에 알맞은 단어를 쓰시오.

01 depose ⊜ _____

02 asset ⊜ _____

03 firm ⊜ _____

04 merge ⊜ _____

05 retail ⇔ _____

06 slump ⇔ _____

07 monopoly ⓥ _____

08 affordable ⓥ _____

09 consumption ⓐ _____

10 bankrupt ⓝ _____

11 financial ⓝ _____

12 commercial ⓝ _____

C 다음 빈칸에 들어갈 알맞은 말을 고르시오. (필요하면 형태를 바꾸시오.)

receipt	guarantee	barter	budget	monetary

01 The _____ exchange rate changes from day to day.

02 Make sure to keep your _____ for every item purchased.

03 The jewelry store _____ to fix the watch if it breaks during the first two years.

04 As an organization we need a spending _____ so that our funds can be well maintained.

05 Before money appeared, _____ was the principal method of exchange in ancient communities.

Crossword Puzzle

앞에서 배운 어휘를 기억하며 퍼즐을 풀어보세요.

Across

2 related to business and the buying and selling of goods and services

4 relating to money or the management of money

7 to combine, or to join things together to form one thing

8 a part of the cost of something you are buying that you pay some time before you pay the rest of it

9 to make a formal written promise to repair or replace a product if it breaks within a specific period of time

10 without enough money to pay what you owe

Down

1 inexpensive; reasonably priced

2 the amount of energy, oil, electricity, etc. that is used

3 someone who gets services or advice from a professional person, company, or organization

5 the process of finding new people to join a company, organization, the army, etc.

6 to remove a leader or ruler from a position of power

Unit 11 Culture of the World

01 ☑ steadfast
[stédfæst]

ⓐ 확고부동한, 고정된

steadfast loyalty 한결같은 충성심

The two nations maintain a steadfast alliance.

ⓝ steadfastness 확고부동

---

02 ☑ advent
[ǽdvent]

ⓝ 도래, 출현

the advent of the Internet 인터넷의 출현

We watched the rising sun announce the advent of a new year.

---

03 ☑ ancient
[éinʃənt]

ⓐ 옛날의, 고대의 ⓞ modern 현대의

an ancient civilization 고대 문명

Archaeologists are studying ancient artifacts.

---

04 ☑ superstition
[sù:pərstíʃən]

ⓝ 미신, 미신적 관습

superstition tales 미신 이야기

Americans have a superstition that breaking a mirror is bad luck.

ⓐ superstitious 미신적인

---

05 ☑ antecedent
[æntəsí:dənt]

ⓝ 선례, 전례

a historical antecedent 역사적인 전례

People look up similar antecedents to understand the present.

ⓝ antecedence 선행

---

06 ☑ antiquity
[æntíkwəti]

ⓝ 낡음, 고대, 유물

a city of great antiquity 아주 오래된 도시

Many tourists find the antiquity of Rome beautiful.

ⓐ antique 고대의

---

01 두 국가는 확고한 동맹관계를 유지하고 있다. 02 우리는 떠오르는 태양이 새해를 선언하는 광경을 지켜보았다. 03 고고학자들이 고대 유물들을 연구하고 있다. 04 미국인들에게는 거울을 깨는 것이 불길하다는 미신이 있다. 05 사람들은 현재를 파악하기 위해 비슷한 전례를 찾아본다. 06 많은 관광객은 로마의 오래된 모습이 아름답다고 생각한다.

07 archaeology
[à:rkiáləd3i]

ⓝ archaeologist 고고학자

ⓝ 고고학　　　　　　　　　　**urban archeology** 도시 고고학

The study of archaeology has discovered many things about the past.

08 architect
[á:rkitèkt]

ⓝ architecture 건축, 건축 양식

ⓝ 건축가, 건설가　　　　　　**a landscape architect** 경관 건축가

The architect that built this temple must have been a genius.

09 throne
[θroun]

ⓥ enthrone 왕위에 앉히다
ⓥ dethrone 폐위하다

ⓝ 왕위, 왕권　　　　　　　　**ascend the throne** 즉위하다

He wanted to abandon the throne and become a normal person.

10 originality
[ərìd3ənǽləti]

ⓐ original 최초의, 독창적인

ⓝ 독창력, 독창성　　　　　　**great originality** 풍부한 독창력

This artist shows greater originality than any other.

11 stable
[stéibl]

ⓝ stability 안정성, 영속성

ⓐ 안정된, 견고한, 영속적인　ⓔ unstable 변하기 쉬운

stable conditions 안정된 환경

The population of this area has been quite stable.

12 variation
[vὲəriéiʃən]

ⓥ vary 변화하다, 변이하다

ⓝ 변화, 변이　　　　　　　　**a slight variation** 약간의 변화

Some languages have slight regional variations, like English.

13 conventional
[kənvénʃənəl]

ⓝ convention 관례

ⓐ 전통적인, 형식적인　ⓔ traditional 전통적인

conventional culture 기성문화

Many people think it's important to preserve conventional methods.

---

07 고고학 연구는 과거에 대한 많은 것들을 밝혀냈다.　08 이 사원을 지은 건축가는 분명히 천재였을 것이다.　09 그는 왕위를 포기하고 보통 사람이 되길 원했다.　10 이 화가는 다른 누구보다 뛰어난 독창성을 보여준다.　11 이 지역의 인구는 비교적 안정된 상태를 유지했다.　12 영어처럼 어떤 언어들은 약간의 지역적 변화를 보인다.　13 많은 사람은 전통 방식을 보존하는 것이 중요하다고 생각한다.

14 convert
[kənvə́ːrt]

ⓐ convertible 바꿀 수 있는
ⓝ conversion 전환, 변환

ⓥ 전환하다, 변환하다   ⓢ change, transform
convert sugar into alcohol 설탕을 알코올로 바꾸다

Many things had been converted to a modern fashion.

15 cosmopolitan
[kàzməpálətən]

ⓥ cosmopolitanize
세계적으로 하다

ⓐ 국제적인, 시야가 넓은 ⓝ 세계인, 세계주의자   ⓢ international 국제적인
a cosmopolitan city 국제 도시

★ New York City is very cosmopolitan as many tourists and immigrants live and work together.

★ He became a cosmopolitan after traveling around the world.

16 diversity
[divə́ːrsəti]

ⓐ diverse 다양한

ⓝ 다양성, 변화   ⓢ difference   **cultural diversity** 문화적 다양성

People are trying to accept the diversity among themselves.

17 dynasty
[dáinəsti]

ⓝ 왕조, 왕가   ⓢ empire   **the Joseon Dynasty** 조선 왕조

I believe the people who built this palace were of a great dynasty.

18 era
[íərə]

ⓝ 기원, 연대, 시대   **the Victorian era** 빅토리아 여왕 시대

The era this artifact was made in is still uncertain.

19 ethnic
[éθnik]

ⓝ ethnicity 민족성

ⓐ 민족의, 인종의, 소수 민족의   **an ethnic minority** 소수민족

I enjoy having ethnic food when I visit different countries.

20 exotic
[igzátik]

ⓝ exoticism 이국풍

ⓐ 이국적인, 외국산의   ⓢ foreign 외국산의   **an exotic plant** 외래 식물

Sam brought exotic clothes from his trip to India.

---

14 많은 것들이 현대식으로 전환되었다. 15 뉴욕은 많은 관광객과 이주자들이 함께 살고, 일하는 매우 국제적인 도시다. / 그는 전 세계를 여행하고 나서 세계인이 되었다. 16 사람들은 서로의 다양성을 받아들이려 노력하고 있다. 17 나는 이 궁전을 지은 사람들이 실로 대단한 왕조였을 것으로 생각한다. 18 이 유물이 만들어진 시기는 아직도 불확실하다. 19 나는 다른 나라를 방문할 때, 그 나라의 전통 음식을 즐겨 먹는다. 20 Sam은 인도 여행에서 돌아왔을 때 이국적인 옷을 가지고 왔다.

21 feudal
[fjúːdl]

ⓝ feud 봉건 시대의 토지

ⓐ 봉건 시대의, 중세의　　　　　the feudal system 봉건 제도

Ancient China had a feudal system based on bloodlines.

---

22 globalization
[glòubəlizéiʃən]

ⓝ globe 지구
ⓐ global 세계적인
ⓥ globalize 세계화하다

ⓝ 세계화　　　　　globalization age 세계화 시대

The Internet has accelerated globalization to a great height.

---

23 heritage
[héritidʒ]

ⓝ 상속 재산, 유산　ⓔ legacy　World Heritage Site 세계 유산 등록지

This monument is a priceless national heritage.

---

24 imperialism
[impíəriəlìzəm]

ⓐ imperial 제국의

ⓝ 제국주의　　　　　Social Imperialism 사회 제국주의

The general fought against the invasion of imperialism.

---

25 indigenous
[indídʒənəs]

ⓥ indigenize 현지화하다

ⓐ 토착의, 자생의, 고유의　ⓔ native　indigenous population 토착민

Taekwondo is the indigenous martial art of Korea.

---

26 joint
[dʒɔint]

ⓥ join 결합하다, 접합하다

ⓐ 공동의, 합동의 ⓝ 이음매, 관절　Joint Security Area (JSA) 공동경비구역

★ This parade is the result of joint work of Spain and Mexico.
★ Jack has just glued the joints of the chair.

---

27 knight
[nait]

ⓝ (중세의) 기사, 무사 ⓥ ～에게 기사 작위를 수여하다
the Knights of the Round Table 원탁(圓卓)의 기사

★ England is famous for its tales of medieval knights.
★ Paul McCartney was knighted by Queen Elizabeth II in 1996.

---

21 고대 중국에는 혈통을 바탕으로 한 봉건 제도가 있었다. 22 인터넷은 세계화를 크게 가속화했다. 23 이 기념비는 값으로 따질 수 없는 국가적 유산이다. 24 장군은 제국주의의 침략에 맞서 싸웠다. 25 태권도는 한국의 고유 무술이다. 26 이 행진은 스페인과 멕시코의 합동의 결과다. / Jack은 의자의 이음매를 접착제로 붙였다. 27 영국은 중세 기사에 대한 이야기로 유명하다. / 폴 메카트니는 1996년 엘리자베스 2세에게 기사 작위를 받았다.

28 multiracial
[mʌltiréiʃəl]

ⓐ 다민족의 ⓢ multicultural 다문화의   **a multiracial country** 다민족 국가

ⓝ multiracialism
다민족 평등사회

The high school I attended in America was a multiracial school.

29 nobility
[noubíləti]

ⓝ 귀족, 고귀함 ⓢ aristocracy 귀족, 귀족 정치

marry into the nobility 귀족 가문과 결혼하다

ⓐ noble 귀족의, 고귀한

In some countries, there are still people of nobility.

30 pottery
[pátəri]

ⓝ 도기, 도기류 ⓢ ceramics 도자기류   **a pottery shop** 도자기 가게

ⓝ pot 원통형의 그릇, 항아리

The pottery on display at the museum was made in the 16th century.

31 practicable
[préktikəbəl]

ⓐ 실용적인, 실리적인   **a practicable gift** 실용적인 선물

ⓥ practice 실행하다, 실천하다

Tools that are more practicable were developed throughout history.

32 predominant
[pridámənənt]

ⓐ 지배적인, 우세한   **the predominant color** 두드러진 색

ⓥ predominate 우세하다
ⓝ predominance 지배, 출중

Around the world, English is the predominant language.

33 privilege
[prívəlidʒ]

ⓝ 특권, 명예   **a breach of privilege** 특권 침해

ⓐ privileged 특권이 있는

Remember that not all countries have the privileges we have.

34 racial
[réiʃəl]

ⓐ 인종(상)의, 종족의   **racial discrimination** 인종차별

ⓝ race 인종, 종족

You need to learn to tolerate racial differences.

---

28 내가 미국에서 다녔던 고등학교는 다민족 학교였다. 29 몇몇 나라에서는 아직 귀족이 있다. 30 박물관에서 전시 중인 도자기는 16세기에 만들어진 것이다. 31 더 실용적인 도구들이 역사 속에서 개발되었다. 32 영어는 전 세계에서 지배적으로 사용되는 언어다. 33 모든 나라가 우리와 같은 특권을 가지는 것은 아니라는 것을 기억하라. 34 너는 인종의 차이를 받아들이는 방법을 배워야 한다.

35 radical
[rǽdikəl]

ⓝ radicalism 급진주의
ad radically 급진적으로

ⓐ 급진적인 **ⓝ** 급진주의자　**≡** revolutionary 혁명적인

radical reforms 과감한 개혁

★ Many countries went through radical changes after the World War.
★ The political radicals are requesting the media law revision.

36 realm
[relm]

ⓝ 왕국, 영역　**≡** kingdom 왕국, field 영역　**the realm of religion** 종교적 영역

★ The idea does not belong in the realm of science fiction.
★ The border is to indicate the realm of each country.

37 relic
[rélik]

ⓝ 유적, 유물　**relics of antiquity** 고대의 유물

Experts study relics to understand the culture of ancient civilizations.

38 revolution
[rèvəlúːʃən]

ⓥ revolve 회전하다
ⓐ revolutionary 혁명적인

ⓝ 혁명, 회전　**the Industrial Revolution** 산업혁명

★ The invention of the wheel is one of history's greatest revolutions.
★ The Earth makes one revolution around the sun each year.

39 ruins
[rúːins]

ⓐ ruined 멸망한

ⓝ 폐허, 유적, 파멸　**ancient ruins** 고대 유적

Archaeologists discovered the ruins of an ancient kingdom.

40 initiative
[iníʃiətiv]

ⓥ initiate
시작하다, 개시하다, 창시하다

ⓝ 주도, 시작, 발의　**a new diplomatic initiative** 새로운 외교적 주도권

It seems that Pakistan took the initiative in opening negotiations.

35 많은 나라가 세계 대전 이후에 급진적인 변화를 겪었다. / 정치 급진주의자들은 미디어법 개정을 요구하고 있다. 36 그 아이디어는 공상과학소설 영역에 속하지 않는다. / 국경은 각 나라의 영역을 표시하기 위한 것이다. 37 전문가들은 고대 문명의 문화를 이해하기 위해 유적을 연구한다. 38 바퀴의 발명은 역사상 가장 위대한 혁명 중 하나다. / 지구는 매년 태양 주변을 한번 회전한다. 39 고고학자들은 고대 왕국의 유적을 발견했다. 40 파키스탄이 협상을 여는 데에 주도권을 쥔 것 같다.

EXERCISE

A 다음 영어는 우리말로, 우리말은 영어로 옮기시오.

01	heritage _____	07	도래, 출현 _____
02	multiracial _____	08	제국주의 _____
03	originality _____	09	특권, 명예 _____
04	nobility _____	10	실용적인, 실리적인 _____
05	realm _____	11	세계화 _____
06	archaeology _____	12	기사, 무사 _____

B 다음 빈칸에 알맞은 단어를 쓰시오.

01	conventional ⊜ _____	07	variation ⓥ _____
02	dynasty ⊜ _____	08	initiative ⓥ _____
03	indigenous ⊜ _____	09	superstition ⓐ _____
04	cosmopolitan ⊜ _____	10	revolution ⓐ _____
05	stable ⇔ _____	11	feudal ⓝ _____
06	ancient ⇔ _____	12	exotic ⓝ _____

C 다음 빈칸에 들어갈 알맞은 말을 고르시오. (필요하면 형태를 바꾸시오.)

throne	ethnic	convert	antecedent	feudal

01 It is possible for scientists to _____ most solids into liquids.

02 There was no _____ to this case, so the jury had a hard time convicting him.

03 Hitler committed _____ cleansing for the sake of racism during the Second World War.

04 According to history books, the _____ lords were not kind to their subjects.

05 The king and queen sat on their respective _____ and received honor from their subjects.

Across

6. the study of ancient societies by examining what remains of their buildings, graves, tools, etc.

7. originating in or characteristic of a distant foreign country

8. a family of kings or other rulers whose parents, grandparents etc. have ruled the country for many years

Down

1. a special advantage that is given only to one person or group of people

2. the fact of including many different types of people or things

3. to change something into a different form, or to change something so that it can be used for a different purpose or in a different way

4. originating or occurring naturally in a particular place

5. someone whose job is to design buildings

01 ☑ appropriate
[əpróupriət]

ad appropriately
적당히, 적절하게

ⓐ 적합한, 적절한 ⊜ suitable

appropriate attitude for a job interview 구직 면접에 적절한 태도

My brother is not an appropriate person to serve others.

---

02 ☑ atheist
[éiθiist]

ⓝ atheism 무신론

ⓝ 무신론자, 무신앙자 **a confirmed atheist** 확고한 무신론자

My sister is an atheist and thinks the Bible is fiction.

---

03 ☑ pilgrim
[pílgrim]

ⓝ pilgrimage 순례

ⓝ 순례자 **pilgrim sign** 순례의 표시

Pilgrims visit Mecca every year according to their faith.

---

04 ☑ ban
[bæn]

ⓝ 금지, 금지령 ⓥ 금지하다 ⊜ prohibition 금지, prohibit 금지하다

a press ban 보도 금지

★ Smoking is banned within this area.

★ Cindy was banned from driving for three months.

---

05 ☑ cardinal
[káːrdənl]

ⓝ 추기경 **a cardinal's hat** 추기경의 빨간 모자

Many Catholics were shocked by the death of the cardinal.

---

06 ☑ cathedral
[kəθíːdrəl]

ⓝ 대성당 **the Cathedral of Notre Dame** 노트르담 대성당

Myeondong Cathedral is one of the oldest cathedrals in Korea.

---

01 나의 오빠는 다른 사람에게 봉사하기에 적합하지 않은 사람이다. 02 내 여동생은 무신론자이고, 성서가 허구라고 생각한다. 03 순례자들은 자신들의 신념에 따라 매년 메카를 방문한다. 04 이 지역에서 흡연이 금지되어 있다. / Cindy는 3개월 동안 운전을 금지당했다. 05 많은 천주교도가 추기경의 선종에 충격을 받았다. 06 명동성당은 한국에 있는 가장 오래된 성당 중 하나다.

07 ceremony
[sérəmòuni]
ⓐ ceremonial 의식의

ⓝ 의식, 의례 ⓔ ritual, rite **stand on ceremony** 격식을 차리다
The people stood silent during the religious ceremony.

08 chapel
[tʃǽpəl]

ⓝ 예배당 **a school chapel** 학교 예배당
The priest preaches in the chapel every Sunday.

09 charity
[tʃǽrəti]
ⓐ charitable 너그러운

ⓝ 자비, 자선 **ask for charity** 자비를 구하다
She donated a considerable amount of money to charity.

10 clergy
[klə́ːrdʒi]

ⓝ 목사, 성직자들 **the Catholic clergy** 가톨릭 성직자
All the clergy attended the ceremony that took place at the monument.

11 conscience
[kánʃəns]
ⓐ conscientious 양심적인
ⓐd conscientiously 양심적으로

ⓝ 양심 **a guilty conscience** 양심의 가책
Our conscience is what guides us in the right direction.

12 courteous
[kə́ːrtiəs]
ⓝ courtesy 예의 바름, 공손함

ⓐ 예의 바른, 친절한 ⓔ polite ⓞ impolite 버릇없는, 무례한
a courteous manner 예의 바른 태도
The staff will pay courteous attention to any requirement and make your stay pleasant.

13 creed
[kriːd]

ⓝ 신념, 신조 ⓔ faith, belief **a political creed** 정치적 신조
Her creed is to be polite and to behave herself all the time.

07 사람들은 종교의식 동안에 침묵을 지켰다. 08 목사가 일요일마다 예배당에서 설교한다. 09 그녀는 상당한 금액의 돈을 자선단체에 기부했다. 10 모든 성직자가 기념비에서 열리는 행사에 참석했다. 11 우리의 양심이 우리를 바른길로 인도하는 것이다. 12 직원들은 어떤 요청에도 정중하게 대할 것이며, 당신이 편안하게 머물도록 할 것입니다. 13 그녀의 신조는 늘 공손하고 올바르게 행동하는 것이다.

14 divine
[diváin]
ⓝ divinity 신, 신성

ⓐ 신의, 신성한   ⓔ sacred 신성한   **the divine power** 신력

Religions have their own concept of a divine being.

15 dogma
[dɔ́(:)gmə]
ⓐ dogmatic 교리에 관한

ⓝ 교의, 교리   ⓔ doctrine 교의, 교리   **a political dogma** 정치적 독단론

Many people try to live according to their religious dogma.

16 esteem
[istíːm]

ⓝ 존경, 경의 ⓥ 존경하다   ⓔ honor, respect   **self-esteem** 자존감

★ Please accept the small gift as a mark of my esteem.

★ I hold the president of my university in high esteem as he has contributed much to the community.

17 faithful
[féiθfəl]
ⓝ faith 신앙, 신념, 충실

ⓐ 충실한, 헌신적인   ⓔ disloyal 불성실한 **a faithful companion** 충실한 동반자

If a couple swear to be faithful until death, they should truly honor that vow.

18 holy
[hóuli]
ⓝ holiness 신성함

ⓐ 신성한, 경건한   **a holy life** 신앙생활

This area is regarded as holy ground by the natives.

19 misdeed
[mìsdíːd]
ⓥ misdo 잘못하다, 실수하다

ⓝ 악행, 비행, 범죄   **commit a misdeed** 비행을 저지르다

He became a new man after repenting for his misdeeds.

20 missionary
[míʃənèri]
ⓝ mission 선교, 임무

ⓝ 선교사, 전도사   **a foreign missionary** 외국인 선교사

A group of people went abroad as missionaries.

---

14 종교들은 각기 그들만의 신적 존재에 대한 개념이 있다. 15 많은 사람은 자신들의 종교적 교리에 따라 살려고 노력한다. 16 나의 존경의 표시로 주는 이 선물을 받아주세요. / 나는 우리 대학교 총장님이 지역 사회에 많은 공헌을 해 오셨기 때문에 그를 매우 존경한다. 17 부부가 죽을 때까지 헌신할 것을 맹세하면 그 맹세를 진정 존중해야 한다. 18 토착민들은 이 지역을 성지로 생각한다. 19 그는 자신의 악행을 회개한 후로 새로운 사람이 되었다. 20 몇 명의 사람들이 선교사로 외국에 나갔다.

21 monk
[mʌŋk]

n 수사(修士)

a religious monk 수도사

The monks welcomed us into the temple.

22 morality
[mɔ(:)rǽləti]
a moral 도덕의

n 도덕, 윤리성

personal morality 개인적 도덕성

We are working hard to boost the morality of the people.

23 pagan
[péigən]
v paganize 이교도가 되다

a 이교도의 **n** 이교도

convert the pagan 이교도를 개종하다

Some religions tend to regard other religions as pagan.

24 pastor
[pǽstər]
a pastoral 목사의

n 목사

a respected pastor 존경받는 목사

I consulted the pastor about the sins I had made in the past.

25 persecute
[pə́:rsikjù:t]
n persecution 박해
a persecutive 박해하는

v 박해하다, 학대하다 **≒** torture

persecute a religion 종교를 박해하다

In the past, people were persecuted for their religious beliefs.

26 pious
[páiəs]
n piety 경건, 신앙심

a 신앙심이 깊은, 독실한 **≒** religious

a pious Muslim 독실한 이슬람교도

My father became pious after he went through several troubles.

27 Protestant
[prátəstənt]
n Protestantism 개신교

n 개신교도

the Protestant church 교회

People who are Protestant go to their own churches on Sundays.

---

21 수도사들은 우리를 사원 안으로 환대했다. 22 우리는 사람들의 도덕성을 높이기 위해 노력하고 있다. 23 어떤 종교들은 다른 종교가 이교도라고 생각하는 경향이 있다. 24 나는 내가 과거에 저지른 죄에 대해 목사님과 상담했다. 25 과거에 사람들은 종교적 신념 때문에 박해받았다. 26 아버지는 여러 고난을 겪고 나서 독실해지셨다. 27 개신교도인 사람들은 일요일마다 자신들의 교회에 다닌다.

28 providence
[právədəns]

ⓐ provident 선견지명이 있는

ⓝ 섭리, 신   **divine providence** 신의 섭리

After doing all they could do, the rest was up to providence.

29 psychology
[saikálədʒi]

ⓐ psychological 심리적인
ⓝ psychologist 심리학자

ⓝ 심리학, 심리 (상태)   **mob psychology** 군중 심리

I study social psychology to understand the people in our society.

30 benevolent
[bənévələnt]

ⓝ benevolence 자비심

ⓐ 자선의, 호의적인   **a benevolent donor** 자비로운 기증자

It was very benevolent of him to share his wealth with the poor.

31 sacred
[séikrid]

ⓐ 신성한, 종교적인   ⓔ blessed, holy 신성한   **a sacred building** 신전

In some religions, certain animals are held sacred.

32 salvation
[sælvéiʃən]

ⓥ salvage 구출하다

ⓝ 구세, 구조   **the Salvation Army** 구세군

The people gathered in the church in seek of salvation.

33 sanctuary
[sǽŋktʃuèri]

ⓝ 신전, 성역, 성당   **violate sanctuary** 성역을 침범하다

The young men entered a sanctuary to escape from the police.

34 sermon
[sə́:rmən]

ⓐ sermonic 설교적인
ⓥ sermonize 설교하다

ⓝ 설교, 잔소리   **preach a sermon** 설교하다

I was deeply touched by the minister's sermon.

---

28 그들이 할 수 있는 모든 것을 한 후, 나머지는 신의 뜻에 달렸었다. 29 나는 우리 사회의 사람들을 이해하기 위해 사회 심리학을 공부한다. 30 그가 가난한 사람들에게 부를 나눠준 것은 참으로 자비로운 행동이었다. 31 어떤 종교에서는, 특정한 동물들이 신성시된다. 32 사람들은 구원을 받기 위해 교회에 모였다. 33 젊은 남자들이 경찰로부터 도망치기 위해 성당 안으로 들어갔다. 34 나는 목사님의 설교에 나는 크게 감동했다.

35 ☑ **sin**
[sin]

ⓝ 죄, 죄악

commit a sin 죄를 범하다

The old man wished to confess his sin of the past.

---

36 ☑ **taboo**
[təbúː]

ⓝ 금기, 금단 **⊜** prohibition, restriction

a taboo word 금기어

There once was a taboo against drinking alcohol.

---

37 ☑ **temple**
[témpəl]

ⓝ 신전, 성당, 절

a Buddhist temple 절

The Greeks built great temples to please their gods.

---

38 ☑ **theology**
[θiːálədʒi]
ⓝ theologist 신학자
ⓐ theological 신학적인

ⓝ 신학, 신학 과정

a theological school 신학교

Some believe that history can be interpreted from theology.

---

39 ☑ **worship**
[wə́ːrʃip]
ⓐ worshipful 숭배하는

ⓝ 예배, 숭배 **ⓥ** 숭배하다

the worship of idols 우상 숭배

It is our tradition to worship our ancestors.

---

40 ☑ **altar**
[ɔ́ːltər]

ⓝ 제단, 제대

a church altar 교회 제단

At the man's funeral, many people laid down flowers on the altar.

---

35 노인은 자신의 과거의 죄를 고백하고 싶어 했다. 36 한때는 술을 마시는 것에 대한 금기가 있었다. 37 그리스인들은 자신들의 신을 기쁘게 하기 위해 훌륭한 신전을 지었다. 38 어떤 사람들은 신학을 통해 역사를 해석할 수 있다고 믿는다. 39 조상을 숭배하는 것이 우리의 풍습이다. 40 그 남자의 장례식 때, 많은 사람이 제단에 꽃을 놓았다.

EXERCISE

A 다음 영어는 우리말로, 우리말은 영어로 옮기시오.

01 pilgrim   _____

02 morality   _____

03 taboo   _____

04 clergy   _____

05 misdeed   _____

06 providence   _____

07 무신론자, 무신앙자   _____

08 선교사, 전도사   _____

09 심리학, 심리 (상태)   _____

10 예배당   _____

11 목사   _____

12 예배, 숭배   _____

B 다음 빈칸에 알맞은 단어를 쓰시오.

01 ceremony ⊜ _____

02 esteem ⊜ _____

03 ban ⊜ _____

04 pious ⊜ _____

05 faithful ⇔ _____

06 courteous ⇔ _____

07 salvation ⓥ _____

08 sermon ⓥ _____

09 dogma ⓐ _____

10 charity ⓐ _____

11 divine ⓝ _____

12 benevolent ⓝ _____

C 다음 빈칸에 들어갈 알맞은 말을 고르시오. (필요하면 형태를 바꾸시오.)

creed	pagan	persecute	sanctuary	appropriate

01 One is to enter the _____ with an attitude of respect.

02 Many people are _____ for their Christian beliefs in the Middle East.

03 It is believed that Halloween is a holiday that originated from _____ customs.

04 The executives agreed that it was _____ to announce the new company policy to their employees.

05 Even though there are laws that protect employees, discrimination on the basis of religious _____ is common.

Crossword Puzzle

앞에서 배운 어휘를 기억하며 퍼즐을 풀어보세요.

Across

4 beliefs or ideas about what is right and wrong and about how people should behave

5 to treat someone cruelly or unfairly over a period of time, especially because of their religious or political beliefs

8 an organization that gives money, goods, or help to people who are poor, sick, etc.

9 the part of your mind that tells you whether what you are doing is morally right or wrong

Down

1 to show respect and love for a god, especially by praying in a religious building

2 the mental processes involved in believing in something or doing a certain activity

3 correct or suitable for a particular time, situation, or purpose

6 polite and showing respect for other people

7 coming from or relating to God or a god

Law & Society

---

01 ☑ **testimony**
[téstəmòuni]

n a testimonial 증명서; 증명의

n 증언, 증명　**=** statement 진술　　**a false testimony** 거짓 증언

Her testimony was the conclusive turning point of the case.

---

02 ☑ **apprehend**
[æprihénd]

n apprehension 체포

v 체포하다　　**apprehend a suspect** 용의자를 체포하다

The police apprehended the thief at the crime scene.

---

03 ☑ **constitution**
[kànstətjúːʃən]

v constitute (법을) 제정하다

n 헌법, 구성, 조직　　**the court of constitution** 헌법재판소

★ Freedom of the press is guaranteed under the Constitution of the U.S.

★ What is the constitution of the company?

---

04 ☑ **auction**
[ɔ́ːkʃən]

n 경매, 공매　　**an auction house** 경매 회사

Tom's house was put up for auction because he couldn't pay his debt.

---

05 ☑ **banish**
[bǽniʃ]

n banishment 추방

v 추방하다, 내쫓다　**=** expel　　**banish one's worries** 걱정거리를 없애다

James was banished from his community for his crimes.

---

06 ☑ **bar**
[baːr]

n 법정, 법조계, 변호사단　　**the bar exam** 변호사 시험

He is a member of the bar.

---

01 그녀의 증언이 그 사건의 결정적인 전환점이었다. 02 경찰이 도둑을 범죄 현장에서 체포했다. 03 언론의 자유는 미국 헌법에 보장되어 있다. / 이 회사는 어떻게 조직되어 있습니까? 04 Tom이 빚을 갚지 못했기 때문에 그의 집은 경매에 부쳐졌다. 05 James는 자신의 죄 때문에 지역사회에서 추방당했다. 06 그는 변호사이다.

07 bill
[bil]

ⓝ 법안, 계산서   **submit a bill** 법안을 제출하다

★ The National Assembly passed a bill that aims to boost commerce.

★ You can pay your public utility bills at that counter.

---

08 bribe
[braib]

ⓐ bribable 매수할 수 있는

ⓝ 뇌물 **ⓥ** 매수하다, 뇌물로 꾀다   **bribe with money** 돈으로 매수하다

★ It was wrong for the politician to accept the bribe from his supporter.

★ She bribed her coworker with money to hide her faults.

---

09 burglar
[bə́:rglər]

ⓝ burglary 강도, 절도

ⓝ 강도, 빈집털이, 사기꾼   ⊜ thief   **a burglar alarm** 도난 경보기

A burglar stole from almost every house in the neighborhood.

---

10 certify
[sə́:rtəfài]

ⓝ certification 증명

ⓥ 증명[보증]하다, 확인하다   ⊜ verify 확인하다

CPA (certified public accountant) 공인 회계사

The man was certified dead at the scene.

---

11 Congress
[káŋgris]

ⓝ 의회, 국회   **a member of Congress** 국회의원

Politicians will vote for the bill at the coming regular Congress.

---

12 attorney
[ətə́:rni]

ⓝ 변호사, 대리인   **a defense attorney** 피고 측 변호인

My goal after graduating from law school is to be an attorney.

---

13 convict
[kánvikt / kənvíkt]

ⓝ 죄인, 죄수 **ⓥ** 유죄를 선고하다   **an ex-convict** 전과자

★ The convict was released after three years in jail.

★ The criminal was convicted of two counts of murder.

---

07 국회에서 상거래를 증진시키려는 법안을 통과시켰다. / 공공요금은 저 창구에서 내면 됩니다. 08 그 정치인이 후견인으로부터 뇌물을 받은 것이 잘못이었다. / 그녀는 자신의 잘못을 감추기 위해 동료를 돈으로 매수했다. 09 한 강도가 동네의 거의 모든 집을 털었다. 10 그는 현장에서 사망한 것이 확인되었다. 11 정치인들이 이번 정기 국회에서 법안에 대해 투표할 것이다. 12 로스쿨을 졸업한 후의 내 목표는 변호사가 되는 것이다. 13 그 죄인은 3년간 복역하고 나서 풀려났다. / 그 범인은 두 건의 살인으로 유죄 판결을 받았다.

14 corrupt
[kərʌ́pt]

ⓝ corruption 부패, 부정

ⓐ 부정한, 타락한   **a corrupt politician** 부패한 정치인

The government is distancing itself from the people, and is growing more corrupt.

15 valid
[vǽlid]

ⓥ validate 확인하다, 비준하다
ⓝ validity 정당함

ⓐ 근거가 확실한, 유효한   ⓔ reasonable   **a valid contract** 유효한 계약

The investigators were able to come up with a valid conclusion.

16 criminal
[krímənəl]

ⓝ crime 범죄

ⓝ 범인 ⓐ 형사상의, 범죄의   ⓔ convict 죄인, 죄수   **criminal law** 형법

★ The man was a lifetime criminal with a long history of crime.
★ Scientific methods are important in criminal investigations.

17 decree
[dikríː]

ⓝ 법령, 판결   **the enforcement decree** 시행령

The man paid for the damages he made by decree.

18 trial
[tráiəl]

ⓝ 재판, 공판, 시도   **a trial procedure** 재판 절차
trial and error 시행착오

★ Every man has the right to get a fair trial.
★ It is important to let students learn by trial and error.

19 evidence
[évidəns]

ⓐ evident 명백한

ⓝ 증거, 증언, 증인   **material evidence** 물증

We searched for any kind of evidence at the crime scene.

20 stabilize
[stéibəlàiz]

ⓐ stable 안정된

ⓥ 안정시키다, 견고하게 하다   **stabilize prices** 물가를 안정시키다

The U.S. has expressed support for the Chinese government's measures to stabilize the situation.

---

14 정부는 국민에게서 멀어지고 더욱 부패해가고 있다. 15 수사관들은 타당한 결론을 내릴 수 있었다. 16 그 남자는 많은 전과기록을 가진 범죄자로 평생을 살았다. / 범죄수사에서 과학적 방법들이 중요하다. 17 그 남자는 판결에 따라 자신이 끼친 피해를 배상했다. 18 모든 사람은 공정한 재판을 받을 권리가 있다. / 시행착오를 통해 학생들을 배우게 하는 것이 중요하다. 19 우리는 범죄현장에서 모든 종류의 증거를 찾으려고 했다. 20 미국은 상황을 안정시키려는 중국 정부의 조치에 대한 지지를 표명했다.

21 execution
[èksikjúːʃən]
ⓥ execute 처형하다, 집행하다

ⓝ 처형, 사형 집행

a public execution 공개 처형

No executions have been carried out in Korea for over twenty years.

---

22 fake
[feik]

ⓐ 위조의, 가짜의 ⓝ 위조품, 가짜 ⓔ genuine 진짜의

fake money 위조지폐

★ A teenager was caught trying to enter a bar with a fake ID.

★ The painting was a fake and this was proved by the expert art dealer.

---

23 forgery
[fɔ́ːrdʒəri]
ⓥ forge 위조하다, 꾸며내다

ⓝ 위조, 모조

forgery of documents 문서 위조

The documents we had found turned out to be a forgery.

---

24 fraud
[frɔːd]
ⓐ fraudulent 부정의, 사기의

ⓝ 비리, 사기 ⓔ deception

electoral fraud 선거 비리

Recently, cases of fraud by telephone are increasing.

---

25 fugitive
[fjúːdʒətiv]

ⓝ 도망자, 탈주자 ⓐ 도망하는

a fugitive soldier 탈영병

★ The police obtained information of where the fugitive was hiding.

★ The vehicle was found, but the fugitive solider is still on the run.

---

26 guilty
[gílti]
ⓝ guilt 유죄, 죄의식

ⓐ 유죄의, 범죄성의

guilty of murder 살인죄가 있는

I am not guilty of the hit-and-run accident.

---

27 smuggle
[smʌ́gl]
ⓝ smuggler 밀수입자

ⓥ 밀수하다, 밀입국하다

drug smuggling 마약 밀수

They smuggled drugs into Korea by sea.

---

21 한국에서는 20년이 넘게 사형이 집행되지 않았다. 22 한 10대 청소년이 위조 신분증을 가지고 술집에 들어가려다 붙잡혔다. / 그 그림은 모조품이었고, 이것은 전문 미술상에 의해 입증되었다. 23 우리가 찾은 문서들은 결국 위조로 판명되었다. 24 최근 전화를 이용한 사기가 증가하고 있다. 25 경찰은 도망자가 어디에 숨어 있는지에 대한 제보를 받았다. / 차량은 발견되었지만, 탈영병은 아직 도주 중이다. 26 나는 뺑소니 사고에 대한 죄가 없다. 27 그들은 바다를 통해 한국으로 마약을 밀수했다.

28 judicial
[dʒu:díʃəl]

ⓝ judiciary 사법부, 사법제도

ⓐ 사법의, 재판의   **a judicial procedure** 소송 절차

For the judicial procedure, you need to bring more evidence.

29 justify
[dʒʌ́stəfài]

ⓝ justice 정의
ⓝ justification 정당화

ⓥ 정당화하다   **justify oneself** 자신의 행위를 변명하다, 자신의 옳음을 밝히다

She tried to justify her actions as self-defense.

30 lawsuit
[lɔ́:sù:t]

ⓝ 소송, 고소   ● case 소송   **drop a lawsuit** 소송을 취하하다

The workers filed a lawsuit against the executives.

31 legal
[lí:gəl]

ⓝ legality 합법, 적법
ⓥ legalize 적법화하다

ⓐ 법률의, 합법적인   ● illegal 불법의   **legal status** 법적 지위

In Korea, the legal age for alcohol is twenty.

32 legislation
[lèdʒisléiʃən]

ⓥ legislate 법률을 제정하다
ⓐ legislative 입법상의

ⓝ 법률 제정, 입법   **a new legislation** 새로운 법령

We are working to make legislation against hunting in this area.

33 legitimate
[lidʒítəmət]

ⓝ legitimacy 합법성, 적법성

ⓐ 합법적인, 적법의   ● illegitimate 불법의   **a legitimate right** 합법적 권리

It is legitimate to have firearms in America as long as it's registered.

34 observe
[əbzə́:rv]

ⓝ observance 준수
ⓝ observation 관찰

ⓥ 준수하다, 관찰하다   **observe a speed limit** 제한 속도를 지키다

★ We ought to observe the law whether we like it or not.
★ The policeman observed his behavior closely.

---

28 너는 소송절차를 위해서 증거를 더 가져와야 한다. 29 그녀는 자신의 행동을 정당방위로 정당화하려 했다. 30 근로자들이 간부들을 상대로 소송했다. 31 한국에서 술을 마실 수 있는 법적 나이는 20세다. 32 우리는 이 지역에서 사냥을 금지하는 법률을 만들기 위해 노력하고 있다. 33 미국에서는 등록되어 있다면, 총기류를 소지하는 것이 합법적이다. 34 우리가 좋든 싫든 간에 법을 지켜야 한다. / 그 경찰은 그의 행동을 면밀히 관찰했다.

35 patent
[pǽtənt]

n 특허, 특허권 **≡** copyright **patent law** 특허법

Other companies can't use your designs if you have a patent.

36 penalty
[pénəlti]

a penal 처벌의, 형벌의

n 형벌, 벌금 **≡** punishment 형벌, fine 벌금 **the death penalty** 사형 선고

He is to pay the plaintiff the penalty of nine million dollars.

37 prosecute
[prάsikjùːt]

n prosecution 기소, 고소
n prosecutor 검사

v 기소하다 **prosecute for theft** 절도 혐의로 기소하다

She has been prosecuted for the murder of her friend.

38 punishment
[pʌ́niʃmənt]

v punish 벌주다

n 처벌, 형벌 **≡** penalty **capital punishment** 사형제도

His lawyer put great effort in lightening his punishment.

39 rein
[rein]

n 구속, 고삐 **≡** restraint 구속, 속박 **without rein** 구애 없이, 자유롭게

The workers declared a strike against the owner's tight reins.

40 senator
[sénətər]

a senatorial 상원 의원의

n 의원, 상원 의원 **a senior senator** 원로 상원 의원

The senator had to come to the court for a bribery case.

35 특허를 받았다면 다른 회사들이 당신의 디자인을 쓸 수 없다. 36 그는 원고에게 벌금으로 9백만 달러를 내야 한다. 37 그녀는 자신의 친구를 살해한 혐의로 기소되었다. 38 그의 변호사는 그의 형량을 낮추는 데 부단히 노력했다. 39 직원들은 사장의 심한 구속에 반대하는 파업을 선언했다. 40 그 상원 의원은 뇌물 사건으로 법정에 출두해야 했다.

EXERCISE

A 다음 영어는 우리말로, 우리말은 영어로 옮기시오.

01 burglar _____

02 fugitive _____

03 lawsuit _____

04 testimony _____

05 patent _____

06 corrupt _____

07 체포하다 _____

08 범인, 형사상의 _____

09 준수하다 _____

10 처형, 사형 집행 _____

11 기소하다 _____

12 변호사, 대리인 _____

B 다음 빈칸에 알맞은 단어를 쓰시오.

01 certify ⊜ _____

02 penalty ⊜ _____

03 banish ⊜ _____

04 rein ⊜ _____

05 legitimate ⇔ _____

06 fake ⇔ _____

07 constitution ⓥ _____

08 valid ⓥ _____

09 bribe ⓐ _____

10 evidence ⓐ _____

11 judicial ⓝ _____

12 legal ⓝ _____

C 다음 빈칸에 들어갈 알맞은 말을 고르시오. (필요하면 형태를 바꾸시오.)

convict	fraud	smuggle	senator	bill

01 The parents were _____ of neglect and abuse toward their children.

02 The terrorists attempted to _____ illegal chemicals through airport security.

03 The politician was guilty of _____ and was found to have accepted a large sum of money for his own gain.

04 The parents of the missing child helped pass a _____ for faster search efforts when a child is reported missing.

05 The _____ did his best to represent his state and relied on the opinion of his constituents to make decisions.

Crossword Puzzle

앞에서 배운 어휘를 기억하며 퍼즐을 풀어보세요.

1 c

2 t

3 b 4 v 5 l

6 p 7 f

8 s 9 c

10 c

11 a

Across

1 someone who is involved in illegal activities or has been proved guilty of a crime

3 to illegally give someone, especially a public official, money or a gift in order to persuade them to do something for you

4 legally or officially acceptable

10 a set of basic laws and principles that a country or organization is governed by

11 a person, typically a lawyer, appointed to act for another in business or legal matters

Down

1 using your power in a dishonest or illegal way in order to get an advantage for yourself

2 a formal statement saying that something is true, especially one a witness makes in a court of law

5 conforming to the law or to rules

6 to charge someone with a crime and try to show that they are guilty of it in a court of law

7 someone who is trying to avoid being caught by the police

8 to take something or someone illegally from one country to another

9 to prove or officially announce that someone is guilty of a crime after a trial in a law court

Politics & Administration

---

01 ☑ **abolish**
[əbáliʃ]

ⓥ 폐지하다, 철폐하다 ⊜ end, eliminate

abolish slavery 노예 제도를 폐지하다

ⓝ **abolition** 폐지, 사형 폐지

Many people think the death penalty should be abolished.

---

02 ☑ **ambassador**
[æmbǽsədər]

ⓝ 대사, 대표 ⊜ representative 대표

the American ambassador to Korea 주한 미국 대사

The ambassador from Mexico went to America
for a meeting.

---

03 ☑ **assembly**
[əsémbli]

ⓝ 집회, 의회 ⊜ congress 의회 **the National Assembly** 국회

The assembly for this week is scheduled on Wednesday.

ⓥ **assemble** 모으다

---

04 ☑ **autocracy**
[ɔːtákrəsi]

ⓝ 독재 정치, 절대 권력 **autocracy and democracy** 독재 정치와 민주주의

The people revolted against the cruel autocracy.

ⓝ **autocrat** 독재자
ⓐ **autocratic** 독재적인

---

05 ☑ **autonomy**
[ɔːtánəmi]

ⓝ 자치(권), 자치 국가 ⊜ self-government 자치 **local autonomy** 지방 자치

We have autonomy to decide what to do for our community.

ⓐ **autonomic** 자치의

---

06 ☑ **ballot**
[bǽlət]

ⓝ 투표, 투표용지 ⊜ vote 투표 **a secret ballot** 비밀 선거

The candidates waited for the results of the ballot counting.

---

01 많은 사람이 사형제도가 폐지되어야 한다고 생각한다. 02 멕시코 대사는 회의하기 위해 미국으로 갔다. 03 이번 주 집회는 수요일로 예정되어 있다.
04 사람들이 잔혹한 독재에 대항하여 반란을 일으켰다. 05 우리는 지역사회를 위해 무엇을 해야 할지 결정할 수 있는 자치권이 있다. 06 후보들은 개표
결과를 기다렸다.

07 □ border
[bɔ́:rdər]

ⓝ 경계, 국경 ⊜ frontier 국경

a border army 국경 수비대

North Korea and South Korea have a tightly guarded border.

08 □ bureau
[bjúərou]

ⓝ (관청의) 국, 사무국, 사무소

an employment bureau 직업소개소

Politicians try to keep a close relation with the news bureau.

09 □ candidate
[kǽndidèit]

ⓝ 후보, 지원자

a strong candidate 유력한 후보

You must be prudent when you decide which candidate to vote for.

10 □ designation
[dèzignéiʃən]
ⓥ designate 지명하다

ⓝ 지정, 지명, 임명

official designation 공식 지정

The designation of this area as greenbelt was a good decision.

11 □ diplomatic
[dìpləmǽtik]
ⓝ diplomacy 외교

ⓐ 외교의, 외교 관계의

diplomatic dispute 외교 분쟁

We face a diplomatic difficulty with a few countries.

12 □ doctrine
[dáktrin]
ⓐ doctrinal 교리의

ⓝ 공식적 외교 정책, 〈종교〉 교리

military doctrine 군사 정책

★ People are discussing the benefits of a free trade doctrine.
★ The priest has led his life as close to the doctrine as he could.

13 □ dominate
[dámənèit]
ⓝ domination 지배

ⓥ 지배[통치]하다

dominate the world 세계를 지배하다

There were several attempts to dominate the world in history.

---

07 북한과 한국은 삼엄하게 경계하는 국경이 있다. 08 정치인들은 보도부와 친밀한 관계를 유지하려고 한다. 09 어느 후보에게 투표할 것인지 결정할 때 신중해야 한다. 10 이 지역을 그린벨트로 지정한 것은 현명한 판단이었다. 11 우리는 몇몇 나라와 외교적 어려움을 겪고 있다. 12 사람들은 자유무역 정책의 이점에 대해 논의하고 있다. / 사제는 가능한 교의에 충실한 삶을 살았다. 13 역사적으로 세계를 지배하려는 몇 번의 시도가 있었다.

14 election
[ilékʃən]
ⓥ elect 선거하다

ⓝ 선거, 선정   **election campaign** 선거 운동

Who can predict how the elections will turn out?

15 eligible
[élidʒəbəl]
ⓝ eligibility 자격, 적격

ⓐ 적임의, 적격의   ⊜ qualified   ⊜ unqualified 부적격의

an eligible voter 유권자

A hearing will be held to see if the man is eligible to be a minister.

16 council
[káunsəl]

ⓝ 회의, 의회, 협의회   **a council member** 의원

The city council held a meeting to discuss several issues.

17 exile
[égzail]
ⓐ exiled 추방당한

ⓝ 국외 추방, 망명자 ⓥ 추방하다   ⊜ banishment 추방, banish 추방하다

be forced into exile 추방되다

The author of the controversial novel was forced to live in exile for ten years.

18 anarchy
[ǽnərki]
ⓝ anarchism 무정부주의

ⓝ 무정부, 무정부 상태   **a state of anarchy** 무정부 상태

The people were left in complete anarchy after the war.

19 ideology
[àidiálədʒi]
ⓐ ideologic 이념의

ⓝ (사회적, 정치적) 이데올로기, 이념   **ideological propaganda** 이념 선전

Politics should be focused on the welfare of people rather than ideologies.

20 impose
[impóuz]
ⓝ imposition 과세

ⓥ (의무, 세금, 벌 등을) 부과하다   **impose a fine** 벌금을 부과하다

Everybody who has an income is imposed of taxes.

---

14 선거 결과가 어떻게 될지 누가 예측할 수 있겠습니까? 15 그 남자가 장관이 되기에 적합한지를 보기 위해 청문회가 열릴 것이다. 16 시의회는 여러 안건에 대해 논의하기 위해 회의를 열었다. 17 논란이 되었던 소설의 저자는 10년 동안 망명생활을 해야만 했다. 18 전쟁이 끝나고 사람들은 완전한 무정부 상태로 남았다. 19 정치는 이념보다는 사람들의 복지에 이바지해야 한다. 20 수입이 있는 모든 사람에게는 세금이 부과된다.

21 monarch
[mánərk]

n monarchy 군주제, 군주 국가

n 군주, 왕　**⊜** ruler

an absolute monarch 전제 군주

The monarch has the strong power to dismiss the government.

22 municipal
[mju:nísəpəl]

n municipality 지방 자치제

a 시(市)의, 지방 자치의　**⊜** civic

the municipal council 시 의회

The role of municipal governments in America is very important.

23 nominate
[námənèit]

n nomination 지명
n nominee 지명된 사람

v 지명하다, 임명하다

nominate a leader 지도자를 지명하다

Steve has been nominated as a candidate for the class president.

24 parliament
[pá:rləmənt]

a parliamentary
의회의, 국회의

n 의회, 국회　**⊜** assembly

convene [dissolve] a parliament 의회를 소집[해산]하다

Many things will change if the bill is passed by the parliament.

25 petition
[pitíʃən]

a petitionary 청원의, 탄원의

n 청원, 탄원　**⊜** appeal

a direct petition 직접 청원

The staff members submitted a petition against the decision.

26 pledge
[pledʒ]

n 공약, 맹세　**⊜** promise

an election pledge 선거 공약

We were disappointed as the mayor didn't fulfill his pledge.

27 politics
[pálitiks]

a political 정치적인

n 정치, 정치학

practical politics 실용 정치

There are many complex factors influencing international politics.

---

21 군주는 정부를 해산할 수 있는 강력한 힘이 있다.　22 미국에서는 지방 자치 정부의 역할이 매우 중요하다.　23 Steve는 반장 후보로 지명되었다.
24 법안이 국회에서 통과되면 많은 것이 변할 것이다.　25 직원들이 결정된 사항에 반대하는 청원을 제출했다.　26 우리는 시장이 자신의 공약을 지키지
않아 실망했다.　27 국제 정치에 영향을 끼치는 복잡한 변수들이 아주 많다.

28 **poll**
[poul]

ⓝ 득표집계, 투표　　　　　　　　　　**exit polls** 출구 조사

★ The press often conducts polls to predict the election results.

★ A group of people started a poll about the general opinion.

---

29 **rebel**
[rébəl]

ⓝ **rebellion** 반란, 폭동
ⓐ **rebellious** 반역하는

ⓝ 반역자, 반항자　　　　　　　　　　**a rebel army** 반란군

A group of rebels attacked a government building.

---

30 **regime**
[reiʒíːm]

ⓝ 정권, 통치 (방식)　ⓔ government　　**a repressive regime** 억압적인 정권

The people's revolution brought down the old regime.

---

31 **regulate**
[régjəlèit]

ⓝ **regulation** 규제, 단속

ⓥ 규제하다, 단속하다　ⓔ control, moderate **regulate a flow** 흐름을 조절하다

The city is in charge of regulating the traffic system.

---

32 **reign**
[rein]

ⓥ 지배하다, 주권을 잡다 ⓝ 통치, 지배　ⓔ rule 지배(하다)
　　　　　　　　　　　　　　　　　　the reign of law 법의 지배

★ It is quite difficult to reign over the entire kingdom and please all its inhabitants.

★ We all wish for an age which is under the reign of peace.

---

33 **rural**
[rúərəl]

ⓐ 지방의, 시골의　ⓔ urban 도시의　　　　**rural life** 전원생활

Unlike my ambitious brother, I wish for a quiet rural life.

---

34 **secretary**
[sékrətèri]

ⓐ **secretarial** 장관의, 비서의

ⓝ 장관, 비서　　　　　　　　　　**the Secretary of State** 국무 장관

★ The new Secretary of Defense has a new plan for the military.

★ His secretary takes care of all his appointments.

---

28 언론은 흔히 선거결과를 예측하기 위해 여론조사를 시행한다. / 몇 명의 사람들이 여론에 대한 투표를 시작했다. 29 한 무리의 반역자가 정부 건물을 공격했다. 30 시민혁명은 구정권을 끌어내렸다. 31 시 당국은 교통체계를 통제할 책임이 있다. 32 전 왕국을 통치하고 그 왕국의 모든 거주민들을 만족하게 하는 것은 꽤 힘든 일이다. / 우리는 모두 오랫동안 평화가 지배하는 시대를 희망한다. 33 야심이 있는 우리 형과 달리, 나는 조용한 시골생활을 원한다. 34 새 국방부 장관은 군대에 대한 참신한 계획이 있다. / 그의 비서가 그의 모든 약속을 담당한다.

35 statesman
[stéitsmən]

ⓐ statesmanlike 정치력 있는

ⓝ (훌륭한) 정치가   **a prominent statesman** 저명한 정치가

A great statesman is made by great followers.

36 traitor
[tréitər]

ⓐ traitorous 배반적인, 반역의

ⓝ 배반자, 반역자   ⓢ betrayer   **a traitor to the nation** 매국노

They say "Once a traitor, always a traitor."

37 tyranny
[tírəni]

ⓝ tyrant 폭군, 전제 군주

ⓐ tyrannical
포악한, 전제 군주적인

ⓝ 폭정, 전제 정치   **the struggle against tyranny** 폭정에 맞선 투쟁

The people stood up against the tyranny of the king.

38 veto
[ví:tou]

ⓝ 거부권 ⓥ 거부하다, 반대하다   **a veto power** 거부권

a presidential veto 대통령의 거부권

★ The President delivered his veto to Congress.

★ The President is allowed to veto any bills passed by Congress.

39 administration
[ædmìnistréiʃən]

ⓥ administrate 통치하다

ⓝ 행정, 통치, 관리, 경영   ⓢ management 관리, 경영

a college administration 대학 행정처

★ The administration couldn't decide what and how to do.

★ Denny has majored in business administration at Baruch College.

40 ministry
[mínistri]

ⓝ minister 장관

ⓝ (정부의) 부   ⓢ department, bureau   **the Ministry of Defense** 국방부

The Ministry of Labor is working on a new policy.

35 위대한 정치가는 위대한 추종자들을 통해 만들어진다. 36 사람들은 "한번 배신자는 영원히 배신자다."라고 한다. 37 백성은 왕의 폭정에 저항하였다. 38 대통령은 그의 거부 의사를 의회에 전달했다. / 대통령은 국회에서 통과된 어떤 법안에도 거부권을 행사할 수 있다. 39 행정기관은 무엇을 어떻게 해야 하는지 결정할 수 없었다. / Denny는 버룩 대학에서 경영학을 전공했다. 40 노동부는 새로운 정책을 세우고 있다.

EXERCISE

A 다음 영어는 우리말로, 우리말은 영어로 옮기시오.

01 ballot _____

02 monarch _____

03 rebel _____

04 bureau _____

05 veto _____

06 impose _____

07 독재 정치, 절대 권력 _____

08 지명하다, 임명하다 _____

09 폭정, 전제 정치 _____

10 정권, 통치 (방식) _____

11 무정부, 무정부 상태 _____

12 지배[통치]하다 _____

B 다음 빈칸에 알맞은 단어를 쓰시오.

01 petition ⊜ _____

02 assembly ⊜ _____

03 traitor ⊜ _____

04 ambassador ⊜ _____

05 rural ⇔ _____

06 eligible ⇔ _____

07 designation ⓥ _____

08 administration ⓥ _____

09 autonomy ⓐ _____

10 parliament ⓐ _____

11 regulate ⓝ _____

12 diplomatic ⓝ _____

C 다음 빈칸에 들어갈 알맞은 말을 고르시오. (필요하면 형태를 바꾸시오.)

candidate	council	abolish	diplomatic	reign

01 Each _____ put up posters with their picture and slogan around town.

02 The new king is expected to _____ successfully for many years over the nation.

03 The _____ of schools is expected to make decisions for the greater good of all children.

04 They _____ slavery, putting an end to the savage practice of mistreatment to humanity.

05 _____ decisions require much skill and negotiation among the various parties involved.

Crossword Puzzle

앞에서 배운 어휘를 기억하며 퍼즐을 풀어보세요.

정답

Across

3 to officially suggest someone or something for an important position, duty, or prize

5 having the right to do or obtain something; satisfying the appropriate conditions

8 to control an activity or process, especially by rules

10 to control someone or something or to have more importance than other people or things

Down

1 the official line that separates two countries, states, or areas, or the area close to this line

2 someone who is being considered for a job or is competing in an election

4 someone who opposes or fights against people in authority

6 to require (a duty, charge, or penalty) to be undertaken or paid

7 a system of voting, usually in secret, or an occasion when you vote in this way

9 a constitutional right to reject a decision or proposal made by a lawmaking body

Geography & Traffic

---

01 ☑ anchor
[ǽŋkər]

ⓝ anchorage 정박, 정박지

ⓝ닻 ⓥ닻을 내려 멈추다, 정박시키다   **drop anchor** 닻을 내리다

★ Without the ship's anchor, the waves would have pushed it out to sea.

★ He anchored his boat in the middle of the lake.

---

02 ☑ basin
[béisən]

ⓝ분지, 대야   **a peaceful basin** 평화로운 분지

★ The climate conditions in basins are good for fruit gardens.

★ I put water in the basin to wash my hands.

---

03 ☑ brook
[bruk]

ⓝ시내, 개천 ⊜ stream   **small brook** 작은 시냇물

I went fishing with my father in a nearby brook last summer.

---

04 ☑ charter
[tʃáːrtər]

ⓐ **chartered** 전세 낸

ⓥ전세 내다, 빌리다 ⓝ전세   **charter a plane** 비행기를 전세 내다

★ He sat in the airplane alone as if he had chartered it.

★ Sixty percent of European tourists have used charter flight services.

---

05 ☑ civic
[sívik]

ⓐ시민의, 시의 ⊜ municipal   **a civic group** 시민 단체
civic center 관청가, 시민 회관

Their civic traffic regulations are very strict.

---

06 ☑ congestion
[kəndʒéstʃən]

ⓝ혼잡, 밀집 ⊜ jam 혼잡   **the traffic congestion** 교통 혼잡

He was late because of terrible traffic congestion.

---

01 함선에 닻이 없었다면 풍랑에 의해 함선이 바다로 떠내려갈 수도 있었다. / 그는 호수 한가운데 배를 정박시켰다. 02 분지의 기후 조건은 과수원을 하기에 좋다. / 나는 손을 씻기 위해 대야에 물을 담았다. 03 나는 지난여름에 아버지와 함께 가까운 개천으로 낚시하러 갔다. 04 그는 마치 비행기를 전세 낸 깃처럼 홀로 앉아 있었다. / 유럽 관광객의 60%가 전세 비행기 편을 이용했다. 05 그들의 시의 교통 법규는 매우 엄하다. 06 그는 몹시 심한 교통 혼잡 때문에 지각했다.

07 ☑ continent
[kántinənt]

ⓐ continental 대륙의

ⓝ 대륙, 육지　　　the Old Continent 구대륙(유럽, 아시아, 아프리카)

Columbus thought he reached India when he found the new continent.

---

08 ☑ deck
[dek]

ⓝ 갑판, 바닥　　　a slippery deck 미끄러운 갑판

The sailors watched the sunset on the main deck.

---

09 ☑ destination
[dèstinéiʃən]

ⓥ destine 운명 짓다

ⓝ 목적지, 행선지　　　a vacation destination 휴양지

The destination of this airplane is Singapore.

---

10 ☑ detour
[díːtuər]

ⓝ 우회, 도는 길　ⓔ diversion　　　make a detour 우회하다

We had to make a detour around the construction site.

---

11 ☑ direction
[dirékʃən]

ⓥ direct 지시하다

ⓝ 방향, 지시　　　wind direction 풍향

★ They stopped the car to ask for directions to the museum.
★ The chief gave directions to the workers.

---

12 ☑ slope
[sloup]

ⓝ 기울기, 비탈　ⓔ incline, slant 경사(면)　measure a slope 기울기를 측정하다

The slope of the mountain is too steep to climb on foot.

---

13 ☑ embark
[embáːrk]

ⓝ embarkation 탑승, 승선

ⓥ (배, 비행기 등에) 탑승하다, 싣다　ⓔ board 탑승하다

embark passengers 승객을 태우다

The passengers embarked for Jeju island.

---

07 콜럼버스가 신대륙을 발견했을 때, 그는 자신이 인도에 도착했다고 생각했다.　08 선원들은 주 갑판에서 석양을 바라보았다.　09 이 비행기의 목적지는 싱가포르다.　10 우리는 건설 현장을 돌아서 우회해야 했다.　11 그들은 박물관 가는 길을 물으려고 차를 세웠다. / 상사는 직원들에게 지시를 내렸다.　12 그 산의 경사는 걸어서 오르기에는 너무 가파르다.　13 승객들이 제주도행 배에 탔다.

14 erosion
[iróuʒən]

v erode 부식하다

n 침식, 부식

soil erosion 토양 침식

We must take care of the erosion before the river overflows.

15 eruption
[irʌ́pʃən]

v erupt 분출하다, 분화하다
a eruptive 폭발적인, 분출하는

n (화산의) 폭발, 분화

a volcanic eruption 분화

Many people were injured during a volcanic eruption in Japan.

16 expedition
[èkspədíʃən]

a expeditionary 탐험의

n 긴 여행, 원정 **=** journey, quest **an exploring expedition** 탐험 여행

Several countries have expedition teams in the Arctic.

17 geography
[dʒiːágrəfi]

a geographic
지리학의, 지리적인

n 지리, 지세, 지형

physical geography 자연 지리학

I learned much about the world during my geography class.

18 intersection
[ìntərsékʃən]

v intersect 가로지르다, 교차하다

n 교차로 **=** junction **a busy intersection** 교통량이 많은 교차로

We need to take a right at the intersection to go to the bookstore.

19 landfill
[lǽndfil]

n 쓰레기 매립지

a sanitary landfill 위생 매립

Most of our household wastes are buried in a landfill.

20 creek
[kriːk]

n 시내, 샛강 **=** stream, brook **the Cheonggye Creek** 청계천

Jumping into the creek from a height is not permitted.

---

14 강이 범람하기 전에 강의 침식을 관리해야 한다. 15 일본에서 화산이 폭발했을 때 많은 사람이 다쳤다. 16 여러 나라가 북극에 탐사단을 보냈다.
17 나는 지리 시간에 세계에 대해 많은 것을 배웠다. 18 우리가 서점에 가기 위해서는 교차로에서 우회전해야 한다. 19 우리의 생활 쓰레기는 대부분 매립지에 묻힌다. 20 높은 데서 시냇물에 뛰어들어가는 것은 금지되어 있다.

21 ☑ **Mediterranean**
[mèdətəréiniən]

ⓝ 지중해 **ⓐ** 지중해의

a **Mediterranean climate** 지중해성 기후
the **Mediterranean** 지중해 지역

You can find the best view of the Mediterranean Sea on a ferry.

---

22 ☑ **metropolitan**
[mètrəpálitən]

ⓝ metropolis 대도시, 중심도시

ⓐ 대도시의, 수도의

a **metropolitan area** 대도시권

A large portion of the Korean population lives in metropolitan areas.

---

23 ☑ **monument**
[mánjəmənt]

ⓐ monumental 기념비의

ⓝ 기념비, 기념물

a **national monument** 국가 기념물

This monument was built in memory of a great king.

---

24 ☑ **nomadic**
[noumǽdik]

ⓝ nomad 유목민, 방랑자

ⓐ 유목의, 방랑의

nomadic life 유목 생활

Gypsies are famous for their free and nomadic lifestyles.

---

25 ☑ **oriental**
[ɔ̀:riéntl]

ⓝⓐ orient 동양; 동양의
ⓝ orientalism 동양식, 동양학

ⓐ 동양 (문명)의 ⬌ occidental 서양의

oriental civilization 동양 문명

The westerners were fascinated by the oriental culture.

---

26 ☑ **Pacific**
[pəsífik]

ⓝ 태평양 **ⓐ** 태평양의

the **Pacific Ocean** 태평양

The Korean settlers crossed the Pacific Ocean to America.

---

27 ☑ **pavement**
[péivmənt]

ⓥ pave (도로를) 포장하다

ⓝ 포장도로

a **concrete pavement** 콘크리트 포장도로

The mountain roads became safer after pavement was installed.

---

21 너는 지중해의 가장 멋진 경관을 배에서 볼 수 있다. 22 대한민국 인구의 큰 비중이 대도시권에 살고 있다. 23 이 기념비는 위대한 왕을 기리기 위해 만들어졌다. 24 집시는 자유롭고 방랑하는 생활방식으로 유명하다. 25 서양인들은 동양 문화에 매혹되었다. 26 한국 이주민들은 태평양을 건너 미국으로 갔다. 27 포장도로가 놓이고 나서 산길이 더욱 안전해졌다.

28 pedestrian
[pədéstriən]

n 보행자 **a** 도보의, 보행의   ⊜ walker 보행자   **a pedestrian bridge** 육교

★ The cars should always allow the pedestrians to pass first when driving.

★ It is dangerous to cross the road when there is no pedestrian crossing.

29 peninsula
[pənínsələ]

n 반도   **the Korean Peninsula** 한반도

A peninsula is a piece of land surrounded by sea and attached to a larger land.

30 pole
[poul]

a polar 극지의, 남[북]극의

n 극, 극지   **the North [South] Pole** 북극[남극]

The South Pole is the point that is furthest south on the Earth.

31 province
[právins]

a provincial 지방의

n 지방, 지역   **an autonomous province** 자치주

Seoul is surrounded by Gyeonggi Province.

32 ridge
[ridʒ]

a ridgy 솟아오른

n 산등성이, 융기(隆起)   **a mountain ridge** 산등성이

The cat is afraid to come down from the ridge of the roof.

33 sector
[séktər]

n 구역, 분야   ⊜ part   **a different sector** 다른 지역

★ The city has several sectors that have different development plans.

★ This policy is expected to strengthen the industrial sector.

34 lorry
[lɔ́(:)ri]

n 화물 자동차, 트럭   ⊜ truck   **a coal lorry** 석탄차

My car couldn't enter because two lorries blocked the entrance.

---

28 운전할 때는 항상 보행자가 먼저 건널 수 있도록 해야 한다. / 건널목이 없을 때 길을 건너는 것은 위험하다. 29 반도는 바다로 둘러싸이고 더 큰 육지에 붙어있는 땅 덩어리를 말한다. 30 남극은 지구상에서 최남단인 지점이다. 31 서울은 경기도에 둘러싸여 있다. 32 고양이가 지붕의 용마루에서 내려오기를 무서워하고 있다. 33 도시는 서로 다른 개발 계획이 있는 여러 구역으로 나뉜다. / 이 정책은 산업 분야를 강화할 것으로 기대된다. 34 큰 트럭 두 대가 입구를 막고 있어서 내 차가 들어갈 수 없었다.

35 ☑ spectacle
[spéktəkəl]

ⓐ spectacular 구경거리의, 장관의

ⓝ 광경, 장관, 구경거리 ⓢ wonder 감탄할 만한 것

a public spectacle 대중의 구경거리

★ The night scene in Las Vegas was a real spectacle.
★ Sidney has several spectacles for tourists.

36 ☑ stopover
[stápòuvər]

ⓝ 단기 체류, 도중하차

a brief stopover 단기 체류

★ I'm just staying at Paris for a short stopover.
★ Our flight will have a three-hour stopover at Hong Kong.

37 ☑ suburb
[sʌ́bəːrb]

ⓐ suburban 교외의

ⓝ 교외, 근교

a suburb of Los Angeles 로스앤젤레스 근교

Many people work in the city while living in the suburbs.

38 ☑ swamp
[swɑmp]

ⓐ swampy 질퍽질퍽한

ⓝ 늪, 습지

drain swamps 습지에 물을 빼내다[배수하다]

Many reptiles, such as alligators, live in swamps.

39 ☑ terrain
[təréin]

ⓝ 지형, 지역 ⓢ ground, land

a mountainous terrain 산악 지형

Certain symbols on maps represent different terrain.

40 ☑ transportation
[trænspərtéiʃən]

ⓥ transport 수송하다, 운반하다

ⓝ 교통, 운송

air transportation 항공 교통

The public transportation system in Seoul is very convenient to use.

---

35 라스베이거스의 야경은 대단한 장관이었다. / 시드니에는 관광객을 위한 여러 가지 구경거리가 있다. 36 나는 파리에 단기 체류로 잠시 머무르고 있을 뿐이다. / 우리 비행기는 홍콩에서 3시간 동안 도중하차할 예정입니다. 37 많은 사람이 도시에서 일하고 교외에서 생활한다. 38 악어 등과 같은 다양한 파충류들은 늪에 산다. 39 지도에 있는 특정한 상징들은 각기 다른 지형을 나타낸다. 40 서울의 대중교통 체계는 이용하기에 매우 편리하다.

EXERCISE

A 다음 영어는 우리말로, 우리말은 영어로 옮기시오.

01 pavement _____　　07 혼잡, 밀집 _____

02 basin _____　　08 늪, 습지 _____

03 sector _____　　09 지리, 지세, 지형 _____

04 landfill _____　　10 광경, 장관 _____

05 suburb _____　　11 기념비, 기념물 _____

06 slope _____　　12 반도 _____

B 다음 빈칸에 알맞은 단어를 쓰시오.

01 brook ⊜ _____　　07 direction ⓥ _____

02 detour ⊜ _____　　08 erosion ⓥ _____

03 embark ⊜ _____　　09 continent ⓐ _____

04 civic ⊜ _____　　10 eruption ⓐ _____

05 expedition ⊜ _____　　11 nomadic ⓝ _____

06 oriental ⇔ _____　　12 metropolitan ⓝ _____

C 다음 빈칸에 들어갈 알맞은 말을 고르시오. (필요하면 형태를 바꾸시오.)

destination	expedition	nomadic	charter	pedestrian

01 The gypsies follow a(n) _____ way of life.

02 We _____ a huge fishing boat for the company-wide fishing trip last week.

03 The _____ walkway should be respected and all vehicles should remain on the streets.

04 Our _____ was the northernmost part of town, and the estimated travel time was three hours.

05 The explorer makes several dangerous _____ each year, focusing on a new unexplored region each time.

Crossword Puzzle

앞에서 배운 어휘를 기억하며 퍼즐을 풀어보세요.

정답

Across

2 someone who is walking, especially along a street or other place used by cars

3 the problem of too much traffic in a place

4 a place where roads, lines, etc. cross each other, especially where two roads meet

6 a building, statue, or other large structure that is built to remind people of an important event or famous person

7 the place that someone or something is going to

8 a sudden outbreak of something, typically something unwelcome or noisy

Down

1 a system or method for carrying passengers or goods from one place to another

5 traveling from place to place and not living in any one place for very long

_____ 재정적인

_____ 소비, 소비량

_____ 채용, 보충

_____ 상업의, 광고방송

_____ 보증하다

_____ 인종의

_____ 미신

_____ 특권

_____ 양심

_____ 충실한

Economy & Finance
경제와 금융

Culture & Ethics
문화와 윤리

Society and Culture
사회와 문화

Politics & Society
정치와 사회

Geography & Traffic
지리와 교통

_____ 유죄의

_____ 증거

_____ 규제하다

_____ 적임의

_____ 폐지하다

_____ 목적지

_____ 보행자

_____ (화산의) 폭발

_____ 혼잡, 밀집

_____ 교통, 운송

Chapter
04

Science and Technology

Biology & Chemistry

---

01 additive
[ǽdətiv]

ⓥ add 더하다, 추가하다

ⓝ 첨가물, 첨가제

food additives 식품 첨가물

The toxic industrial additive level of the river was dangerously high.

---

02 vapor
[véipər]

ⓥ vaporize 기화시키다

ⓝ 증기

water vapor 수증기
vapor engine 증기 기관

A hydrogen car emits only water vapor as exhaust.

---

03 biological
[bàiəládʒikəl]

ⓝ biology 생물학

ⓐ 생물학적인

biological parents 생물학적 부모, 친부모

Unhealthy food can disrupt our biological balance.

---

04 biotechnology
[bàioʊteknáːlədʒi]

ⓝ 생명공학

medical biotechnology 의료 생명공학

People hope that biotechnology will come up with new treatments.

---

05 blend
[blend]

ⓝ blending 혼합(물)

ⓥ 섞다 **ⓝ** 혼합물 ⊜ mix, combine

blended tea 혼합차

★ Blending different medicines arbitrarily can be very dangerous.

★ He wrote a song with a blend of jazz, hip-hop, and classical music.

---

06 breed
[briːd]

ⓝ 종류, 품종 **ⓥ** 낳다, 기르다

a dying breed 사라져 가는 품종

A new breed of plant can be made by mixing two different trees.

---

01 그 강의 독성 산업 첨가물 수치가 위험할 정도로 높았다. 02 수소 자동차는 배기가스로 수증기만을 배출한다. 03 건강에 해로운 음식은 우리의 생물학적 균형을 교란시킬 수 있다. 04 사람들은 생명공학을 통해 새로운 치료법이 개발될 것을 기대한다. 05 마음대로 다른 약을 섞는 것은 매우 위험할 수 있다. / 그는 재즈, 힙합, 클래식 음악을 혼합한 노래를 만들었다. 06 다른 나무 두 개를 섞음으로써 새로운 품종의 식물을 만들 수 있다.

07 carbohydrate
[kɑ̀ːrbouháidreit]

ⓝ 탄수화물 　intake of carbohydrates 탄수화물 섭취(량)

Sufficient amount of carbohydrates is recommended before exercise.

08 carbon
[káːrbən]

ⓝ 탄소 　carbon dioxide [monoxide] 이산화탄소[일산화탄소]

Many experts agree that carbon dioxide is a main factor of global warming.

09 chemistry
[kémistri]
ⓝ chemist 화학자

ⓝ 화학 　a chemistry lab 화학 실험실

Chemistry was born in the attempt to make gold from plain metals.

10 chromosome
[króuməsòum]

ⓝ 염색체 　Y chromosome Y 염색체

The goal of the Human Genome Project was to make human chromosome map.

11 compound
[kámpaund / kəmpáund]

ⓝ 합성물, 혼합물 ⓥ 합성하다, 혼합하다 　a chemical compound 화합물

Compounding two materials without caution can cause an explosion.

12 cultivate
[kʌ́ltəvèit]
ⓝ cultivation 배양, 경작

ⓥ 배양하다, 경작하다 　cultivate land 땅을 경작하다

The chemists cultivated bacteria for experimental purposes.

13 decay
[dikéi]
ⓐ decayed 썩은

ⓥ 썩다, 부식하다 ⓝ 부식, 충치 ⊜ rot 썩다

vulnerable to decay 부식에 취약한

★ You can use certain chemicals to treat decayed metal.

★ Not brushing your teeth regularly can cause tooth decay.

14 detergent
[ditə́ːrdʒənt]

ⓝ 세제 　a synthetic detergent 합성세제

A detergent works by merely making oil dissolve in water.

07 운동 전에 충분한 양의 탄수화물이 권장된다. 08 많은 전문가는 이산화탄소가 지구온난화의 주요인이라는 것에 동의한다. 09 화학은 평범한 금속에서 황금을 만들려는 시도에서 탄생했다. 10 인간 게놈 프로젝트의 목표는 인간 염색체 지도를 만드는 것이었다. 11 두 물질을 부주의하게 합성하면 폭발이 일어날 수도 있다. 12 화학자들은 실험을 목적으로 박테리아를 배양했다. 13 부식한 금속을 복원하는 데 특정한 화학물질을 쓸 수 있다. / 이를 규칙적으로 닦지 않는 것은 충치를 초래할 수 있다. 14 세제는 단순히 기름을 물에 녹이는 기능을 한다.

15 sprout
[spraut]

ⓥ 싹트다, 발아하다, 발육하다 **ⓝ** 싹　**ⓔ** bud 싹트다, 싹　　**a bean sprout** 콩나물

★ Spring was finally announced as plants started to sprout.

★ The little seed grew, and the many sprouts turned into a huge plant.

16 dissolve
[dizálv]

ⓝ dissolution 용해, 분해

ⓥ 녹이다, 용해하다　**ⓔ** melt　　**dissolve in water** 물에 녹다

If you mix sugar in water, it dissolves and makes a clear solution.

17 duplicate
[djú:pləkèit / djú:plikət]

ⓝ duplication 복제

ⓥ 복제하다 **ⓐ** 복제의 **ⓝ** 복제품　　**a duplicate copy** 사본

★ A clone is a living thing that was artificially duplicated from another.

★ The thief unlocked the door with a duplicate key.

★ Which painting do you have, the duplicate or the original?

18 evaporate
[ivǽpərèit]

ⓝ evaporation 증발, 발산

ⓥ 증발하다　　**evaporated by the sun** 태양에 의해 증발된

Water evaporates more quickly on a hot and dry day.

19 evolution
[èvəlú:ʃən]

ⓥ evolve 발전시키다, 진화하다

ⓝ 진화, 발전　　**the theory of evolution** 진화론

Through evolution, certain organs are more developed than others.

20 ferment
[fəːrmént]

ⓝ fermentation 발효 작용

ⓥ 발효시키다　　**fermented drink** 발효주

As kimchi is fermented, many healthy components are formed.

---

15 식물의 싹이 트면서 드디어 봄의 시작을 알렸다. / 작은 씨앗이 자라고 많은 새싹은 큰 나무로 성장했다. 16 설탕을 물에 용해하면 설탕이 녹아서 투명한 용액이 된다. 17 클론은 다른 생물로부터 인공적으로 복제된 생물이다. / 도둑은 복제 열쇠로 문을 열었다. / 복제품과 진품 중 어떤 그림을 가지고 있습니까? 18 물은 덥고 건조한 날에 더 빨리 증발한다. 19 진화를 통해, 특정한 기관들이 다른 기관들보다 더 발달하였다. 20 김치는 발효되면서 건강에 좋은 성분들이 많이 만들어진다.

21 ☑ fume
[fju:m]

ⓝ 증기, 가스 ⓥ (연기, 가스 등을) 뿜다, 증발하다　**poisonous fumes** 유독가스

★ Many cars in the street give off fumes.

★ The exhaust gas fuming out of cars pollutes the air seriously.

22 ☑ fungus
[fʌ́ŋgəs]

ⓝ 버섯, 균류　**a deadly fungus** 치명적인 곰팡이

A fungus is not only used for food, but also for medicine like penicillin.

23 ☑ fusion
[fjú:ʒən]

ⓥ fuse 녹이다, 융합하다

ⓝ 용해, 융합　**nuclear fusion** 핵융합
a fusion bomb (= a hydrogen bomb) 수소폭탄

Energy from nuclear fusion can supply power for a vast area.

24 ☑ gene
[dʒi:n]

ⓝ 유전자　**a dominant [recessive] gene** 우성[열성] 유전자

Offspring resemble their parents because they share the same genes.

25 ☑ genetic
[dʒinétik]

ⓝ genetics 유전학

ⓐ 유전자의, 유전학적인　**genetic modification/manipulation** 유전자 조작

The genetic codes of a living thing are stored in its DNA.

26 ☑ germ
[dʒə:rm]

ⓝ 세균, 병균　● virus　**a germ carrier** 보균자

Always keep your hands clean to avoid being infected by germs.

27 ☑ hatch
[hætʃ]

ⓥ 부화하다　**take ~ to hatch** 부화하는 데 ~가 걸리다

I saw a chick hatching out from an egg at my grandmother's farm.

---

21 거리에 있는 많은 차가 연기를 내뿜는다. / 자동차에서 배출되는 배기가스는 공기를 심각하게 오염시킨다.　22 균류는 식용뿐만 아니라, 페니실린과 같은 약에도 사용된다.　23 핵융합을 통한 에너지는 광범위한 지역에 전력을 공급할 수 있다.　24 자손은 부모와 같은 유전자를 공유하기 때문에 부모를 닮는다.　25 생물의 유전 암호는 DNA에 저장되어 있다.　26 세균에 감염되는 것을 피하려면 항상 손을 청결히 해라.　27 나는 할머니의 농장에서 병아리가 알에서 부화하는 것을 보았다.

28 hydrogen
[háidrədʒən]

ⓝ 수소

a hydrogen vehicle 수소 자동차

A hydrogen bomb has the firepower to destroy a whole city.

29 sperm
[spəːrm]

ⓝ 정자, 정액

a sperm bank 정자 은행

Some lab results suggest that smoking may damage sperm activity.

30 incubation
[ìnkjəbéiʃən]

ⓥ incubate 알을 품다

ⓝ 알을 품음

artificial incubation 인공 부화

A chick is born after three weeks of incubation.

31 microbe
[máikròub]

ⓝ 미생물, 세균

a microbe war 세균전

Microbes can only be observed through microscopes.

32 molecule
[máləkjùːl]

ⓐ molecular 분자의, 분자로 된

ⓝ 분자

a nuclear molecule 원자핵 분자

The molecule is the smallest unit that has a chemical nature.

33 species
[spíːʃi(ː)z]

ⓝ 〈생물〉 종(種), 종류 ⊜ category, breed

an endangered species 멸종 위기 종

Darwin suggested that various species shared common ancestors.

34 organism
[ɔ́ːrgənìzəm]

ⓐ organic 유기체의

ⓝ 유기체

a living organism 살아 있는 유기체[생명체]

The bodies of all living things on the Earth consist of organisms.

---

28 수소 폭탄은 도시 전체를 날려 버릴 만큼 강력한 화력을 가지고 있다. 29 일부 실험 결과에 의하면 흡연이 정자 활동을 저하할 수 있다고 한다. 30 병아리는 대게 3주간의 부화를 거쳐 태어난다. 31 미생물은 현미경을 통해서만 관찰할 수 있다. 32 분자는 화학적 성질을 가진 가장 작은 단위다. 33 다윈은 다양한 종이 공통된 조상을 가진다고 주장했다. 34 지구에 있는 모든 생물체의 몸은 유기체로 구성되어 있다.

35 bleed
[bliːd]

ⓝ blood 피
ⓐⓝ bleeding 피나는; 출혈

ⓥ 피가 나다   **bleed to death** 출혈하여 죽다

His nose suddenly started to bleed from his fatigue.

36 phenomenon
[finámənàn]

ⓐ phenomenal
현상적인, 경이로운

ⓝ 현상 ● circumstance   **a natural phenomenon** 자연 현상

There was no connection between the two scientific phenomena.

37 tissue
[tíʃuː]

ⓝ 조직   **skin tissue** 피부 조직

We examined the tissue under a microscope.

38 reproduction
[rìːprədʌkʃən]

ⓐ reproductive 생식의
ⓥ reproduce 재생하다, 생식하다

ⓝ 재생산, 생식   **reproduction by division** 분열을 통한 생식

Animals all have different strategies and methods for reproduction.

39 solution
[səljúːʃən]

ⓥ solve 용해하다

ⓝ 용액, 용해 ● mixture   **saline solution** 식염수

A solution is a chemical compound in the form of a liquid.

40 specimen
[spésəmən]

ⓝ 견본, 표본 ● sample   **zoological specimens** 동물 표본

Scientists collect specimens of animals to study their biology.

---

35 그는 피로 때문에 갑자기 코피가 나기 시작했다.   36 두 과학적 현상 사이에는 아무런 관련이 없었다.   37 우리는 현미경으로 그 조직을 관찰했다.
38 동물들은 모두 각기 다른 생식 전략과 방법이 있다.   39 용액은 액체 상태의 화학적 혼합물이다.   40 과학자들은 동물의 생명 작용을 연구하기 위해 표본을 모은다.

EXERCISE

A 다음 영어는 우리말로, 우리말은 영어로 옮기시오.

01 evaporate _____
02 germ _____
03 biotechnology _____
04 tissue _____
05 hydrogen _____
06 chromosome _____

07 탄수화물 _____
08 미생물, 세균 _____
09 녹이다, 용해하다 _____
10 (연기, 가스 등을) 내뿜다 _____
11 버섯, 균류 _____
12 수증기 _____

B 다음 빈칸에 알맞은 단어를 쓰시오.

01 blend ⊜ _____
02 sprout ⊜ _____
03 specimen ⊜ _____
04 dissolve ⊜ _____
05 solution ⊜ _____
06 decay ⊜ _____

07 evolution ⓥ _____
08 incubation ⓥ _____
09 molecule ⓐ _____
10 organism ⓐ _____
11 biological ⓝ _____
12 cultivate ⓝ _____

C 다음 빈칸에 들어갈 알맞은 말을 고르시오. (필요하면 형태를 바꾸시오.)

| ferment | phenomenon | duplicate | additive | genetic |

01 The copier is able to create a(n) _____ of any item we choose to copy.

02 The _____ was added to the ingredients of the cake to increase its shelf-life.

03 When cabbage is _____ with various spices and other ingredients, it is called kimchi.

04 Her green eyes are _____ as both her parents have green eyes themselves.

05 There are supernatural _____ that cannot be explained and the best-known one would be the UFO.

Crossword Puzzle

앞에서 배운 어휘를 기억하며 퍼즐을 풀어보세요.

Across

1. something that happens or exists in society, science, or nature, especially something that is studied because it is difficult to understand
3. a substance that is added to food to improve its taste, appearance, etc.
5. to keep animals or plants in order to produce babies or new plants, especially ones with particular qualities
7. an animal, plant, human, or any other living thing
9. to prepare and use land for growing crops and plants
10. a substance containing atoms from two or more elements

Down

2. the smallest unit into which any substance can be divided without losing its own chemical nature, usually consisting of two or more atoms
4. a liquid or powder used for washing clothes, dishes, etc.
6. a small amount or piece that is taken from something, so that it can be tested or examined
8. (of an egg) open and produce a young animal

Earth & Universe

01 alien
[éiljən]

ⓥ alienate 멀리하다, 따돌리다

ⓐ 외국의, 외계의 ⓝ 외국인, 외계인 ⊜ foreign 외국의, foreigner 외국인

alien beings 외계 생물체

★ Many sci-fi movies depict aliens as invaders to the Earth.

★ Illegal aliens should not be allowed to get a job in the country.

02 astrology
[əstrálədʒi]

ⓐ astrologic 점성술의

ⓝ 점성학, 점성술

Chinese astrology 중국 점성학

Early astrology believed that the future could be foretold.

03 astronaut
[ǽstrənɔ̀:t]

ⓝ 우주비행사

astronaut training 우주비행사 훈련

Astronauts receive special training to carry out missions in space.

04 astronomy
[əstránəmi]

ⓐ astronomical 천문학적인

ⓝ 천문학

statistical astronomy 통계 천문학

The field of astronomy studies the origin of the universe.

05 atmosphere
[ǽtməsfìər]

ⓝ 대기, 분위기

the upper atmosphere 대기 상층부

Most meteors burn up and disappear when they enter the atmosphere.

06 aviation
[èiviéiʃən]

ⓥ aviate 비행하다
ⓝ aviator 비행가

ⓝ 항공, 비행

civil aviation 민간 항공

Pilots wear specialized aviation garments to protect themselves.

---

01 많은 공상 과학 영화에서는 외계인을 지구의 침략자로 묘사한다. / 불법 외국인들은 국내에서 취직할 수 없게 해야 한다. 02 초기 점성학은 미래가 예견될 수 있다고 믿었다. 03 우주비행사들은 우주에서 임무를 수행할 수 있도록 특수 훈련을 받는다. 04 천문학 분야는 우주의 기원을 연구한다. 05 운석 대부분은 대기권에 들어올 때 타버려서 사라진다. 06 조종사들은 자신을 보호하기 위해 특수한 항공복을 입는다.

07 chaos
[kéiɑs]
ⓐ chaotic 무질서한

ⓝ 혼돈, 무질서, 대혼란　ⓢ disorder　**social chaos** 사회적 혼란

Scientists are trying to reveal how the cosmos was born from chaos.

08 comet
[kámit]
ⓐ cometary 혜성의, 혜성 같은

ⓝ 혜성　**a comet seeker[finder]** 혜성 관측 망원경

A comet is actually a mass of dust that moves around the sun.

09 constellation
[kànstəléiʃən]

ⓝ 별자리, 성운　**the constellation of Orion** 오리온자리

In the past, sailors used constellations to navigate their ships.

10 cosmos
[kázməs]
ⓐ cosmic 우주의, 우주론의

ⓝ 우주, 천지만물　ⓢ universe　**the entire cosmos** 전 우주

I always dream of being an astronaut, traveling through the cosmos.

11 crust
[krʌst]

ⓝ 지각, 표면　ⓢ surface　**the Earth's crust** 지각

The most outer part of the Earth's surface is called the crust.

12 earthly
[ə́:rθli]

ⓐ 지구의, 지상의　**an earthly paradise** 지상 낙원

Many space voyagers carry information on earthly life.

13 equator
[ikwéitər]
ⓐ equatorial 적도의

ⓝ 적도　**the equator of the planet** 지구의 적도

The hottest areas on the Earth are the ones along the equator.

07 과학자들은 혼돈에서 우주가 어떻게 탄생하게 되었는지 밝히려고 한다. 08 혜성은 실제로 태양 주위를 도는 먼지 덩어리다. 09 과거에 선원들은 항해하는 데 별자리를 이용했다. 10 나는 항상 우주비행사가 되어 우주를 항해하는 꿈을 꾼다. 11 지구의 가장 바깥쪽 표면을 지각이라고 한다. 12 많은 우주 탐사선에는 지구의 생활에 대한 정보가 담겨 있다. 13 지구에서 가장 뜨거운 지역은 적도를 따라 있는 곳이다.

14 exploration
[èkspləréiʃən]

v explore 탐사하다

n 탐사, 탐험　　　　　　　　**space exploration** 우주 탐사

We have made much advancement through attempts of exploration.

15 galaxy
[gǽləksi]

n 은하, 은하계　　　　　　　**a spiral galaxy** 나선 은하

Our solar system is in a spiral galaxy called the "Milky Way."

16 adventure
[ædvéntʃər]

a adventurous
모험적인, 모험을 좋아하는

n 모험　　　　　　　　　　**an adventure novel** 모험소설

Many people wish to escape their daily lives and go on an adventure.

17 gravitation
[græ̀vətéiʃən]

n 인력, 중력　　　　**the law of universal gravitation** 만유인력의 법칙

It is said that Newton developed the law of gravitation after he saw an apple drop from a tree.

18 gravity
[grǽvəti]

n 중력　　　　　　　　　　**zero gravity** 무중력 상태

The gravity on the moon is only 1/6 of that on the Earth.

19 hemisphere
[hémisfìər]

a hemispheric 반구의

n 반구　　　　　　　　**the Southern Hemisphere** 남반구

The Earth is divided into two hemispheres by the equator.

20 infrared
[ìnfrəréd]

a 적외선의　　　　　　　**an infrared detector** 적외선 탐지기

On each side of the visible light spectrum, there are infrared and ultraviolet rays.

21 magnetic
[mægnétik]

n magnet 자석

a 자석의, 자기의　　　　　　**a magnetic body** 자성체

The Earth has a magnetic field between its two poles.

---

14 우리는 탐험 시도를 통해서 큰 발전을 이루었다.　15 태양계는 '은하수'라고 하는 나선 은하 속에 있다.　16 많은 사람이 자신의 일상을 벗어나 모험을 떠나고 싶어 한다.　17 뉴턴은 나무에서 사과가 떨어지는 것을 보고 만유인력의 법칙을 개발했다고 전해진다.　18 달의 중력은 지구의 1/6밖에 되지 않는다. 19 지구는 적도를 따라 2개의 반구로 나뉜다.　20 가시광선 스펙트럼의 양쪽에는 적외선과 자외선이 있다.　21 지구는 두 개의 극지방 사이에 자기장이 있다.

22 universal
[jùːnəvə́ːrsəl]

ⓝ universe 우주

ⓐ 전 세계의, 우주의 **ⓢ** global, worldwide 전 세계의

Universal Time(UT) 세계 표준시

Let me know how to convert the Universal Time into local time.

23 launch
[lɔːntʃ]

ⓥ 발사하다, 착수하다 **ⓝ** 발진, 발사　　　　　**a launch pad** 발사대

★ The control center approved the satellite to be launched.

★ The government announced that the launch of the artificial satellite was a great success.

24 Mars
[mɑːrz]

ⓝⓐ Martian 화성인; 화성의

ⓝ 화성　　　**the distance of Mars from the Earth** 지구와 화성 간의 거리

Some people believe that aliens live on Mars.

c.f.) Mercury 수성 Venus 금성 Jupiter 목성 Saturn 토성 Uranus 천왕성 Neptune 해왕성

25 mercury
[mə́ːrkjəri]

ⓝ 수은, 수성(M-)　　　　　　　　　　**mercury poisoning** 수은 중독

★ The mercury in the thermometer rises as the temperature increases.

★ Mercury is the closest planet to the sun.

26 meteor
[míːtiər]

ⓐ meteoric 유성의, 유성 같은

ⓝ 유성, 운석　　　　　　　　　　　**a meteor shower** 유성우

Scientists discovered a meteor rock that fell to the Earth ages ago.

27 navigation
[nὰvəgéiʃən]

ⓥ navigate 항해하다

ⓝ 항해　　　　　　　　　　　　**aerial navigation** 항공

The North Star was essential to the navigation of ships.

---

22 세계 표준시를 지역 시간으로 전환하는 방법을 알려주세요. 23 작전 본부는 인공위성의 발사를 허가했다. / 정부는 인공위성의 발사가 대성공이라고 발표했다. 24 어떤 사람들은 화성에 외계인이 산다고 생각한다. 25 온도가 올라가면, 온도계 안에 있는 수은도 올라간다. / 수성은 태양에서 가장 가까운 행성이다. 26 과학자들은 매우 오래전에 지구에 떨어진 운석을 발견했다. 27 북극성은 항해에 있어서 매우 중요한 별이었다.

28 observatory
[əbzə́ːrvətɔ̀ːri]

v observe 관찰하다

n 관측소, 천문대   **a meteorological observatory** 기상대

The people gathered at the observatory to observe the comet.

29 orbit
[ɔ́ːrbit]

a orbital 궤도의

n 궤도   **out of orbit** 궤도 밖으로

Korea has seven satellites that are operating in the Earth's orbit.

30 probe
[proub]

n 탐사기, 탐사   **⊜** scrutiny, exploration   **space probe** 우주 탐사기

China's first Mars probe has completed testing and is getting ready for launch.

31 asteroid
[ǽstərɔ̀id]

n 소행성   **asteroid impact** 소행성 충돌

The space shuttle attempted to land on the asteroid to collect samples, but failed to do so.

32 revolve
[riválv]

n revolution 회전

v 회전하다, 공전하다   **⊜** rotate   **a revolving door** 회전문

Some planets have one or more moons revolving around them.

33 satellite
[sǽtəlàit]

n 위성   **an artificial satellite** 인공위성

Satellites move around planets along paths called orbits.

34 shuttle
[ʃʌ́tl]

n 왕복선, 왕복 운행   **a space shuttle** 우주왕복선

People wished for the astronaut's safe return as the shuttle left the Earth.

---

28 사람들은 혜성을 관찰하기 위해 천문대에 모여들었다. 29 한국은 지구의 궤도상에서 작동하는 인공위성이 일곱 개가 있다. 30 중국의 첫 화성 탐사선이 테스트를 끝내고 발사 준비를 하고 있다. 31 우주왕복선이 표본을 모으기 위해 소행성에 착륙하려고 시도했지만 실패했다. 32 몇몇 행성은 그 주위를 도는 위성이 한 개 이상 있다. 33 위성들은 궤도라고 하는 길을 따라 행성 주변을 돈다. 34 사람들은 우주왕복선이 지구를 떠나자, 우주비행사의 무사귀환을 빌었다.

35 ☑ supernatural
[sùːpərnǽtʃərəl]

ⓝ supernaturalism 초자연주의

ⓐ 초자연적인, 불가사의한 ⊜ uncanny

a supernatural being 초자연적인 존재

There are some supernatural events that cannot be explained scientifically.

36 ☑ sonic
[sánik]

ⓐ supersonic 초음속의

ⓐ 음속의, 음의

a sonic speed 음속

A sonic boom occurs when an object moves faster than sound.

37 ☑ spacecraft
[spéiskrὰft]

ⓝ 우주선 **a manned [an unmanned] spacecraft** 유인[무인] 우주선

A spacecraft has a special engine that can operate in outer space.

38 ☑ starry
[stáːri]

ⓐ 별의, 별이 많은

a starry night 별이 빛나는 밤

I am always astonished every time I look up to the starry heavens.

39 ☑ stellar
[stélər]

ⓐ interstellar 별과 별 사이의

ⓐ 별의, 별 같은

a stellar night 별이 총총한 밤

You can see the North Star on a stellar night.

40 ☑ state-of-the-art

ⓐ 최첨단 기술을 사용한, 최신의 **a state-of-the-art cell phone** 최첨단 휴대폰

The government promoted the development of state-of-the-art space technology.

---

35 과학적으로 설명되지 않는 초자연적 사건들이 다소 있다. 36 소닉붐(음속 폭발음)은 물체가 소리보다 빠르게 이동할 때 발생한다. 37 우주선은 우주에서 작동할 수 있는 특수한 엔진이 있다. 38 나는 별이 가득한 하늘을 올려다볼 때마다 항상 경외감이 든다. 39 너는 별이 빛나는 밤에 북극성을 볼 수 있다. 40 정부는 최첨단 기술을 활용한 우주 기술의 발달을 촉진했다.

EXERCISE

A 다음 영어는 우리말로, 우리말은 영어로 옮기시오.

01 satellite _____   07 대기, 분위기 _____

02 astrology _____   08 수은 _____

03 infrared _____   09 궤도 _____

04 navigation _____   10 반구 _____

05 stellar _____   11 우주선 _____

06 constellation _____   12 천문학 _____

B 다음 빈칸에 알맞은 단어를 쓰시오.

01 chaos ⊜ _____   07 aviation ⓥ _____

02 revolve ⊜ _____   08 observatory ⓥ _____

03 probe ⊜ _____   09 equator ⓐ _____

04 supernatural ⊜ _____   10 comet ⓐ _____

05 alien ⊜ _____   11 magnetic ⓝ _____

06 crust ⊜ _____   12 universal ⓝ _____

C 다음 빈칸에 들어갈 알맞은 말을 고르시오. (필요하면 형태를 바꾸시오.)

| gravity | revolve | earthly | launch | supernatural |

01 Many religious beliefs involve a trust in a(n) _____ being.

02 The space shuttle will _____ when the weather improves.

03 When a ball is thrown up in the air, it returns to the ground due to _____.

04 The various planets _____ around the sun, and the earth is one of them.

05 Some scientists are in search of the evidence that _____ life comes from other planets.

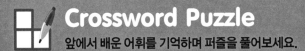

Crossword Puzzle

앞에서 배운 어휘를 기억하며 퍼즐을 풀어보세요.

정답

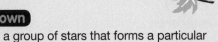

Across

2 the mixture of gases that surrounds a planet

4 to send a weapon or spacecraft into the sky or into space

6 an imaginary line drawn around the middle of the Earth that is exactly the same distance from the North Pole and the South Pole

8 a natural object that moves around a planet

9 the force that causes something to fall to the ground or to be attracted to another planet

Down

1 a group of stars that forms a particular pattern and has a name

2 one of the many small planets that move around the Sun, especially between Mars and Jupiter

3 the scientific study of the stars and planets

5 the study of the positions and movements of the stars and how they might influence people and events

7 to move in a circular orbit around

Unit 18 Industry & Resources

01 ☑ geology
[dʒiːɑ́lədʒi]

ⓐ geological 지질학적인

ⓝ 지질학   **the geology department** 지질학과

Geology studies the origins and structure of the Earth, especially its rocks.

---

02 ☑ alchemy
[ǽlkəmi]

ⓝ alchemist 연금술사

ⓝ 연금술   **the decline of alchemy** 연금술의 쇠퇴

Alchemy was the attempt to change lead into solid gold.

---

03 ☑ apparatus
[æ̀pəréitəs]

ⓝ 장치, 기구 ⊜ device, equipment   **a safety apparatus** 안전장치

The man caught a cold after his heating apparatus broke down.

---

04 ☑ artificial
[àːrtəfíʃəl]

ⓝ artificiality 가짜, 인공물

ⓐ 인공의, 인조의 ⊜ genuine 진짜의   **an artificial flavor** 인공 조미료

Plastic is praised to be the greatest artificial substance ever made.

---

05 ☑ atomic
[ətɑ́mik]

ⓝ atom 원자

ⓐ 원자의, 원자력에 의한   **atomic energy** 원자력
                               an atomic bomb 원자폭탄

An atomic power plant can be both useful and dangerous.

---

06 ☑ brass
[bræs]

ⓐ brassy 놋쇠로 만든

ⓝ 놋쇠, 황동   **a brass instrument** 금관 악기

This factory makes the finest brass dishes and bowls in the country.

---

01 지질학은 지구의 기원과 구조, 특히 암석의 기원과 구조를 연구한다. 02 연금술은 납을 순금으로 바꾸려는 시도였다. 03 난방장치가 고장 난 후 남자는 감기에 걸렸다. 04 플라스틱은 지금까지 만들어진 가장 훌륭한 인공물이라는 평을 받는다. 05 원자력 발전소는 쓸모 있는 동시에 위험할 수도 있다. 06 이 공장은 전국에서 가장 질 좋은 놋쇠 접시와 사발을 만든다.

07 bronze
[brɑnz]

ⓝ 청동   **a bronze medal** 동메달

The invention of bronze greatly changed prehistoric life.

08 cast
[kæst]

ⓥ 주조하다 **⊜** mold 틀에 넣어 본뜨다   **be cast in bronze** 청동으로 주조되다

Blacksmiths used to cast steel with their bare hands.

09 challenge
[tʃǽlindʒ]

ⓐ challenging 도전적인, 힘든

ⓝ 도전, 난관, 과제 **ⓥ** 도전하다   **challenge authority** 권한에 도전하다

Companies face a challenge as the industry undergoes great change.

10 cluster
[klʌ́stər]

ⓝ 무리, 집단 **ⓥ** 밀집하다 **⊜** gather, assemble 모이다

cluster around 주위에 떼를 지어 모이다

★ The cluster of stars formed a bright light in the night sky.

★ The people clustered to the city to find work at factories.

11 component
[kəmpóunənt]

ⓝ 성분, 구성 요소 **⊜** part, element

a component of a weapon 무기의 구성 요소

We have a factory in China that makes electronic components.

12 emergence
[imə́ːrdʒəns]

ⓥ emerge 출현하다, 부상하다
ⓐ emergent 출현하는, 나타나는

ⓝ 출현, 발생 **⊜** appearance   **sudden emergence** 갑작스러운 출현

Many entrepreneurs noticed the emergence of well-being products.

13 facilitate
[fəsílətèit]

ⓐ facile 손쉬운, 힘들지 않는
ⓝ facility 시설, 편의, 재능

ⓥ 쉽게 하다, 용이하게 하다   **facilitate the understanding** 이해를 쉽게 하다

New inventions are born in the attempt to facilitate daily life.

07 청동의 발명은 선사시대의 생활을 크게 변화시켰다. 08 대장장이는 과거에 맨손으로 철을 주조했다. 09 산업이 큰 변화를 겪음에 따라 기업들이 난관에 처해 있다. 10 별무리가 밤하늘에 밝은 빛을 만들었다. / 사람들은 공장 일을 찾기 위해 도시에 밀집했다. 11 우리는 중국에 전자 부품을 만드는 공장이 있다. 12 많은 기업가가 웰빙 제품의 출현을 인지했다. 13 새로운 발명품은 일상생활을 쉽게 하려는 시도로 탄생한다.

14 **handicraft**
[hǽndikræft]

Ⓝ 수공예(품), 손재주   **artistic handicrafts** 미술 공예

Because of complex machinery, handicraft is becoming less and less important.

---

15 **hydroelectric**
[hàidrouiléktrik]

Ⓝ hydroelectricity 수력 전기

Ⓐ 수력 전기의   **a hydroelectric power plant** 수력 발전소

Hydroelectric power is in the limelight as a clean energy source.

---

16 **industrial**
[indʌ́striəl]

Ⓝ industry 산업

Ⓐ 산업의, 공업의   **an industrial exhibition** 산업 박람회

The Industrial Age was possible by the invention of the steam engine.

---

17 **ingredient**
[ingrí:diənt]

Ⓝ 성분, 원료, 재료   ⊜ component   **principal ingredients** 주요 성분

The special ingredient of the company's product is kept secret.

---

18 **institute**
[ínstətʲùːt]

Ⓝ institution 기관, 제도

Ⓝ 학회, 시설, 제도 Ⓥ 세우다, 설립하다   ⊜ establish 세우다

        a language institute 어학 연구소

★ Researchers are developing new material at the research institute.

★ Starting with the freshman class, a new class was instituted to raise cultural awareness.

---

19 **dig**
[dig]

Ⓥ 땅을 파다, 채굴하다   **dig a tunnel** 터널을 파다

We removed a massive pile of soil after finishing the digging.

---

20 **lead**
[léd]

Ⓝ 납   **lead poisoning** 납중독

In the past, alchemists tried to convert lead into gold.

---

14 복잡한 기계설비 때문에, 수공예는 점점 중요성이 떨어지고 있다. 15 수력 전기는 무공해 에너지원으로서 주목을 받고 있다. 16 산업사회는 증기기관의 발명으로 가능했다. 17 그 회사 제품의 특수성분은 비밀로 유지되고 있다. 18 연구원들이 연구소에서 신소재를 개발하고 있다. / 1학년 수업을 시작으로, 문화적 인식을 높이는 새로운 수업이 시행되었다. 19 우리는 땅을 파내고 나서 거대한 흙더미를 치웠다. 20 과거에 연금술사들은 납을 금으로 바꾸려고 노력했다.

21 leather
[léðər]

n 가죽, 가죽제품　　　　　　**a leather jacket** 가죽 재킷

The film industry surpassed traditional businesses, such as the leather manufacture.

22 copper
[kápər]

n 구리　　　　　　**a copper wire** 구리선

Our company joined in Chile's development of natural resources, including copper.

23 cell
[sel]

n 전지　　　　　　**a dry cell** 건전지

Hybrid cars use special fuel cells as a complement to gasoline.

24 neutron
[njú:trɑn]

n 중성자　　　　　　**a neutron star** 중성자별

A neutron is bigger than an electron and smaller than a proton.

25 nuclear
[njú:kliər]

a 원자핵의, 원자력의　　　　　　**nuclear waste** 방사성 폐기물

The real danger of a nuclear explosion is the toxic radiation.

26 nutrient
[njú:triənt]

n 영양분　　　　　　**basic nutrients** 필수 영양소

In natural conditions, the soil provides minerals and other nutrients for plants.

27 steel
[sti:l]

n 강철　　　　　　**stainless steel** 스테인리스

The price of heavy steel plates has soared 50 percent since 2005.

28 petroleum
[pitróuliəm]

n 석유　　　　　　**liquefied petroleum gas(LPG)** 액화 석유 가스

Petroleum is made by fossils that are millions of years old.

---

21 영화산업은 가죽 제조업과 같은 전통적인 업종을 능가했다. 22 우리 회사는 구리를 포함한 칠레의 천연자원 개발에 참여했다. 23 하이브리드 자동차는 휘발유를 보충하기 위해 특수한 연료 전지를 사용한다. 24 중성자는 전자보다 크고, 양성자보다는 작다. 25 핵폭발의 진정한 위험성은 유독성 방사능이다. 26 자연조건에서 토양은 식물에 무기질과 다른 영양소를 제공한다. 27 강철판의 가격은 2005년 이래로 50%가 상승했다. 28 석유는 수백만 년 된 화석에서 만들어진다.

29 radioactive
[rèidiouǽktiv]

ⓐ 방사능의, 방사성의

ⓝ radiation 방사능

a radioactive leak 방사능 누출
radioactive waste 방사성 폐기물

Nuclear waste is highly radioactive and very dangerous.

---

30 resource
[ríːsɔːrs]

ⓝ 자원, 물자

depletion of resources 자원 고갈

Developing reusable resources is essential to our survival.

---

31 rubber
[rʌ́bər]

ⓝ 고무

ⓐ rubber 고무 같은

a rubber band 고무 밴드

The invention of rubber greatly changed our lives along with plastic.

---

32 rust
[rʌst]

ⓝ 녹

ⓐ rusty 녹슨, 색이 바랜

be covered with rust 녹슬다

Our company makes a product that can get rid of rust from steel.

---

33 stuff
[stʌf]

ⓝ 재료, 원료 **ⓥ** ~에 채우다

a stuffed animal 솜으로 채운 동물 인형

★ Sometimes it's hard to tell what kind of stuff things are made of.

★ The turkey was stuffed with many vegetables and seasonings.

---

34 substance
[sʌ́bstəns]

ⓝ 물질, 재료 **⊜** material, stuff

ⓐ substantial 많은

a sticky substance 끈끈한 물질

Toxic substance has been detected in the nearby river.

---

29 핵폐기물은 방사능 수치가 매우 높고 굉장히 위험하다. 30 재사용이 가능한 자원을 개발하는 것은 우리의 생존에 매우 중요하다. 31 고무의 발명은 플라스틱과 함께 우리의 생활을 크게 변화시켰다. 32 우리 회사는 강철에서 녹을 제거할 수 있는 제품을 만든다. 33 가끔 어떤 종류의 재료로 만들어지는지 파악하기가 어렵다. / 칠면조는 많은 채소와 양념으로 채워져 있었다. 34 가까운 강에서 유독성 물질이 검출되었다.

35 textile
[tékstail]

ⓝ 직물

the textile industry 섬유산업

A wide variety of clothes are made of a chemical textile.

36 thermometer
[θərmάmitər]

ⓝ 온도계

a clinical thermometer 체온계
Celsius [Fahrenheit] thermometer 섭씨[화씨] 온도계

Mercury is no longer used in thermometers due to its toxicity.

37 timber
[tímbər]

ⓝ 목재, 재목 **ⓔ** wood, log

timber harvesting 목재 수확

Various items of furniture such as desks and couches are still made of timber.

38 tin
[tin]

ⓐ tinny 주석의, 깡통 소리가 나는

ⓝ 주석

a tin tube 주석관

Tin is widely used to protect iron from decaying.

39 barometer
[bərάmitər]

ⓝ 기압계

a mercury barometer 수은 기압계

Pilots pay attention to the barometer to check air pressure.

40 beam
[bíːm]

ⓝ 광선 **ⓥ** (전파를) 보내다, (빛을) 비추다

a light beam 광선

★ With a beam projector, we can watch movies practically anywhere.

★ The sun beamed its powerful rays, and no one could look up at the sky.

35 다양한 종류의 옷들이 화학섬유로 만들어졌다. 36 수은은 독성 때문에 더 이상 온도계에 사용하지 않는다. 37 책상이나 소파와 같은 다양한 가구들은 아직도 목재로 만들어진다. 38 주석은 철이 부식되는 것을 막기 위해 널리 쓰인다. 39 조종사들은 기압을 확인하기 위해 항상 기압계를 주목한다. 40 빔프로젝터가 있으면, 실질적으로 어디에서든지 영화를 볼 수 있다. / 태양은 강한 빛을 내뿜어서 어떤 사람도 하늘을 올려다볼 수 없었다.

EXERCISE

A 다음 영어는 우리말로, 우리말은 영어로 옮기시오.

01 bronze	_____	07 무리, 집단	_____
02 neutron	_____	08 구리	_____
03 textile	_____	09 영양분	_____
04 lead	_____	10 원자의, 원자력에 의한	_____
05 barometer	_____	11 자원, 물자	_____
06 component	_____	12 수공예(품), 손재주	_____

B 다음 빈칸에 알맞은 단어를 쓰시오.

01 institute	⊜ _____	07 rust	ⓐ _____
02 emergence	⊜ _____	08 geology	ⓐ _____
03 apparatus	⊜ _____	09 challenge	ⓐ _____
04 ingredient	⊜ _____	10 facilitate	ⓝ _____
05 substance	⊜ _____	11 radioactive	ⓝ _____
06 artificial	⊜ _____	12 hydroelectric	ⓝ _____

C 다음 빈칸에 들어갈 알맞은 말을 고르시오. (필요하면 형태를 바꾸시오.)

facilitate	industrial	alchemy	leather	radioactive

01 I prefer _____ bags to nylon bags, as they last longer and are sturdier.

02 The science of _____ was studied in an effort to change ordinary metals into gold.

03 The discussion leader _____ the topics of discussion during the group session last week.

04 Since the emergence of modern _____ societies in the 19th century, our values have shifted significantly.

05 The study shows that many people exposed to _____ wastes will undergo genetic changes.

Across

3 not real or not made of natural things but made to be like something that is real or natural

5 a chemical or food that provides what is needed for plants or animals to live and grow

7 to make an object by pouring liquid metal, plastic, etc. into a mold

8 one of the foods that you use to make a particular food or dish

Down

1 relating to or involving the nucleus of an atom, or the energy produced when the nucleus of an atom is either split or joined with the nucleus of another atom

2 a particular type of solid, liquid, or gas

4 one of several parts that together make up a whole machine, system, etc.

6 any type of woven cloth that is made in large quantities used especially by people in the business of making clothes, etc.

Unit 19 Information & Technology

01 ☑ adjust
[ədʒΛst]

ⓝ adjustment 조정, 정리

ⓥ 조절하다, 조정하다 ⊜ modify **adjust the settings** 설정을 조정하다

The engineer adjusted the engine to increase its performance.

---

02 ☑ appliance
[əpláiəns]

ⓝ 기구, 설비 ⊜ tool, machine **medical appliances** 의료기기

There is plenty of space for all the kitchen appliances.

---

03 ☑ automobile
[ɔ́:təməbì:l]

ⓝ 자동차 **automobile insurance** 자동차 보험

The first gasoline automobile was made by Karl Benz in 1885.

---

04 ☑ censorship
[sénsərʃip]

ⓥ censor 검열하다

ⓝ 검열 **press censorship** 신문 검열

Some people are strongly against censorship of the Internet.

---

05 ☑ portal
[pɔ́:rtl]

ⓝ 입구, 문, 포털(사이트) **an Internet portal site** 인터넷 포털 사이트

Portal sites provide various links to websites you wish to visit.

---

06 ☑ conductor
[kəndΛktər]

ⓥ conduct
(전기나 열을) 전도하다

ⓝ 도체, 전도체 **a lightning conductor** 피뢰침

Metals that are good conductors for heat are widely used for pans.

---

01 기술자는 엔진의 성능을 향상하기 위해 엔진을 조정했다. 02 모든 주방용품이 들어갈 충분한 공간이 있다. 03 최초의 휘발유 자동차는 1885년에 칼 벤츠가 만들었다. 04 어떤 사람들은 인터넷에 대한 검열을 강하게 거부한다. 05 포털 사이트는 여러분이 방문하고자 하는 사이트로 가는 다양한 링크가 있다. 06 열 전도성이 높은 금속은 프라이팬으로 널리 쓰인다.

07 craft
[kræft]
ⓐ crafty 교활한, 교묘한

ⓝ 기능, 재주, 공예 **ⓢ skill** 기능, 숙련

arts and crafts 미술공예

The recent trend is to combine crafts with high-tech devices.

08 detector
[ditéktər]
ⓥ detect 탐지하다

ⓝ 탐지기, 발견자

a metal detector 금속 탐지기
a smoke detector 화재경보기

A lie detector can pick up even the smallest signs of a lie.

09 device
[diváis]
ⓥ devise 고안하다, 발명하다

ⓝ 장치, 고안 **ⓢ gadget**

a portable device 휴대용 장치

All sorts of devices have penetrated the lives of modern people.

10 electronic
[ilèktránik]
ⓝ electronics 전자공학

ⓐ 전자의

an electronic microscope 전자현미경

Due to electronic banking, you rarely need to visit the bank yourself.

11 embroider
[embrɔ́idər]
ⓝ embroidery 자수, 자수품

ⓥ 수놓다

embroider flowers on a dress 옷에 꽃을 수놓다

The logo or design is usually embroidered on the back of the shirt.

12 equipment
[ikwípmənt]

ⓝ 장비, 비품 **ⓢ apparatus** 장치, 기구

electronic equipment 전자 장비

Engineers use highly sophisticated equipment for their work.

13 flashlight
[flǽʃlàit]

ⓝ 손전등, 섬광

a pocket flashlight (매우 작은) 손전등

The explorers had to rely on their own flashlights in the cave.

---

07 오늘날의 추세는 공예와 첨단기기를 결합하는 것이다. 08 거짓말 탐지기는 거짓말의 아주 작은 신호조차도 감지할 수 있다. 09 각종 기기는 현대인의 생활 속에 침투해 들어왔다. 10 전자화된 은행 업무 때문에 은행에 직접 가야 하는 일이 거의 없다. 11 로고나 디자인은 주로 셔츠의 뒤에 수놓아져 있다. 12 기술자들은 작업하는 데 매우 복잡한 장비를 사용한다. 13 탐험가들은 동굴 안에서 자신의 손전등에 의지해야 했다.

14 gear
[giər]

ⓝ 기어, 톱니바퀴 장치   **landing gear** 착륙 장치

The motor's rotation is transferred to the wheels by several gears.

15 generator
[dʒénərèitər]

ⓥ generate
(전기 등을) 발생시키다

ⓝ 발전기   **a high-voltage generator** 고압 발전기

Our facility has its own generator in case of blackouts.

16 identification
[aidèntəfikéiʃən]

ⓥ identify 확인하다

ⓝ 신원 확인, 신분증   **an identification card** 신분증

The cyber police use IP addresses for identification of Internet users.

17 identity
[aidéntəti]

ⓐ identical 동일한

ⓝ 동일함, 신원   **reveal one's identity** ~의 신원을 밝히다

Many people hide their identities when they use the Internet.

18 implement
[ímpləmənt]

ⓐ implemental 도구의

ⓝ 도구 **ⓢ** tool, instrument   **writing implements** 필기도구

Our company manufactures high quality agricultural implements.

19 indicator
[índikèitər]

ⓥ indicate 표시하다, 가리키다

ⓝ 표시기, 지표 **ⓢ** gauge   **a direction indicator** 방향 지시기

This machine has an indicator that tells when it's low on fuel.

20 lag
[læg]

ⓝ 지체, 지연   **a jet lag** 시차 피로

As the Internet speed improved, we experience lags much less.

---

14 모터의 회전은 여러 톱니바퀴를 통해 바퀴로 전달된다. 15 우리 시설은 정전을 대비해 고유의 발전기가 따로 있다. 16 사이버 경찰은 인터넷 사용자의 신원 확인을 위해 IP 주소를 사용한다. 17 많은 사람은 인터넷을 사용할 때 자신의 정체를 숨긴다. 18 우리 회사는 고품질의 농기구를 제조한다. 19 이 기계에는 연료가 부족할 때를 알려주는 표시기가 장착되어 있다. 20 인터넷 속도가 향상되어서, 예전과 비교하면 훨씬 적게 지체됨을 경험한다.

21 transform
[trænsfɔ́ːrm]

ⓝ transformation 변형

ⓥ 변형시키다, 바꾸다, 변환하다

transform electricity into mechanical energy
전기를 기계 에너지로 바꾸다

He was able to transform my idea into a useful driving device.

22 manufacture
[mænjəfǽktʃər]

ⓥ 제조하다 **ⓝ** 제조, 제조업   **the manufacturing industry** 제조업

★ Automatic machinery is widely used to manufacture goods massively.

★ The government approved the manufacture of nuclear weapons.

23 mechanism
[mékənìzəm]

ⓝ 기계 장치, 부품 **≒** machine 기계, process 절차

a safety mechanism 안전장치

★ There was something wrong with the mechanism of my DVD player.

★ Most airplanes have escape mechanisms in case of an emergency.

24 reactor
[riːǽktər]

ⓥ react 반응하다

ⓝ 반응 장치, 원자로   **a nuclear reactor** 원자로

Nuclear reactions in reactors generate a huge amount of energy.

25 transmission
[trænsmíʃən]

ⓥ transmit (정보를) 전송하다, (빛·열 따위를) 전도하다

ⓝ 전송 **≒** transfer 전송   **data transmission speed** 데이터 전송 속도

The company upgraded the transmission speeds of their Internet services.

26 optics
[áptiks]

ⓐ optic 눈의, 시력의
ⓐ optical 광학의, 빛의

ⓝ 광학   **electron optics** 전자 광학

Using fiber optics, Internet speed has been enhanced greatly.

---

21 그는 내 아이디어를 유용한 추진 장치로 변환할 수 있었다. 22 자동화 기계들은 대규모로 제품을 제조하기 위하여 널리 쓰인다. / 정부는 핵무기 제조를 승인했다. 23 내 DVD 플레이어 부품에 문제가 있었다. / 비행기에는 대부분 긴급 상황을 대비하는 탈출 장치가 있다. 24 원자로 내에서의 핵반응은 엄청난 양의 에너지를 만들어낸다. 25 회사는 인터넷 서비스의 속도를 향상시켰다. 26 광섬유를 이용하여, 인터넷 속도는 매우 증가했다.

27 principle
[prínsəpl]

ⓝ 원리, 원칙 **ⓢ** rule   **a general principle** 일반 원칙

You can predict the outcome by applying scientific principles.

28 procedure
[prəsí:dʒər]

ⓥ proceed 나아가다, 계속하다

ⓝ 순서, 절차 **ⓢ** process 과정   **an experimental procedure** 실험 절차

This machine can make the whole procedure very simple.

29 prompt
[prɑmpt]

ⓝ promptitude 신속

ⓐ 즉석의, 신속한 **ⓢ** immediate   **prompt delivery** 신속한 배달

We can gain prompt access to all sorts of information by the Internet.

30 qualified
[kwáləfàid]

ⓥ qualify 자격을 주다
ⓝ qualification 자격, 자격 부여

ⓐ 자격 있는   **a qualified doctor** 자격 있는 의사

We must make sure all equipment is qualified for operation.

31 scan
[skæn]

ⓝ 정밀 검사 **ⓥ** 정밀 검사하다, 유심히 보다 **ⓢ** examine   **a CT scan** CT 촬영

This software scans your computer for any harmful viruses.

32 sophisticated
[səfístəkèitid]

ⓥ sophisticate
복잡하게 하다, 정교하게 하다

ⓐ 정교한, 세련된 **ⓢ** simple 단순한   **a sophisticated machine** 정교한 기계

Many scientists use sophisticated equipment to gain accurate results.

33 surpass
[sərpǽs]

ⓥ ~보다 낫다, ~을 능가하다 **ⓢ** outdo

surpass expectations 기대를 능가하다

Humans use tools for work that surpasses their physical ability.

---

27 과학적 원리를 적용하여 결과를 예측할 수 있다. 28 이 기계는 모든 절차를 매우 간단하게 만들 수 있다. 29 우리는 인터넷을 통해 모든 정보에 신속하게 접근할 수 있다. 30 우리는 모든 장비가 작동하기에 적합한지 확인해야 한다. 31 이 소프트웨어는 당신의 컴퓨터에 악성 바이러스가 있는지 검사해준다. 32 많은 과학자는 정확한 결과를 얻기 위해 정교한 장비를 사용한다. 33 사람들은 자신의 육체적 능력을 능가하는 도구를 사용한다.

34 technical
[téknikəl]

① technique 기술, 기법

ⓐ 기술적, 전문의

a technical term 기술적 용어
a technical difficulty 기술적 어려움

There seems to be a technical problem that is beyond our ability.

35 utensil
[juːténsəl]

① 도구, 기구 **ⓢ** tool

a farming utensil 농기구

Stainless steel is an alloy widely used to make kitchen utensils.

36 pioneer
[pàiəníər]

ⓐ pioneering 선구적인

① 개척자, 선구자 **ⓥ** 개척하다

the pioneering industry 첨단산업

★ Bill Gates is considered as a great pioneer of the computer industry.
★ The scientists pioneered the study of the new flu vaccine.

37 vacuum
[vǽkjuəm]

① 진공 **ⓥ** 진공청소기로 청소하다

a vacuum package 진공 포장

★ Housekeeping becomes an easy task if you have a vacuum cleaner.
★ You should vacuum the carpet in your house at least every other day.

38 vehicle
[víːikəl]

① 탈것, 차

a recreational vehicle (RV) 여가용 차량

An amphibious vehicle is designed to run on both land and water.

39 weave
[wiːv]

ⓥ (천을) 짜다, 뜨다

weave thread into cloth 실을 짜서 천을 만들다

Steam engines were first used for spinning and weaving machinery.

40 windmill
[wíndmìl]

① 풍차

The modern windmill is used to convert wind power to electricity.

34 우리의 능력을 넘어선 기술적 문제가 있는 것 같다. 35 스테인리스는 주방 도구를 만드는 데 널리 쓰이는 합금이다. 36 빌 게이츠는 컴퓨터 산업의 대단한 선구자로 여겨진다. / 그 과학자들은 새로운 독감 백신 연구를 개척했다. 37 진공청소기가 있다면 가사는 쉬운 일이 된다. / 집에 있는 카펫을 적어도 이틀에 한 번은 진공청소기로 청소해야 한다. 38 수륙 양용차는 육지와 물 모두에서 작동하도록 설계되었다. 39 증기기관은 처음에 방직기를 만드는 데 사용되었다. 40 현대의 풍차는 풍력을 전기로 전환하는 데 쓰인다.

EXERCISE

A 다음 영어는 우리말로, 우리말은 영어로 옮기시오.

01 lag _____

02 mechanism _____

03 utensil _____

04 appliance _____

05 procedure _____

06 electronic _____

07 도체, 전도체 _____

08 전송 _____

09 원리, 원칙 _____

10 손전등, 섬광 _____

11 (천을) 짜다, 뜨다 _____

12 제조, 제조하다 _____

B 다음 빈칸에 알맞은 단어를 쓰시오.

01 scan ⊜ _____

02 adjust ⊜ _____

03 indicator ⊜ _____

04 prompt ⊜ _____

05 surpass ⊜ _____

06 sophisticated ⊕ _____

07 generator ⓥ _____

08 censorship ⓥ _____

09 identity ⓐ _____

10 pioneer ⓐ _____

11 embroider ⓝ _____

12 transform ⓝ _____

C 다음 빈칸에 들어갈 알맞은 말을 고르시오. (필요하면 형태를 바꾸시오.)

| implement | transform | detector | sophisticated | technical |

01 Ever since Sophie moved to the city, her style of dress has become very _____.

02 The fire _____ can pick up the smell of smoke and prevent the loss of many lives.

03 The forklift is a(n) _____ that can lift enormous amounts of items during construction.

04 By losing one hundred pounds, the young man was _____ into a built and attractive individual.

05 I would like to study the _____ aspects of movie making, by enrolling in film school.

Across

1   the process of sending out electronic signals, messages, etc., using radio, television, or other similar equipment

3   the suppression or prohibition of any parts of books, films, news, etc. that are considered obscene, politically unacceptable, or a threat to security

4   a thing such as a knife, spoon, etc. that you use when you are cooking

6   done quickly, immediately, or at the right time

7   a piece of equipment, especially electrical equipment, such as a cooker or washing machine, used in people's homes

8   the fact of being who or what a person or thing is

Down

2   developed to a high degree of complexity

3   something that allows electricity or heat to travel along it or through it

5   to make cloth, a carpet, a basket, etc. by crossing threads or thin pieces under and over each other by hand or on a loom

Unit 20

Medicine & Health

---

01 ☑ **abortion**
[əbɔ́ːrʃən]
ⓥ abort 유산하다, 낙태하다

ⓝ 유산, 낙태   **opposition to abortion** 낙태 반대

There is a great controversy about legalizing abortion.

---

02 ☑ **therapy**
[θérəpi]
ⓝ therapist 치료 전문가

ⓝ 치료법, 요법   **an alternative therapy** 대체 요법

Our clinic provides therapy that is harmless to the human body.

---

03 ☑ **antibiotic**
[æntibaiátik]

ⓝ 항생제   **antibiotic treatment** 항생제 치료

Germs may build a resistance to antibiotics if used improperly.

---

04 ☑ **antibody**
[æntibàdi]

ⓝ 항체   **an antibody reaction** 항체 반응

Our body makes antibodies to fight off invading germs.

---

05 ☑ **bruise**
[bruːz]

ⓝ 멍 ⓥ 멍들게 하다   **get a bruise** 멍이 들다

★ The bluish color of a bruise is actually blood collected under the skin.

★ Jamie fell off the ladder and bruised his elbow.

---

06 ☑ **cavity**
[kǽvəti]

ⓝ 충치   **the prevention of cavities** 충치 예방

The dentist said that brushing teeth improperly could cause cavities.

---

07 ☑ **diabetes**
[dàiəbíːtis]

ⓝ 당뇨병   **develop diabetes** 당뇨병에 걸리다

People with diabetes need to take insulin shots on a regular basis.

---

01 낙태를 합법화하는 것에 대한 큰 논쟁이 있다. 02 우리 진료소는 인체에 해가 없는 치료법을 제공한다. 03 항생제를 부적절하게 쓰면 세균이 이에 대한 내성을 키울 수 있다. 04 우리 몸은 침입하는 세균을 물리치기 위해 항체를 만든다. 05 파란 멍은 실제로 피부 밑에 피가 고인 것이다. / Jamie는 사다리에서 떨어져서 팔꿈치에 멍이 들었다. 06 치과의사는 잘못된 방법으로 양치하면 충치가 생길 수 있다고 했다. 07 당뇨병을 앓는 사람은 정기적으로 인슐린 주사를 맞아야 한다.

---

08 ☑ chronic
[kránik]

ⓐ 만성의, 고질적인   ⓔ acute 급성의

chronic fatigue 만성피로

My father has suffered from diabetes as a chronic disease for several years.

---

09 ☑ clinical
[klínikəl]

ⓝ clinic 진료소, 의원

ⓐ 임상의

a clinical trial 임상 실험

The medical magazine covered an interesting clinical test on cancer.

---

10 ☑ clone
[klóun]

ⓝ cloning 복제

ⓝ 클론, 복제 생물

a human clone 복제인간

Dolly the sheep was the first successful clone of a mammal in the world.

---

11 ☑ contagious
[kəntéidʒəs]

ⓝ contagion 접촉 전염, 전염병

ⓐ 전염성의, 전염병을 일으키는

a contagious disease 전염병

The patient had to be isolated because of his contagious disease.

---

12 ☑ choke
[tʃouk]

ⓐ choky 숨 막히는

ⓥ 질식시키다, 숨이 막히다   ⓔ suffocate **choke one to death** 질식시켜 죽이다

A person can actually die by choking on large pieces of food.

---

13 ☑ diagnose
[dáiəgnòus]

ⓝ diagnosis 진단

ⓥ 진단하다, 원인을 밝혀내다

diagnose as cancer 암으로 진단하다

Doctors often use sophisticated instruments when diagnosing patients.

---

14 ☑ transfuse
[trænsfjúːz]

ⓝ transfusion 수혈, 주입

ⓥ 수혈하다, 주입하다   **transfuse blood into a patient** 환자에게 수혈하다

The patient needs to be transfused with blood as fast as possible.

---

08 아버지는 지병인 당뇨병으로 수년 동안 고생하고 계신다. 09 의학 잡지에서 암에 대한 흥미로운 임상시험을 다뤘다. 10 복제 양 돌리는 세계에서 최초로 복제에 성공한 포유류였다. 11 환자는 자신의 전염병 때문에 격리되어야 했다. 12 사람은 실제로 커다란 음식물 때문에 질식사할 수 있다. 13 의사들은 환자를 진단할 때 종종 복잡한 기구를 사용한다. 14 환자는 가능한 한 빨리 수혈을 받아야 했다.

15 doze
[douz]

ⓥ 졸다, 선잠 자다   **doze over a book** 책을 읽다가 졸다

I dozed off during class after taking medicine for my cold.

16 exhale
[ekshéil]

ⓝ exhalation 발산, 증발

ⓥ 내쉬다, 내뿜다   ↔ inhale 들이쉬다   **exhale smoke** 연기를 내뿜다

The therapist told me to breathe deeply and exhale slowly.

17 syndrome
[síndroum]

ⓝ 증후군   **Down's Syndrome** 다운 증후군

AIDS is an abbreviation for acquired immune deficiency syndrome.

18 handicapped
[hǽndikæpt]

ⓝ handicap 장애, 곤란

ⓐ 신체적 장애가 있는   **the visually handicapped** 시각 장애인들

There are several facilities that help the handicapped to adapt to society.

19 hygiene
[háidʒiːn]

ⓐ hygienic 위생적인, 위생학의

ⓝ 위생, 위생학   ≈ sanitation   **personal hygiene** 개인위생

Many people are concerned with hygiene issues at restaurants.

20 immune
[imjúːn]

ⓝ immunity 면역

ⓐ 면역성의, 면한

Acquired Immune Deficiency Syndrome (AIDS)
후천성 면역 결핍 증후군(에이즈)

AIDS is a disease that disrupts a person's immune system.

21 infection
[infékʃən]

ⓥ infect 감염시키다

ⓝ 전염(병), 감염   **pass on infection** 병을 전염시키다

We need to treat his wounds before an infection occurs.

---

15 나는 감기약을 먹고 나서, 수업 중에 깜빡 졸았다. 16 치료사는 내게 숨을 깊게 마시고 천천히 뱉으라고 말했다. 17 에이즈는 후천성 면역 결핍 증후군의 약자다. 18 장애인들이 사회에 적응할 수 있도록 도움을 주는 시설이 여러 개 있다. 19 많은 사람이 식당의 위생 문제에 관심이 있다. 20 에이즈는 사람의 면역 체계를 교란시키는 질병이다. 21 우리는 그의 상처 부위가 감염되기 전에 상처를 치료해야 한다.

22 injection
[indʒékʃən]

ⓥ inject 주사하다, 주입하다

ⓝ 주사, 주입

insulin injections 인슐린 주사

The patient had to receive medication by injection.

23 insomnia
[insámniə]

ⓝ 불면증   **ⓢ** sleeplessness

suffer from insomnia 불면증에 걸리다

One way to tackle insomnia is to avoid beverages with caffeine.

24 vomit
[vámit]

ⓝ vomiting 구토

ⓥ 구토하다   **ⓢ** throw up

vomit food 음식을 토해내다

Vomiting habitually can bring serious pain to the stomach and throat.

25 intoxicate
[intáksikèit]

ⓐ intoxicated 술 취한
ⓝ intoxication 취함

ⓥ 취하게 하다

an intoxicating beverage 주류

The amount of alcohol needed to get intoxicated is different from person to person.

26 metabolism
[mətǽbəlìzəm]

ⓝ 신진대사

basal metabolism 기초 대사

People with fast metabolism tend to gain weight more slowly.

27 symptom
[símptəm]

ⓝ 증상, 징후

allergic symptoms 알레르기 증상
withdrawal symptoms 금단 증상

A physician treats diseases by test results and symptoms of patients.

28 nurture
[nə́:rtʃər]

ⓥ 양육하다, 영양물을 주다   **ⓢ** raise

nurture plants 식물에 영양분을 주다

Premature infants need to be nurtured with extreme caution.

---

22 그 환자는 주사로 약물치료를 받아야 했다. 23 불면증을 극복하는 방법의 하나는 카페인이 든 음료를 피하는 것이다. 24 습관적으로 구토하는 것은 위와 목에 심한 통증을 가져올 수 있다. 25 사람을 취하게 하는 술의 양은 사람에 따라 매우 다르다. 26 신진대사가 빠른 사람은 살이 덜 찌는 경향이 있다. 27 내과 의사는 검사 결과와 환자의 증상으로 질병을 치료한다. 28 조산아들은 매우 조심스럽게 양육되어야 한다.

29 ☑ obesity
[oubíːsəti]

ⓐ obese 비만의, 뚱뚱한

ⓝ 비만

abdominal obesity 복부 비만

Recently, obesity of children is becoming a huge social problem.

30 ☑ ointment
[ɔ́intmənt]

ⓝ 연고

apply an ointment 연고를 바르다

There are different kinds of ointments for different injuries.

31 ☑ operation
[àpəréiʃən]

ⓥ operate 수술하다, 작동하다

ⓝ 수술, 가동, 작동 **ⓢ** surgery

a minor operation 간단한 수술

★ The doctor said my father has to go through a major operation soon.

★ The factory stopped its operation after the terrible accident.

32 ☑ pharmacy
[fáːrməsi]

ⓝ pharmacist 약사

ⓝ 약국, 약학

the college of pharmacy 약학 대학

We need a doctor's prescription to buy certain drugs at the pharmacy.

33 ☑ physician
[fiziʃən]

ⓝ (내과) 의사 **ⓢ** doctor

a practicing physician 개업 의사

People with heart disease should talk to their physician before traveling abroad.

34 ☑ plague
[pleig]

ⓝ 전염병, 역병 **ⓢ** epidemic

the Black Plague 흑사병

In 1664, about 70,000 people died from the Great Plague of London.

35 ☑ paralyze
[pǽrəlàiz]

ⓝ paralysis 마비

ⓥ 마비시키다 **ⓢ** numb, disable **be partly paralyzed** 부분적으로 마비되다

Both his legs were paralyzed in the car accident.

---

29 최근에 소아 비만은 큰 사회 문제로 떠오르고 있다. 30 상처 종류에 따라 쓰이는 연고가 가지각색이다. 31 의사는 아버지가 곧 대수술을 받아야 한다고 말했다. / 공장은 끔찍한 사고가 난 후 가동을 멈추었다. 32 약국에서 특정한 약품을 사기 위해서는 의사의 처방전이 필요하다. 33 심장병이 있는 사람들은 해외여행을 가기 전에 의사에게 알려야 한다. 34 1664년에 약 7만 명의 사람이 런던 대역병으로 목숨을 잃었다. 35 교통사고로 그의 두 다리가 마비되었다.

36 premature
[prè:mətjúər]

n prematurity 조산, 조숙

a 조숙한　**↔** mature 성숙한

a premature delivery 조산

An infant that is born within 34 weeks is considered as a premature baby.

37 prescribe
[priskráib]

n prescription 처방전

v 처방하다, 지시하다

prescribe pills 약을 처방하다

The attending physician prescribed some medicine for my stomach pain.

38 pulse
[pʌls]

n 맥박　**↔** beat

a regular pulse 규칙적인 맥박

a pulse rate 맥박 수

In emergencies, the pulse is used to tell if someone is dead or not.

39 respiration
[rèspəréiʃən]

v respire 호흡하다
a respiratory 호흡의

n 호흡

artificial respiration 인공호흡

Ever since I was a kid, I have had trouble with my respiration.

40 sanitary
[sǽnətèri]

n sanitation 위생, 위생 시설

a 위생의, 위생적인

a sanitary inspection 위생 검사

A hospital with poor sanitary conditions can be the cause of secondary infection.

---

36 34주가 되기 전에 태어난 아기들은 조산아로 간주한다.　37 주치의는 복통약을 처방해 주었다.　38 위급한 상황에서 사람이 죽었는지 아닌지를 맥박으로 알아본다.　39 어렸을 때부터 나는 호흡에 문제가 있었다.　40 위생 상태가 허술한 병원은 2차 감염의 원인이 될 수 있다.

EXERCISE

A 다음 영어는 우리말로, 우리말은 영어로 옮기시오.

01 transfuse _____
02 metabolism _____
03 diabetes _____
04 prescribe _____
05 vomit _____
06 pharmacy _____

07 멍, 멍들게 하다 _____
08 증상, 징후 _____
09 신체적 장애가 있는 _____
10 연고 _____
11 만성의, 고질적인 _____
12 증후군 _____

B 다음 빈칸에 알맞은 단어를 쓰시오.

01 plague ⊜ _____
02 hygiene ⊜ _____
03 paralyze ⊜ _____
04 choke ⊜ _____
05 exhale ⇔ _____
06 premature ⇔ _____

07 abortion ⓥ _____
08 infection ⓥ _____
09 obesity ⓐ _____
10 respiration ⓐ _____
11 diagnose ⓝ _____
12 immune ⓝ _____

C 다음 빈칸에 들어갈 알맞은 말을 고르시오. (필요하면 형태를 바꾸시오.)

| contagious | nurture | antibiotic | sanitary | insomnia |

01 Due to _____, he was only able to sleep for two hours every night.

02 The doctor prescribed a strong _____ for the large wound I suffered.

03 Be careful that you do not catch the _____ flu, by washing your hands frequently.

04 You can _____ your plant by placing it under moderate sunlight and providing it with fresh water.

05 It is _____ to use antibacterial lotion and wipes to prevent the spread of germs.

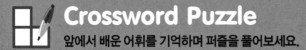

Crossword Puzzle

앞에서 배운 어휘를 기억하며 퍼즐을 풀어보세요.

정답

Across

1 a drug that is used to kill bacteria and cure infections

3 something wrong with your body or mind which shows that you have a particular illness

6 a disease that affects a particular part of your body and is caused by bacteria or a virus

9 the process of cutting into someone's body to repair or remove a part that is damaged

10 to say what medicine or treatment a sick person should have

Down

2 resistant to a particular infection or toxin owing to the presence of specific antibodies or sensitized white blood cells

4 (of a disease) spread from one person or organism to another, typically by direct contact

5 to find out what illness someone has, or what the cause of a fault is, after doing tests, examinations, etc.

7 relating to the ways that dirt, infection, and waste are removed so that places are clean and healthy for people to live in

8 to feed and take care of a child or a plant while it is growing

Unit 21 Nature, Animal & Plant

01 ☑ **beast**
[biːst]

ⓝ 동물, 짐승, 야수　　　　　　　　**a wild beast** 야수

The zoologists explored the jungle to study a rare beast.

02 ☑ **blizzard**
[blízərd]

ⓝ 눈보라　　　　　　　**an unexpected blizzard** 예상치 못한 눈보라

The crops were severely damaged by a winter blizzard.

03 ☑ **blossom**
[blásəm]

ⓝ 꽃, 개화 ⓥ 꽃이 피다　⊜ bloom 개화　**come into blossom** 꽃피기 시작하다

★ We went to the park to enjoy the beautiful view of the new blossoms of spring.

★ In late March, flowers in our garden start to blossom.

04 ☑ **botany**
[bátəni]

ⓝ **botanist** 식물학자

ⓝ 식물학　　　　　　　**geographical botany** 식물 지리학

As zoology studies the different kinds of animals, botany studies plants.

05 ☑ **bough**
[bau]

ⓝ 큰 가지　　　　　　　**a broken bough** 부러진 나뭇가지

Birds usually make nests on the tree boughs to hatch their offspring.

06 ☑ **breeze**
[briːz]

ⓐ **breezy** 산들바람이 부는

ⓝ 산들바람　　　　　　　**a fresh breeze** 시원한 바람

The workers rested in the shade, letting the breeze cool them down.

---

01 동물학자들은 희귀 동물을 연구하고자 정글을 탐험했다. 02 겨울 눈보라에 농작물이 심각한 손해를 입었다. 03 우리는 봄에 새로 핀 꽃의 아름다운 전망을 구경하러 공원에 갔다. / 3월 하순에 우리 집 정원의 꽃들이 피기 시작한다. 04 동물학이 여러 종류의 동물을 연구하는 것처럼, 식물학은 식물을 연구한다. 05 새들은 새끼를 부화하기 위해서 대개 큰 나뭇가지 위에 둥지를 튼다. 06 근로자들은 그늘에 쉬면서, 산들바람에 땀을 식혔다.

07 □ bud
[bʌd]

ⓝ 싹, 눈, 봉오리　　　　　　　　　　　　　**a flower bud** 꽃눈

I could see spring coming from the little flower buds in trees.

08 □ tropical
[trápikəl]

ⓐ 열대의, 열대성의　　　　　　　　　　　**a tropical night** 열대야

Tropical fruits such as pineapples and coconuts can only be grown in certain areas.

09 □ caterpillar
[kǽtərpìlər]

ⓝ (나비·나방 따위의) 유충, 모충　　　**a green caterpillar** 배추벌레

A caterpillar protects itself with a cocoon to become a butterfly.

10 □ chilly
[tʃíli]

ⓝ chill 냉기, 한기

ⓐ 찬, 으스스한　　　　　　　　　　　　　**a chilly wind** 찬바람

The weather is usually chilly in areas with high altitudes.

11 □ cocoon
[kəkúːn]

ⓝ 고치　　　　　　　　　　　　　**spin a cocoon** 고치를 만들다

Larvae spend several weeks in cocoons before reaching adulthood.

12 □ crude
[kruːd]

ⓝ crudity 미숙, 조잡

ⓐ 천연의, 날것의　　　　　　　　　　　　　　　**crude oil** 원유

This area has an abundant amount of crude iron buried in the ground.

13 □ damp
[dæmp]

ⓐ 축축한　**ⓔ** moist　**ⓐ** dry 건조한　　**damp weather** 축축한 날씨

★ In the monsoon season, the climate becomes very damp.

★ As soon as I went into the basement, I was overwhelmed by the damp smell.

---

07 나무에 맺힌 작은 꽃봉오리에서 봄이 오고 있음을 느낄 수 있었다. 08 파인애플과 코코넛과 같은 열대 과일은 특정한 지역에서만 자란다. 09 유충은 나비가 되기 위해 자신을 고치로 보호한다. 10 고도가 높은 지역은 날씨가 주로 쌀쌀하다. 11 유충은 성충이 되기 전에 몇 주 동안을 고치 안에서 보낸다. 12 이 지역에는 땅속에 매장된 풍부한 양의 천연 철이 있다. 13 장마철에는 기후가 매우 습해진다. / 지하실에 들어서자마자, 나는 축축한(눅눅한) 냄새에 압도당했다.

14 ☑ decompose
[dì:kəmpóuz]

ⓥ 분해하다, 부패하다

ⓝ decomposition 분해

a decomposed body 부패한 시체

When animals die, their bodies decompose into the soil.

---

15 ☑ ditch
[ditʃ]

ⓝ 수로, 도랑

dig a ditch 수로를 파다

The campers made a ditch around their tents in case it rains heavily.

---

16 ☑ downpour
[dáunpɔ̀:r]

ⓝ 호우

a sudden downpour 갑작스러운 폭우

The dike prevents the river from overflowing during local downpours.

---

17 ☑ drizzle
[drízl]

ⓝ 이슬비 **ⓥ** 이슬비가 내리다

drizzling rain 부슬부슬 내리는 비

★ The light drizzle stopped by the time they arrived home.

★ I did not need an umbrella as it was only drizzling outside.

---

18 ☑ veterinarian
[vètərənέəriən]

ⓝ 수의사 **ⓔ** vet

a local veterinarian 그 지역의 수의사

Veterinarians are doctors who treat sick animals.

---

19 ☑ ebb
[eb]

ⓝ 썰물 **ⓔ** flow 밀물

the ebb and flow 조수의 간만

The gravitation of the moon causes the ebb and flow of the tide.

---

20 ☑ fountain
[fáuntin]

ⓝ 분수, 샘

a drinking fountain 식수대

There are legends about the fountain that brings eternal youth.

---

14 동물이 죽으면, 그 시체는 땅속에서 부패한다. 15 야영하는 사람들은 큰 비가 올 것을 대비하여 텐트 주위로 수로를 만들었다. 16 제방은 집중 호우가 내릴 때 강이 범람하는 것을 방지한다. 17 그들이 집에 도착했을 때 이슬비는 그쳤다. / 밖에 이슬비가 내리고 있었기 때문에 나는 우산이 필요하지 않았다. 18 수의사는 병든 동물을 돌보는 의사다. 19 달의 인력이 밀물과 썰물을 일으킨다. 20 영원한 젊음을 주는 샘에 대한 전설들이 있다.

21 freeze
[friːz]
ⓐ frozen 얼은

ⓥ 얼다, 얼리다　　　　　　**the freezing point** 어는점[빙점]

★ We can walk across the river when it freezes in winter.

★ You must be very careful when skating on a frozen lake.

22 frost
[frɔːst]
ⓐ frosty 서리가 내리는, 싸늘한

ⓝ 서리　　　　　　**a degree of frost** 영하

Crops are often damaged by unexpected frost.

23 graze
[greiz]

ⓥ 풀을 뜯어먹다, 방목하다　　　**graze cattle** 소를 방목하다

In mountain regions, many cows and horses graze in meadows.

24 surge
[səːrdʒ]
ⓐ surgy 파도가 밀려드는

ⓝ 파도, 쇄도 **ⓥ** 파도가 일다　　**a storm surge** 폭풍 해일

★ The surge protector was old, and repairs were needed to be made.

★ During the tsunami, the ocean's waves surged and destroyed many homes.

25 hail
[heil]

ⓝ 우박 **ⓥ** 우박이 내리다, 환호하다　**a hail storm** 우박을 동반한 폭풍

★ Hail is rainfall in the form of small pieces of ice.

★ The people all hailed the hero as he returned from his journey.

26 leaflet
[líːflit]

ⓝ 작은 잎　　　**a number of leaflets** 여러 개의 작은 잎

Leaflets are not born on stems but on the veins of other leaves.

27 lizard
[lízərd]

ⓝ 도마뱀　　　**the tail of a lizard** 도마뱀의 꼬리

When in danger, a lizard cuts off its own tail to escape.

21 겨울에 강이 얼면 우리는 강을 걸어서 건널 수 있다. / 얼어붙은 호수에서 스케이트를 탈 때는 매우 주의해야 한다. 22 곡식은 종종 예기치 못한 서리에 손해를 입는다. 23 산간지역에서는, 많은 소와 말이 목초지에서 풀을 뜯어 먹는다. 24 방파제는 매우 낡아서 보수공사가 필요했다. / 쓰나미 중에 파도가 밀려와서 많은 집을 파괴했다. 25 우박은 작은 얼음조각의 형태로 비가 내리는 것이다. / 사람들은 모두 영웅이 여행에서 돌아오자 그를 환호했다. 26 작은 잎은 식물의 줄기가 아니라 다른 잎사귀의 잎맥에서 자란다. 27 위험에 닥치면, 도마뱀은 도망치기 위해 자신의 꼬리를 자른다.

28 stem
[stem]

n 줄기 ● stalk

a plant stem 식물 줄기
a stem cell 줄기 세포

Water absorbed by roots moves up to the leaves through the stem.

29 marsh
[mɑːrʃ]

a marshy 습지의, 축축한

n 습지, 늪 ● swamp

a marsh plant 습생 생물

Certain animals such as frogs are fit to live in marshes.

30 meadow
[médou]

n 풀밭, 녹초지 ● pasture

an open meadow 사방이 트인 목초지

Meadows mainly have non-woody plants such as grass.

31 torrent
[tɔ́ːrənt]

a torrential 급류의

n 급류, 억수

a mountain torrent 산 계곡의 급류

A torrent of lava will melt anything that is caught in its path.

32 reptile
[réptil]

a reptilian 파충류의

n 파충류

the Age of Reptiles 파충류 시대

Reptiles are animals that are cold-blooded and have hard skin.

33 tide
[taid]

a tidal 조수의

n 조수, 조류 ● current

a red tide 적조

The people had to get out of the water as the tide was on the flow.

34 orchard
[ɔ́ːrtʃərd]

n 과수원

a peach orchard 복숭아 과수원

Daegu is famous for having the finest apple orchards in Korea.

---

28 뿌리를 통해 흡수된 물은 줄기를 통해 잎사귀로 올라온다. 29 개구리 같은 특정 동물들은 습지대에 살기 적합하다. 30 녹초지에는 나무가 아닌 잔디 같은 식물이 주로 자란다. 31 용암 급류는 그 길에 있는 것을 모두 녹여버릴 것이다. 32 파충류는 단단한 피부를 가진 냉혈동물이다. 33 조수가 들어오기 시작하자 사람들은 바닷물에서 나와야 했다. 34 대구는 한국에서 가장 좋은 사과 과수원들이 있기로 유명하다.

35 ☑ pasture
[pǽstʃər]

ⓝ 목초, 목장   ● meadow

pasture land 목초지

put (animals) out to pasture (가축을) 목초지에 내놓다

Sheepdogs protect a herd of cows when they are taken to the pasture.

36 ☑ temperate
[témpərit]

ⓐ 온대성의, 온화한

a temperate climate 온대성 기후

★ The forest was temperate compared to the outside plains.

★ The monk gave me a temperate smile and returned to the temple.

37 ☑ petal
[pétl]

ⓝ 꽃잎

rose petals 장미 꽃잎

I decorated my room with rose petals.

38 ☑ pollen
[pálən]

ⓥ pollinate 꽃에 수분시키다

ⓝ 꽃가루

a pollen allergy 꽃가루 알레르기

Because I have an allergy to pollen, I don't like spring.

39 ☑ ranch
[ræntʃ]

ⓝ 대목장, 대농장

a chicken ranch 양계장

Many western movies have scenes where cowboys work on ranches.

40 ☑ submarine
[sʌ́bmərìːn]

ⓐ 해저의 **ⓝ** 잠수함

a submarine volcano 해저 화산

★ The government is planning to build a submarine tunnel.

★ The submarine fired a missile at the enemy battleship.

---

35 양치기 개는 소를 목초지로 데려갈 때 소떼를 보호한다. 36 숲은 바깥쪽 평원과 비교하면 기후가 따뜻했다. / 스님은 내게 온화한 미소를 짓고 나서 사찰 안으로 돌아갔다. 37 나는 내 방을 장미꽃잎으로 장식했다. 38 나는 꽃가루에 알레르기가 있어서 봄을 좋아하지 않는다. 39 많은 서부영화에는 카우보이들이 목장에서 일하는 장면이 나온다. 40 정부는 해저터널을 건설할 계획을 하고 있다. / 잠수함은 적의 전함에 미사일을 발사했다.

EXERCISE

Unit 21

A 다음 영어는 우리말로, 우리말은 영어로 옮기시오.

01 blizzard _____   07 과수원 _____

02 drizzle _____   08 열대의, 열대성의 _____

03 freeze _____   09 분수, 샘 _____

04 petal _____   10 방목하다 _____

05 caterpillar _____   11 식물학 _____

06 submarine _____   12 호우 _____

B 다음 빈칸에 알맞은 단어를 쓰시오.

01 tide ⊜ _____   07 pollen ⓥ _____

02 marsh ⊜ _____   08 breeze ⓐ _____

03 stem ⊜ _____   09 reptile ⓐ _____

04 pasture ⊜ _____   10 torrent ⓐ _____

05 damp ⇔ _____   11 decompose ⓝ _____

06 ebb ⇔ _____   12 chilly ⓝ _____

C 다음 빈칸에 들어갈 알맞은 말을 고르시오. (필요하면 형태를 바꾸시오.)

crude	marsh	blossom	frost	temperate

01 After the tree is planted, it will _____ in the springtime.

02 Due to the sudden drop in temperature, _____ was found on the crops.

03 By trying to cross the _____ by foot, Mary found herself stuck in the muddy grass.

04 Compared to the southwestern part of the U.S., the northeastern region is _____ in climate.

05 The _____ oil industry is highly dependent on the major oil producing countries such as Iran, Iraq, and Saudi Arabia.

Crossword Puzzle

앞에서 배운 어휘를 기억하며 퍼즐을 풀어보세요.

정답

Across

1 (of a tree or bush) to produce flowers or masses of flowers

3 coming from or existing in the hottest parts of the world

5 to decay or make something decay

7 slightly wet, often in an unpleasant way

8 in a natural or raw state; not yet processed or refined

9 a long narrow hole dug at the side of a field, road, etc. to hold or remove unwanted water

10 to eat grass in a field

Down

1 a severe snowstorm

2 a sudden powerful forward or upward movement, especially by a crowd or by a natural force such as the tide

3 relating to or denoting a region or climate characterized by mild temperatures

4 land or a field that is covered with grass and is used for cattle, sheep, etc. to feed on

6 a type of animal, such as a snake or lizard, whose body temperature changes according to the temperature around it, and that usually lays eggs to have babies

정답

Science
과학

_____ 현상

_____ 분해하다, 부패하다

_____ 회전하다, 공전하다

_____ 탐사, 탐험

_____ 대기, 분위기

Industry & Resources
산업과 자원

_____ 자원, 물자

_____ 영양분

_____ 성분, 구성 요소

_____ 인공의

_____ 용이하게 하다

Science and Technology
과학과 기술

Information & Technology
정보와 기술

_____ 검열

_____ 제조하다

_____ 신원 확인, 신분증

_____ 순서, 절차

_____ 정교한

Medicine & Health
의학과 건강

_____ 전염성의

_____ 증상, 증후

_____ 감염

_____ 진단하다

_____ 위생의

Chapter
05

Expression of
Current Affairs

Mass Media

01 ☑ sensation
[senséiʃən]

ⓐ **sensational** 선풍적인 인기의

ⓝ 감동, 대사건　●excitement

an overnight sensation 하룻밤 사이에 일어난 큰 일

The new invention created a great sensation among scientists.

---

02 ☑ inquisitive
[inkwízətiv]

ⓥ **inquire** 묻다, 문의하다

ⓐ 호기심이 많은　●curious　**an inquisitive question** 꼬치꼬치 캐는 질문

The inquisitive reporter finally discovered the truth.

---

03 ☑ monitor
[mánitər]

ⓝ 감독자 ⓥ 감시하다, 관찰하다　●watch, observe

a test monitor 시험 감독관

★ The UN is ready to send peace monitors to the area.

★ TV stations monitor their programs to filter immoral content.

---

04 ☑ advertising
[ǽdvərtàiziŋ]

ⓝ 광고(업)　**an advertising agency** 광고 대행업

Advertising has become a very important factor in marketing recently.

---

05 ☑ appendix
[əpéndiks]

ⓥ **append** 덧붙이다, 추가하다

ⓝ 부속물, 부록　**add an appendix** 부록을 추가하다

The tour guide has the city's subway map in its appendix.

---

06 ☑ article
[áːrtikl]

ⓝ 한 품목, 신문기사　**a newspaper article** 신문기사

★ Department stores usually organize the floors by article.

★ The reporter wrote an article about the economic challenges.

---

01 새로운 발명품은 과학자들 사이에서 대단한 화젯거리가 되었다. 02 호기심이 많은 기자는 마침내 진실을 알아냈다. 03 UN은 그 지역에 평화 감시단을 보낼 준비가 되어 있다. / 방송국들은 비윤리적인 내용을 걸러내기 위해 프로그램을 감시한다. 04 최근에 마케팅에서 광고는 매우 중요한 요인이 되었다. 05 그 여행책자에는 부록에 도시의 지하철 노선도가 들어 있다. 06 백화점은 흔히 층별로 품목을 나눈다. / 그 기자는 경제적 난점에 대한 기사를 작성했다.

07 broadcast
[brɔ́:dkæst]

ⓥ ~을 방송하다 **ⓝ** 방송, 방영　　　**broadcast the news** 뉴스를 방송하다

★ Twelve thousand people attended her funeral, which was broadcast on television nationwide.

★ I was just listening to a broadcast, when the plane crashed into the field.

08 bulletin
[búlətin]

ⓝ 게시, 공보　**ⓢ** message　　　**a bulletin board** 온라인 게시판

The city's official website has a bulletin board for the citizens.

09 catalogue
[kǽtəlɔ̀:g]

ⓝ 목록, 카탈로그　　　　**a library catalogue** (도서관의) 장서목록

I ordered a skirt I saw in the catalogue last week.

10 celebrity
[səlébrəti]

ⓝ 유명인사　**ⓢ** star, personality

an international celebrity 세계적인 유명인사

The woman became a celebrity after her TV appearance.

11 circulation
[sə̀:rkjəléiʃən]

ⓥ circulate 순환하다

ⓝ 발행 부수, 유통　　　**mass circulation** 많은 발행 부수

★ The newspaper failed to get a large circulation.

★ The fliers were withdrawn from circulation due to an error.

12 classified
[klǽsəfàid]

ⓥ classify 분류하다

ⓐ 분류된, 기밀의　　　**classified information** 기밀 정보

★ The documents are classified by topic, not by alphabetical order.

★ The military reported that classified documents were stolen.

13 narration
[næréiʃən]

ⓥ narrate 말하다, 서술하다, (영화·텔레비전 등의) 해설자가 되다

ⓝ 서술, 이야기하기　　　**first person narration** 1인칭 서술

He has worked as the writer of the narration for many documentaries since he graduated from college.

---

07 만이천 명이 그녀의 장례식에 참석했고, 이것이 텔레비전으로 전국에 방송되었다. / 비행기가 들판에 추락했을 때, 나는 방송을 듣고 있었다. 08 시의 공식 사이트에는 시민을 위한 게시판이 마련되어 있다. 09 나는 지난주에 카탈로그에서 본 치마를 주문했다. 10 그 여자는 텔레비전에 출연한 후로 유명인사가 되었다. 11 그 신문은 많은 발행 부수를 얻는 데 실패했다. / 오류 때문에 전단지를 회수했다. 12 그 문서들은 알파벳 순서가 아니라 주제별로 분류되어 있다. / 군은 기밀문서를 도난당했다고 발표했다. 13 그는 대학 졸업 후 많은 다큐멘터리의 이야기 작가로 일했다.

14 release
[rilíːs]

ⓥ 공개하다, 출시하다 **ⓝ** 발표, 공개 **⊜** make public 공개하다

release a film 영화를 개봉하다

The musician released his new album at the music stores in the city.

15 editorial
[èdətɔ́ːriəl]

ⓝ editor 편집자

ⓝ 사설, 논설 **ⓐ** 사설의, 논설의　　**an editorial page** 사설 페이지

★ Articles are based on fact while editorials are based on opinion.

★ The author expressed his disapproval of the mayor's plans through the editorial piece.

16 compile
[kəmpáil]

ⓝ compilation 편집

ⓥ 수집하다, 편집하다 **⊜** collect, gather

compile a database 데이터베이스를 구축하다

★ The editor compiled folk tales into a book.

★ A group of people compiled a guidebook to the city.

17 virtual
[vɔ́ːrtʃuəl]

ⓝ virtuality 실질, 본질

ⓐ 가상의, 실질적인　　**virtual reality** 가상현실

a virtual dictator 실질적인 독재자

★ The air force is using a virtual simulation for flight training.

★ Even though he denies it, he is the virtual leader of our religious group.

18 publication
[pʌ̀bləkéiʃən]

ⓥ publish 출판하다

ⓝ 발표, 출판, 출판물　　**a monthly publication** 월간 출판물

The main items on their publication list are books for children and young adults.

19 clipping
[klípiŋ]

ⓥ clip 자르다, 베다

ⓝ 오려낸 기사　　**newspaper clippings** 신문 스크랩

I accumulated newspaper clippings related to the issue.

---

14 그 음악가는 도시의 음반 가게에서 새 앨범을 출시했다. 15 신문기사는 사실에 기초하는 반면, 사설은 주장에 기초한다. / 글쓴이는 사설란을 통해서 시장의 계획에 대한 불만을 표현했다. 16 편집장은 민담을 모아서 책으로 엮었다. / 몇 명의 사람들이 도시에 대한 안내책자를 만들었다. 17 공군에서는 비행훈련을 위해 가상 시뮬레이션을 사용한다. / 비록 그가 부정할지라도 그는 우리 종교 단체의 실질적인 지도자다. 18 그들의 주요 출판물은 아동 관련 서적과 청소년 관련 서적이다. 19 나는 이 이슈와 관련된 신문기사를 스크랩하여 모아두었다.

20 vogue
[voug]

ⓐ voguish 유행의

ⓝ 유행, 성행 **have a great[short] vogue** 대인기[짧은 인기]이다

The accessories and clothes actresses wear on TV often come into vogue.

21 disclose
[disklóuz]

ⓝ disclosure 폭로

ⓥ 나타내다, 드러내다 ⓢ reveal **disclose details** 상세한 내용을 밝히다

Reporters are doing their best to disclose the truth to the public.

22 dispatch
[dispǽtʃ]

ⓝ 급파, 급보 ⓥ 급송하다 **a foreign dispatch** 외신

★ The news dispatch was urgent and delivered within a matter of minutes to the next town.

★ The news was dispatched throughout the nation very quickly yesterday.

23 distract
[distrǽkt]

ⓝ distraction 주의 산만, 혼란
ⓐ distractive 주의를 산만하게 하는

ⓥ (주의를) 딴 데로 돌리다 **distract one's attention** ~의 관심을 딴 곳으로 돌리다

Some people argue that the press distracts people from certain issues.

24 coverage
[kʌ́vəridʒ]

ⓥ cover 덮다

ⓝ 취재, 적용 범위 **in-depth news coverage** 심층 취재

★ Every major newspaper gave front-page coverage about the trial.

★ The coverage of the service will be as wide as possible.

25 epilogue
[épilɔ̀ːg]

ⓝ 에필로그, 후기 ⓐ prologue 프롤로그, 머리말 **write an epilogue** 후기를 쓰다

There is a short epilogue from the author at the end of the book.

26 feature
[fíːtʃər]

ⓝ (신문 등의) 특집 기사, 연재물 **a Sunday feature** 일요 특집판

The magazine has a feature story about the life of a writer.

20 여배우들이 TV에서 착용하는 장신구와 의상이 유행하는 일은 흔하다. 21 기자들은 대중에게 진실을 밝히기 위해 온 힘을 기울이고 있다. 22 뉴스 특보는 긴급했고, 몇 분 내로 옆 동네에 전달되었다. / 그 소식은 어제 전국적으로 매우 빠르게 급파되었다. 23 어떤 사람들은 언론이 대중의 관심을 특정한 이슈에서 돌린다고 주장한다. 24 모든 주요 신문들이 그 재판 내용을 1면 기사로 보도했다. / 서비스의 적용 범위는 가능한 한 넓을 것이다. 25 책 뒤에는 작가가 쓴 짧은 후기가 있다. 26 잡지에는 어떤 작가의 일생에 대한 특집 기사가 있다.

27 correspondent
[kɔ̀:rəspándənt]

v correspond 교신하다

n 특파원, 통신인   **a foreign correspondent** 해외 특파원

War correspondents took several shocking pictures during the war.

28 impartial
[impá:r\ʃəl]

a 공정한, 편파적이지 않은   **↔ partial, biased** 편견적인

an impartial opinion 공정한 의견

Reporters should try to maintain an impartial view about all issues.

29 journalism
[dʒə́:rnəlìzəm]

n journal 신문, 잡지

n 언론, 저널리즘   **yellow journalism** 옐로 저널리즘, 선정적 보도

Journalism is often referred to as the watchdog of the government.

30 transmit
[trænsmít]

n transmission 전달, 방송

v (보도, 지식 등을) 전하다, 방송하다   **≒ broadcast, televise** 방송하다

transmit news 뉴스를 보내다

These days, TV stations use satellites to transmit their broadcast.

31 multimedia
[mʌ̀ltimí:diə]

a 멀티미디어의, 다중 매체의 **n** 멀티미디어, 다중 매체

digital multimedia broadcasting (DMB) 디엠비 방송

★ The multimedia industry is expanding and developing very fast today.

★ Multimedia is one of the fastest growing industries in the world today.

32 trend
[trend]

a trendy
최신 유행의, 유행을 따르는

n 경향, 동향, 유행

A fashion magazine brings fashion news, latest trends, and beauty tips.

33 neutral
[njú:trəl]

a 중립의, 공평한   **≒ impartial**   **a neutral territory** 중립지역

The press is obliged to be neutral with coverage on elections.

---

27 종군 기자들은 전쟁 당시에 충격적인 사진을 여러 장 촬영했다. 28 기자들은 모든 이슈에 대해 공정한 입장을 유지하도록 노력해야 한다. 29 언론은 흔히 정부의 감시견이라고 불린다. 30 요즘에는 방송국에서 방송을 내보낼 때 인공위성을 사용한다. 31 오늘날 멀티미디어 산업은 매우 빠르게 확장되고 발전하고 있다. / 멀티미디어는 오늘날 전 세계에서 가장 빨리 성장하는 산업 중 하나다. 32 패션 잡지는 패션 뉴스, 최신의 동향과 미용 정보를 가져다준다. 33 언론은 선거와 관련된 보도에서 중립을 지켜야 한다.

34 ☑ shorthand
[ʃɔ́ːrthænd]

ⓝ 속기 **⊜** longhand 보통 서법　　　　**a shorthand typist** 속기사

Knowing shorthand is very useful when you take down a speech.

35 ☑ notify
[nóutəfai]

ⓥ 통지하다, 통보하다 **⊜** inform, announce

notify someone in advance ~에게 사전에 통지하다

ⓝ notification 통지, 통고

I was notified by the editor that the schedule was to be changed due to heavy rain.

36 ☑ pressing
[présiŋ]

ⓐ 긴급한, 절박한 **⊜** urgent, important　　**a pressing issue** 시급한 문제

The reporters hastily relayed the pressing news.

37 ☑ propaganda
[prὰpəgǽndə]

ⓝ 선전, 선전 활동　　　　　　　　**propaganda films** 선전 영화

In the past, the press was often used to spread political propaganda.

ⓥ propagate 선전하다, 전하다

38 ☑ publicity
[pʌblísəti]

ⓝ 홍보, 광고, 명성 **⊜** advertising 광고　　**a publicity campaign** 홍보 활동

The man gained publicity after the story about his life was reported by the press.

ⓐ public 소문난, 저명한

39 ☑ relay
[ríːlei]

ⓥ 말을 전달하다, 중계하다 **⊜** carry, spread

be relayed by satellite 위성으로 중계되다

A long time ago, news was relayed from mouth to mouth.

40 ☑ column
[kάləm]

ⓝ 칼럼, 기고란　　　　　　　　　**agony columns** 고민 상담란

The editor asked the professor to write a column about politics.

ⓝ columnist 칼럼니스트

---

34 연설을 기록할 때 속기할 줄 아는 것이 매우 유용하다. 35 편집장이 나에게 폭우로 계획이 바뀔 거라고 통보했다. 36 기자들은 서둘러서 긴급 뉴스를 전했다. 37 과거에는 언론이 정치적 선전을 퍼트리는 데 사용되는 일이 잦았다. 38 언론이 남자의 인생에 대한 이야기를 보도하고 나서, 그는 유명해졌다. 39 옛날에 뉴스는 입에서 입으로 전달되었다. 40 편집장은 교수에게 정치에 대한 칼럼을 써달라고 부탁했다.

EXERCISE

A 다음 영어는 우리말로, 우리말은 영어로 옮기시오.

01 publication _____
02 publicity _____
03 advertising _____
04 pressing _____
05 distract _____
06 article _____

07 공개하다, 발표 _____
08 급파, 급송하다 _____
09 특파원, 통신원 _____
10 방송, 방영 _____
11 선전, 선전 활동 _____
12 유명인사 _____

B 다음 빈칸에 알맞은 단어를 쓰시오.

01 compile ⊜ _____
02 notify ⊜ _____
03 disclose ⊜ _____
04 sensation ⊜ _____
05 impartial ⇔ _____
06 epilogue ⇔ _____

07 inquisitive ⓥ _____
08 circulation ⓥ _____
09 vogue ⓐ _____
10 distract ⓐ _____
11 transmit ⓝ _____
12 virtual ⓝ _____

C 다음 빈칸에 들어갈 알맞은 말을 고르시오. (필요하면 형태를 바꾸시오.)

virtual	editorial	trend	monitor	classified

01 Young people often set the _____ for the popular culture to follow.

02 The _____ expressed the author's view on race relations in America.

03 The doctors will _____ the condition of the patient until she has fully recovered.

04 All _____ information is kept in a locked cabinet located in a separate building.

05 The dating website created a(n) _____ space where singles could easily mingle and date.

Crossword Puzzle

앞에서 배운 어휘를 기억하며 퍼즐을 풀어보세요.

Across

1 to take someone's attention away from something by making them look at or listen to something else

5 to make a book, list, record, etc., using different pieces of information, music, etc.

6 a feeling that you get from one of your five senses, especially the sense of touch

7 not involved in a particular situation, and therefore able to give a fair opinion or piece of advice

9 to let news or official information be known and printed

10 to make something publicly known, especially after it has been kept secret

Down

2 an article on a particular subject or by a particular writer that appears regularly in a newspaper or magazine

3 interested in a lot of different things and wanting to find out more about them

4 the treatment of an issue by the media

8 a general tendency in the way a situation is changing or developing

Unit 23 Conflict & Dispute

---

01 ☑ **absurd**
[əbsə́ːrd]
ⓝ **absurdity** 불합리, 어리석은 일

ⓐ 불합리한, 어리석은 ⓢ ridiculous　　**an absurd idea** 터무니없는 생각

It is absurd to expect us to finish the work within a day.

---

02 ☑ **abuse**
[əbjúːs / əbjúːz]
ⓐ **abusive** 학대하는, 남용하는

ⓝ 학대, 남용 ⓥ 학대하다, 남용하다　　**drug abuse** 약물 남용
sexual abuse 성적 학대

The protesters demonstrated against the abuse of public power.

---

03 ☑ **adverse**
[ædvə́ːrs]
ⓝ **adversary** 적, 상대편

ⓐ 거스르는, 반대하는 ⓢ hostile　　**adverse effects** 해로운 영향

The two debaters continuously made adverse comments at each other.

---

04 ☑ **anguish**
[ǽŋgwiʃ]

ⓝ 고통, 괴로움 ⓢ pain　　**in anguish** 괴로워하며

The woman felt bitter anguish over her husband's words.

---

05 ☑ **clash**
[klæʃ]

ⓝ 충돌, 대립　　**the clash of cultures** 문화의 충돌

There was a clash between the politicians' viewpoint on the issue.

---

06 ☑ **collapse**
[kəlǽps]

ⓥ 무너지다, 붕괴하다 ⓝ 붕괴　　**collapse from hunger** 배고픔으로 쓰러지다

There was a great confusion after the stock market collapsed last year.

---

01 우리가 그 일을 하루 안에 끝낼 것이라고 기대하는 것은 불합리하다. 02 시위자들은 공권력 남용에 항의하는 시위를 했다. 03 두 토론자는 계속해서 서로에게 반대 의견을 내놓았다. 04 여자는 남편이 한 말 때문에 크게 괴로워했다. 05 이 사안에 대한 정치인들의 의견 충돌이 있었다. 06 지난해 주식 시장이 폭락하고 나서 엄청난 혼란이 초래되었다.

07 torment
[tɔ́ːrment]

ⓝ 고통, 고뇌 ⓥ 괴롭히다 ⊜ pain 고통, torture 괴롭히다

be tormented by poverty 가난에 시달리다

★ After two years of mental torment, he finally realized that he needed treatment.

★ The ruthless king tormented his subjects with his greed.

08 torture
[tɔ́ːrtʃər]

ⓐ torturous 고통스러운

ⓥ 고문하다, 괴롭히다 ⓝ 고문, 심한 고통　　**a torture chamber** 고문실

★ The investigators found proof that the suspect was tortured.

★ In the past, torture was used to make people confess.

09 consequent
[kánsikwènt]

ⓝ consequence 결과, 결말
ⓐ consequently
그 결과, 따라서

ⓐ 결과로서 생기는, 결과적인　　**consequent changes** 결과로서 생기는 변화

The fight between the two men was consequent to abuse of alcohol.

10 controversial
[kàntrəvə́ːrʃəl]

ⓝ controversy 논쟁

ⓐ 논쟁의 여지가 있는, 논쟁을 좋아하는　⊜ debatable, disputed

a controversial issue 쟁점

Many people found the politician's statement very controversial.

11 discrimination
[diskrìmənéiʃən]

ⓥ discriminate
차별하다, 구별하다

ⓝ 차별, 구별　　**race discrimination** 인종 차별

★ Discrimination based on race, sex, or religion is against the law.

★ A strict discrimination of terms is important in all fields of science.

12 disrupt
[disrʌ́pt]

ⓝ disruption 분열, 와해

ⓥ 혼란하게 하다, 붕괴시키다　⊜ disturb　**disrupt a meeting** 회의를 방해하다

The young men were accused of disrupting social order.

07 2년 동안의 정신적 고통을 겪고 나서 그는 치료가 필요하다는 것을 깨달았다. / 무자비한 왕은 자신의 이기심 때문에 백성을 괴롭혔다. 08 조사관들은 용의자가 고문당했다는 증거를 발견했다. / 과거에 사람들을 자백하게 하기 위해서 고문이 사용되었다. 09 두 남자 사이의 싸움은 술을 너무 마신 결과로 일어났다. 10 많은 사람이 그 정치인의 발언이 논쟁의 여지가 크다고 생각했다. 11 인종, 성별, 종교에 대한 차별 대우는 법에 저촉된다. / 용어의 엄격한 구분은 과학의 모든 분야에서 중요하다. 12 청년들은 사회질서를 혼란하게 만들었다는 비난을 받았다.

13 dispute
[dispjúːt]
ⓐ disputable 논쟁의 여지가 있는

ⓝ 분쟁, 논쟁 **ⓥ** 논쟁하다　**ⓔ** argument 논쟁, argue 논쟁하다

a trade dispute 무역 마찰

★ There was a fierce dispute between the workers and the executives.

★ The custody of the children was disputed in court by the two parents.

*custody : 양육권

14 eject
[idʒékt]
ⓝ ejection 방출

ⓥ 몰아내다, 쫓아내다　**ⓔ** expel　**eject someone from** ~에서 쫓아내다

The man was ejected from the meeting for his improper actions.

15 exclusive
[iksklúːsiv]
ⓥ exclude 제외시키다
ⓝ exclusion 제외, 배제

ⓐ 배타적인, 독점적인　　**an exclusive interview** 독점 인터뷰

★ You cannot support two ideas that are mutually exclusive.

★ You can get an exclusive right over a product if you submit a patent.

16 expel
[ikspél]
ⓝ expulsion 추방, 제명

ⓥ 내쫓다, 방출하다　　**be expelled from school** 퇴학당하다

Illegal aliens should be expelled from the country.

17 forbid
[fərbíd]
ⓐ forbidden 금지된

ⓥ 금지하다　**ⓔ** prohibit　　**forbid smoking** 흡연을 금지하다

The law forbids the usage of alcohol by minors.

18 hostage
[hástidʒ]

ⓝ 인질　　**be taken hostage** 인질로 잡히다

The police asked the terrorists to release the hostages.

19 hostile
[hástil]
ⓝ hostility 적의, 전쟁 행위

ⓐ 적대적인　**ⓔ** friendly 친근한　　**a hostile territory** 적지

Our nation will not tolerate any hostile activity against us.

---

13 노사 간에 격렬한 분쟁이 있었다. / 두 부모는 아이들의 양육권을 두고 법정에서 다투었다.　14 남자는 부적절한 행동 때문에 회의에서 쫓겨났다.
15 서로 배타적인 두 의견을 모두 지지할 수는 없다. / 특허를 신청하면 그 상품에 대한 독점권을 가질 수 있다.　16 불법체류자는 나라에서 추방당해야
한다.　17 법령은 미성년자의 음주를 금지한다.　18 경찰은 테러리스트들에게 인질을 석방하여 달라고 요구했다.　19 우리나라는 우리를 향한 적대적 행
동을 용납하지 않을 것이다.

20 □ hypocrisy
[hipάkrəsi]

ⓝ hypocrite 위선자

ⓝ 위선, 위선적인 행위   **ⓔ** sincerity 정직, 성실

religious hypocrisy 종교적 위선

The people were not able to see through the man's hypocrisy.

21 □ inferior
[infíəriər]

ⓝ inferiority 하위, 열등

ⓐ 하위의, 열등한   **ⓔ** superior 보다 나은, 우수한   **inferior to** ~보다 열등한

He had to work harder to compete in such an inferior position.

22 □ interfere
[ìntərfíər]

ⓝ interference 방해, 훼방

ⓥ 간섭하다, 훼방을 놓다   **ⓔ** intrude   **interfere with** ~을 방해하다

The opposing party kept interfering with our plans.

23 □ intimidate
[intímədèit]

ⓝ intimidation 협박

ⓥ 위협하다, 협박하다   **ⓔ** threaten, frighten

intimidate one into ~을 하도록 위협하다

The defendant said that he was intimidated into committing the crime.

24 □ irreversible
[ìrivə́:rsəbəl]

ⓥ reverse 거꾸로 하다, 뒤집다

ⓐ 거꾸로 할 수 없는, 되돌릴 수 없는   **irreversible damage** 회복할 수 없는 손해

Keep in mind that words are irreversible once they are spoken.

25 □ isolate
[áisəlèit]

ⓝ isolation 고립, 격리

ⓥ 고립시키다, 분리하다, 격리하다   **ⓔ** separate

isolate a patient 환자를 격리시키다

We need to isolate the facts and the opinions from his argument.

26 □ minority
[minɔ́:riti]

ⓐ minor 보다 작은, 중요치 않은

ⓝ 소수파, 소수자   **ⓔ** majority   **a minority government** 소수당 정부

It is important not to neglect the interest of the minority.

---

20 사람들은 남자의 위선을 꿰뚫어보지 못했다. 21 그는 불리한 상황에서 경쟁하기 위해 더욱 부단히 노력해야 했다. 22 반대파들이 우리의 계획을 계속해서 방해했다. 23 피고인은 범죄를 저지르라는 협박을 받았다고 말했다. 24 말을 한번 하면 되돌릴 수 없다는 것을 명심해라. 25 우리는 그의 주장에서 사실과 의견을 분리시켜야 한다. 26 소수자의 이권을 도외시하지 않는 것이 중요하다.

27 negotiate
[nigóuʃièit]

n negotiation 협상

v 협상하다, 교섭하다

negotiate a treaty 조약을 협상하다

The leaders of two nations met to negotiate the peace treaty.

28 obstacle
[ábstəkəl]

n 장애물, 장애 ● obstruction **overcome an obstacle** 장애물을 극복하다

We are facing several obstacles to our activities.

29 obstruct
[əbstrʌ́kt]

n obstruction 방해, 장애
a obstructive 방해하는

v 막다, 방해하다 ● block

obstruct a view 전망을 가로막다

I believe greed is the biggest thing that obstructs peace.

30 occupancy
[ákjəpənsi]

v occupy 차지하다, 점령하다

n 점유, 점령 ● occupation

unlawful occupancy 불법 점유

The people in the country rebelled against the Japanese occupancy.

31 oppose
[əpóuz]

a opposite 반대의, 반대편의

v ~에 반대하다 ● support

oppose a bill 법안에 반대하다

The dictator ordered his troops to kill all who opposed him.

32 quarrel
[kwɔ́:rəl]

n 싸움, 말다툼 **v** 다투다

lead to a quarrel 언쟁을 가져오다

★ You should be careful not to turn a debate into a quarrel.

★ The children quarreled about who should play the video game first.

33 reconcile
[rékənsàil]

n reconciliation 조화, 화해

v 조화시키다, 화해시키다 ● adjust **reconcile a dispute** 논쟁을 조정하다

I tried to reconcile my parents with each other.

---

27 두 나라의 지도자들이 평화 조약에 대해 협상하기 위해 만났다. 28 우리는 우리의 활동을 방해하는 장애물에 직면하고 있다. 29 나는 평화를 막는 가장 큰 장애물이 욕심이라고 생각한다. 30 그 나라의 사람들은 일본의 점령에 저항했다. 31 독재자는 그에게 반대하는 모든 사람을 죽이라고 명령했다. 32 토론을 말다툼으로 만들지 않도록 조심해야 한다. / 아이들은 누가 먼저 비디오게임을 할지를 두고 싸웠다. 33 나는 부모님을 화해시키려고 노력했다.

34 repress
[riprés]

repression 진압, 제지
repressive 억압적인

ⓥ 억제하다, 억누르다 = control, suppress

repress a sneeze 재채기를 참다

Intellects say that the government is repressing the people's freedom.

---

35 compromise
[kámprəmàiz]

ⓝ 타협, 화해, 양보 = agreement **reject a compromise** 타협안을 거부하다

It wasn't easy to decide on a compromise with his point of view.

---

36 restrict
[ristríkt]

restriction 제한, 한정
restrictive 제한적인

ⓥ 규제하다, 제한하다 = limit, regulate **a restricted area** 통제구역

In the present day, it is thought to be unjust to restrict certain ideas.

---

37 soothe
[suːð]

soothing 달래는, 위로하는

ⓥ 달래다, 위로하다 = relieve, calm **soothe a child** 아이를 달래다

Sweet words could no longer soothe the angry people.

---

38 reverse
[rivə́ːrs]

reversal 반전, 역전

ⓥ 거꾸로 하다 ⓐ 반대의, 거꾸로의 **reverse order** 역순

His book is expected to reverse the current trend in marketing.

---

39 segregation
[sègrigéiʃən]

segregate 분리하다, 격리하다

ⓝ (인종, 성별에 따른) 분리, 격리, 차별 = integration 통합

segregation of men and women 남, 녀의 분리

Martin Luther King worked hard to eliminate racial segregation.

---

40 concede
[kənsíːd]

concession 양보, 용인

ⓥ 인정하다, 양보하다 **concede defeat** 패배를 인정하다

I conceded that I made a lot of mistakes.

---

34 지식인들은 정부가 국민의 자유를 억압한다고 이야기한다. 35 그의 관점과 타협하기로 결정한 것은 쉽지 않았다. 36 오늘날에는 특정한 사상을 규제하는 것이 부당한 것으로 간주한다. 37 달콤한 말은 더는 화난 사람들을 위로하지 못했다. 38 그의 책은 현재 마케팅의 경향을 뒤집을 것으로 기대된다. 39 마틴 루터 킹은 인종 차별을 없애기 위해 열심히 노력했다. 40 나는 많은 실수를 저질렀음을 인정했다.

EXERCISE

A 다음 영어는 우리말로, 우리말은 영어로 옮기시오.

01 forbid _____

02 torment _____

03 reconcile _____

04 consequent _____

05 obstruct _____

06 absurd _____

07 배타적인, 독점적인 _____

08 인질 _____

09 협상하다, 교섭하다 _____

10 고립시키다, 분리하다 _____

11 달래다, 위로하다 _____

12 붕괴, 무너지다 _____

B 다음 빈칸에 알맞은 단어를 쓰시오.

01 intimidate ⊜ _____

02 dispute ⊜ _____

03 repress ⊜ _____

04 minority ⇔ _____

05 segregation ⇔ _____

06 inferior ⇔ _____

07 discrimination ⓥ _____

08 occupancy ⓥ _____

09 torture ⓐ _____

10 abuse ⓐ _____

11 disrupt ⓝ _____

12 adverse ⓝ _____

C 다음 빈칸에 들어갈 알맞은 말을 고르시오. (필요하면 형태를 바꾸시오.)

compromise	hypocrisy	expel	abuse	controversial

01 After the divorce, the parents _____ by sharing custody of their children.

02 It is sheer _____ for my parents to forbid something that they actually do.

03 Michael was _____ from school for his bad behavior.

04 Since you are so nice, people may _____ your kindness and take advantage of it.

05 His new released book is considered _____ because it unveils the truth about the Iraq War.

Crossword Puzzle

앞에서 배운 어휘를 기억하며 퍼즐을 풀어보세요.

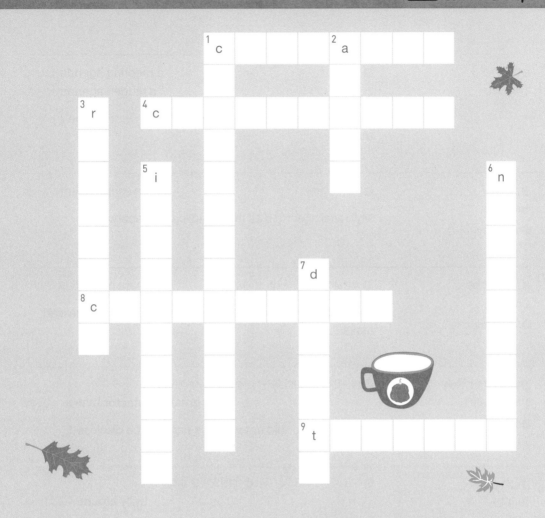

Across

1 (of a structure) suddenly fall down or give way

4 happening as a result of a particular event or situation

8 an agreement that is achieved after everyone involved accepts less than what they wanted at first, or the act of making this agreement

9 to deliberately hurt someone in order to force them to give you information, to punish them, or to be cruel

Down

1 causing a lot of disagreement, because many people have strong opinions about the subject being discussed

2 cruel or violent treatment of someone

3 to limit or control the size, amount, or range of something

5 to frighten or threaten someone into making them do what you want

6 to discuss something in order to reach an agreement, especially in business or politics

7 a serious argument or disagreement

Group & Activity

01 agenda
[ədʒéndə]

ⓝ 안건, 의제

a meeting agenda 회의 안건
a hidden agenda 숨은 의도

The members brought up an important agenda for the meeting.

02 agent
[éidʒənt]

ⓝ agency 대리점

ⓝ 대리인, 중개인

a secret agent 비밀 요원

My travel agent did all the complicated paperwork for me.

03 allocate
[æləkèit]

ⓝ allocation 할당, 배치

ⓥ 배분하다, 할당하다　ⓔ distribute

allocate money 돈을 배당하다

Each team of our organization is allocated with specialized tasks.

04 benefactor
[bénəfæ̀ktər]

ⓝ beneficence 선행, 은혜

ⓝ 자선을 베푸는 사람, 후원자　ⓔ sponsor 후원자

a great benefactor 기부를 많이 하는 사람

The benefactor did not want his name to be disclosed.

05 bully
[búli]

ⓝ 약한 사람을 괴롭히는 사람 ⓥ (약한 사람을) 괴롭히다

bully around ~을 괴롭히다

It was very courageous of you to stand up to those bullies.

06 civil
[sívəl]

ⓝ civilian 민간인

ⓐ 민간의, 문명의

civil law 민법

★ Many organizations work hard to make sure civil rights aren't violated.

★ I cannot understand how such crimes can happen in a civil world.

---

01 회원들이 매우 중요한 회의 안건을 제기했다.　02 여행사 직원이 나 대신 복잡한 서류 업무를 해주었다.　03 우리 조직의 각 부서에 특수 업무가 할당된다.　04 그 후원자는 자신의 이름이 밝혀지는 것을 원하지 않았다.　05 네가 약자를 괴롭히는 애들에게 대항한 것은 용기 있는 일이었다.　06 많은 단체가 시민권이 침해되는 것을 막기 위해 노력한다. / 나는 문명화된 세계에서 어떻게 그런 범죄들이 일어날 수 있는지 이해할 수 없다.

07 companionship
[kəmpǽnjənʃìp]

n companion 친구, 동료

n 교우관계, 교제 **=** company   **close companionship** 친한 관계

I cherish the companionship which I shared with my former colleagues.

08 confidential
[kὰnfidénʃəl]

n confidentiality 기밀성

a 기밀의, 신뢰할 수 있는 **=** secret 기밀의   **confidential papers** 기밀서류

★ I'm afraid the information you requested is confidential.

★ Steve and I became confidential when we collaborated on a project.

09 cooperate
[kouápərèit]

n cooperation 협력, 협조
a cooperative 협력적인

v 협력하다, 협동하다   **cooperate with** ~와 협력하다

The policeman asked us to cooperate with the investigation into the car accident.

10 correlation
[kɔ̀:rəléiʃən]

v correlate 서로 관련시키다

n 상관관계, 인과관계   **a close correlation** 밀접한 상관관계

Our work has a close correlation with government policy.

11 delegate
[déligət / déligèit]

n delegation 대표단, 파견단

n 대표, 파견 **v** 파견하다 **=** representative 대표
a party delegate 당(黨) 대표

★ The delegates of each group gathered to discuss the economic recession.

★ Keith will be delegated to attend a conference in Chicago.

12 department
[dipá:rtmənt]

n 부서, 부문 **=** section, bureau   **the PR department** 홍보부

Tom said that the human resources department would assign me to a new section.

13 commission
[kəmíʃən]

n 위원회, 임무   **an investigating commission** 조사 위원회

The government agreed on the establishment of a commission for the project.

07 나는 옛 동료와의 교우관계를 소중히 여긴다. 08 유감스럽게도 귀하가 요청하신 정보는 기밀입니다. / Steve와 나는 프로젝트를 함께 하면서 신뢰할 수 있게 되었다. 09 경찰은 우리에게 교통사고 수사에 협조해달라고 요청했다. 10 우리 일은 정부정책과 밀접한 관계가 있다. 11 각 단체의 대표자들이 경기침체에 대해 토의하려고 모였다. / Keith는 시카고에서 열리는 회의에 참석하도록 파견될 것이다. 12 인사부가 나를 새로운 부서로 배정할 것이라고 Tom이 말했다. 13 정부는 프로젝트를 위한 위원회의 설립에 동의했다.

14 vow
[vau]

n 맹세 **v** 맹세하다 **≒** swear 맹세하다 **a vow of silence** 침묵의 서약

The newly assigned CEO vowed to boost the growth of the company.

15 division
[divíʒən]

v divide 나누다

n 부서, 분할, 구분 **equal division** 균등한 분할

★ I work for the marketing division of my corporation.

★ In the past, there was a sharp division among the class of people.

16 register
[rédʒistər]

n registration 등록

n 등록부 **v** 등록하다, 기재하다 **register an invention** 발명품을 등록하다

★ After the marriage, the couple's names were added to the family register.

★ Unauthorized usage of a registered trademark is prohibited by law.

17 entry
[éntri]

v enter ~에 들어가다

n 들어감, 입장 **allow [refuse] entry** 입장을 허가[거부]하다

A person who wishes entry into our group needs to meet our standards.

18 feminist
[fémənist]

n feminism
페미니즘, 여권신장운동

n 페미니스트, 여권신장론자 **the feminist movement** 여권신장운동

The main argument of feminists is that women are repressed by men.

19 flock
[flɑk]

n 떼 **v** 떼 짓다 **a flock of visitors** 많은 수의 방문자

★ The flock of chickens filled the yard on the farm.

★ People who have similar interests tend to flock together.

---

14 새로 부임한 CEO가 회사 성장 촉진에 박차를 가할 것이라고 단언했다. 15 나는 우리 회사의 마케팅 부서에서 일한다. / 과거에는 사람들의 계급이 뚜렷하게 구분되었다. 16 결혼하고 나서 그 부부의 이름이 호적에 추가되었다. / 등록 상표를 허가 없이 사용하는 것은 법으로 금지되어 있다. 17 우리 단체에 들어오려는 사람은 우리 기준에 들어맞아야 한다. 18 여권주의자들의 주된 주장은 여성이 남성에 의해 억압받는다는 것이다. 19 한 무리의 닭이 농장 마당을 가득 채웠다. / 관심사가 비슷한 사람끼리 뭉치는 경향이 있다.

20 ☑ **gathering**
[gǽðəriŋ]
v gather 모으다, 모이다

n 모임, 집회 **●** assembly, meeting   **a social gathering** 친목 모임

Steve announced his engagement at his family gathering.

---

21 ☑ **reflex**
[rí:fleks]
a reflexive 반응하는, 반사의

n 반사, 반영   **a reflex action** 반사 작용

Certain behavior can be made into a conditioned reflex.

---

22 ☑ **guild**
[gild]

n 조합, 회, 길드 **●** union, association   **an industrial guild** 산업 조합
Screen Actors Guild 미국 영화배우 조합

People who enjoy online games often form groups called guilds.

---

23 ☑ **headquarters**
[hédkwɔ̀:rtərz]

n 본부, 본사   **general headquarters** 총사령부, 총본부

The headquarters of our company is located in Seoul.

---

24 ☑ **shield**
[ʃi:ld]
a shieldless 무방비의

n 방패, 보호물 **v** 보호하다 **●** protection 보호(물), protect 보호하다
a sword and a shield 칼과 방패

★ Our organization tries to act as a shield for those who need help.

★ The mother shielded her baby from the sun's strong rays.

---

25 ☑ **majority**
[mədʒɔ́(:)rəti]
a major 큰 쪽의, 주요한

n 대부분, 대다수   **a majority vote** 다수결 투표

In many cases, the principle of decision by the majority is adopted.

---

26 ☑ **mission**
[míʃən]

n 임무, 사명, 선교   **carry out one's mission** 임무를 수행하다

★ The members of a group must always keep in mind their mission.

★ Sally wanted to go to a mission school to study theology.

---

20 Steve는 가족모임에서 자신의 약혼 사실을 발표했다. 21 특정한 행동을 조건반사로 만들 수 있다. 22 온라인 게임을 즐기는 사람들은 흔히 길드라는 모임을 만든다. 23 우리 회사의 본점은 서울에 있다. 24 우리 조직은 도움이 필요한 사람들에게 방패 역할을 해주고자 노력한다. / 어머니는 강렬한 태양광선으로부터 아이를 보호했다. 25 많은 경우에 다수결의 원칙이 적용된다. 26 단체의 일원은 항상 자신의 사명을 명심해야 한다. / Sally는 신학을 공부하기 위해 신학교에 가고 싶어 했다.

27 mob
[mɑb]

Ⓝ 군중, 대중, 폭도   ⊜ mass, crowd   **mob psychology** 군중 심리

A mob of soccer fans called hooligans stormed the streets in England.

28 unity
[júːnəti]

Ⓥ unite 결합하다

Ⓝ 통일성, 조화, 개체   **family unity** 집안의 화합

In times of a national crisis, social unity is needed to overcome it.

29 novice
[návis]

Ⓝ 풋내기, 초심자   ⊜ beginner   **a novice driver** 초보 운전자

Every expert in any field used to be a novice in the past.

30 assimilation
[əsìməléiʃən]

Ⓥ assimilate 동화시키다

Ⓝ 동화, 융화   **cultural assimilation** 문화적 동화

Traces of the assimilation between two different cultures were found.

31 organization
[ɔ̀ːrgənəzéiʃən]

Ⓥ organize 정리하다, 조직하다

Ⓝ 단체, 조직   **an international organization** 국제기구

Many non-profit organizations work hard for good causes.

32 partake
[pɑːrtéik]

Ⓝ partaker 분담자, 관여자

Ⓥ 참여하다, 함께하다   ⊜ participate 참여하다
partake in a festival 축제에 참여하다

The man refused to partake in the project without his colleagues.

33 superior
[səpíəriər]

Ⓝ superiority 우월, 우위

ⓐ 상급의, 우수한   ⊜ inferior 하급한, 열등한   **superior quality** 우수한 품질

The company has a reputation for superior technology and design.

---

27 영국에서 훌리건이라고 불리는 축구광 무리가 거리를 휩쓸었다. 28 국가적 위기상황에서는, 이를 극복하기 위해 사회 통합이 필요하다. 29 그 어떤 분야의 전문가들도 모두 과거에는 초보자였다. 30 두 문화 사이에 융화의 흔적이 발견되었다. 31 많은 비영리단체가 대의를 위해 열심히 일한다. 32 남자는 자신의 동료 없이 프로젝트에 참여하기를 거부했다. 33 그 회사는 기술과 디자인이 우수하다고 평판이 나 있다.

34 rally
[rǽli]

n 대규모 집회 **v** 다시 모으다, 불러 모으다　　　**an anti-war rally** 반전 집회

★ To protest the capture of the author, a rally was held in the center of the city.

★ The men rallied their fellow workers to negotiate with the executives.

35 voluntary
[váləntèri]

n volunteer 지원자, 봉사자
ad voluntarily 자발적으로

a 자발적인, 임의의　　　**voluntary help** 자발적 도움

Many voluntary organizations helped the victims of the flood.

36 representative
[rèprizéntətiv]

v represent 나타내다, 대리하다

n 대표자, 대리인　　　**representative of the people** 국민의 대표

The National Assembly consists of elected representatives.

37 riot
[ráiət]

a riotous 폭동의, 떠들썩한

n 폭동, 반란　　　**a huge riot** 거대한 폭동

Many people were injured during a serious riot in L.A.

38 partisan
[pá:rtizən]

n 일당, 당원 **a** 당파심이 강한　　　**a communist partisan** 공산당원

★ During the war, the partisans were key to the success of securing peace on the island.

★ The congressmen met to solve the problem and stop partisan politics.

39 throng
[θrɔ(:)ŋ]

n 군중, 집합 **v** 몰려들다　**=** crowd 군중, 몰려들다

a throng of spectators 한 무리의 관중

★ A throng of reporters and photographers gathered at the airport to cover our national soccer team's arrival.

★ The people thronged the town hall to listen to the announcement.

40 staff
[stæf]

n 직원, 간부　　　**a staff meeting** 간부회의

Only staff members are authorized to go behind stage.

---

34 그 작가의 체포에 대해 항의하기 위해서 도심에서 집회가 열렸다. / 그 사람들이 임원들과 협상하기 위해 동료 근로자들을 불러 모았다.　35 많은 자원봉사 단체들이 홍수 피해자들을 도왔다.　36 국회는 선출된 대표들로 구성된다.　37 LA에서 큰 폭동이 일어났을 때 많은 사람이 다쳤다.　38 전쟁 중에 비밀 결사대원들이 섬의 평화를 보장하는 성공의 열쇠였다. / 국회의원들이 문제를 해결하고 당파싸움을 그만두기 위해 회동했다.　39 많은 기자와 사진사들이 국가대표 축구팀의 도착을 취재하기 위해 공항에 모였다. / 사람들이 발표를 들으려고 마을회관으로 몰려들었다.　40 무대 뒤에는 오직 직원들만 출입이 허락된다.

EXERCISE

A 다음 영어는 우리말로, 우리말은 영어로 옮기시오.

01	benefactor	_____	07	기밀의, 신뢰할 수 있는	_____
02	mob	_____	08	대표자, 대리인	_____
03	division	_____	09	여권신장론자	_____
04	reflex	_____	10	풋내기, 초심자	_____
05	cooperate	_____	11	임무, 사명, 선교	_____
06	partisan	_____	12	안건, 의제	_____

B 다음 빈칸에 알맞은 단어를 쓰시오.

01	delegate	⊜ _____	07	unity	ⓥ _____
02	shield	⊜ _____	08	assimilation	ⓥ _____
03	throng	⊜ _____	09	riot	ⓐ _____
04	allocate	⊜ _____	10	reflex	ⓐ _____
05	vow	⊜ _____	11	civil	ⓝ _____
06	partake	⊜ _____	12	superior	ⓝ _____

C 다음 빈칸에 들어갈 알맞은 말을 고르시오. (필요하면 형태를 바꾸시오.)

flock	correlation	bully	headquarters	voluntary

01 The donation of blood is done on a _____ basis.

02 After a careful study, a _____ was found between second-hand smoke and lung disease.

03 The survey shows that 32 percent of students have been involved in _____ or being _____ .

04 The young teenagers _____ to the mall when they learned that their favorite singer would be performing there.

05 The outbreak of the swine flu led to many meetings among the staff at the _____ of the World Health Organization.

Across

1 to work with someone else to achieve something that you both want

6 someone who has been elected or chosen to speak, vote, or take decisions for a group

7 the process of becoming an accepted part of a country or group

8 someone who gives money for a good purpose

Down

1 spoken or written in secret and intended to be kept secret

2 someone who has been chosen to speak, vote or make decisions for someone else

3 an action that is performed without conscious thought as a response to a stimulus

4 a group of people who have been given the official job of finding out about something or controlling something

5 a violent disturbance of the peace by a crowd

Unit 25 War & Peace

---

01 ☑ **admiral**
[ǽdmərəl]

ⓝ 해군 대장　　　　　　　　　　　　　　**a Navy admiral** 해군 대장

Admiral Lee Sun-Shin defeated the Japanese navy at the South Sea.

---

02 ☑ **alert**
[əlɔ́ːrt]

ⓐ 방심하지 않는, 조심하는　ⓝ 경보, 경계　ⓥ 경고하다　● careless 부주의한

a red alert 적색경보

★ The soldiers stood alert and watched the enemy's movement all night.

★ The news alert warned the town of the strong winds and rain.

★ There are advertisements to alert people to the dangers of bird flu infection.

---

03 ☑ **alliance**
[əláiəns]

ⓥ ⓝ ally 동맹시키다; 동맹국

ⓝ 동맹, 결연　● union　　　　　　**a military alliance** 군사동맹

The two nations hold a firm alliance against a mutual enemy.

---

04 ☑ **treaty**
[tríːti]

ⓝ 조약, 협정　　　　　　　　　**a commercial treaty** 통상 조약

Both countries finally reached an agreement on the treaty.

---

05 ☑ **ambitious**
[æmbíʃəs]

ⓝ ambition 야망, 야심

ⓐ 야심적인, 대망을 품은　● unambitious 야심이 없는, 수수한

an ambitious plan 야심찬 계획

In history, several ambitious leaders caused terrible wars.

---

06 ☑ **annihilate**
[ənáiəlèit]

ⓝ annihilation 근절, 전멸, 폐지

ⓥ 전멸시키다, 무력하게 하다　　　**annihilate the enemy** 적을 전멸시키다

Experts say that a nuclear war may annihilate mankind.

---

01 이순신 장군은 남해에서 일본 해군을 격퇴했다. 02 병사들은 방심하지 않고 적군의 움직임을 밤새도록 주시했다. / 뉴스 속보가 강풍과 폭우에 대해 마을 사람들에게 알렸다. / 사람들에게 조류 인플루엔자 감염의 위험성을 경고하는 광고가 있다. 03 두 국가는 공통의 적을 상대로 굳건한 동맹을 유지하고 있다. 04 두 나라는 마침내 조약에 합의했다. 05 역사적으로, 여러 야심 찬 지도자들이 끔찍한 전쟁을 일으켰다. 06 전문가들은 핵전쟁이 인류를 전멸시킬 수 있다고 말한다.

---

07 ☑ **spear**
[spiər]

n 창

thrust a spear into ~을 창으로 찌르다

The spear is one of the earliest weapons developed by men.

---

08 ☑ **armament**
[ά:rməmənt]

v arm 무장하다

n 군비, 무장

an armament race 군비 경쟁

Many nations try to prevent the expansion of atomic armaments.

---

09 ☑ **subdue**
[səbdʒú:]

n subdual 정복

v 정복하다, 복종시키다 ● conquer

a subdued laugh 숨죽인 웃음

Alexander the Great subdued most of Europe from 356 B.C. to 323 B.C.

---

10 ☑ **assassinate**
[əsǽsənèit]

n assassin 암살자
n assassination 암살

v 암살하다 ● murder, kill

get assassinated 암살당하다

Many people were shocked when John F. Kennedy was assassinated in Texas.

---

11 ☑ **assault**
[əsɔ́:lt]

a assaultive 공격적인

n 습격 **v** 습격하다

a military assault 군대의 습격
commit an assault 공격을 감행하다

★ Mr. Simpson was put in prison for assault.
★ The sergeant led his troop to assault the enemy base.

---

12 ☑ **bombard**
[bɑmbá:rd]

v 폭격하다, 퍼붓다 ● attack

bombard the enemy 적군을 폭격하다

The enemy bombarded the city with massive explosives.

---

13 ☑ **bullet**
[búlit]

n 총탄, 탄약통

a bullet wound 총상

My grandfather died by an enemy bullet during the war.

---

07 창은 인간이 만든 초기 무기 중 하나다. 08 많은 나라가 핵무장의 확장을 막으려고 노력한다. 09 알렉산더 제왕은 기원전 356년부터 323년까지 유럽 대부분을 정복했다. 10 존 F. 케네디가 텍사스에서 암살되었을 때 많은 사람이 큰 충격을 받았다. 11 Simpson 씨는 폭행으로 교도소에 수감되었다. / 상사가 자신의 부대를 이끌고 적진을 공격했다. 12 적군은 도시에 엄청난 양의 폭탄을 퍼부었다. 13 우리 할아버지는 전쟁 중에 적군의 총탄에 맞아 돌아가셨다.

14 civilian
[sivíljən]

ⓝ (군인이 아닌) 민간인, 일반 시민 **ⓐ** (군인이 아닌) 일반인의

civilian life 민간인 생활

★ Many innocent civilians were injured or killed during the Korean War.

★ There were many civilian casualties during the air raid.

---

15 colony
[káləni]

ⓥ colonize 식민지로 개척하다

ⓝ 식민지

a self-governing colony 자치 식민지

Many countries used to be colonies of different countries.

---

16 tactic
[tǽktik]

ⓐ tactical 전술적인

ⓝ 꾀, 전술

a negotiating tactic 협상 전략

In some cases, tactics are more important than strength.

---

17 commander
[kəmǽndər]

ⓥ command 명령하다

ⓝ 사령관, 지휘자 **ⓔ** captain, leader

a military commander 군 장교
a commander in chief 총사령관

The commander ordered his troops to dig a bunker.

---

18 conference
[kánfərəns]

ⓥ confer 협의하다

ⓝ 회견, 회담

a press conference 기자회견

The leaders of several nations gathered for a peace conference.

---

19 conqueror
[káŋkərər]

ⓥ conquer 정복하다
ⓝ conquest 정복, 획득

ⓝ 정복자

a mighty conqueror 강력한 정복자

The defeated army had no choice but to submit to the conqueror.

---

20 counterattack
[káuntərətæk]

ⓝ 역습, 반격 **ⓥ** 역습하다, 반격하다

a rapid counterattack 빠른 역공

★ The general waited for a chance to launch a counterattack.

★ The British Army was waiting for a chance to counterattack.

---

14 한국전쟁 중에 많은 무고한 민간인이 다치거나 목숨을 잃었다. / 공습 도중에 많은 민간인 사상자가 발생했다. 15 많은 나라가 과거에 다른 나라의 식민지였다. 16 어떤 경우에서는 힘보다 전술이 중요할 때가 있다. 17 사령관은 병사들에게 벙커를 파라고 명령했다. 18 여러 나라의 지도자들이 평화회담을 갖기 위해 모였다. 19 패배한 군대는 정복자에게 굴복하는 수밖에 없었다. 20 장군은 반격할 기회를 기다렸다. / 영국군은 반격할 기회를 기다리고 있었다.

21 surrender
[səréndər]

ⓥ 넘겨주다, 항복하다 **ⓝ** 인도, 항복 **an unconditional surrender** 무조건 항복

★ The man surrendered his firearms to the police.

★ The king was forced to surrender to the rebel forces.

22 discord
[dískɔːrd]

ⓐ discordant 부조화의

ⓝ 불화, 불일치 **ⓜ** concord 일치, 조화 **a family discord** 가정불화

The general was troubled with the discord among his commanders.

23 fleet
[fliːt]

ⓝ 함대 **a combined fleet** 연합 함대

A whole fleet of warships was wiped out by a sudden attack.

24 foe
[fou]

ⓝ 원수, 적 **ⓜ** enemy **a political foe** 정치적 원수

The Indian warriors fought against their foes to protect their tribe and territory.

25 intermission
[ìntərmíʃən]

ⓥ intermit 일시 멈추다

ⓝ 휴식시간, 중단 **ⓜ** interval 휴식시간 **a short intermission** 짧은 휴식

The training program went on until morning without intermission.

26 withdraw
[wiðdrɔ́ː]

ⓝ withdrawal 철수, 후퇴

ⓥ 철수하다, 후퇴하다, 인출하다 **withdraw funds** 자금을 회수하다

★ The commander withdrew his troops to lead the enemy into a trap.

★ Today, many people withdraw money by using ATMs instead of visiting the bank.

27 landmine
[lǽndmàin]

ⓝ 지뢰 **lay a landmine** 지뢰를 매설하다

In Cambodia, operations to defuse landmines are carried out to this day.

---

21 남자는 경찰에게 자신의 총을 넘겨주었다. / 왕은 반란군에게 강제로 항복했다. 22 장군은 지휘관들 사이의 불화 때문에 골머리를 앓고 있었다. 23 기습 공격으로 군 함대 전체가 몰살당했다. 24 인디언 전사들은 자신들의 부족과 영토를 보호하기 위해 적들과 맞서 싸웠다. 25 훈련은 휴식시간 없이 아침까지 이어졌다. 26 지휘관은 적을 함정에 빠뜨리기 위해 군대를 후퇴시켰다. / 오늘날, 많은 사람이 은행을 방문하는 것 대신 ATM을 통해 돈을 찾는다. 27 캄보디아에서는 오늘날까지도 지뢰를 제거하는 작업이 이루어지고 있다.

28 marshal
[mɑ́:rʃəl]

n 군 최고 사령관, 보안관 **v** (사람을) 정렬시키다   **a field marshal** 육군 원수

★ The marshal decided to launch a final attack.

★ Mr. Adler marshaled his students, telling them where to go.

29 martial
[mɑ́:rʃəl]

a 군사의, 전쟁의   ● military   **martial music** 군악

There is a rumor that the military will declare martial law.

30 warrior
[wɔ́(:)riər]

n 전사   ● soldier, fighter   **a warrior of the Cross** 십자군 전사

We must remember the warriors that fought to defend our land.

31 morale
[mourǽl]

n 사기, 의욕   ● confidence   **raise the morale** 사기를 북돋다

The soldiers lost their morale as they were outnumbered.

32 naval
[néivəl]

n navy 해군

a 해군의   **a naval base** 해군 기지

The naval forces are protecting the nation's sea territory.

33 occupy
[ɑ́kjəpài]

n occupation 차지, 점령

v 차지하다, 종사하다, 점령하다   ● own, inhabit   **occupy territory** 영토를 점령하다

After World War II, the country was occupied by the Soviet Union.

34 opponent
[əpóunənt]

v oppose ~에 대항하다

n 적수   ● rival, enemy   **a formidable opponent** 강적

They developed a weapon which was designed to kill the opponent with a single shot.

---

28 최고 사령관이 최후의 공격을 펼치기로 했다. / Adler 선생님은 학생들을 집결시키고, 갈 곳을 알려주었다. 29 군부가 계엄령을 선포할 것이라는 소문이 있다. 30 우리는 이 땅을 지키기 위해 싸웠던 용사들을 기억해야 한다. 31 병사들은 수적으로 열세해지자 사기를 잃었다. 32 해군은 국가의 영해를 지키고 있다. 33 2차 세계대전이 끝나고 나서, 그 나라는 소련에 점령당했다. 34 그들은 단 한 방으로 적을 사살할 수 있도록 고안된 무기를 개발했다.

35 peril
[pérəl]

a perilous 위험한

n 위험, 모험 ● danger **in peril** 위험에 직면하여

We were able to avert a great peril as reinforcements arrived.

36 recession
[riséʃən]

v recede 물러가다

n 퇴거, 후퇴 ● boom 갑작스러운 인기, 붐 **an economic recession** 불경기

Many countries are suffering from a recession.

37 revenge
[rivéndʒ]

n 복수 **v** 복수하다 ● vengeance 복수 **in revenge of** ~의 앙갚음으로

★ The victim's family chose not to seek revenge and forgive the criminal.

★ The boy vowed to revenge his father's death.

38 salute
[səlú:t]

n salutation 인사

v 경례하다, 인사하다 ● greet **salute with a hand** 거수경례하다

Soldiers are supposed to salute officers on sight.

39 sergeant
[sá:rdʒənt]

n 하사관 **a drill sergeant** 훈련교관

A sergeant carries out orders from officers by directing his soldiers.

40 siege
[si:dʒ]

v besiege
포위 공격하다, 쇄도하다

n 포위 공격 **under siege** 포위 공격을 받고 있는

The castle couldn't stand the siege for long.

35 지원병이 도착하자 우리는 큰 위험을 모면할 수 있었다. 36 많은 나라가 불경기로 고통을 받고 있다. 37 피해자의 가족은 복수가 아니라, 범죄자를 용서하는 것을 택했다. / 소년은 아버지의 원수를 갚으리라 다짐했다. 38 병사들은 장교를 보면 경례를 해야 한다. 39 부사관은 병사들을 통솔하여 장교가 내린 명령을 수행한다. 40 성은 포위 공격을 오랫동안 막아낼 수는 없었다.

EXERCISE

A 다음 영어는 우리말로, 우리말은 영어로 옮기시오.

01 ambitious	_____	07 암살하다	_____
02 opponent	_____	08 식민지	_____
03 admiral	_____	09 포위 공격	_____
04 surrender	_____	10 함대	_____
05 sergeant	_____	11 전사	_____
06 bombard	_____	12 군비, 무장	_____

B 다음 빈칸에 알맞은 단어를 쓰시오.

01 foe	⊜ _____	07 alliance	ⓥ _____
02 subdue	⊜ _____	08 conference	ⓥ _____
03 revenge	⊜ _____	09 tactic	ⓐ _____
04 recession	⇔ _____	10 peril	ⓐ _____
05 discord	⇔ _____	11 occupy	ⓝ _____
06 alert	⇔ _____	12 withdraw	ⓝ _____

C 다음 빈칸에 들어갈 알맞은 말을 고르시오. (필요하면 형태를 바꾸시오.)

assault	treaty	martial	civilian	salute

01 Many _____ participated in the march for civil rights in the capital city.

02 Bruce Lee is famous for his excellent _____ arts skills and techniques.

03 In order to bring the war to an end, a(n) _____ was established between the two countries.

04 It is a crime to _____ a person because of his or her race, color, nationality, or religion.

05 As the general passed their way, all the military cadets paid their respects and _____.

Across

1 determined to be successful, rich, powerful, etc.

4 to say officially that you want to stop fighting, because you realize that you cannot win

5 connected with war and fighting

7 a situation in which an army or the police surround a place and try to gain control of it

9 giving all your attention to what is happening

10 something you do in order to punish someone who has harmed or offended you

11 someone who you try to defeat in a competition, game, fight, or argument

Down

2 a formal written agreement between two or more countries or governments

3 to murder an important person

6 to destroy something or someone completely

8 the crime of physically attacking someone

Unit 26 Environment & Ecology

---

01 **Antarctic**
[æntɑ́ːrktik]

ⓝ Antarctica 남극대륙

ⓐ 남극의 ● arctic 북극의　　　　**the Antarctic expedition** 남극 탐험

Scientists are researching alternative fuel at the Antarctic base.

---

02 **barren**
[bǽrən]

ⓐ 불모의, 임신을 못하는 ● fertile 비옥한　　　**a barren land** 불모지

★ This area became barren because of industrial pollution.

★ The barren couple adopted a child from the orphanage.

---

03 **circumference**
[sərkʌ́mfərəns]

ⓝ 둘레, 원주　　　**the circumference of a pond** 연못의 둘레

The circumference of the Earth at the equator is 40,232.5 km.

---

04 **community**
[kəmjúːnəti]

ⓝ 사회, 공동체 ● society　　　**the international community** 국제 사회

Our community strengthened the local environmental standards.

---

05 **contaminate**
[kəntǽmənèit]

ⓝ contamination 오염

ⓥ 오염시키다 ● pollute

contaminate food with dioxins 다이옥신으로 음식을 오염시키다

The river became contaminated by household wastewater.

---

06 **deforestation**
[diːfɔ̀ːristéiʃən]

ⓝ 삼림 벌채, 산림 개간　　　**rainforest deforestation** 열대 우림 파괴

Rapid deforestation can be critical to the global environment.

---

01 과학자들이 남극기지에서 대체 연료를 연구하고 있다. 02 이 지역은 산업공해 때문에 불모지가 되었다. / 불임부부가 보육원에서 아이를 입양했다. 03 적도에서 지구의 둘레는 40,232.5km다. 04 우리 공동체는 지역 환경 기준을 강화했다. 05 강이 생활폐수로 오염되었다. 06 삼림벌채가 빠르게 진행되는 것은 지구 환경에 치명적일 수 있다.

07 ☑ deluge
[déljuːdʒ]

ⓝ 대홍수　**ⓢ** flood

the Noachian deluge 노아의 대홍수

Many people lost their homes by a serious deluge.

08 ☑ depletion
[diplíːʃən]

ⓥ deplete 고갈되다

ⓝ 고갈, 소모

depletion of the ozone layer 오존층 파괴

We need to be prepared for the depletion of fossil fuel.

09 ☑ desertification
[dizəːrtəfikéiʃən]

ⓝ desert 사막

ⓝ 사막화

rapid desertification 급속한 사막화

Many experts say that global warming is boosting desertification.

10 ☑ desolate
[désələt]

ⓝ desolation 황폐화, 쓸쓸함

ⓐ 황량한, 쓸쓸한

a desolate land 황량한 땅

Many people put a lot of effort to restore the desolate area.

11 ☑ reinforce
[rìːinfɔ́ːrs]

ⓝ reinforcement 보강, 강화

ⓥ 강화하다　**ⓢ** strengthen

reinforce the standard 기준을 강화하다

The city plans to reinforce the safety standards and prevent pollution.

12 ☑ ecology
[iːkálədʒi]

ⓐ ecological 생태학의

ⓝ 생태(학)

the ecological pyramid 생태 피라미드

Foreign animals can sometimes disrupt the local ecology.

13 ☑ ecosystem
[íːkousìstəm]

ⓝ 생태계

a closed ecosystem 폐쇄 생태계

Even a small pond can have a very complicated ecosystem.

---

07 많은 사람이 심각한 홍수로 집을 잃었다.　08 우리는 화석연료의 고갈에 대비해야 한다.　09 많은 전문가는 지구온난화가 사막화를 촉진한다고 이야기한다.　10 많은 사람이 황무지를 복원하는 데 많은 노력을 기울였다.　11 시 당국은 안전을 강화하고, 오염을 예방할 계획이다.　12 외래종은 때때로 지역 생태계를 교란시킬 수 있다.　13 작은 연못에도 매우 복잡한 생태계가 있을 수 있다.

14 emission
[imíʃən]

v emit 방출하다, 발산하다

n 방사, 방출, 배출　**⊜** release　　**control emissions** 배출량을 규제하다

The Kyoto Protocol is an agreement to decrease carbon emissions.

15 equilibrium
[ìːkwəlíbriəm]

n 균형, 평형　**⊜** balance　　**an economic equilibrium** 경제적 균형

Human activity often breaks the equilibrium of nature.

16 evacuate
[ivǽkjuèit]

n evacuation 대피, 철수

v 대피시키다, 철수시키다　**⊜** withdraw

evacuate the residents 거주민들을 대피시키다

The villagers were evacuated from the town to escape the forest fire.

17 extinct
[ikstíŋkt]

n extinction 멸종

a 멸종한, 활동을 멈춘　**⊜** dead　　**an extinct species** 멸종된 종

The extinct volcano became a worldwide tourist site.

18 filth
[filθ]

a filthy 더러운

n 오물, 쓰레기　　**filth-treating equipment** 오물 처리 시설

This new equipment can filter filth more efficiently.

19 fossilize
[fάsəlàiz]

n fossil 화석

v 화석이 되다　　**a fossilized dinosaur bone** 화석이 된 공룡 뼈

The scientist was extremely excited when he found a fossilized dinosaur egg.

20 greenhouse
[gríːnhàus]

n 온실　　**the greenhouse effect** 온실효과

Because of greenhouses, all sorts of fruit are available at any season.

---

14 교토 의정서는 탄소 배출량을 줄이는 것에 대한 협약이다. 15 인간 활동은 종종 자연의 균형을 무너뜨린다. 16 주민들은 산불을 피하려고 마을에서 대피했다. 17 그 사화산은 세계적으로 유명한 관광지가 되었다. 18 이 새 장비는 오물을 더 효율적으로 여과할 수 있다. 19 그 과학자는 화석이 된 공룡 알을 발견했을 때 극도로 흥분했다. 20 온실 덕분에 계절에 관계없이 각종 과일을 구할 수 있다.

21 habitat
[hǽbitæt]

n habitation 거주

n 서식지

a natural habitat 자연 서식지

Every day, many animals lose their habitat by deforestation.

22 humidity
[hju:mídəti]

a humid 습한
v humidify 적시다

n 습기 ⊜ moisture

absolute [relative] humidity 절대[상대] 습도

The humidity is very high in swamp areas.

23 inevitable
[inévitəbəl]

n inevitability 불가피함

a 불가피한, 필연적인 ⊜ avoidable 피할 수 있는

an inevitable conclusion 당연한 결론

We will encounter an inevitable disaster if we keep polluting the Earth.

24 irrigate
[írəgèit]

n irrigation 물을 댐, 관개

v (토지 등에) 물을 대다

irrigate farms [crops] 농장에[곡물에] 물을 대다

Volunteers tried to irrigate desert areas to make them fertile.

25 junk
[dʒʌŋk]

n 폐물 ⊜ waste, rubbish, garbage

junk food 정크 푸드, (고열량·저영양의) 불량 식품

Nowadays, people consider old things as junk too easily.

26 biodegradable
[bàioʊdigréidəbəl]

v degrade 분해되다
v biodegrade
생물 분해를 일으키다

a 자연 분해되는, 생물 분해성의

a biodegradable plastic bag 자연 분해 비닐봉지

The use of biodegradable products has increased in the past years.

27 mess
[mes]

a messy 어질러진, 지저분한

n 엉망, 혼란, 난잡

make a mess 어질러 놓다

People are concerned about the mess left behind at the beach.

---

21 삼림 개간으로 말미암아 매일 많은 동물이 서식지를 잃는다. 22 늪지대는 습도가 매우 높다. 23 우리가 지구를 계속 오염시키면 불가피한 재난에 직면하게 될 것이다. 24 자원봉사자들은 사막 지역을 비옥하게 하기 위하여 물을 대려고 노력했다. 25 요즘, 사람들은 오래된 물건을 너무 쉽게 폐물로 생각한다. 26 지난 몇 년 동안 자연 분해되는 제품의 사용이 증가했다. 27 사람들은 해변에 버려지는 쓰레기를 걱정한다.

28 **wasteland**
[wéistlæ̀nd]

ⓝ 불모지, 황무지

an industrial wasteland 산업 황무지

The once fertile farm became a wasteland after the fire.

29 **pesticide**
[péstəsàid]

ⓝ 구충제, 살충제

pesticide-free vegetables 무농약 야채

Excessive use of pesticide on crops can be harmful to people.

30 **pollutant**
[pəlú:tənt]

ⓝ **pollution** 오염

ⓝ 오염물질, 오염원

toxic air pollutants 독성이 있는 공기 오염물질

Many researchers are developing fuel with less pollutants.

31 **predator**
[prédətər]

ⓝ 포식 동물, 약탈자 ● prey 먹이

marine predators 해양 포식 동물

In every ecosystem, predators always struggle with their prey.

32 **preserve**
[prizə́:rv]

ⓝ **preservation** 보존, 보호

ⓥ 보호하다, 보존하다 ● protect

preserve a custom 관습을 보존하다

We need to change several daily habits in order to preserve the Earth.

33 **purification**
[pjùərəfikéiʃən]

ⓥ **purify** 정화하다, 청결하게 하다

ⓝ 정화, 정제 ● contamination 오염

self-purification 자연 정화
water purification system 정수 장치

It was too late to conduct any purification methods for the lake.

34 **refuge**
[réfju:dʒ]

ⓝ **refugee** 피난민

ⓝ 피난, 피난처 ● shelter

a house of refuge 빈민 수용소, 양육원

The government designated this area as a wildlife refuge.

---

28 한때 비옥했던 농장은 화재로 황무지가 되었다. 29 농작물에 살충제를 지나치게 많이 사용하면 사람들에게 해로울 수 있다. 30 많은 연구원이 오염물질이 더 적은 연료를 개발하고 있다. 31 모든 생태계에서 포식자는 항상 먹이와 치열한 싸움을 한다. 32 우리는 지구를 보호하기 위해 여러 가지 생활 습관을 바꿔야 한다. 33 그 어떤 방법으로도 호수를 정화하기에는 너무 늦었다. 34 정부가 이 지역을 야생동물 보호지역으로 지정했다.

35 □ **rubbish**
[rʌ́biʃ]

n 쓰레기　**≒** waste, garbage　　**talk rubbish** 쓸데없는 소리를 하다

Some people don't believe in global warming and think of it as rubbish.

36 □ **unchangeable**
[ʌ̀ntʃéindʒəbəl]

n unchangeability 불변

a 불변의, 변하지 않는　**⊜** changeable 변하기 쉬운

the unchangeable truth 불변의 진리

The fact that fossil fuel will be depleted someday is unchangeable.

37 □ **substitute**
[sʌ́bstitjùːt]

n substitution 대체

v 대신하다, 대리하다　**n** 대리인, 대용품　**≒** replace, replacement

substitute food 대용식

Scientists are trying to use solar power as a substitute for gasoline.

38 □ **sufficient**
[səfíʃənt]

n sufficiency 충분, 족함

a 충분한, 적당한　**≒** adequate　　**sufficient resources** 충분한 자원

People dispute whether the protection measure is sufficient or not.

39 □ **threaten**
[θrétn]

n threat 위협, 협박

v 위협하다, 협박하다　**≒** intimidate　　**a threatened species** 멸종 위기 종

In a sense, we are threatening our own lives through pollution.

40 □ **trash**
[træʃ]

n 쓰레기, 폐물　**≒** rubbish　　**a trash can** 쓰레기통

Burning trash can discharge harmful chemicals into the air.

---

35 어떤 사람들은 지구온난화를 믿지 않고, 이를 쓸데없는 걱정이라고 생각한다.　36 화석연료가 언젠가 고갈될 것이라는 사실은 변하지 않는다.　37 과학자들은 휘발유의 대용품으로 태양 에너지를 이용하려고 노력한다.　38 사람들은 보호조치가 충분한가의 여부에 대해 논쟁을 한다.　39 어떤 의미에서 우리는 환경오염을 통해 자신의 생명을 위협하고 있다.　40 쓰레기를 소각하는 것은 공기 중에 해로운 물질을 방출할 수 있다.

EXERCISE

A 다음 영어는 우리말로, 우리말은 영어로 옮기시오.

01 deforestation   _____
02 extinct   _____
03 habitat   _____
04 pesticide   _____
05 refuge   _____
06 desolate   _____

07 대신하다, 대리하다   _____
08 둘레, 원주   _____
09 균형, 평형   _____
10 습기   _____
11 오염물질, 오염원   _____
12 대홍수   _____

B 다음 빈칸에 알맞은 단어를 쓰시오.

01 threaten   ⊜ _____
02 reinforce   ⊜ _____
03 contaminate   ⊜ _____
04 predator   ⇔ _____
05 barren   ⇔ _____
06 inevitable   ⇔ _____

07 emission   ⓥ _____
08 purification   ⓥ _____
09 ecology   ⓐ _____
10 filth   ⓐ _____
11 preserve   ⓝ _____
12 evacuate   ⓝ _____

C 다음 빈칸에 들어갈 알맞은 말을 고르시오. (필요하면 형태를 바꾸시오.)

fossilize	sufficient	desertification	ecosystem	inevitable

01 Many of the farmers were saddened by the _____ of their land.

02 People should accept the fact that it is _____ to get old and die in the end.

03 The archaeologist discovered that the remains of the dinosaur had become _____.

04 In order to preserve the _____, all people must be responsible and take care of the earth.

05 The young couple had _____ funds for the purchase of their first home.

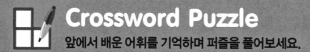

Crossword Puzzle

앞에서 배운 어휘를 기억하며 퍼즐을 풀어보세요.

Across

3 all the animals and plants in a particular area, and the way in which they are related to each other and to their environment

8 (of a species, family, or other larger group) having no living members

9 to send people away from a dangerous place to a safe place

10 shelter or protection from someone or something

Down

1 a chemical substance used to kill insects and small animals that destroy crops

2 reduction in the number or quantity of something

4 a substance that makes air, water, soil, etc. dangerously dirty, and is caused by cars, factories, etc.

5 (of land) too poor to produce much or any vegetation

6 to use something new or different instead of something else

7 to give support to an opinion, idea, or feeling, and make it stronger

_____ (주의를) 딴 데로 돌리다

_____ 발표, 출판

_____ 취재, 적용 범위

_____ 분류된, 기밀의

_____ 논쟁의 여지가 있는

_____ 위협하다

_____ 적대적인

_____ 차별, 구별

Mass Media
언론과 매체

Conflict & Dispute
갈등과 분쟁

**Expression of
Current Affairs**
시사적 표현

**Environment &
Ecology**
환경과 생태

_____ 오염시키다

_____ 멸종한

_____ 고갈, 소모

_____ 보호하다

Group & Activity
단체와 활동

War & Peace
전쟁과 평화

_____ 대표자, 대리인

_____ 협력하다

_____ 동화

_____ 상관관계

_____ 차지하다, 점령하다

_____ 넘겨주다, 항복하다

_____ 동맹, 결연

_____ 야심적인

Chapter
06

Human Life

Food, Clothing & Shelter

---

01 accommodation
[əkàmədéiʃən]

ⓥ accommodate 숙박시키다

ⓝ 숙박 시설, 편의 ⊜ housing

hotel accommodations 호텔 시설

The city is offering accommodations for flood victims.

---

02 acid
[ǽsid]

ⓝ 산 **ⓐ** 산성의, 신맛이 나는

acid rain 산성비

★ Amino acids are substances that form the basic structure of proteins.

★ The science laboratory had a strong solution of acid that was kept in a safe container.

---

03 starvation
[sta:rvéiʃən]

ⓥ starve 굶어 죽다, 굶주리다

ⓝ 기아, 아사

death by starvation 아사

Even now, there are thousands of people dying by starvation.

---

04 attic
[ǽtik]

ⓝ 다락방

an attic bedroom 다락방 침실

My parents keep items that aren't frequently used in the attic.

---

05 banquet
[bǽŋkwit]

ⓝ 연회, 진수성찬 ⊜ feast

a wedding banquet 결혼 피로연

There was a grand banquet to celebrate the city's 100th anniversary.

---

06 barn
[bá:rn]

ⓝ 헛간, 광

a cow barn 외양간

The farmer allowed the travelers to spend the night in his barn.

---

01 시 당국이 홍수 피해자들에게 숙박시설을 제공하고 있다. 02 아미노산은 단백질의 기본 구조를 형성하는 물질이다. / 과학 실험실에 안전한 용기에 보관된 강 염산 용액이 있었다. 03 지금 이 순간에도, 수천 명의 사람이 굶주림으로 죽고 있다. 04 부모님은 자주 쓰지 않는 물건들을 다락방에 보관한다. 05 시(市)의 백 주년을 축하하기 위한 성대한 연회가 열렸다. 06 농부는 여행객들이 자신의 헛간에서 하룻밤 잘 수 있게 허락했다.

07 dormitory
[dɔ́:rmətɔ̀:ri]

ⓝ 기숙사   **a dormitory inspector** 기숙사 사감

I live in a school dormitory on campus.

08 spice
[spais]

ⓐ spicy 향신료를 넣은, 매콤한

ⓝ 양념, 향신료, 풍미   **a spice jar** 양념 병

★ Salt is a basic spice that everybody has in his/her home.
★ Variety is the spice of life.

09 broth
[brɔ(:)θ]

ⓝ 수프, 국물   **beef broth** 쇠고기 수프

My mother used to make me chicken broth when I was sick.

10 chef
[ʃef]

ⓝ 주방장, 요리사   **a pastry chef** 제빵사

The chef came up with a new dish that suited every single guest.

11 chimney
[tʃímni]

ⓝ 굴뚝   **chimney sweeping** 굴뚝 청소

I always wondered how Santa enters a house that has no chimney.

12 chore
[tʃɔ:r]

ⓝ 지루한 일, 잡일 **ⓢ** task, duty   **domestic chores** 집안일

It is unfair for only women to do the chores around the house.

13 corridor
[kɔ́:ridər]

ⓝ 복도 **ⓢ** hallway, aisle   **an empty corridor** 텅 빈 복도

My room is at the end of the corridor upstairs.

14 diaper
[dáiəpər]

ⓝ 기저귀   **a disposable diaper** 일회용 기저귀

Babies just start to cry when they need to change their diapers.

---

07 나는 캠퍼스 내에 있는 학교 기숙사에 산다. 08 소금은 모든 사람들이 집에 기본적으로 가지고 있는 양념이다. / 〈속담〉 다양함은 인생의 양념이다. (= 변화는 인생을 즐겁게 한다.) 09 어머니는 내가 아플 때 닭고기 수프를 끓여주시곤 했다. 10 요리사는 모든 손님이 만족할 수 있는 새로운 요리를 생각해냈다. 11 나는 항상 산타 할아버지가 굴뚝이 없는 집에는 어떻게 들어가는지 궁금했다. 12 집안의 허드렛일을 여자만 도맡아서 하는 것은 불공평하다. 13 내 방은 위층 복도 맨 끝에 있다. 14 아기들은 기저귀를 갈아야 할 때 무작정 울기 시작한다.

15 ☑ **domestic**
[douméstik]

ⓐ 가정의, 국내의 　⊜ foreign 외국의, 외국산의

the domestic market 국내시장

★ In some countries, asking too much about domestic affairs is rude.

★ The domestic economy is steadily recovering each day.

16 ☑ **estate**
[istéit]

ⓝ 소유지, 재산 　⊜ property 재산

real estate 부동산

★ Public schools along with other public facilities are country estates.

★ Steve has accumulated a considerable estate over the years.

17 ☑ **leftover**
[léftòuvər]

ⓝ 남은 음식, 나머지

leftover food 먹고 남은 음식

Thanks to the refrigerator, leftovers can be stored for a long time.

18 ☑ **famine**
[tǽmin]

ⓝ 굶주림, 기아

a potato famine 감자 흉작

Many low developed countries are still suffering from famine.

19 ☑ **faucet**
[fɔ́ːsit]

ⓝ 수도꼭지 　⊜ tap

a water faucet 수도꼭지

I couldn't shave this morning because my water faucet wasn't working.

20 ☑ **fiber**
[fáibər]

ⓝ 섬유, 실

dietary fiber 식이섬유

Bathing suits are made of an elastic fiber to be water-resistant.

21 ☑ **ceiling**
[síːliŋ]

ⓝ 천장

a high ceiling 높은 천장

Painting the ceiling proved nearly impossible without a ladder.

---

15 어떤 나라에서는 가정사에 대해 너무 꼬치꼬치 캐묻는 것은 무례한 일이다. / 국내 경제가 매일 꾸준하게 회복하고 있다. 16 공공시설을 비롯하여 공립학교도 모두 국가 소유지다. / Steve는 수년간 상당한 재산을 모았다. 17 냉장고 덕분에 남은 음식을 오랫동안 보관할 수 있게 되었다. 18 여러 저개발 국가들은 여전히 굶주림으로 고통받고 있다. 19 오늘 아침에 수도꼭지가 제대로 작동하지 않아서 면도할 수 없었다. 20 수영복은 물에 강하도록 탄력이 있는 섬유로 만들어진다. 21 사다리 없이 천장을 칠하는 것은 거의 불가능했다.

22 garment
[gáːrmənt]

n 의류, 옷 **≡** clothes

woolen garments 모직 의류

To compliment a lady's garments is part of being a gentleman.

---

23 gourmet
[gúərmei]

a (음식이) 고급인, 값비싼 **n** 미식가

gourmet food 고급 음식

★ The hotel offers a gourmet menu of international foods.

★ Gourmets that are specialized in wine are called sommeliers.

---

24 grain
[grein]

n 곡물, 곡류

a grain of rice 쌀 한 톨

For a long time, rice has been the most important grain to people living in Asia.

---

25 greasy
[gríːsi]

n grease 지방, 유지

a 기름진, 기름이 묻은

greasy food 기름진 음식

Western food seems to be more greasy than that of the Eastern.

---

26 decoration
[dèkəréiʃən]

v decorate 장식하다

n 장식

interior decoration 실내 장식

For Christmas decorations, we hung long lines of light bulbs on trees.

---

27 leakage
[líːkidʒ]

v leak 누출되다, 새다

n 누출

oil leakage 기름 누출

We need to make sure that there is not any gas leakage at all times.

---

28 litter
[lítər]

n 쓰레기 **v** 쓰레기를 버리다

No Litter. 쓰레기를 버리지 마시오.

★ The community decided to clear the litter from the streets of their neighborhood.

★ You will be fined if you litter the streets.

---

22 숙녀의 옷을 칭찬하는 것은 신사가 지녀야 하는 예절이다. 23 그 호텔은 세계적인 음식들로 구성된 고급 메뉴를 제공한다. / 포도주를 전문으로 하는 미식가를 일컬어 소믈리에라고 한다. 24 오랜 세월 동안 쌀은 아시아에 사는 사람들 가장 중요한 곡식이었다. 25 서양 음식은 동양 음식보다 더 기름진 것 같다. 26 우리는 크리스마스 장식으로 나무에 줄로 연결된 전구를 걸었다. 27 우리는 항상 가스 누출이 없는지 확인해야 한다. 28 그 지자체는 인근 거리의 쓰레기를 치우기로 했다. / 길거리에 쓰레기를 버리면 벌금을 물게 될 것이다.

29 ☑ lodge
[lɑdʒ]

ⓝ 산장, 별장, 여관 **ⓥ** 숙박하다, 숙박시키다   **lodge for the night** 하룻밤 묵다

★ The family spends many summers at their country lodge where they can enjoy water activities.

★ The lodging house where we stayed at was small and cozy.

30 ☑ recipe
[résəpìː]

ⓝ 조리법, 비법   **a recipe book** 요리책

You can substitute oil for butter according to this recipe.

31 ☑ nourish
[nə́ːriʃ]

ⓝ nourishment 자양분

ⓥ 자양분을 주다, 기르다   **ⓔ** nurture, feed

nourish an infant with milk 아기에게 우유를 먹이다

Women need to have nourishing food after they give birth.

32 ☑ paste
[peist]

ⓝ 반죽, 연고 **ⓥ** 붙이다   **tomato paste** 토마토소스

The art teacher instructed the children to paste the different shapes onto their colored paper.

33 ☑ mop
[mɑp]

ⓝ 대걸레 **ⓥ** 대걸레로 닦다   **mop the floor** (대걸레로) 바닥을 닦다

I brought a mop to clean the juice I spilt on the floor.

34 ☑ texture
[tékstʃər]

ⓝ 질감   **ⓔ** surface, feel   **a smooth texture** 부드러운 질감

She knew the dress wasn't really made of silk by its coarse texture.

35 ☑ vegetarian
[vèdʒətɛ́əriən]

ⓝ 채식주의자   **vegetarian food** 채식요리

Our restaurant has a special dish for those who are vegetarians.

---

29 가족은 물놀이를 즐길 수 있는 시골 별장에서 많은 여름을 보낸다. / 우리가 머물렀던 하숙집은 작고 안락했다. 30 이 요리법에 따르면, 버터 대신 식용유를 써도 된다. 31 여성들은 출산하고 나서는 영양가 높은 음식을 섭취해야 한다. 32 미술 선생님은 아이들에게 색종이에 다른 모양을 붙이라고 지시했다. 33 나는 바닥에 흘린 주스를 닦기 위해 대걸레를 가져왔다. 34 그녀는 드레스의 거친 질감을 통해 실제로는 그것이 비단으로 만든 것이 아니라는 것을 알았다. 35 우리 식당에는 채식주의자를 위한 특별 메뉴가 있다.

36 residence
[rézidəns]
v reside 거주하다

n 주거, 거주　　**permanent [temporary] residence** 영구[임시] 거주

I plan to take up residence in the countryside after my retirement.

37 resident
[rézidənt]
a residential 거주에 적합한

n 거주자 **a** 거주하는, 고유의, 내재의　　**resident registration** 주민 등록

★ The local residents were strongly against the development plan.

★ Every person has both resident evil and goodness within him or her.

38 sewage
[súːidʒ]
n sewer 하수구

n 하수　　**a sewage system** 하수도

The river has been contaminated by household sewage.

39 shelter
[ʃéltər]

n 은신처, 피난처 **=** refuge　　**a homeless shelter** 노숙자 쉼터

We had to take shelter from the sudden rain under a tree.

40 season
[síːzən]
n seasoning 조미, 양념

v 양념하다 **=** flavor

season the beef with salt and pepper 소금, 후추로 소고기를 양념하다

The chef knew how to season each dish to create the most flavorful dish possible.

36 나는 은퇴하고 나서 시골에 살 계획이다. 37 인근 주민들은 개발 계획에 강하게 반발했다. / 모든 사람은 내재적 선과 악이 모두 있다. 38 강이 생활 하수로 오염되었다. 39 우리는 나무 밑에서 소나기를 피해야 했다. 40 요리사는 요리마다 어떻게 양념하면 가장 맛있는 요리를 만들 수 있는지 알고 있었다.

EXERCISE

A 다음 영어는 우리말로, 우리말은 영어로 옮기시오.

01 famine _____

02 acid _____

03 lodge _____

04 gourmet _____

05 chimney _____

06 resident _____

07 섬유, 실 _____

08 헛간, 광 _____

09 질감 _____

10 지루한 일, 잡일 _____

11 하수 _____

12 곡물, 곡류 _____

B 다음 빈칸에 알맞은 단어를 쓰시오.

01 corridor ⊜ _____

02 estate ⊜ _____

03 accommodation ⊜ _____

04 garment ⊜ _____

05 nourish ⊜ _____

06 banquet ⊜ _____

07 decoration Ⓥ _____

08 leakage Ⓥ _____

09 starvation Ⓥ _____

10 spice ⓐ _____

11 season Ⓝ _____

12 greasy Ⓝ _____

C 다음 빈칸에 들어갈 알맞은 말을 고르시오. (필요하면 형태를 바꾸시오.)

| starvation | dormitory | domestic | greasy | litter |

01 The table was covered with _____ dishes.

02 Do not _____ in public places, but rather use the garbage cans.

03 Teenagers look forward to living on their own in their college _____.

04 Any kind of _____ abuse should be reported to the local police station.

05 Despite food aid from rich countries, _____ is a major issue of global concern in Africa.

Crossword Puzzle

앞에서 배운 어휘를 기억하며 퍼즐을 풀어보세요.

정답

Across

1 a place to live, considered as one of the basic needs of life

3 suffering or death caused by lack of food

4 a situation in which a large number of people have little or no food for a long time and many people die

6 relating to or happening in one particular country and not involving any other countries

10 a place for someone to stay, live or work

11 the way a surface or material feels when you touch it, especially how smooth or rough it is

Down

2 the accidental admission or escape of liquid or gas through a hole or crack

5 someone who lives or stays in a particular place

7 a long narrow passage on a train or between rooms in a building, with doors leading off it

8 the mixture of waste from the human body and used water, that is carried away from houses by pipes under the ground

9 a soft thick mixture that can easily be shaped or spread

Leisure & Sports

---

01 ☑ aging
[éidʒiŋ]

ⓥⓝ age 나이를 먹다; 나이

ⓝ 나이 먹음, 노화　　　　　　　**an aging society** 고령화 사회

There is nothing in the world to stop the process of aging.

---

02 ☑ anniversary
[ænəvə́:rsəri]

ⓝ 기념일, 기념제　　　　　　**a wedding anniversary** 결혼기념일

Today, I will be celebrating my parent's 30th wedding anniversary.

---

03 ☑ vital
[váitl]

ⓝ **vitality** 생명력

ⓐ 생명의, 절대로 필요한　⊜ essential 절대로 필요한
vital signs (혈압, 맥박, 호흡 등의) 생명 징후, 바이탈 사인

Exercising on a regular basis gives vital energy to our lives.

---

04 ☑ attraction
[ətrǽkʃən]

ⓥ **attract** 매혹시키다

ⓝ 매력, 유혹　　　　　　　　**a tourist attraction** 관광 명소

The main attraction of the show was a wonderful stunt by dolphins.

---

05 ☑ belly
[béli]

ⓝ 배, 복부　　　　　　　　　　**a belly button** 배꼽
belly dancing 밸리댄싱

I started to go to the gym to get rid of my beer belly.

---

06 ☑ competitive
[kəmpétətiv]

ⓥ **compete** 경쟁하다
ⓝ **competition** 경쟁

ⓐ 경쟁의, 경쟁에 의한　　　　**a competitive spirit** 경쟁심

I prefer sports that are competitive such as basketball.

---

01 노화가 진행되는 것을 막을 방법은 세상에 없다. 02 오늘 나는 부모님의 30주년 결혼기념일을 축하 해드릴 것이다. 03 규칙적인 운동은 우리 생활에 활력을 준다. 04 쇼에서 가장 큰 흥밋거리는 돌고래가 펼친 멋진 묘기였다. 05 나는 맥주로 생긴 뱃살을 없애려고 체육관에 다니기 시작했다. 06 나는 농구처럼 경쟁하는 운동을 좋아한다.

07 □ corporal
[kɔ́ːrpərəl]

ⓐ 육체의, 신체의　　　　　　　**corporal punishment** 체벌

Some people put more value in mental stability than corporal pleasure.

08 □ endurance
[indʒúərəns]

ⓥ endure 견디다, 참다

ⓝ 인내력, 지구력　　　　　　　**physical endurance** 신체 지구력

He must have powers of endurance or he is just lazy.

09 □ cruise
[kruːz]

ⓥ 순항하다 ⓝ 선박여행　ⓔ voyage, sail　　**a cruise ship** 유람선

★ With the new car, the driver was able to cruise smoothly along the highway.

★ During summer vacation, I went on a cruise around Europe.

10 □ excursion
[ikskə́ːrʒən]

ⓝ 소풍, 유람　　　　　　　**an excursion train** 유람 열차

I went on an excursion to the park near my house with my family last Sunday.

11 □ feast
[fiːst]

ⓝ 축제, 축하연　　　　　　　**a feast day** 잔칫날

His family gave a feast celebrating Mr. Parnell's 60th birthday.

12 □ frail
[freil]

ⓝ frailty 약함

ⓐ 허약한, 무른　　　　　　　**frail health** 허약한 건강상태

I try to keep myself busy to prevent becoming frail in mind.

13 □ gamble
[ɡǽmbəl]

ⓝ gambling 도박, 내기

ⓥ 도박을 하다, 내기를 하다　　　**a gambling casino** 도박장

It is only legal to gamble in authorized areas like casinos.

---

07 어떤 사람들은 육체적 쾌락보다 정신적 안정감에 더 큰 가치를 둔다. 08 그는 대단한 인내력을 가졌거나, 매우 게으른 것이다. 09 새 차를 탄 운전사는 고속도로를 따라 미끄러지듯이 달릴 수 있었다. / 지난 여름방학 때 나는 유람선을 타고 유럽을 돌았다. 10 나는 지난 일요일에 가족과 집 근처에 있는 공원으로 소풍을 갔다. 11 Parnell 씨의 가족은 그의 60세 생일을 축하하는 잔치를 마련했다. 12 나는 정신적으로 약해지지 않기 위해 바쁘게 지내려고 노력한다. 13 카지노와 같이 허가된 장소에서 하는 도박만이 합법적이다.

14 gymnastics
[dʒimnǽstiks]

ⓝ 체조, 체육　　　　　　　**gymnastics competition** 체조 경기

Gymnastics is scientifically designed to help develop a healthy body.

15 lame
[leim]

ⓐ 절름발이의, 불구의　　**a lame duck president** 정권 말기의 (권력이 없는) 대통령

I took my dog to a veterinarian as soon as I noticed he became lame.

16 leisurely
[líːʒərli]

ⓝ leisure 여가, 틈

ⓐ 느긋한, 여유 있는　　　　　　**a leisurely pace** 한가한 걸음

I played a leisurely game of golf with one of my friends last Sunday.

17 limb
[lim]

ⓝ 팔다리　　　　　　　　**an artificial limb** 의족

My limbs felt like lead after my first day at the gym.

18 luggage
[lʌ́gidʒ]

ⓝ 수화물, 여행용 짐　　　**check in one's luggage** 짐을 부치다

The airplane was so small that we had to carry our luggage on board.

19 magician
[mədʒíʃən]

ⓝ magic 마술

ⓝ 마법사, 마술사　　　　　**a magician of words** 언어의 마술사

For a hobby, I'm taking lessons to be an amateur magician.

20 repose
[ripóuz]

ⓐ reposeful 평온한, 조용한

ⓝ 휴식 **ⓥ** 쉬다, 쉬게 하다　**ⓔ** rest 휴식, 쉬다　　**seek repose** 휴식하다

★ The old lady was able to take repose at the assisted-living facility.

★ I'll be fine if I repose in bed for a while.

---

14 체조는 건강한 발육을 돕기 위해 과학적으로 만들어졌다. 15 나는 강아지가 다리를 저는 것을 보자마자 수의사에게 데려갔다. 16 나는 지난 일요일에 친구와 느긋하게 골프 한 게임을 쳤다. 17 체육관에 다니기 시작한 첫날에 팔다리가 납덩이처럼 무거웠다. 18 우리는 비행기가 너무 작아서 짐을 들고 타야 했다. 19 나는 취미 삼아 아마추어 마술사가 되기 위한 수업을 받는다. 20 노부인은 노인 생활 시설에서 휴양할 수 있었다. / 잠깐 침대에 누워서 쉬면 괜찮아질 거야.

---

21 ☑ **meager**
[míːgər]

ⓐ 빈약한, 야윈 ⊜ thin 얇은, 야윈   **a meager salary** 박한 봉급

He supplemented his meager income by doing various jobs.

---

22 ☑ **mobile**
[móubəl]

ⓝ **mobility** 가동성, 이동성

ⓐ 이동할 수 있는, 휴대가 용이한 ⊜ portable   **a mobile phone** 휴대전화

People today can watch movies anywhere on their mobile phones.

---

23 ☑ **organ**
[ɔ́ːrgən]

ⓥ **organize** 조직하다

ⓝ 장기, 기관   **vital organs** 신체 중요 장기

Organ transplanting includes replacing a kidney, heart or lung.

---

24 ☑ **palm**
[pɑːm]

ⓝ 손바닥   **read one's palm** ~의 손금을 보다

He noticed that the sweat in his palm was cool now.

---

25 ☑ **pant**
[pænt]

ⓥ 숨차다, 헐떡거리다 ⊜ gasp   **pant for breath** 숨을 헐떡거리다

On long-distance races, avoid panting by keeping a steady pace.

---

26 ☑ **physiology**
[fìziálədʒi]

ⓐ **physiological**
생리학, 생리적인

ⓝ 생리학   **exercise physiology** 운동 생리학

Physiology helped boost sports science greatly in several ways.

---

27 ☑ **posture**
[pástʃər]

ⓝ 자세, 몸가짐   **body posture** 몸의 자세

Typically in all sports, posture is the most important thing to master.

---

21 그는 다양한 일을 하여 부족한 수입을 보충했다. 22 오늘날 사람들은 휴대전화로 어디서든지 영화를 볼 수 있다. 23 장기 이식은 신장, 심장, 폐 등을 교체하는 것을 포함한다. 24 그는 자기의 손안에 땀이 이제 식었음을 알았다. 25 장거리 경주를 할 때는 일정한 페이스를 유지하여 숨이 차지 않도록 하라. 26 생리학은 여러 방법으로 스포츠 과학이 크게 발전할 수 있게 도왔다. 27 대체로 모든 스포츠에서 자세는 익혀야 하는 가장 중요한 것이다.

28 random
[rǽndəm]

ⓐ 임의의, 닥치는 대로의　　　　　　　　　**a random search** 무작위 조사

Today's contestants were chosen at random from the audience.

29 recess
[ríːses]

ⓝ 휴식, 휴가　**ⓢ** break　　　　　　　　**be in recess** 휴식 중이다

At lunchtime, my colleagues and I often take a recess at a nearby park.

30 recreational
[rèkriéiʃənəl]

ⓝ recreation 휴양, 레크리에이션

ⓐ 휴양의, 오락의　　　　　　　　**recreational purposes** 오락용 목적

Sports is one of the most important recreational activities in modern society.

31 roam
[roum]

ⓥ 배회하다, 방랑하다　**ⓢ** wander　**roam about the forest** 숲속을 돌아다니다

I took a short vacation from work and roamed about the country.

32 slumber
[slʌ́mbər]

ⓝ 잠　**ⓢ** sleep　　　　　　　　　　**a deep slumber** 깊은 잠

I usually stay at home on weekends and just enjoy my deep slumber.

33 spectator
[spékteitər]

ⓥ spectate (경기 등을) 구경하다

ⓝ 구경꾼, 관객　**ⓢ** bystander, onlooker

　　　　　　　　　　the seats for the spectators 관중석

The spectators poured out of the stadium onto the street.

34 spinal
[spáinl]

ⓝ spine 척추

ⓐ 척추의, 등뼈의　　　　　　　　　**a spinal injury** 척추 손상

The doctor recommended a special exercise for my spinal injury.

---

28 오늘 경기 참가자들은 관객 중에서 무작위로 선발되었다. 29 나는 점심시간에 직장 동료와 가까운 공원에서 종종 휴식을 취한다. 30 스포츠는 현대 사회에서 가장 중요한 오락 활동 중 하나다. 31 나는 직장에 잠시 휴가를 내고 지방을 두루 돌아다녔다. 32 나는 주말에 대체로 집에 있으면서 잠을 푹 자는 걸 즐긴다. 33 관객이 경기장에서 거리로 쏟아져 나왔다. 34 의사는 내 척추 부상의 치료를 위해 특수한 운동을 권했다.

35 sprint
[sprint]

n sprinter 단거리 주자

n 단거리 경주, 전력 질주   **a sprint race** 단거리 경주

Most people go on light jogs rather than sprints for leisure sports.

36 onlooker
[ánlùkər]

a onlooking 방관적인

n 방관자, 구경꾼   **e** spectator   **a curious onlooker** 호기심 많은 구경꾼

Although there were many onlookers, nobody reached out to help me.

37 thigh
[θai]

n 넓적다리   **thigh muscles** 허벅지근육

Maria took yoga lessons expecting it to make her thighs thinner.

38 thumb
[θʌm]

n 엄지손가락   **be all thumbs** 손재주가 없다

The critics praised the new action film and gave it two thumbs up.

39 tread
[tred]

v 밟다, 걷다   **e** step, walk   **tread under foot** 짓밟다, 경멸하다

My partner kept treading on my foot during the dance party!

40 versus
[və́ːrsəs]

prep 대(對), ~와 대비하여

capitalism versus communism 자본주의 대 공산주의

Everybody was greatly interested in games of Korea versus Japan.

---

35 사람들은 대부분 레저스포츠로 전력질주보다는 가벼운 조깅을 즐긴다.   36 구경하는 사람들은 많았지만, 누구도 나를 도우려 하지 않았다.
37 Maria는 허벅지가 얇아질 것이라는 기대로 요가를 배우기 시작했다.   38 비평가들은 새 액션 영화에 대해 칭찬을 했으며, 양 엄지손가락을 세웠다.
(= 극찬했다) 39 내 파트너가 댄스파티에서 계속 내 발을 밟았어! 40 모두가 한국 대 일본 경기에 큰 관심을 보였다.

EXERCISE

A 다음 영어는 우리말로, 우리말은 영어로 옮기시오.

01 anniversary _____

02 thigh _____

03 leisurely _____

04 versus _____

05 random _____

06 excursion _____

07 육체의, 신체의 _____

08 이동할 수 있는 _____

09 잠 _____

10 자세, 몸가짐 _____

11 휴양의, 오락의 _____

12 도박을 하다 _____

B 다음 빈칸에 알맞은 단어를 쓰시오.

01 repose ⊜ _____

02 spectator ⊜ _____

03 roam ⊜ _____

04 vital ⊜ _____

05 meager ⊜ _____

06 cruise ⊜ _____

07 competitive ⓥ _____

08 attraction ⓥ _____

09 physiology ⓐ _____

10 onlooker ⓐ _____

11 spinal ⓝ _____

12 frail ⓝ _____

C 다음 빈칸에 들어갈 알맞은 말을 고르시오. (필요하면 형태를 바꾸시오.)

vital	limb	meager	roam	endurance

01 Wounded soldiers of war often have lost one of their _____.

02 The wild buffalos _____ the fields in search of food and mates.

03 Water is _____ to the existence of all living organisms on the earth.

04 A marathon runner needs to build his _____ if he is to run for a long period of time.

05 To supplement her _____ income as a singer, Martha works as a waitress.

Across

2 a time during the day or year when no work is done, especially in parliament, law courts, etc.

6 a date on which something special or important happened in a previous year

9 weak and delicate

Down

1 relating to or denoting activity done for enjoyment when one is not working

3 the branch of biology that deals with the normal functions of living organisms and their parts.

4 the ability to continue doing something difficult or painful over a long period of time

5 to play games of chance for money; bet

7 extremely important and necessary for something to succeed or exist

8 to walk or travel, usually for a long time, with no clear purpose or direction

Occupation & Asset

---

01 absentee
[ǽbsəntíː]

ⓐ absent 결석한

ⓝ 부재자, 결석자   **an absentee vote** 부재자 투표

Before the meeting, there was briefing for the absentees of last week.

---

02 accumulate
[əkjúːmjəlèit]

ⓝ accumulation 축적

ⓐ accumulative
축적하는, 누적적인

ⓥ 모으다, 쌓다   **⊜** build up   **accumulate knowledge** 지식을 쌓다

I have to pay off the interest that accumulated over the past few years.

---

03 profession
[prəféʃən]

ⓐ ⓝ professional
직업의, 전문의; 전문가

ⓝ (교사 · 문필가 등 학문적 소양을 필요로 하는) 직업

            the teaching profession 교직

The Richards have been practicing medicine as a family profession.

---

04 affluent
[ǽflu(ː)ənt]

ⓝ affluence 풍족

ⓐ 풍족한   **⊜** poor 가난한   **an affluent society** 풍요로운 사회
      the life style of the affluent 부유한 사람들의 생활방식

I work as a clerk in a shop located in the affluent district of the city.

---

05 allowance
[əláuəns]

ⓥ allow 허락하다, 지급하다

ⓝ 수당, 용돈, 허용 **⊜** pocket money 용돈 **a daily allowance** 매일 주는 용돈

★ Some countries give unemployment allowance until one finds a job.

★ There is a baggage allowance for each person that boards this plane.

---

06 blacksmith
[blǽksmìθ]

ⓝ 대장장이   **a blacksmith's shop** 대장간

In the past, the main job of a blacksmith was to repair horseshoes.

---

01 회의 전에 지난주에 참석하지 못했던 사람들을 위한 브리핑이 있었다. 02 나는 지난 몇 년간 쌓인 이자를 갚아야 한다. 03 Richard의 집안은 대대로 의료업을 직업으로 삼아 왔다. 04 나는 도시의 부유한 지역에 있는 가게에서 점원으로 일한다. 05 몇몇 국가에서는 직업을 구할 때까지 실업수당을 지급한다. / 이 항공기는 각각의 승객에게 할당되는 수하물 허용량이 있다. 06 과거에 대장장이의 주된 업무는 말편자를 수리하는 것이었다.

---

07 ☑ **broke**
[brouk]

ⓐ 파산한, 무일푼의

go broke (회사 등이) 파산하다, 부도나다
flat broke 완전히 파산한

He went completely broke after that foolish investment in stock.

---

08 ☑ **usher**
[ʌ́ʃər]

ⓥ 안내하다 ⓝ 안내원, 접수원 ⊜ guide 안내하다, 안내원
usher the guests into the room 손님들을 방 안으로 안내하다

★ During the summer vacation, James worked at the theater, ushering people to their seats.

★ On weekends, I have a part time job at the wedding hall as an usher.

---

09 ☑ **errand**
[érənd]

ⓝ 심부름, 볼일, 용건

run an errand for ~가 시킨 심부름을 하다

Susan got mad because her boss made her do his personal errands.

---

10 ☑ **expenditure**
[ikspénditʃər]

ⓥ expend 지출하다

ⓝ 지출, 소비 ⊜ expense, spending **a capital expenditure** 자본 지출

The accountant pointed out our expenditures that were unnecessary.

---

11 ☑ **extravagant**
[ikstrǽvəgənt]

ⓝ extravagance 사치, 낭비

ⓐ 돈을 함부로 쓰는, 낭비벽이 있는 ⊜ wasteful
an extravagant gift 사치스러운 선물

The woman thought her husband was too extravagant with money.

---

12 ☑ **vocational**
[voukéiʃənəl]

ⓝ vocation 직업

ⓐ 직업의, 직업상의 **vocational education** 직업 교육

The company is using a vocational aptitude test for this year's employment.

---

13 ☑ **fiscal**
[fískəl]

🆎 fiscally 재정상, 회계상

ⓐ 재정의, 회계의 ⊜ financial **a fiscal year** 회계 연도
a fiscal crisis 재정 위기

Experts expect the new fiscal policy will boost the economy.

---

07 그는 주식에 어리석은 투자를 한 후 완전히 파산해버렸다. 08 James는 여름 방학 동안, 극장에서 사람들을 자리로 안내하는 일을 했다. / 나는 주말마다 예식장에서 안내원 아르바이트를 한다. 09 Susan은 상사가 개인적인 심부름을 시켜서 화가 났다. 10 회계사가 우리의 불필요한 지출을 지적해주었다. 11 여자는 자신의 남편이 돈을 너무 함부로 쓴다고 생각했다. 12 올해 회사채용 시험으로 직업 적성 검사를 실시하고 있다. 13 전문가들은 새로운 재정 정책이 경제에 활력을 넣을 것으로 기대한다.

14 frugal
[frú:gəl]

ⓝ frugality 절약, 검소

ⓐ 간소한, 절약하는

a frugal life 검소한 생활

My wife told me that we needed to be more frugal to buy our own house.

15 gross
[grous]

ⓐ (비용, 세금 등을 빼기 전) 모두 합친, 전체의 ⓢ whole, entire

the gross amount 총액

gross domestic product(GDP) 국내 총생산

The wealth of a country is measured by the gross national product.

16 impoverish
[impávəriʃ]

ⓝ impoverishment 가난

ⓥ 가난하게 하다, (질을) 저하시키다

be impoverished by war 전쟁으로 황폐해지다

★ The CEO worked up to his position from an impoverished background.

★ The soil was impoverished by excess use of chemical fertilizers.

17 janitor
[dʒǽnətər]

ⓝ 경비, 관리인 ⓢ caretaker

a school janitor 학교 관리인

The janitors have night shifts to secure the building at all times.

18 dismiss
[dismís]

ⓝ dismissal 면직, 해고

ⓥ 해고하다, 해산하다, 잊어버리다

dismiss oneself from office 공직에서 물러나다

★ The company dismisses its employees in cases of gross misconduct.

★ He tried to dismiss the suspicions from his mind.

19 thrifty
[θrífti]

ⓝ thrift 검약, 검소
ⓥ thrive 번창하다, 번영하다

ⓐ 아끼는, 검소한

a thrifty man 검소한 남자

Ever since I was a kid, I have been told to live a thrifty life.

---

14 아내가 내게 우리가 집을 장만하려면 더 검소해져야 한다고 말했다. 15 나라의 부는 국민 총생산으로 측정된다. 16 그 CEO는 가난한 배경에서 노력을 통해 현재 위치까지 올라왔다. / 과도한 화학비료의 사용으로 토양이 황폐해졌다. 17 관리인은 항시 건물을 지켜야 하기 때문에 야간 교대 근무를 한다. 18 그 회사는 중대한 실책을 범했을 경우에 한해서 직원을 해고한다. / 그는 마음속에서 의혹을 지워 버리려고 애썼다. 19 나는 어렸을 때부터 검소하게 생활하라는 말을 많이 들어왔다.

20 low-budget
[loubʌ́dʒit]

ⓐ 저예산의   **a low-budget film** 저예산 영화

Our low-budget production is looking for talented young directors.

21 master
[mǽstər]

ⓝ 대가, 거장 ⓥ 숙련하다   **a master of disguise** 변장의 달인

★ The man was known to be the master of computer graphics.

★ The young child was able to master the new video game after an hour of playing.

22 deprivation
[dèprəvéiʃən]

ⓥ deprive 빼앗다, 해임시키다

ⓝ 상실, 파면, 빈곤

deprivation caused by unemployment 실업으로 야기된 빈곤

We estimated that most of them had died from starvation or deprivation.

23 nuisance
[njúːsəns]

ⓝ 성가심, 방해 ⊜ trouble, bother   **a public nuisance** 공적인 폐해

Phone calls in the middle of the night are a real nuisance.

24 occupation
[àkjəpéiʃən]

ⓥ occupy 점령하다, 종사사키다

ⓝ 직업 ⊜ job, employment   **out of occupation** 실업 중인

Please state your name, age, and occupation on the form.

25 opening
[óupəniŋ]

ⓝ 공석, 개방   **a job opening** 일자리

★ There aren't enough job openings for everybody looking for a job.

★ The market opening is small, but it seems like a good opportunity.

26 paycheck
[péitʃèk]

ⓝ 급료, 임금   **a monthly paycheck** 월급

This job is very tiresome and harsh, but promises a fat paycheck.

---

20 우리 저예산 제작사는 재능 있는 젊은 감독들을 찾고 있다. 21 그 남자는 컴퓨터 그래픽의 대가로 알려졌다. / 그 어린 아이는 새로운 게임을 한 시간 동안 한 후에 그 게임의 사용법을 모두 익힐 수 있다. 22 우리는 그들 대부분이 기아나 빈곤으로 사망했다고 추정했다. 23 한밤중에 걸려오는 전화는 매우 성가시다. 24 그 양식에 당신의 이름, 나이, 직업을 기술하세요. 25 직업을 구하는 모든 이들에게 돌아갈 만큼 일자리가 충분하지 않다. / 시장 개방은 소규모이지만, 좋은 기회인 것 같다. 26 이 일은 매우 고되고 거칠지만, 두둑한 임금을 보장한다.

27 ☑ peasant
[pézənt]

ⓝ 소작농   **a peasant community** 소작농 사회

In the past, nobles didn't care about working conditions for peasants.

28 ☑ pension
[pénʃən]

ⓝ pensioner 연금 수령자

ⓝ 연금   **ⓢ** welfare, benefit   **a pension fund** 연금 기금

After retirement, I plan on living off governmental pensions.

29 ☑ plumber
[plʌ́mər]

ⓝ 배관공   **a master plumber** 솜씨가 뛰어난 배관공

I had to call a plumber because I couldn't fix the water pipes myself.

30 ☑ teller
[télər]

ⓝ (은행의) 금전 출납원   **ATM (automated teller machine)** 현금인출기

He told the bank teller he would like to open an account.

31 ☑ property
[prápərti]

ⓝ 재산, 자산   **ⓢ** possession, asset   **private property** 사적재산

This public facility is the property of the Korean government.

32 ☑ compensate
[kámpənsèit]

ⓝ compensation 보상

ⓥ 보상하다   **ⓢ** make up for   **compensate for a loss** 손해를 배상하다

My boss told me he would compensate me for working overtime.

33 ☑ retirement
[ritáiərmənt]

ⓥ retire 은퇴하다, 퇴직하다

ⓝ 은퇴, 퇴직   **a retirement pension** 퇴직 연금

I'm having a hard time deciding at what age my retirement should be.

---

27 과거에 귀족들은 소작농의 노동환경에 대해 신경 쓰지 않았다. 28 나는 은퇴 후에 국가 연금을 받으며 살 계획이다. 29 나는 수도관을 직접 수리할 수 없었기 때문에 배관공을 불러야 했다. 30 그는 은행원에게 계좌를 개설하고 싶다고 말했다. 31 이 공공시설은 한국 정부의 소유다. 32 직장상사가 나에게 초과 근무한 것을 보상해 주겠다고 이야기했다. 33 나는 몇 살에 은퇴할지 정하는 데 어려움을 겪고 있다.

34 revenue
[révənjùː]

ⓝ 소득, 수익 **⊜** income

advertising revenue 광고 수입

Most of the government's revenue came from the export of oil.

35 self-employed
[sélfimplɔ́id]

ⓐ 자영업의, 자유업의

a self-employed operation 자영업

I plan to become self-employed after working at a firm for five years.

36 servant
[sə́ːrvənt]

ⓝ 고용인, 하인 **⊜** slave, maid

a civil servant 공무원

Priests are people who dedicate themselves as servants of God.

37 spare
[spɛər]

ⓐ 여분의 **ⓥ** 절약하다, 할애하다 **⊜** extra 여분의

spare time 여가

★ The spare tire was kept in the trunk of the car to be used when needed.

★ Tom asked me if I could spare some time to help with his project.

38 stingy
[stíndʒi]

ⓐ 인색한, 너무 아끼는 **⊜** generous 잘 베푸는, 관대한

a stingy person 구두쇠

Sometimes, it's rude to be too stingy to other people.

39 subsidy
[sʌ́bsidi]

ⓥ subsidize 보조금을 주다

ⓝ 보조금, 기부금

a government subsidy 정부 보조금

Our factory receives a subsidy for employing the disabled.

40 surplus
[sə́ːrplʌs]

ⓝ 나머지, 잉여 **⊜** shortage 부족

trade surplus 무역 흑자

There was a surplus of used clothing after everyone had donated generously to the thrift store.

---

34 정부 수익의 대부분은 석유 수출에서 나왔다. 35 나는 회사에서 5년간 근무하고 나서 자영업을 시작할 계획이다. 36 성직자들은 자신을 하느님의 하인으로서 헌신하는 사람들이다. 37 필요하면 사용할 수 있도록 여분의 타이어가 트렁크에 있다. / Tom은 내게 자신의 프로젝트를 도와주기 위해 시간을 낼 수 있는지 물었다. 38 때로는 다른 사람들에게 지나치게 인색한 것은 예의에 어긋난다. 39 우리 공장은 장애인을 고용하면 보조금을 받는다. 40 관대하게도 모든 사람이 중고 할인점에 기부를 해주어서 중고 의류가 넘쳐 났다.

EXERCISE

A 다음 영어는 우리말로, 우리말은 영어로 옮기시오.

01 nuisance _____

02 absentee _____

03 retirement _____

04 paycheck _____

05 janitor _____

06 errand _____

07 간소한, 절약하는 _____

08 여분의, 할애하다 _____

09 연금 _____

10 재산, 자산 _____

11 수당, 용돈, 허용 _____

12 소작농 _____

B 다음 빈칸에 알맞은 단어를 쓰시오.

01 fiscal ⊜ _____

02 extravagant ⊜ _____

03 expenditure ⊜ _____

04 stingy ⇔ _____

05 surplus ⇔ _____

06 affluent ⇔ _____

07 deprivation ⓥ _____

08 thrifty ⓥ _____

09 profession ⓐ _____

10 accumulate ⓐ _____

11 dismiss ⓝ _____

12 impoverish ⓝ _____

C 다음 빈칸에 들어갈 알맞은 말을 고르시오. (필요하면 형태를 바꾸시오.)

vocational	gross	usher	subsidy	compensate

01 She would like to be _____ for her hard work by being paid more.

02 I have calculated my _____ annual income to be greater than $40,000.

03 For the musical performance, I volunteered by _____ audience members to their seats.

04 Our office tries to meet the _____ needs of the unemployed members of the community.

05 Fortunately, the _____ allowed the community to enjoy lower costs and a better quality of life.

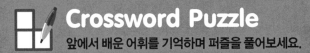
Crossword Puzzle
앞에서 배운 어휘를 기억하며 퍼즐을 풀어보세요.

정답

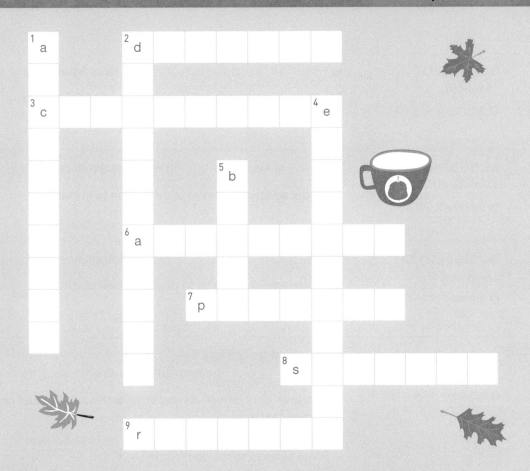

1 a
2 d
3 c
4 e
5 b
6 a
7 p
8 s
9 r

Across

2 to remove someone from a job

3 to pay someone money because they have suffered injury, loss or damage

6 an amount of money that you are given regularly or for a special purpose

7 an amount of money paid regularly by the government or company to someone who does not work anymore

8 money that is paid by a government or organization to make prices lower, reduce the cost of producing goods, etc.

9 money that a business or organization receives over a period of time, especially from selling goods or services

Down

1 to gradually get more and more money, possessions, knowledge, etc. over a period of time

2 the lack of something that you need in order to be healthy, comfortable or happy

4 the total amount of money that a government, organization, or person spends during a particular period of time

5 having no money

Human Relationship

01 ☑ accidental
[æ̀ksidéntl]

ⓝ accident 우연, 사고

ⓐ 우연한, 고의가 아닌 ⊜ deliberate 의도적인 **accidental death** 사고사

My father forgave me, knowing that what I had done was accidental.

02 ☑ acquaintance
[əkwéintəns]

ⓥ acquaint 알리다

ⓝ 아는 사이 ⊜ associate **a new acquaintance** 새로 알게 된 사람

I introduced an old acquaintance of mine to my family.

03 ☑ adolescence
[æ̀dəlésəns]

ⓐ adolescent 사춘기의

ⓝ 사춘기, 청소년기 ⊜ youth **reach adolescence** 사춘기에 접어들다

It's never easy for parents to deal with their child's adolescence.

04 ☑ appointment
[əpɔ́intmənt]

ⓥ appoint 지명하다, 임명하다

ⓝ 약속, 임명 ⊜ arrangement 약속

miss an appointment 약속한 자리에 못 나가다

★ I made an appointment to go fishing with my father and my brother next week.

★ The president announced the appointment of the new Prime Minister to the commission.

05 ☑ tolerate
[tálərèit]

ⓝ tolerance 관용, 인내
ⓐ tolerant 관대한

ⓥ 참다, 견디다 ⊜ endure, stand **tolerate criticism** 비판을 참다

I couldn't tolerate anymore of his complaining.

06 ☑ colleague
[káli:g]

ⓝ 동료 **a colleague at work** 회사 동료

My colleagues complimented my wife's cooking at the housewarming party.

---

01 아버지는 내가 한 일이 고의가 아니라는 것을 알고 용서해주셨다. 02 나는 오래된 지인을 가족에게 소개했다. 03 부모가 사춘기의 자녀를 대하기는 결코 쉽지 않다. 04 나는 다음 주에 아버지하고 형과 낚시하러 가기로 약속했다. / 대통령은 위원회에 새 국무총리의 임명을 발표했다. 05 나는 더 이상 그의 불평을 참을 수 없었다. 06 직장 동료들이 집들이에서 아내의 요리 솜씨를 칭찬했다.

07 association
[əsòusiéiʃən]

ⓥ associate 연합시키다

ⓝ 연합, 협회, 관계   **in association with** ~와 공동으로

★ My family keeps a close association with most of our relatives.

★ The people founded a trade association to promote fair trade.

08 committee
[kəmíti]

ⓝ 위원회, 위원   **an advisory committee** 자문 위원회

The decision of the committee will start to have effect tomorrow.

09 relevant
[réləvənt]

ⓝ relevance 관련

ⓐ 관련된, 적절한   **⊜ irrelevant** 관련 없는   **relevant information** 관련 정보

The police investigated people relevant to the murder case.

10 contract
[kántrækt]

ⓝ 계약, 약정   **⊜ agreement**   **the terms of the contract** 계약 조건

My family signed a two-year contract with the landlord for the house.

11 destiny
[déstəni]

ⓥ destine 운명으로 정해지다

ⓝ 운명, 숙명

I believe that it was my destiny to meet my wife.

12 directory
[diréktəri]

ⓝ 주소 성명록, 전화번호부   **a telephone directory** 전화번호부

The businessman keeps close relations with those in his directory.

13 divorce
[divɔ́ːrs]

ⓝ 이혼, 분리   **⊜ break-up, split-up**   **get a divorce** 이혼하다

A divorce not only affects the parting couple, but the child as well.

---

07 우리 가족은 대부분의 친척들과 가까이 지낸다. / 그 사람들이 공정거래를 장려하기 위해 무역 협회를 설립했다. 08 위원회에서 내린 결정은 내일부터 효력이 발생한다. 09 경찰은 그 살인사건과 관련된 사람들을 조사했다. 10 우리 가족은 집에 대해 집주인과 2년짜리 계약을 맺었다. 11 나는 내 아내와 만난 것이 운명이라고 생각한다. 12 그 사업가는 자신의 주소록에 기록된 사람들과 가까운 관계를 유지한다. 13 이혼은 헤어지는 부부뿐만 아니라, 자녀에게도 영향을 끼친다.

14 ego
[íːgou]
ⓐ egoistic 이기적인, 자기본위의

ⓝ 자아, 자존심   **a person with a big ego** 자존심이 센 사람

★ The ego of a person is known to be developed during childhood.

★ I wouldn't hate him so much if it weren't for his big ego.

15 immigration
[ìməgréiʃən]
ⓥ immigrate 이주하다

ⓝ 이민, 이주   **illegal immigration** 불법 이민

He was opposed to the mass immigration from Eastern Europe into France.

16 engagement
[engéidʒmənt]
ⓥ engage 속박하다, 약혼시키다

ⓝ 약속, 맹세, 약혼   **⊜** appointment 약속   **an engagement ring** 약혼반지

People were shocked when the famous actor announced the sudden engagement.

17 folk
[fóuk]

ⓝ 사람들, 가족, 부모   **old folks** 노인들

★ There were thousands of folks waiting for the official statement.

★ My folks were happy when I introduced my fiancée to them.

18 formation
[fɔːrméiʃən]
ⓥ form 형성하다

ⓝ 형성, 구성   **⊜** establishment, development

         battle formation 전투 대형

The townsmen agreed that the formation of a committee was needed.

19 foster
[fɔ́(ː)stər]

ⓐ 양육하는, 기르는 **ⓥ** 양육하다, 기르다   **a foster child** 수양 자녀

★ Britney was officially adopted by her foster parents.

★ They've fostered over sixty children in the last ten years.

---

14 사람의 자아는 유년기에 발달하는 것으로 알려져 있다. / 그의 센 자존심만 아니었어도 나는 그를 그렇게 싫어하진 않을 거야. 15 그는 동유럽에서 프랑스로 들어오는 대거 이민에 반대했다. 16 사람들은 그 유명한 배우가 갑작스러운 약혼을 발표했을 때 놀랐다. 17 수천 명의 사람이 공개 성명을 기다리고 있었다. / 우리 가족은 내가 약혼녀를 소개하자 크게 기뻐하셨다. 18 마을 사람들은 위원회의 구성이 필요하다는 것에 동의했다. 19 Britney는 공식적으로 자신의 양부모에게 입양되었다. / 그들은 지난 10년 동안 60명의 아이들을 양육했다.

20 gender
[dʒéndər]

ⓝ 성(性) **⊜** sex **gender equality** 양성 평등

Gender differences influence boys' and girls' learning and emotions.

21 heir
[ɛər]

ⓝ heiress 상속녀

ⓝ 상속인, 계승자 **⊜** successor 계승자 **an heir to the throne** 왕위 계승자

My grandfather appointed my father as his heir in a will.

22 heredity
[hərédəti]

ⓐ hereditary 유전적인, 세습의

ⓝ 유전, 상속 **the law of heredity** 유전의 법칙

★ Heredity plays an important role in determining one's personality and traits.

★ The heredity was carried out according to the old man's will.

23 descendant
[diséndənt]

ⓥ descend 내려가다, 전해지다

ⓝ 후손 **a direct descendant** 직계 자손

The descendants tried to clear their ancestor's name of the disgrace.

24 inherit
[inhérit]

ⓝ inheritance 상속, 유산

ⓥ 상속하다, 물려받다 **⊜** succeed **inherit property** 재산을 상속하다

I inherited my father's business when he passed away last year.

25 spouse
[spaus]

ⓐ spousal 결혼의

ⓝ 배우자 **⊜** husband or wife **a faithful spouse** 헌신적인 배우자

The CEO brought her spouse to the company's Christmas party.

26 mistress
[místris]

ⓝ 여주인, 여왕 **a mistress of cooking** 요리의 대가

The master and the mistress were kind to their servants.

---

20 성의 차이는 남자아이와 여자아이의 학습과 감정에 영향을 미친다. 21 할아버지는 유서를 통해 아버지를 자신의 상속인으로 지정하셨다. 22 유전은 성격과 특성을 결정하는 데 중요한 역할을 한다. / 상속은 노인의 유서에 따라 진행되었다. 23 후손들은 조상의 오명을 씻기 위해 노력했다. 24 나는 작년에 아버지가 돌아가셨을 때 아버지의 회사를 물려받았다. 25 CEO는 회사 크리스마스 파티에 자신의 배우자를 데려왔다. 26 주인과 여주인은 하인들에게 친절하게 대했다.

27 juvenile
[dʒúːvənəl]

ⓐ 청소년의, 소년[소녀]의　ⓔ adult 어른의, 성인의

juvenile delinquency 청소년 비행

I bought some juvenile literature for my young cousin.

28 widow
[wídou]

ⓝ 미망인　ⓔ widower 홀아비　**a war widow** 남편이 전쟁에서 목숨을 잃은 미망인

The young widow couldn't find a way to bring up her two sons.

29 legacy
[légəsi]

ⓝ 유산, 물려받은 것　ⓔ inheritance　**hand down a legacy** 유산을 물려주다

There were several rumors about a young man and his legacy from his parents.

30 marital
[mǽrətl]

ⓐ 결혼의, 부부의

marital life 결혼생활

★ Nowadays, it's not polite to directly ask someone's marital status.

★ My wife complains that I'm not faithful to my marital vows.

31 masculine
[mǽskjəlin]

ⓝ masculinity 남자다움

ⓐ 남성의, 남자다운　ⓔ feminine 여자의, 여성 같은

masculine pride 남자로서의 자존심

My wife said she loved my deep, masculine voice.

32 intimate
[íntəmət]

ⓝ intimacy 친밀
ⓐⓓ intimately 친밀하게

ⓐ 친밀한, 개인적인　ⓔ close 친밀한, private 개인적인

an intimate relationship 친밀한 관계

I became intimate with my brother's friends after his wedding.

33 monogamy
[mənɑ́ugəmi]

ⓝ 일부일처　**a monogamy [polygamy] society** 일부일처제[일부다처제] 사회

In the modern world, monogamy is the predominant form of marriage.

---

27 나는 어린 사촌을 위해 아동도서를 몇 권 샀다. 28 그 젊은 미망인은 두 아들을 키울 방법을 찾을 수 없었다. 29 한 젊은 남자와 그가 부모로부터 물려받은 유산에 대한 소문이 무성했다. 30 요즘은 결혼 여부를 직접적으로 묻는 것은 무례한 것이다. / 내 아내는 내가 부부의 맹세를 충실히 지키지 않는다고 불평한다. 31 아내는 내 깊고 남자다운 목소리가 좋다고 이야기했다. 32 나는 형의 결혼식 이후로 형의 친구들과 친해졌다. 33 현대 사회에서는 일부일처제가 주된 결혼 형태다.

34 mutual
[mjú:tʃuəl]

ⓝ mutuality 상호관계

ⓐ 서로의, 상호관계가 있는 **㊀** common

mutual respect 상호 존중

I was introduced to my husband by a mutual friend from college.

35 orphanage
[ɔ́:rfənidʒ]

ⓝ orphan 고아

ⓝ 고아원, 보육원

an orphanage resident 보육원 거주자

After both of his parents died, Tommy was sent to an orphanage.

36 paternity
[pətə́:rnəti]

ⓐ paternal 아버지의

ⓝ 부성(父性), 부계(父系)

paternity leave 남편의 육아휴가

Scientific advancements increased the accuracy of paternity tests.

37 peer
[piər]

ⓝ 동시대 사람, 동료 **㊀** fellow, contemporary

P2P (peer to peer) file sharing 일대일 파일 공유

peer pressure 동료 집단의 사회적 압력

I asked my peers to review my paper before I published it.

38 pregnancy
[prégnənsi]

ⓐ pregnant 임신한

ⓝ 임신

a false pregnancy 상상 임신

a pregnancy test 임신 검사

The role of the husband is very important during pregnancy.

39 puberty
[pjú:bərti]

ⓝ 사춘기

reach puberty 사춘기에 접어들다

Jenny felt confused when her first stage of puberty started to show.

40 status
[stéitəs]

ⓝ 상태, 지위, 자격

equal status 동등한 자격

I tried to behave myself considering my father's social status.

---

34 나는 대학 때 남편과 나를 둘 다 아는 친구에게서 남편을 소개받았다. 35 Tommy는 부모님이 돌아가시고 나서 보육원으로 보내졌다. 36 과학의 발전으로 친자확인 검사의 정확도가 증가했다. 37 나는 논문을 발표하기 전에 동료에게 검토를 부탁했다. 38 임신 중에는 남편의 역할이 매우 중요하다. 39 Jenny는 사춘기의 초기 단계가 나타나기 시작하자 혼란스러웠다. 40 나는 아버지의 사회적 신분을 고려하여 예의 바르게 행동하려고 노력했다.

EXERCISE

A 다음 영어는 우리말로, 우리말은 영어로 옮기시오.

01 appointment _____

02 monogamy _____

03 orphanage _____

04 directory _____

05 pregnancy _____

06 engagement _____

07 동료 _____

08 후손 _____

09 이민, 이주 _____

10 결혼의, 부부의 _____

11 성 _____

12 연합, 협회 _____

B 다음 빈칸에 알맞은 단어를 쓰시오.

01 tolerate ⊜_____

02 legacy ⊜_____

03 inherit ⊜_____

04 widow ⇔_____

05 masculine ⇔_____

06 accidental ⇔_____

07 destiny ⓥ_____

08 formation ⓥ_____

09 heredity ⓐ_____

10 ego ⓐ_____

11 intimate ⓝ_____

12 mutual ⓝ_____

C 다음 빈칸에 들어갈 알맞은 말을 고르시오. (필요하면 형태를 바꾸시오.)

relevant	acquaintance	foster	intimate	spouse

01 We are _____, having met at a summer camp as teenagers.

02 In total, my parents have _____ ten children during the course of twenty years.

03 I am able to say that my _____ is not only my best friend, but is also my great mentor.

04 During the court hearing, the _____ details of the relationship were not discussed.

05 The teacher stopped him halfway since his opinions were not _____ to the topic of discussion.

Across

1 the time, usually between the ages of 12 and 18, when a young person is developing into an adult

2 to receive money, property, etc. from someone after they have died

4 an organization that consists of a group of people who have the same aims

8 to allow people to do, say, or believe something without criticizing or punishing them

9 (of a feeling or action) experienced or done by each of two or more parties towards the other or others

Down

1 someone you know, but who is not a close friend

3 having an extremely close friendship

5 the official legal position or condition of a person, group, country, etc.

6 something that happens or exists as a result of things that happened at an earlier time

7 directly relating to the subject or problem being discussed or considered

앞에서 배운 어휘를 기억하며 빈칸을 채워 보세요.

정답

_____ 기아, 아사

_____ 거주자, 거주하는

_____ 자양분을 주다, 기르다

_____ 조리법, 비법

_____ 숙박 시설, 편의

_____ 경재의, 경쟁에 의한

_____ 인내력, 지구력

_____ 매력, 유혹

_____ 휴식, 휴가

_____ 생명의, 절대로 필요한

Food, Clothing & Shelter
의. 식. 주

Leisure & Sports
여가와 운동

Human Life
인간의 생활

Occupation & Asset
직업과 재산

Human Relationship
인간관계

_____ 모으다, 쌓다

_____ 보상하다

_____ 재산, 자산

_____ 상실, 파면

_____ 아끼는, 검소한

_____ 참다, 견디다

_____ 상속하다, 물려받다

_____ 관련된

_____ 상태, 지위

_____ 청소년의

Chapter
07

Explanation and Description

Unit 31 Description of Emotion 1

01 ☑ **advocate**
[ǽdvəkèit / ǽdvəkət]
ⓝ **advocacy** 옹호, 지지

ⓥ 옹호하다, 주장하다 ⓝ 옹호자 ⊜ support 지지하다

a fervent advocate 열렬한 옹호자

★ We have long advocated that CEO salaries be reasonable.
★ Gandhi was an advocate of nonviolence.

02 ☑ **affection**
[əfékʃən]
ⓥ **affect**
영향을 미치다, 감동시키다

ⓝ 애정, 감동 ⊜ fondness

a motherly affection 모성애

She had a deep affection for the countryside.

03 ☑ **afflict**
[əflíkt]
ⓝ **affliction** 괴로움

ⓥ 괴롭히다 ⊜ distress

be afflicted with disease 병에 시달리다

My father was afflicted with failure and debts.

04 ☑ **antipathy**
[æntípəθi]

ⓝ 반감, 혐오 ⊜ sympathy 동정심

be filled with antipathy 반감으로 가득 차다

He didn't try to hide his antipathy toward Congress.

05 ☑ **apathy**
[ǽpəθi]

ⓝ 무관심, 냉담 ⊜ indifference

political apathy 정치적 무관심

They have shown apathy toward these social issues.

06 ☑ **appeal**
[əpíːl]
ⓐ **appealing** 애원하는

ⓥ 애원하다, 호소하다 ⓝ 호소

a court of appeal 항소 법원

★ He appealed to me that I should show mercy.
★ The mayor made an appeal to the public for donations.

---

01 우리는 최고경영자의 급여가 적절해야 한다고 오랫동안 주장했다. / 간디는 비폭력 지지자였다. 02 그녀는 시골에 깊은 애정이 있었다. 03 아버지는 실패와 빚 때문에 괴로워했다. 04 그는 의회를 향한 자신의 반감을 숨기려고 애쓰지 않았다. 05 그들은 이 사회적 문제들에 대해 무관심을 보여왔다. 06 그는 내가 자비를 베풀어주어야 한다고 호소했다. / 시장은 시민들에게 기부를 호소했다.

07 suspense
[səspéns]

v suspend 매달다, 불안케 하다

n 걱정, 불안, 긴장감   **a suspense novel** 긴장감을 주는 소설

The suspense between him and her wasn't as tight as I thought.

08 astonish
[əstániʃ]

n astonishment 놀람

v 놀라게 하다   ⊜ surprise   **astonishing memory** 놀라운 기억력

I was astonished at the development which has taken place in the colony.

09 beguile
[bigáil]

a beguiling 속이는

v 현혹시키다   **be beguiled by a magician** 마법사에게 속다

Her motions when she is dancing beguile many guys.

10 subconscious
[sʌbkánʃəs]

n subconsciousness 잠재의식

n 잠재의식 **a** 잠재의식의   ⊜ aware, conscious 의식하고 있는

the subconscious self 잠재된 자아

The patient's subconscious thoughts were monitored by the medical machines.

11 bliss
[blis]

v bless 축복하다, 빌다

n 행복, 기쁨   **Ignorance is bliss.** 모르는 게 약이다.

It is my bliss to study without any disturbance.

12 cherish
[tʃériʃ]

v 소중히 하다, 마음에 품다   ⊜ treasure

cherish a tradition 전통을 소중히 하다

I've always cherished my sweet childhood memories.

13 compassion
[kəmpǽʃən]

a compassionate 인정이 많은

n 불쌍히 여김, 동정심   ⊜ sympathy, pity   **out of compassion** 동정심에서

Many people who felt compassion for the flood victims donated money to charity.

---

07 그와 그녀 사이의 긴장감은 생각보다 심각하지 않았다. 08 나는 식민지에서 일어난 발전에 놀랐다. 09 그녀가 춤을 출 때 취하는 동작은 많은 남자들을 현혹시킨다. 10 환자의 무의식적인 사고는 의료 장비들에 의해 감시됐다. 11 아무런 방해 없이 공부하는 것이 나의 행복이다. 12 나는 달콤했던 어린 시절의 추억을 항상 소중히 간직했다. 13 홍수 피해자에 대해 동정심을 느낀 많은 사람들이 자선단체에 기부했다.

14 sober
[sóubər]

ⓝ sobriety 진지함, 침착함

ⓐ 침착한, 심각한, 진지한 ⊜ serious **a sober judgment** 냉정한 판단

Her sober answer surprised all of us.

15 rejoice
[ridʒɔ́is]

ⓥ 기뻐하다, 좋아하다 **rejoice over a victory** 승리를 기뻐하다

Rejoice every day, then you would know what life is like.

16 startle
[stá:rtl]

ⓐ startling 놀라운

ⓥ 깜짝 놀라게 하다 ⊜ surprise **startle the children** 아이들을 깜짝 놀라게 하다

He startled me from behind the door when I came into the room.

17 dreadful
[drédfəl]

ⓝ dread 공포, 불안

ⓐ 무시무시한, 끔찍한 **dreadful storm** 무시무시한 폭풍우

The public bathroom has a dreadful odor.

18 embrace
[embréis]

ⓝ embracement 포옹, 수락

ⓥ 포옹하다, 받아들이다 ⊜ hug **embrace tenderly** 따뜻하게 포옹하다

As soon as we saw each other, we embraced.

19 empathy
[émpəθi]

ⓐ empathic 감정이입의

ⓝ 감정이입 **feel empathy** 공감하다

He felt great empathy for the prisoners.

20 solitude
[sálitʃùːd]

ⓐ solitary 고독한

ⓝ 고독, 외로움 **lonely solitude** 외로운 고독

People need a chance to reflect on spiritual matters in solitude.

---

14 그녀의 진지한 대답이 우리 모두를 놀라게 했다. 15 매일 기뻐하라, 그러면 삶이 어떤 것인지 알게 될 것이다. 16 내가 방으로 들어왔을 때 그는 문 뒤에서 나를 깜짝 놀라게 했다. 17 공중 화장실에서 심한 악취가 난다. 18 우리는 서로 보자마자 껴안았다. 19 그는 수감자들의 처지를 깊이 이해했다. 20 사람들은 고독 속에서 영적인 문제를 생각해 볼 기회가 필요하다.

21 ☑ dismay
[disméi]

ⓝ 당황, 실망, 절망　**◉** anxiety, disappointment

to one's dismay 당황스럽게도

To my great dismay, she was absent from school again.

---

22 ☑ exclamation
[èksklÉméiʃən]

ⓥ exclaim 외치다

ⓝ 감탄, 외침

exclamation mark 느낌표

It was an exclamation of joy to have a chance to go to the concert.

---

23 ☑ fanatic
[fənǽtik]

ⓐ fanatical 광신적인

ⓝ 광신자, 열광자　**◉** zealot

a religious fanatic 종교적 광신자

He was assassinated by a religious fanatic during his term of office.

---

24 ☑ fascinate
[fǽsənèit]

ⓐ fascinating 매혹적인
ⓝ fascination 매혹, 매력

ⓥ 주의를 끌다, 매혹하다　**◉** absorb

be fascinated by one's beauty ～의 미모에 사로잡히다

I was fascinated by the voice of a stranger who asked me for directions.

---

25 ☑ gratify
[grǽtəfài]

ⓝ gratification 만족감, 희열

ⓥ 기쁘게 하다, 만족시키다　**◉** satisfy

gratify one's passion 열정을 만족시키다

I gratified my hunger with an apple and a tangerine.

---

26 ☑ greed
[gri:d]

ⓐ greedy 탐욕스러운

ⓝ 탐욕, 욕심　**◉** desire

greed for money 돈 욕심

My greed for clothing and shoes makes me poor.

---

27 ☑ grief
[gri:f]

ⓥ grieve
몹시 슬프게 하다, 슬퍼하다
ⓐ grievous 슬픈, 통탄할

ⓝ 슬픔, 비탄, 비통　**◉** sadness

a bitter grief 비통한 슬픔

He hid his grief with a bright smile and act.

---

21 당황스럽게도, 그녀는 또 결석했다.　22 그것은 콘서트를 보러 갈 기회가 생긴 것에 대한 기쁨의 탄성이었다.　23 그는 임기 중에 종교 광신자에게 암살당했다.　24 나는 내게 길을 물어본 낯선 이의 목소리에 반했다.　25 나는 사과 하나와 귤 하나로 배고픔을 채웠다.　26 옷과 신발에 대한 나의 욕심이 나를 가난하게 만든다.　27 그는 밝은 웃음과 행동으로 자신의 슬픔을 감췄다.

28 grudge
[grʌdʒ]

Ⓝ 원한, 앙심 Ⓢ resentment

a personal grudge 개인적 원한
pay off a grudge 원한을 갚다

I believe that Kate no longer bears them a grudge.

---

29 hatred
[héitrid]

Ⓥ hate 증오하다

Ⓝ 증오, 원한, 혐오

a racial hatred 인종적 증오

I felt jealousy and hatred for him when he got a higher score than I did.

---

30 overwhelm
[òuvərhwélm]

Ⓐ overwhelming 압도적인

Ⓥ 압도하다, 당황하게 하다

be overwhelmed by ~에 압도되다

I overwhelmed the audience with a perfect speech.

---

31 rage
[reidʒ]

Ⓥ enrage 성나게 하다

Ⓝ 격노, 분노 Ⓢ fury, anger

a violent rage 격렬한 분노

His rage couldn't be controlled by anyone in this room.

---

32 rapture
[ræptʃər]

Ⓐ rapturous 기뻐 날뛰는

Ⓝ 큰 기쁨, 환희 Ⓢ delight

complete rapture 완전한 행복

They listened with rapture to the band perform.

---

33 despair
[dispéər]

Ⓐ desperate 필사적인

Ⓝ 절망, 자포자기 Ⓢ depression

in despair 절망하여

Rick was able to overcome despair thanks to his wife's love and support.

---

34 sorrow
[sárou]

Ⓐ sorrowful 슬퍼하는

Ⓝ 슬픔, 애도 Ⓢ sadness, grief

the joys and sorrow of life 인생의 기쁨과 슬픔

I felt deep sorrow at the death of my best friend.

---

28 나는 Kate가 더 이상 그들에게 원한을 품지 않는다고 믿는다. 29 나는 그가 나보다 높은 점수를 받았을 때 그에 대한 질투와 미움을 느꼈다. 30 나는 완벽한 연설로 청중을 압도했다. 31 그의 분노를 제어할 수 있는 사람은 이 방에 아무도 없었다. 32 그들은 그 밴드가 공연하는 것을 즐겁게 감상했다. 33 Rick은 아내의 사랑과 지원으로 절망을 극복할 수 있었다. 34 나의 가장 친한 친구의 죽음에 몹시 슬펐다.

35 **refrain**
[rifréin]

ⓥ 억제하다, 삼가다   **ⓔ** avoid, stop   **refrain from smoking** 흡연을 삼가다

I try really hard to refrain from coffee, but it's not easy at all.

36 **repentance**
[ripéntəns]

ⓥ repent 후회하다
ⓐ repentant 후회하는

ⓝ 후회, 참회   **true repentance** 진심어린 후회

She showed repentance for the absence of the class.

37 **resent**
[rizént]

ⓐ resentful 분개한

ⓥ 분개하다, 원망하다   **resent bitterly** 몹시 분개하다

I resent you for trying to look like you are the top.

38 **sentiment**
[séntəmənt]

ⓐ sentimental 감정적인

ⓝ 감정, 정서   **ⓔ** feeling, emotion   **patriotic sentiment** 애국심

He is fluent in conveying his sentiment into the music.

39 **sob**
[sɑb]

ⓥ 흐느껴 울다, 흐느끼다   **ⓔ** cry   **sob one's eye out** 눈이 퉁퉁 붓도록 울다

She sobbed when he told her that she was not charming.

40 **solace**
[sáləs]

ⓝ 위안, 위로   **ⓔ** comfort   **find solace in music** 음악에서 위안을 찾다

I find solace in music whenever I get stress from work.

---

35 나는 커피를 끊으려고 매우 노력하지만 절대 쉽지 않다. 36 그녀는 수업에 빠진 것에 대해 후회했다. 37 나는 최고로 보이고 싶어 하는 네가 불쾌하다. 38 그는 자신의 감정을 음악으로 전달하는 데에 능숙하다. 39 그가 그녀에게 매력이 없다고 말했을 때 그녀는 흐느껴 울었다. 40 나는 일로 스트레스를 받을 때마다 음악에서 위안을 찾는다.

EXERCISE

A 다음 영어는 우리말로, 우리말은 영어로 옮기시오.

01 affection _____
02 gratify _____
03 cherish _____
04 repentance _____
05 overwhelm _____
06 solitude _____

07 포옹하다, 받아들이다 _____
08 걱정, 불안, 긴장감 _____
09 주의를 끌다, 매혹하다 _____
10 절망, 자포자기 _____
11 억제하다, 삼가다 _____
12 괴롭히다 _____

B 다음 빈칸에 알맞은 단어를 쓰시오.

01 grief ⊜ _____
02 solace ⊜ _____
03 astonish ⊜ _____
04 grudge ⊜ _____
05 antipathy ⊕ _____
06 subconscious ⊕ _____

07 exclamation ⓥ _____
08 rage ⓥ _____
09 compassion ⓐ _____
10 appeal ⓐ _____
11 afflict ⓝ _____
12 advocate ⓝ _____

C 다음 빈칸에 들어갈 알맞은 말을 고르시오. (필요하면 형태를 바꾸시오.)

rejoice	resent	apathy	dreadful	fanatic

01 He displayed _____ toward the elderly neighbors who struggled to climb the stairs.

02 We _____ when we heard that Jerry had won the grand prize in the cooking contest.

03 I never wish to have another _____ nightmare like the one I experienced last night.

04 The Michael Jackson _____ sobbed when she heard that the singer had passed away.

05 The boy _____ the fact that he was the only one who was left behind.

Crossword Puzzle

앞에서 배운 어휘를 기억하며 퍼즐을 풀어보세요.

Across

1 a strong feeling of sympathy for someone who is suffering and a desire to help them

5 to publicly support a particular way of doing something

7 to surprise someone very much

9 to feel angry or upset about a situation or about something that someone has done, especially because you think that it is not fair

Down

2 to make a serious public request for help, money, information, etc.

3 to have a strong emotional effect on

4 to attract the strong attention and interest of (someone)

5 a feeling of liking or love and caring

6 to stop oneself from doing something

8 not affected by alcohol

Unit 32 Description of Emotion 2

01 ☐ agonizing
[ǽgənàiziŋ]
- ⓥ agonize 괴롭히다, 괴로워하다
- ⓝ agony 고민, 고통

ⓐ 괴로워하는, 고뇌하는   **agonizing pain** 괴로운 고통

It was very agonizing for me to decide to have a surgery.

02 ☐ amiable
[éimiəbəl]

ⓐ 호감을 주는, 상냥한   ⓔ friendly   **an amiable character** 정감 있는 성격

Every boy in the classroom said her amiable personality was attractive.

03 ☐ annoyed
[ənɔ́id]
- ⓥ annoy 괴롭히다, 귀찮게 굴다

ⓐ 귀찮은, 불쾌한   **get annoyed** 짜증나다

He was very annoyed by his dog while he was watching television.

04 ☐ anxious
[ǽŋkʃəs]
- ⓝ anxiety 걱정, 불안

ⓐ 걱정하여, 염려하여   **be anxious about** ~에 관해 걱정하다

I was anxious about his health and tried to visit him.

05 ☐ appreciative
[əprí:ʃətiv]
- ⓥ appreciate 감사하다, 감상하다

ⓐ 감사의   **appreciative words** 감사하는 말

The appreciative look on your face made my heart warm.

06 ☐ ashamed
[əʃéimd]
- ⓝ shame 부끄러움, 창피

ⓐ 부끄러이 여겨, 수줍어하여   **be ashamed of** ~을 수치스러워 하다

There is no need to be ashamed of your faults.

---

01 수술하기로 한 것은 나에겐 매우 괴로운 일이었다. 02 교실에 있던 모든 소년들은 그녀의 붙임성 있는 성격이 매력적이라고 했다. 03 그는 TV를 보는 동안 개 때문에 굉장히 귀찮았다. 04 나는 그의 건강이 걱정되어 그를 방문하려고 했다. 05 너의 감사하는 표정이 나의 마음을 따뜻하게 만들었다. 06 네 실수에 대해 부끄러워할 필요는 없다.

07 assured
[əʃúərd]
v assure 보증하다

ⓐ 자신 있는, 보증된 ⓢ confident   **an assured manner** 자신 있는 태도

I always have an assured attitude to look stately.

08 awesome
[ɔ́ːsəm]
n awe 경외(敬畏), 두려움

ⓐ 굉장한 ⓢ amazing   **an awesome sight** 엄청난 광경

His strength was so awesome that he could push a car with one hand.

09 awkward
[ɔ́ːkwərd]
ad awkwardly
어색하게, 거북하게

ⓐ 어색한, 거북한 ⓐ comfortable 편안한

at an awkward moment 곤란한 때에

He often says things that make the atmosphere more awkward.

10 amazing
[əméiziŋ]
v amaze 깜짝 놀라게 하다

ⓐ 놀랄 정도의, 굉장한   **amazing endurance** 놀라운 인내력

It was amazing that she was able to solve the problem so quickly.

11 bewildered
[biwíldərd]
v bewilder 당황하게 하다

ⓐ 당황한, 갈피를 못 잡은 ⓢ perplexed, puzzled

a bewildered look 당황하는 표정

He was bewildered by an unexpected question at the conference.

12 candid
[kǽndid]
ad candidly 솔직히

ⓐ 솔직한 ⓢ frank   **the candid newspaper article** 노골적인 신문 기사

They have had candid talks about the current crisis.

13 capricious
[kəpríʃəs]
ad capriciously 변덕스럽게

ⓐ 변덕스러운, 변하기 쉬운 ⓢ fickle   **capricious weather** 변덕스러운 날씨

He is very capricious, so his girlfriend is getting tired of him.

07 나는 당당하게 보이기 위해서 항상 자신 있는 태도를 보인다. 08 그는 힘이 매우 세서 한 손으로 차를 밀 수 있었다. 09 그는 종종 분위기를 더 어색하게 만드는 말을 한다. 10 그녀가 그 문제를 그렇게 빨리 풀 수 있다니 놀라웠다. 11 그는 회의에서 예상치 못한 질문을 받고 당황했다. 12 그들은 현재의 위기에 관해서 솔직한 이야기를 나누었다. 13 그는 매우 변덕스러워서 그의 여자친구는 그에게 질려간다.

14 contempt
[kəntémpt]

ⓐ contemptuous
경멸적인, 오만한

ⓝ 경멸, 모욕　ⓔ disrespect

contempt of court 법정 모독죄

I feel contempt for people who treat children cruelly.

---

15 content
[kəntént]

ⓝ contentment 만족

ⓐ 만족하는　ⓔ satisfied

be content with ~에 만족하다

Today, people can't be content with just making a living.

---

16 deplorable
[diplɔ́:rəbl]

ⓥ deplore 한탄하다

ⓐ 통탄할, 비참한

deplorable accident 비통한 사고

I feel deplorable ever since he passed away.

---

17 depressed
[diprést]

ⓝ depression 우울, 불경기

ⓐ 우울한, 불경기의　ⓔ blue 우울한

a depressed market 침체 시장

★ He has been depressed since he broke up with his ex-girlfriend, Jane.

★ The car market has been depressed for several months.

---

18 explicit
[iksplísit]

ⓐ 명백한, 노골적인　ⓔ implicit 함축적인, 암시적인

an explicit reason 명백한 이유

He stated some explicit reasons for why the employees should be fired.

---

19 dismal
[dízməl]

ⓝ dismalness 음울함

ⓐ 우울한, 황량한　ⓔ dark 음울한, depressing 우울한

a dismal tone of voice 우울한 어조

Michael's dismal feeling got worse as he got sick.

---

20 distress
[distrés]

ⓐ distressful 괴로운, 비참한

ⓝ 비탄, 고민　ⓔ grief 슬픔, 비탄

in distress 괴로워서

Trying to relieve her distress didn't make her feel better.

---

14 나는 아이들을 잔인하게 대하는 사람들에 대해서는 경멸감이 든다. 15 요즘 사람들은 생활비를 버는 것만으로는 만족할 수 없다. 16 나는 그가 죽고 난 이후로 비참하다. 17 그는 전 여자친구 Jane과 헤어지고 나서 우울해 있다. / 자동차 시장이 몇 달 동안 침체 상태에 있다. 18 그는 왜 그 직원들이 해 고되어야 하는지에 대한 몇 가지 명백한 이유를 설명했다. 19 Michael의 우울함은 그가 아프면서 더 심해졌다. 20 그녀의 고통을 덜어주려는 노력은 그 녀의 기분을 나아지게 하지 못했다.

21 envious
[énviəs]
ⓥ envy 부러워하다

ⓐ 부러워하는, 시기심이 강한   **envious looks** 부러워하는 표정

She was envious of her sister traveling around the world.

22 vulnerable
[vʌ́lnərəbəl]
ⓝ vulnerability 취약성

ⓐ 취약한, 상처 받기 쉬운   ⓢ weak, helpless
      feel vulnerable and alone 무력하고 외로움을 느끼다

I try to comfort Tina when she feels helpless and vulnerable.

23 timid
[tímid]
ⓝ timidity 겁 많음, 수줍음

ⓐ 겁 많은, 소심한   ⓞ confident 자신 있는
      as timid as a rabbit 토끼처럼 몹시 겁이 많은

The boy was too timid to show his feelings.

24 frustrate
[frʌ́streit]
ⓝ frustration 실망, 좌절

ⓥ 실망시키다, 좌절시키다   ⓢ disappoint
      frustrated ambition 좌절된 야망

We were frustrated that we could find no support.

25 furious
[fjúəriəs]
ⓝ fury 격노, 분노

ⓐ 성난, 격렬한   ⓢ very angry   **a furious debate** 격렬한 토론

Vanessa was furious about her short hair after having her hair cut yesterday.

26 heartfelt
[hɑ́ːrtfèlt]

ⓐ 진심에서 우러난   ⓢ sincere   **heartfelt apology** 진심어린 사과

His heartfelt apology made his parents forgive him.

27 heartwarming
[hɑ́ːrtwɔ̀ːrmiŋ]

ⓐ 마음이 푸근해지는   **a heartwarming hospitality** 극진한 대접

It's a heartwarming story about the rescue of a lonely dog.

---

21 그녀는 자신의 여동생이 세계여행을 하고 있는 것이 부러웠다.   22 나는 Tina가 무력하고 약할 때 그녀를 위로하려고 애쓴다.   23 소년은 너무 소심해서 감정을 드러낼 수 없었다.   24 우리는 도움의 손길을 찾지 못해 좌절했다.   25 Vanessa는 어제 머리를 자르고 나서 짧은 머리에 대해서 화가 났다. 26 그의 진심 어린 사과에 그의 부모님은 그를 용서했다.   27 이것은 외로운 개를 구조해 낸 감동적인 이야기다.

28 ☑ miserable
[mízərəbəl]

ⓐ 비참한, 가련한

a miserable life 비참한 인생

The story of your college life sounds miserable.

ⓝ misery 고통, 불행

29 ☑ jealous
[dʒéləs]

ⓐ 질투심이 많은, 시샘하는 ⊜ envious

a jealous husband 질투심 많은 남편

I am jealous of her skill of speaking three languages fluently.

ⓝ jealousy 시기, 질투

30 ☑ lamentable
[læməntəbəl]

ⓐ 슬퍼할, 통탄할

lamentable result 유감스러운 결과

His lamentable news was that the university didn't accept him.

ⓥ lament 슬퍼하다, 애도하다

31 ☑ memorial
[məmɔ́ːriəl]

ⓐ 기념의, 추도의

a memorial service 추도식

There is a memorial park for the soldiers who died in the Korean War.

32 ☑ sting
[stiŋ]

ⓥ 감정을 해치다, 찌르다 ⓝ 찔린 상처, 아픔 ⊜ hurt

a bee sting 벌침

★ I was stung by her harsh remarks.

★ I felt the sting of conscience after listening to her words.

33 ☑ aggressive
[əgrésiv]

ⓐ 공격적인, 적극적인 ⊜ offensive 공격적인

an aggressive driver 난폭 운전자

His aggressive attitude made me angrier.

ⓥ aggress 공격하다

34 ☑ vile
[vail]

ⓐ 비열한, 야비한

a vile act 야비한 행위

I never thought my closest friend, Tom, could become a vile traitor.

---

28 너의 대학 생활은 비참한 것 같다. 29 나는 3개 국어를 유창하게 할 수 있는 그녀의 능력이 부럽다. 30 슬픈 소식은 그 대학이 그를 받아주지 않았다는 것이었다. 31 한국전쟁에서 전사한 군인들을 위한 추모 공원이 있다. 32 나는 그녀의 가혹한 말에 감정이 상했다. / 그녀의 말을 듣고 나는 양심의 가책을 느꼈다. 33 그의 공격적인 태도는 나를 더 화나게 하였다. 34 나는 나의 가장 친한 친구인 Tom이 야비한 배신자가 되리라곤 생각도 못했다.

35 narrow-minded
[nǽroumàindid]

ⓐ 속 좁은, 옹졸한　　　**a narrow-minded person** 속 좁은 사람

David is so narrow-minded that he never lets me talk to his friends.

---

36 nostalgia
[nɑstǽldʒiə]

ⓝ 옛날을 그리워 함, 향수(병)　ⓔ homesickness 향수병

ⓐ nostalgic 고향을 그리는

feel nostalgia 향수를 느끼다

I had a bad feeling of nostalgia, so I couldn't stop crying.

---

37 oppressive
[əprésiv]

ⓐ 압제적인, 압박적인　ⓔ tyrannical

ⓥ oppress 압박하다, 억압하다

an oppressive king 폭군

Oppressive orders from my boss made me lose the smile on my face.

---

38 panic
[pǽnik]

ⓝ 겁먹음, 당황　ⓔ fear, anxiety

the financial panic 경제 공황

I was in a panic when I heard that one of my friends was in an accident.

---

39 pessimistic
[pèsəmístik]

ⓐ 비관적인　ⓔ optimistic 낙관적인

ⓝ pessimism
비관주의, 염세주의

a pessimistic prediction 비관적 예측

He is always pessimistic about his future.

---

40 regrettable
[rigrétəbəl]

ⓐ 유감스러운, 후회되는　　**a regrettable mistake** 유감스러운 실수

ⓥ regret 후회하다

The most regrettable thing I have ever done is crying in front of my classmates.

---

35 David는 너무 속이 좁아서 내가 자신의 친구들과 이야기하지 못하게 한다.　36 나는 향수병을 심하게 앓아서 울음이 멈추질 않았다.　37 상사의 강압적인 명령은 내 얼굴에서 웃음이 사라지게 하였다. 38 내 친구에게 사고가 났다는 말을 들었을 때 나는 겁을 먹었다. 39 그는 항상 자신의 미래에 대해 비관적이다. 40 내가 한 일 중에 가장 후회되는 일은 반 친구들 앞에서 운 것이다.

EXERCISE

A 다음 영어는 우리말로, 우리말은 영어로 옮기시오.

01 explicit _____   07 걱정하며, 염려하여 _____

02 assured _____   08 비참한, 가려운 _____

03 heartfelt _____   09 상처 받기 쉬운 _____

04 capricious _____   10 유감스러운, 후회되는 _____

05 vile _____   11 슬퍼할, 통탄할 _____

06 appreciative _____   12 음산한, 황량한 _____

B 다음 빈칸에 알맞은 단어를 쓰시오.

01 bewildered ⊜ _____   07 deplorable Ⓥ _____

02 aggressive ⊜ _____   08 oppressive Ⓥ _____

03 amiable ⊜ _____   09 nostalgia ⓐ _____

04 pessimistic ⇔ _____   10 distress ⓐ _____

05 awkward ⇔ _____   11 ashamed ⓝ _____

06 timid ⇔ _____   12 content ⓝ _____

C 다음 빈칸에 들어갈 알맞은 말을 고르시오. (필요하면 형태를 바꾸시오.)

candid	contempt	panic	frustrate	agonizing

01 Most people in the world hold great _____ for the dictator Hitler.

02 It was _____ for her to see children crying for food and warmth on the streets.

03 The rainy weather will not _____ our plans for a spectacular wedding.

04 The young mother experienced _____ when her baby choked on candy.

05 The author was quite _____ when being interviewed about her experience in writing the novel.

Across 1: o p _ _ _ _ _ _ 3: v
Across 4: a 5: m _ _ _ _
Across 6: a
Across 7: a _ _ _
Across 8: f
Across 9: a
Across 10: b _ _ _

Across

1. powerful, cruel, and unfair
4. friendly and easy to like
7. confident about your own abilities
10. totally confused

Down

2. expecting that bad things will happen in the future or that something will have a bad result
3. exposed to the possibility of being attacked or harmed, either physically or emotionally
5. extremely unhappy, for example because you feel lonely, cold, or badly treated
6. feeling very sorry and embarrassed because of something you have done
8. extremely angry
9. making you feel embarrassed so that you are not sure what to do or say

Unit 33 Movement & Motion 1

---

01 ☑ shudder
[ʃʌ́dər]

ⓥ 떨다 ⊜ shiver, tremble

shudder with fear 두려움에 떨다

As my boiler broke down, I shuddered through the entire night.

---

02 ☑ decline
[dikláin]

ⓝ declination 거절, 내리막 경사
ⓐ declining 떨어지는, 하락하는

ⓥ 거절하다, 기울다 ⓝ 경사, 내리막, 하락
⊜ reject 거절하다 ⊖ accept 수락하다

decline an offer 제의를 거절하다

★ He had to decline the job offer because of his health problems.

★ Production output will increase sharply, leading to a decline in prices.

---

03 ☑ activate
[ǽktəvèit]

ⓝ activation 활성화

ⓥ 활동적으로 하다, 활성화하다

activate the economy 경제를 활성화하다

The military activated the defense system against the enemy attack.

---

04 ☑ adhere
[ædhíər]

ⓐ adherent 들러붙는

ⓥ 들러붙다, 접착하다, 고수하다

adhere to a principle 원칙을 고수하다

★ Dog hair keeps adhering to my clothes due to static electricity.

★ Ray is the kind of guy that adheres to his opinion no matter what happens.

---

05 ☑ ascend
[əsénd]

ⓝ ascent 상승, 오름

ⓥ 오르다 ⊖ descend, decline 내려가다

ascend the stairs 계단을 오르다

There are numerous reports that the sea level is ascending yearly.

---

01 나는 보일러가 고장 나서 밤새 추위에 떨었다. 02 그는 건강 문제 때문에 일자리를 거절해야 했다. / 생산량이 급증할 것이고, 가격의 하락으로 이어질 것이다. 03 군 당국은 적군의 공격에 대항하여 방어 시스템을 가동시켰다. 04 정전기 때문에 강아지 털이 자꾸 내 옷에 달라붙는다. / Ray는 무슨 일이 있어도 자기 생각을 고수하는 사람이다. 05 해수면이 매년 상승하고 있다는 보고서가 매우 많다.

06 attach
[ətǽtʃ]

n attachment 부착, 애착

v 붙이다, 달다 ⊜ detach 떼다

be deeply attached to ~에 강한 애착을 느끼다

The discount prices are on the price tags attached to the items.

07 emerging
[imə́:rdʒiŋ]

v emerge 부상하다, 떠오르다

a 최근 생겨난, 신흥의 **an emerging market** 신흥 시장

The secret agents warned headquarters about an emerging danger.

08 befall
[bifɔ́:l]

v (좋지 않은 일이) 일어나다 **A misfortune befalls.** 재난이 일어나다.

Mary was unaware of the fate that was to befall her.

09 burst
[bə:rst]

v 파열하다, 터뜨리다 ⊜ blow up

burst into tears [laughter] 눈물이[웃음이] 터지다

She burst into tears when I told her goodbye at the airport.

10 wither
[wíðər]

v 시들다, 말라죽다 ⊜ fade **wither away** 시들어 버리다

The girl sadly watched the withering flower, pitying its fate.

11 chase
[tʃeis]

v 뒤쫓다, 추구하다 **n** 추격, 추구 **chase flies off** 파리를 쫓아버리다

★ I bought a cat to chase off the rats living inside my walls.
★ Life is nothing more than a never-ending chase of happiness.

12 descend
[disénd]

n descendant 후손

v 내려가다, 전해지다 **a descending air current** 하강 기류

The singer descended from the stage and sang a song with the excited fans.

06 할인 가격은 상품에 부착된 가격표에 표시되어 있다. 07 비밀 요원들은 본부에 새로운 위험에 대해 알렸다. 08 Mary는 그녀에게 일어날 운명을 알지 못했다. 09 내가 공항에서 작별인사를 하자 그녀는 울음을 터뜨렸다. 10 여자아이는 시들어가는 꽃을 슬프게 바라보며, 꽃의 운명을 측은히 여겼다. 11 나는 벽 속에 사는 쥐들을 쫓아내려고 고양이를 한 마리 샀다. / 인생은 끊임없이 행복을 추구하는 것에 지나지 않는다. 12 그 가수는 무대에서 내려와 흥분한 팬들과 함께 노래를 불렀다.

13 reception
[risépʃən]

v receive 받다, 접대하다

n 받아들임, 수신, 환영회　　host a reception 환영회를 주최하다

★ We installed a satellite dish because of the poor television reception.

★ You had better not block others' view during the reception.

14 stumble
[stʌ́mbəl]

v 넘어지다, 비틀거리다　**≒** trip, stagger　**a stumbling block** 방해물, 고민거리

I couldn't avoid breaking my leg when I stumbled down the staircase.

15 whirl
[hwəːrl]

v 소용돌이치다 **n** 회전, 소란　　a social whirl 사회적 혼란

The wind picked up a handful of leaves, whirling them in the air.

16 comply
[kəmplái]

n compliance 응낙

v 따르다, 응하다　**≒** abide by　**↔** disobey 불복종하다

comply with orders 명령에 따르다

My lawyer checked thoroughly if the contract complied with legal regulations.

17 crash
[kræʃ]

v 부서지다, 충돌하다 **n** 충돌　**≒** collide, collision　　a car crash 교통사고

The airplane crashed into the mountains due to engine malfunctions.

18 creep
[kriːp]

v 기다, 살금살금 걷다　**≒** crawl, sneak　　creep into ~에 몰래 들어가다

The runaway crept out of his hiding place and turned himself in.

19 smash
[smæʃ]

v 부수다, 깨다　**≒** break, crush　　smash cans 깡통을 눌러 뭉개다

The biscuits were smashed into pieces when I dropped the box.

---

13 우리는 텔레비전 수신신호가 좋지 않아서 위성 안테나를 설치했다. / 환영회 하는 동안 다른 사람의 시야를 막지 않는 것이 좋겠어. 14 계단 아래로 넘어졌을 때 다리가 부러지는 것을 피할 수 없었다. 15 한 줌의 나뭇잎이 바람에 들려 공중에서 빙빙 돌며 날렸다. 16 내 변호사가 계약서가 법률 규정에 맞는지 철저히 검토했다. 17 항공기가 엔진 오작동으로 산에 충돌했다. 18 도망자는 은신처에서 슬며시 나와 자수했다. 19 내가 상자를 떨어뜨리자, 비스킷이 산산조각이 나버렸다.

---

20 ☑ **snap**
[snæp]

ⓥ 똑 부러지다, 덥석 물다　　　　　**snap twigs** 작은 나뭇가지를 부러뜨리다

★ The stick couldn't hold the weight of the stones and snapped.

★ I watched a crocodile snapping at its lunch when I went to the zoo.

---

21 ☑ **delay**
[diléi]

ⓥ 늦추다, 미루다　ⓢ postpone　　**an unavoidable delay** 불가피한 연기

The ceremony was being delayed due to sudden problems.

---

22 ☑ **chop**
[tʃɑp]

ⓥ 자르다, 잘게 썰다　　　　　**chop down a tree** 나무를 베다

I chopped up sausages into small pieces for my younger sister.

---

23 ☑ **devastate**
[dévəstèit]

ⓝ **devastation** 황폐

ⓥ 황폐화하다　ⓢ ravage, desolate, destroy

a devastating earthquake (파괴적인) 강력한 지진

The hurricane will devastate the whole city if it comes through.

---

24 ☑ **diffuse**
[difjúːz]

ⓝ **diffusion** 살포, 유포

ⓥ 발산하다, 흩뜨리다　ⓢ emit, scatter　　**diffuse light** 빛을 발산하다

It seems that I can see the scent of perfume diffuse through the air.

---

25 ☑ **drain**
[drein]

ⓥ 물을 빼다　ⓝ 배수　　　**drain the land dry** 토지를 배수해서 말리다

★ A terrible flood will happen if we don't drain the dam in time.

★ The water in the bathroom leaves through the drain on the floor.

---

26 ☑ **drift**
[drift]

ⓐ **drifting** 표류하는, 불안정한

ⓥ 표류하다　ⓝ 표류　ⓢ float　　**drift of the current** 해류의 흐름

The shipwreck survivors were drifting around the sea on a lifeboat.

---

20 그 막대기는 돌의 무게를 이기지 못하고 똑 부러졌다. / 나는 동물원에 갔을 때 악어가 점심을 덥석 무는 것을 보았다. 21 갑작스러운 문제 때문에 식이 지연되고 있었다. 22 나는 여동생을 위해 소시지를 작게 잘라주었다. 23 허리케인이 도시를 지나가면 도시 전체를 황폐화할 것이다. 24 나는 마치 향수 냄새가 공중에 퍼지는 것을 볼 수 있는 것 같았다. 25 시간 내에 댐의 물을 빼지 않으면, 끔찍한 홍수가 발생할 것이다. / 욕실에 있는 물은 바닥에 있는 배수구를 통해 흘러나간다. 26 조난사고 생존자들은 구조선을 탄 채 바다 위를 표류하고 있었다.

27 elastic
[ilǽstik]

ⓝ elasticity 탄력, 탄성

ⓐ 탄력 있는, 유연한　⊜ flexible　⊜ rigid, inflexible 빳빳한, 딱딱한

an elastic body 탄성체

We were astonished at the elastic moves of the world-famous figure skater.

28 eradicate
[irǽdəkèit]

ⓝ eradication 근절, 박멸

ⓥ 근절하다, 뿌리째 뽑다　⊜ root out, uproot, exterminate

eradicate crime 범죄를 근절하다

Medical science succeeded in eradicating several deadly diseases.

29 explosion
[iksplóuʒən]

ⓐ explosive 폭발의

ⓝ 폭발　　**a nuclear explosion** 핵폭발

It was a tragedy that the whole family died in a gas explosion.

30 extinguish
[ikstíŋgwiʃ]

ⓝ extinguisher 소화기
ⓝ extinguishment 소화, 전멸

ⓥ 끄다, 소멸시키다　⊜ put out　　**extinguish a fire** 화재를 진압하다

It took a whole week to extinguish the forest fire.

31 flourish
[flə́:riʃ]

ⓐ flourishing 번영하는, 무성한

ⓥ 번영하다, 잘 자라다　⊜ thrive, prosper

a flourishing business 번성하는 사업

The greenhouse was built so that crops could flourish during the winter.

32 flutter
[flʌ́tər]

ⓥ 날개 치다, 퍼덕거리다　　**fluttering leaves** 팔랑거리는 나뭇잎

Birds have developed huge breast muscles to flutter their wings.

33 flux
[flʌks]

ⓝ (물의) 흐름　　**constant flux** 끊임없는 흐름

It's hard to capture market needs that are in a state of flux.

---

27 우리는 세계적으로 유명한 피겨 스케이트 선수의 유연한 동작에 넋을 잃었다.　28 의학은 여러 치명적인 질병을 근절시키는 데 성공했다.　29 가족 전체가 가스 폭발 사고로 목숨을 잃은 것은 참으로 비극적이었다.　30 산불을 진화하는 데 꼬박 일주일이 걸렸다.　31 온실을 설치해서 겨울에도 곡식이 잘 자랄 수 있었다.　32 새는 날갯짓을 하기 위해 큰 가슴 근육을 발달시켰다.　33 항상 변하는 시장에 필요한 것을 잡아내는 것은 어렵다.

34 gasp
[gæsp]

ⓥ 헐떡거리다, 숨이 차다　　**gasp out one's life** 마지막 숨을 거두다

The old man started to gasp for air after only one step of the stairs.

35 insert
[insə́:rt]

ⓝ insertion 삽입, 끼어 넣기

ⓥ 삽입하다　　**insert a coin** 동전을 넣다

The editor inserted an appendix that explained the book's main point.

36 liberate
[líbərèit]

ⓝ liberation 해방, 석방

ⓥ 자유롭게 하다, 해방하다　**ⓔ** release　**ⓐ** imprison 투옥하다
liberate a slave 노예를 해방하다

The Korean people were liberated from the Japanese Empire in 1945.

37 mitigate
[mítəgèit]

ⓝ mitigation 완화, 경감

ⓥ 완화시키다, 누그러뜨리다　**ⓔ** alleviate　**mitigate poverty** 가난을 완화시키다

These pills are meant to mitigate the pain caused by the surgery.

38 plunge
[plʌndʒ]

ⓥ 던져 넣다, 뛰어들다　　**plunge into danger** 위험으로 뛰어들다

We plunged into the sea as soon as we arrived at the beautiful beach.

39 propel
[prəpél]

ⓝ propeller 추진기, 프로펠러

ⓥ 추진하다, 나아가게 하다　　**propelling power** 추진력

A motorboat is propelled by an engine which runs on gasoline.

40 flush
[flʌʃ]

ⓥ 분출하다, 붉어지다　　**a flush of orders** 주문 쇄도

She flushed in embarrassment when the man confessed his love.

---

34 노인은 겨우 계단 하나를 오르고 나서 숨을 헐떡거리기 시작했다. 35 편집자는 책의 요점을 설명하는 부록을 삽입했다. 36 한국인들은 1945년에 일제로부터 해방되었다. 37 이 알약은 수술로 말미암은 고통을 완화하기 위한 것이다. 38 우리는 아름다운 해변에 도착하자마자 바다 속으로 뛰어들어갔다. 39 모터보트는 휘발유로 작동하는 엔진을 통해 추진력을 얻는다. 40 남자가 자신의 사랑을 고백했을 때, 그녀는 부끄러움에 얼굴이 붉어졌다.

EXERCISE

A 다음 영어는 우리말로, 우리말은 영어로 옮기시오.

01 stumble _____   07 시들다, 말라줄다 _____

02 befall _____   08 부수다, 깨다 _____

03 liberate _____   09 근절하다 _____

04 plunge _____   10 거절하다, 기울다 _____

05 chase _____   11 끄다, 소멸하다 _____

06 propel _____   12 물을 빼다 _____

B 다음 빈칸에 알맞은 단어를 쓰시오.

01 delay ⊜ _____   07 reception ⓥ _____

02 flourish ⊜ _____   08 emerging ⓥ _____

03 mitigate ⊜ _____   09 explosion ⓐ _____

04 attach ⇔ _____   10 adhere ⓐ _____

05 comply ⇔ _____   11 devastate ⓝ _____

06 ascend ⇔ _____   12 diffuse ⓝ _____

C 다음 빈칸에 들어갈 알맞은 말을 고르시오. (필요하면 형태를 바꾸시오.)

activate	emerging	elastic	flutter	whirl

01 During the heavy thunderstorm, the leaves _____ in the sky.

02 The cute little bird _____ its wings as it was trying to fly on its own.

03 In order to _____ the machine, you must press the red "start" button.

04 My grandmother prefers to wear _____ clothing, as she is heavy-set.

05 The small company is a(n) _____ electronics firm that was established only a year ago.

Across

1 to do what you have to do or are asked to do

3 to make a fire or light stop burning or shining

5 to make the water or liquid in something flow away

6 to break open or apart suddenly and violently, especially as a result of an impact or internal pressure

8 to free someone from feelings or conditions that make their life unhappy or difficult

9 to develop well and be successful

10 to completely get rid of something such as a disease or a social problem

Down

2 to make a situation or the effects of something less unpleasant, harmful, or serious

4 to move, drive, or push something forward

5 to damage something very badly or completely

7 to decrease in quantity or importance

Unit 34 Movement & Motion 2

---

01 abandon
[əbǽndən]

n abandonment 포기, 유기

v 버리다, 포기하다 **ⓢ** give up 포기하다

abandon one's child 자식을 버리다

Only mice are roaming within the walls of the abandoned building.

---

02 bestow
[bistóu]

n bestowal 증여, 수여

v 수여하다, 증여하다 **ⓢ** present, grant **bestow a medal** 메달을 수여하다

The Christmas spirit is to bestow happiness and joy to others.

---

03 bet
[bet]

n betting 내기에 건 돈, 내기

v (내기를) 걸다

bet one's bottom dollar 매우 확신하다

The two men bet money on the results of tonight's soccer game.

---

04 subside
[səbsáid]

n subsidence 진정, 가라앉음

v 가라앉다, 내려앉다

subside into a chair 의자에 주저앉다

The man did everything he could to make the panic subside.

---

05 perish
[périʃ]

a perishable
(음식 등이) 쉽게 상하기 쉬운

v 죽다, 망가지다 **ⓢ** pass away, expire **perish by famine** 기근으로 죽다

We stood silent for the souls that perished defending this country.

---

06 yield
[ji:ld]

a yielding
다산의, 생산적인, 유순한

n 생산, 산출 **v** 산출하다, 양보하다, 양도하다
ⓢ produce 산출하다, give in 양보하다, surrender 양도하다

an annual yield 연간 생산

★ The company reached the highest yield since its foundation.

★ The man yielded all rights over his estate to his only son.

---

01 버려진 건물 내에는 오로지 쥐만이 살고 있을 뿐이다. 02 크리스마스 정신은 행복과 기쁨을 사람들에게 나눠주는 것이다. 03 두 남자는 오늘 밤 축구경기 결과에 대해 돈을 걸고 내기했다. 04 남자는 혼란이 진정되도록 할 수 있는 것은 다 했다. 05 우리는 이 나라를 지키다가 목숨을 잃은 영혼들을 위해 묵념을 했다. 06 회사는 설립 이래 최고의 생산을 달성했다. / 남자는 재산에 대한 모든 권리를 자신의 외아들에게 양도했다.

07 **conform**
[kənfɔ́ːrm]

ⓥ 따르다, 순응하다 **ⓢ** comply, adjust

ⓝ conformance 적합, 일치

conform to custom 관습에 따라 행동하다

The building has to conform to safety regulations.

---

08 **crumble**
[krʌ́mbl]

ⓥ 빻다, 부수다, 무너지다 **ⓢ** grind 빻다

the crumbling economy 무너지는 경제 상황

The house crumbled into dust after the demolition team did their job.

---

09 **extract**
[ikstrǽkt]

ⓥ 뽑다, 뽑아내다, 추출하다

ⓝ extraction 추출

extract a tooth 이를 뽑다

The therapist extracted medicine from several medical herbs.

---

10 **devour**
[diváuər]

ⓥ 게걸스레 먹다 **ⓢ** wolf

ⓐ devouring
게걸스럽게 먹는, 맹렬한

devour its prey 먹이를 게걸스럽게 먹다

My family devoured the bread as soon as it came out of the oven.

---

11 **disguise**
[disgáiz]

ⓝ 변장 **ⓥ** 변장시키다

a man in disguise 변장한 사람

★ Everyone wore a disguise to the masquerade party.

★ I disguised my voice when I called home to give my wife a surprise.

---

12 **dissipate**
[dísəpèit]

ⓥ 흩뜨리다, 낭비하다 **ⓢ** accumulate, collect

ⓝ dissipation 소실, 낭비

dissipate one's fortune 재산을 낭비하다

The storm dissipated the next day without causing any damage.

---

13 **drag**
[dræg]

ⓥ 끌다, 질질 끌리다

drag one's feet 발을 질질 끌며 걷다

We dragged the fallen tree to the river.

---

07 그 건물은 안전 수칙을 지켜야 한다. 08 건물 철거반이 작업을 끝내고 나서 집은 먼지로 산산조각이 났다. 09 치료사는 여러 약초로부터 약 성분을 추출했다. 10 우리 가족은 오븐에서 빵이 나오자마자 게걸스럽게 먹어 치웠다. 11 모두 가면무도회에 변장을 하고 왔다. / 나는 집에 전화할 때, 아내를 놀려주려고 목소리를 다른 사람처럼 꾸몄다. 12 폭풍은 아무런 손해도 입히지 않고 다음날 사라졌다. 13 우리는 쓰러진 나무를 강 쪽으로 끌었다.

14 endow
[endáu]

ⓝ endowment 기증, 기부

ⓥ (능력 등을) 주다, 기부하다 **ⓢ** bestow 주다, donate 기부하다

endow money to ~에 돈을 기부하다

James was endowed with an extraordinary talent in music.

15 enhance
[enhǽns]

ⓝ enhancement 상승, 증진

ⓥ 개선하다, 향상시키다 **ⓢ** improve **ⓐ** worsen 악화시키다

enhance one's reputation 명성을 높이다

The engineers are looking for a way to enhance the speed of the car.

16 exploit
[éksplɔit]

ⓝ exploitation 이용, 개발, 착취

ⓥ 착취하다, 이용하다 **ⓢ** abuse 이용하다

exploit ruthlessly 무자비하게 착취하다

★ Some multinational companies are accused of exploiting labor from poor countries.

★ We must be smart and exploit this opportunity to its full extent.

17 stagger
[stǽɡər]

ⓥ 비틀거리다 **stagger from dizziness** 어지러움으로 비틀거리다

The man staggered towards the oasis, dragging his feet in thirst.

18 fetch
[fétʃ]

ⓥ 가지고 오다 **ⓢ** bring, deliver **fetch A for** ~을 위해 A를 가져오다

My grandfather asked me to fetch the newspaper for him.

19 flatten
[flǽtn]

ⓐ flat 평평한

ⓥ 평평하게 하다, 단조롭게 하다 **ⓢ** level out 평평하게 하다

flatten a box 상자를 평평하게 하다

The workers are flattening the ground for the building's foundation.

20 forge
[fɔ́ːrdʒ]

ⓝ forgery 위조

ⓥ 위조하다 **ⓢ** counterfeit **forge a document** 문서를 위조하다

The police arrested the women for forging official documents.

---

14 James는 음악적으로 천부적인 재능을 가지고 있었다. 15 정비공들은 자동차의 속도를 높일 방법을 찾고 있다. 16 일부 다국적 회사들은 가난한 나라로부터 노동을 착취한 것으로 비난받고 있다. / 우리는 현명하게 이 기회를 최대한 이용해야 한다. 17 남자는 갈증으로 다리를 질질 끌며, 오아시스를 향해 비틀거리며 걸었다. 18 할아버지께서 내게 신문을 대신 가져와 달라고 하셨다. 19 근로자들이 건물의 토대를 만들기 위해 땅을 평평하게 하고 있다. 20 경찰은 공문서를 위조한 혐의로 여자를 체포했다.

21 forsake
[fərséik]
ⓐ forsaken 버림받은, 버려진

ⓥ 버리다, 떠나다 ⊜ abandon, relinquish 버리다
forsake one's home 집을 버리고 떠나다
The monk forsook the world and lived in the mountains alone.

22 frown
[fraun]
ⓐ frowning 눈살을 찌푸린, 불쾌한

ⓥ 찌푸리다, 얼굴을 찡그리다 ⓝ 찌푸린 얼굴 **frown upon** ~을 못 마땅해 하다
★ The people all frowned at the man smoking near the bus stop.
★ The clown's frown expressed his frustration over the situation at the circus.

23 glimpse
[glimps]

ⓝ 흘끗 봄 ⓥ 흘끗 보다 **catch a glimpse of** ~을 흘끗 보다
★ The groom caught a glimpse of the bride before the wedding ceremony began.
★ I couldn't stop glimpsing at the beautiful girl at the party.

24 impel
[impél]
ⓐ impellent 추진하는, 밀어붙이는

ⓥ 추진하다, 재촉하다 **an impelling force** 추진력
The editor kept impelling me to finish my work before the deadline.

25 linger
[líŋgər]
ⓐ lingering 질질 끄는, 우물쭈물하는

ⓥ 오래 머무르다, 떠나지 못하다
linger to say good-bye 작별 인사를 하려고 남아있다
Her perfume lingered in the room long after she stepped out.

26 penetrate
[pénətrèit]
ⓝ penetration 침투, 관통

ⓥ 뚫다, 침투하다 ⊜ bore, go through
penetrate one's mind ~의 마음을 꿰뚫어 보다
The soldier screamed as he felt a bullet penetrating his body.

21 스님은 속세를 버리고 홀로 산속에서 생활했다. 22 사람들은 모두 버스 정류장에서 담배를 피우는 남자에게 눈살을 찌푸렸다. / 광대의 찡그린 표정은 서커스에서의 상황에 대한 좌절을 표현했다. 23 결혼식이 시작되기 전에 신랑은 신부를 흘끗 쳐다보았다. / 나는 파티장에서 그 아름다운 여자를 흘끗 보는 걸 멈출 수 없었다. 24 편집자는 계속해서 내게 마감 전에 작업을 마치라고 재촉했다. 25 그녀의 향수냄새는 그녀가 밖으로 나가고 나서도 한참 동안 방에 남아있었다. 26 병사는 총알이 몸을 뚫고 들어오는 것을 느끼자 비명을 질렀다.

27 pierce
[piərs]

ⓐ piercing 관통하는, (추위 등이) 살을 에는 듯한

ⓥ 꿰뚫다, 관통하다　　　**pierce one's ear** (귀고리용으로) 귀를 뚫다

My heart was pierced with grief at the bitter news.

---

28 poke
[pouk]

ⓥ 구멍을 내다, 찌르다　**ⓢ** jab　　　**poke a hole** 구멍을 내다

She poked me in the side and said she wanted to leave.

---

29 prolong
[proulɔ́:ŋ]

ⓐ prolonged 오래 끄는, 장기의

ⓥ 늘이다, 연장하다　**ⓢ** lengthen, extend　**ⓐ** shorten 줄이다

a prolonged drought 장기간의 가뭄

I fell in love with the countryside and decided to prolong my stay.

---

30 quiver
[kwívər]

ⓐ quivering 떨고 있는, 진동하는

ⓥ 떨다, 떨리다　**ⓢ** tremble　　　**quiver with fear** 공포로 몸을 떨다

I tried to control myself, but my voice quivered with anger.

---

31 relieve
[rilí:v]

ⓝ relief 경감, 안심, 구원

ⓥ 경감하다, 안도하게 하다　　　**relieve A of B** A에게서 B를 덜어주다

The pills aren't doing a good job in relieving me of my headache.

---

32 spanking
[spǽŋkiŋ]

ⓥ spank 찰싹 때리다

ⓝ (어린이의) 엉덩이를 때리기　　　**give A a spanking** A의 엉덩이를 때리다

My father used to give me a spanking when I did something wrong.

---

33 skim
[skim]

ⓥ 스쳐 지나가다, 대충 읽다, 걷어내다

skim the surface of ~을 피상적으로 다루다

★ I only had enough time to skim through the article.

★ The cook skimmed the fat off the milk to make whipping cream.

---

27 비통한 뉴스를 듣고 나의 가슴은 슬픔으로 찢어질 것 같았다.　28 그녀는 내 옆구리를 찌르고는 나가고 싶다고 말했다.　29 나는 시골마을에 흠뻑 빠져버렸고, 더 오래 머물기로 했다.　30 나는 자제하려고 애썼지만 내 목소리는 분노로 떨렸다.　31 알약은 내 두통을 그다지 효과적으로 완화하지 못하고 있다.　32 아버지는 내가 무얼 잘못하면 매를 들곤 하셨다.　33 나는 기사를 대충 훑어볼 시간밖에 없었다. / 제빵사는 생크림을 만들기 위해 우유에서 지방을 걷어냈다.

34 repel
[ripél]

Ⓥ 쫓아버리다, 격퇴하다　Ⓢ repulse 격퇴하다　**repel insects** 벌레를 퇴치하다

To my disappointment, the board repelled my business proposal.

35 retrieve
[ritríːv]

Ⓥ 되찾다, 만회하다　Ⓢ recover, regain

retrieve a missing item 분실물을 되찾다

Ⓝ retrieval 만회, 회복

I was only able to retrieve half of the money that I lent.

36 scrub
[skrʌb]

Ⓥ 북북 문지르다　Ⓢ rub　**scrub the floor** 바닥을 문질러 닦다

I had to scrub off the drawing some kid left on the outside wall.

37 seclude
[siklúːd]

Ⓥ 격리하다, 분리하다　Ⓢ isolate, separate　Ⓐ mingle 섞다

a secluded beach 외딴 해변

Ⓝ seclusion 격리, 은둔

I have a cottage in the countryside secluded from the city.

38 seize
[siːz]

Ⓥ 잡다, 붙잡다　Ⓢ grasp, snatch　Ⓐ let go, release 풀어주다

Seize the day. 오늘을 즐겨라.

Ⓝ seizure 붙잡기, 강탈

Our company tried to seize the chance to make huge profits.

39 shrink
[ʃriŋk]

Ⓥ 오그라들다, 줄다, 물러서다　**shrink with water** 물에 담그면 줄어든다

They all shrank in horror when they saw the lake monster.

Ⓝ shrinkage 수축, 축소

40 shrug
[ʃrʌg]

Ⓥ (어깨를) 으쓱하다 Ⓝ (어깨를) 으쓱하기

shrug one's shoulders 어깨를 으쓱하다

★ The teenager shrugged when asked if she wanted to talk about her problem.
★ To my question, he answered he had no idea and gave me a shrug.

34 실망스럽게도, 이사회는 내 사업 제안을 거절했다. 35 나는 빌려준 돈의 절반밖에 회수하지 못했다. 36 나는 건물 외벽에 어떤 아이가 남긴 낙서를 지워야 했다. 37 나는 도시로부터 떨어진 시골에 오두막 하나가 있다. 38 우리 회사는 큰 이익을 얻을 기회를 잡기 위해 노력했다. 39 그들은 호수의 괴물을 본 순간 두려움에 뒤로 물러섰다. 40 그 십대 청소년은 자신의 문제에 대해 얘기하고 싶으냐는 질문을 받았을 때 어깨를 으쓱했다. / 내 질문에 그는 전혀 모르겠다며 어깨를 으쓱였다.

EXERCISE

A 다음 영어는 우리말로, 우리말은 영어로 옮기시오.

01 crumble _____

02 flatten _____

03 quiver _____

04 devour _____

05 linger _____

06 stagger _____

07 버리다, 포기하다 _____

08 오그라들다, 물러서다 _____

09 찌푸리다 _____

10 경감하다, 안도하게 하다 _____

11 꿰뚫다, 관통하다 _____

12 뽑다, 추출하다 _____

B 다음 빈칸에 알맞은 단어를 쓰시오.

01 endow ⊜ _____

02 conform ⊜ _____

03 seclude ⊜ _____

04 enhance ⇔ _____

05 prolong ⇔ _____

06 dissipate ⇔ _____

07 yield ⓐ _____

08 impel ⓐ _____

09 perish ⓐ _____

10 bestow ⓝ _____

11 retrieve ⓝ _____

12 forge ⓝ _____

C 다음 빈칸에 들어갈 알맞은 말을 고르시오. (필요하면 형태를 바꾸시오.)

| disguise | repel | glimpse | subside | penetrate |

01 As I took the medicine prescribed by the doctor, the pain gradually _____.

02 Due to the traffic jam, the cars could barely _____ through the tunnel.

03 On Halloween night, kids go from house to house in their _____, ring bells, and shout, "Trick or treat!"

04 With the huge crowds, I could only catch a _____ of the music superstar's performance.

05 When used properly, this spray will _____ the bugs and keep the mosquitoes from biting you.

Crossword Puzzle

앞에서 배운 어휘를 기억하며 퍼즐을 풀어보세요.

정답

Across

5　to reduce someone's pain or unpleasant feelings

6　to behave in the way that most other people in your group or society behave

8　to die, especially in a terrible or sudden way

9　to drive or force (an attack or attacker) back or away

11　to change someone's appearance so that people cannot recognize them

Down

1　to produce a result, answer, or piece of information

2　to leave someone, especially someone you are responsible for

3　to find something and bring it back

4　to eat something quickly because you are very hungry

7　to improve something

10　to take hold of something suddenly and violently

Will & Effort

---

01 ☑ absorbed
[əbsɔ́ːrbd]

ⓥ absorb 열중케 하다

ⓐ 열중한, 몰두한 ⓔ engrossed, preoccupied ⓐ distracted 주위가 산만한

absorbed in thought 생각에 깊이 잠긴

I was absorbed by the philosophy of the great minds of my time.

---

02 ☑ accelerate
[æksélərèit]

ⓝ acceleration 가속

ⓥ 가속시키다, 촉진시키다 ⓔ speed up ⓐ decelerate 속도를 줄이다

accelerate growth 성장을 촉진시키다

The new members accelerated the progress of our project.

---

03 ☑ accessible
[æksésəbəl]

ⓝ access 접근

ⓐ 접근할 수 있는, 이용할 수 있는   **accessible to the public** 대중에 개방된

Lay all of your supplies on a table so they are easily accessible.

---

04 ☑ affirmative
[əfə́ːrmətiv]

ⓥ affirm 확언하다, 단언하다
ⓝ affirmation 확언, 단언, 긍정

ⓐ 긍정적인, 확언적인 ⓔ positive 긍정적인, confirming 확언적인
ⓐ negative 부정적인   **an affirmative reply** 찬성하는 회답

I got an affirmative response from my boss.

---

05 ☑ apt
[æpt]

ⓝ aptitude 경향, 적성

ⓐ 적절한, 적성 있는, 하기 쉬운 ⓔ appropriate, suitable, capable

be apt to 자칫 ~하기 쉽다

★ It is important for you to choose the apt theme for your blog site.

★ Most foods are apt to rot quickly in hot summer.

---

01 나는 나와 동시대를 살아가는 위대한 사상가들의 철학에 흠뻑 빠졌다. 02 새로운 구성원들은 우리 프로젝트의 진행을 촉진했다. 03 쉽게 접할 수 있도록 모든 공급품을 탁자 위에 진열해 두어라. 04 나는 상사로부터 긍정적인 답변을 받았다. 05 네 블로그에 맞는 적절한 주제를 고르는 것이 중요하다. / 더운 여름에는 대부분 음식이 부패하기 쉽다.

06 ascribe
[əskráib]

ⓥ ~의 탓으로 돌리다 **㊀** attribute

ascribe one's failure to a bad luck 실패를 불운 탓으로 돌리다

The CEO ascribed the honor of the award to the staff members.

07 attribute
[ətríbjuːt]

ⓝ attribution 돌림, 귀속

ⓥ ~의 탯[덕분]으로 하다 **attribute A to B** A를 B탓으로 돌리다

He attributed his success in business to diligence and hard work.

08 avoid
[əvɔ́id]

ⓝ avoidance 회피, 기피

ⓥ 피하다 **㊀** avert, evade **avoid contact** 연락을 피하다

You must try to avoid contradictions when arguing about an issue.

09 beware
[biwέər]

ⓥ 경계하다, 주의하다 **beware of strangers** 낯선 사람들을 경계하다

You must beware of strangers who approach you at night.

10 cautious
[kɔ́ːʃəs]

ⓝ caution 조심, 경고

ⓐ 조심성 있는 **㊀** careful **㊁** careless 부주의한

cautious optimism 신중한 낙관론

You should be cautious not to give offense to others.

11 collaborate
[kəlǽbərèit]

ⓝ collaboration 협동

ⓥ 공동으로 일하다, 협동하다 **collaborate with** ~와 협동하다

I have collaborated on this project with Jeffrey for over a year.

12 urge
[əːrdʒ]

ⓐ urgent 긴급한

ⓥ 재촉하다 **ⓝ** 충동 **㊀** incite, impel 재촉하다, impulse 충동

a sudden urge 갑작스러운 충동

★ We urged the family to seriously consider adopting a child of their own.

★ As civilized men, we need to know how to control our natural urges.

06 CEO는 수상의 영광을 모두 직원에게 돌렸다. 07 그는 사업의 성공이 근면함과 노력 덕분이라고 했다. 08 어떤 사안에 대해 주장을 할 때 모순을 피해야 한다. 09 너는 밤에 접근하는 낯선 사람들을 조심해야 한다. 10 당신은 다른 사람의 감정을 상하게 하지 않도록 매우 조심해야 한다. 11 나는 일 년 넘게 이 프로젝트를 Jeffrey와 공동으로 작업하고 있다. 12 우리는 그 가족에게 아이를 입양하는 것을 진지하게 고려해 보라고 재촉했다. / 우리는 문화인으로서 자연적인 충동을 억제할 줄 알아야 한다.

13 consciousness
[kánʃəsnis]

ⓐ conscious 의식하는

ⓝ 의식, 자각　**ⓔ subconsciousness** 잠재의식, 무의식

recover consciousness 의식을 회복하다

She lost consciousness when she had the car accident the other day.

14 selection
[silékʃən]

ⓥ select 선택하다, 선발하다

ⓝ 선택, 선발　**natural selection** 자연선택

In life, you will have to make a selection between different virtues.

15 dare
[dɛər]

ⓐⓝ daring 대담한; 대담성

ⓥ 감히 하다, 무릅쓰다　**I dare say** ~라고 감히 말하다

Don't you dare turn your back on me when I'm talking to you!

16 uphold
[ʌphóuld]

ⓥ 떠받치다, 지지하다　**ⓔ support, maintain**

uphold one's dignity 위신을 지키다

The man formed a party to uphold the principles that he believed in.

17 defer
[difə́:r]

ⓝ deferment 연기

ⓥ 연기하다　**ⓔ delay, put off, postpone**

defer the departure 출발을 연기하다

The people couldn't come to an agreement and deferred the decision.

18 demanding
[dimǽndiŋ]

ⓐ 큰 노력을 요하는, 지나친 요구를 하는　**demanding work** 힘든 일

The waiter couldn't grant everything the demanding customer wanted.

19 deserve
[dizə́:rv]

ⓥ ~을 받을 가치가 있다　**deserve the prize** 상을 받아 마땅하다

I don't get the respect I deserve from my family.

---

13 그녀는 저번에 교통사고를 당했을 때 의식을 잃었다.　14 살아가면서, 여러 가치 중에서 선택해야 할 것이다.　15 내가 이야기할 때 감히 내게 등 돌리지 마라!　16 그 남자는 자신이 믿는 원칙을 지지하기 위해 정당을 창설했다.　17 사람들은 합의점을 찾지 못하고 결정을 연기하기로 했다.　18 웨이터는 너무 많은 것을 요구하는 손님이 원하는 걸 전부 들어줄 수 없었다.　19 나는 가족으로부터 받아야 하는 존중을 충분히 받지 못한다.

20 ☑ zeal
[ziːl]

ⓐ **zealous** 열심인, 열광적인
ⓝ **zealot** 열광자, 광신도

ⓝ 열심

excessive zeal 지나친 열의

After a big failure, the writer felt he lost his zeal to write.

---

21 ☑ efface
[iféis]

ⓝ **effacement** 말소, 소멸

ⓥ 지우다, 말살하다　ⓔ erase 지우다, eliminate 말살하다
efface one's memory ~의 기억을 지우다

The author effaced a few controversial lines from the book.

---

22 ☑ enthusiasm
[enθúːziæzəm]

ⓐ **enthusiastic** 열광적인

ⓝ 열광, 열의, 열정　ⓔ passion, fervor
demonstrate enthusiasm 열의를 보이다

I complained that he no longer felt enthusiasm for his practice.

---

23 ☑ exert
[igzɔ́ːrt]

ⓝ **exertion** 노력

ⓥ 노력하다, 발휘하다
exert one's influence 영향력을 발휘하다

I exerted pressure on my brother to study more and play less during weekends.

---

24 ☑ feasible
[fíːzəbəl]

ⓝ **feasibility** 가능성

ⓐ 실행 가능한, 그럴듯한　ⓔ possible 실행 가능한, plausible 그럴듯한
a feasible solution 실행 가능한 해결책

I need to come up with a feasible excuse to postpone the deadline.

---

25 ☑ fervor
[fɔ́ːrvər]

ⓐ **fervent** 열렬한

ⓝ 열정, 열렬함　ⓔ enthusiasm
religious fervor 종교적 열정

We were touched by the fervor of the musician on stage.

---

26 ☑ flee
[fliː]

ⓝ **flight** 도주, 탈출

ⓥ 달아나다, 도망치다　ⓔ run away
flee for safety 피난하다

The criminal fled from the police pursuit and tried to stay unseen.

---

20 커다란 실패를 겪고 나서, 작가는 글쓰기에 대한 열의를 잃은 느낌이 들었다. 21 저자는 책에서 논란이 되는 몇 줄을 삭제했다. 22 나는 그가 더 이상 연습에 열정을 느끼지 않는 것에 대해 불평했다. 23 나는 주말에 동생이 공부를 더하고 덜 놀도록 압력을 주었다. 24 나는 마감일을 뒤로 미룰 그럴듯한 구실을 생각해내야 한다. 25 우리는 무대에 있는 음악가의 열정에 감동했다. 26 범죄자는 경찰의 추격으로부터 달아나, 몸을 숨기려고 했다.

27 flexible
[fléksəbəl]
- **v** flex 구부리다
- **n** flexibility 유연성

ⓐ 융통성 있는, 탄력적인　**ⓢ** pliable　**a flexible plan** 융통성 있는 계획

It's important to be open-minded and flexible about different ideas.

28 induce
[indjúːs]
- **n** induction 유도, 귀납

v 권유하다, 유도하다　**ⓢ** persuade 권유하다 cause 유도하다

induce electricity 전기를 유도하다

My teacher induced me to study harder and go to college.

29 intense
[inténs]
- **n** intensity 강렬, 격렬

ⓐ 격렬한, 강렬한　**ⓢ** acute 격렬한 **ⓞ** moderate 보통의, 적당한

intense competition 치열한 경쟁

I had to mediate the intense debate between my two friends.

30 intensive
[inténsiv]
- **v** intensify 강하게 하다, 증대하다

ⓐ 집중적인, 강한　**ⓢ** concentrated 집중적인

intensive instruction 집중 교육

He filed an application to be admitted to the intensive course.

31 liable
[láiəbl]
- **n** liability 책임, 의무

ⓐ 책임을 져야 할, ~하기 쉬운　**ⓢ** responsible, inclined
ⓞ unlikely 할 수 없을 것 같은　　**be liable for** ~에 대한 책임이 있다

★ You will not be liable for any illegal use of the lost card.
★ Patients with cancer are more liable to infection.

32 mania
[méiniə]
- **n** **ⓐ** maniac
  미치광이, ~광; 미친, 광기의

n 열광, 열중　**baseball mania** 야구에 대한 열광

I am looking for a job that will fit my mania for jazz music.

33 motivation
[mòutəvéiʃən]
- **v** motivate 동기를 부여하다

n 동기 부여, 자극　**ⓢ** incentive, motive　**lack of motivation** 동기 부족

The executives are trying to manage employee motivation.

---

27 다른 의견에 대해 열린 마음과 융통성이 있는 것은 매우 중요하다.　28 선생님은 내게 공부를 더 열심히 하고 대학에 진학할 것을 권유했다.　29 나는 두 친구의 열띤 토론 사이에서 중재해야 했다.　30 그는 집중 교과 과정을 밟기 위해서 신청서를 냈다.　31 분실된 카드의 어떠한 불법적 사용에 대해 당신에게는 책임이 없습니다. / 암에 걸린 환자들은 더 감염되기 쉽다.　32 나는 내 재즈 음악에 대한 열정에 맞는 직업을 찾고 있다.　33 간부들은 직원들에게 동기부여를 하고자 노력한다.

34 oblige
[əbláidʒ]

n obligation 의무, 책임

v 주장하다, 강요하다   **⊜** compel, force   **be obliged to do** 하는 수 없이 ~하다

By law, we are obliged to pay taxes based on our income.

35 option
[ápʃən]

v opt 선택하다

n 선택, 선택권   **⊜** choice, selection   **take an option on** ~을 선택하다

I had no other option but to follow the plan he proposed.

36 passionate
[pǽʃənit]

n passion 열정

a 열렬한, 정열적인   **⊜** enthusiastic 정열적인

a passionate speech 열렬한 연설

John is a passionate reporter who never gives up finding the truth.

37 conversely
[kənvə́:rsli]

a converse 역의, 거꾸로의

ad 거꾸로   **turn conversely** 거꾸로 돌리다

Conversely to Jimmy, I do not think that is the issue at all.

38 perspiration
[pə̀:rspəréiʃən]

v perspire 땀을 흘리다
a perspiratory
땀나는, 발한 작용의

n 땀, 발한   **⊜** sweat   **beads of perspiration** 구슬땀

I practically bathed in perspiration when I stood before the crowd.

39 strive
[straiv]

n strife 투쟁, 경쟁

v 노력하다, 애쓰다   **⊜** struggle, try   **strive for peace** 평화를 위해 힘쓰다

I personally believe that it is important to strive for success.

40 presume
[prizú:m]

n presumption 추정

v 가정하다, 추정하다   **⊜** suppose   **the presumed value** 추정 가격

She must be presumed innocent until proven guilty.

---

34 우리는 법에 따라 수입에 따른 세금을 내야 한다. 35 그가 제안한 계획에 따르는 것 외에 내가 선택할 수 있는 것이 없었다. 36 John은 진실을 파헤치는 것을 절대 포기하지 않는 열정적인 기자다. 37 Jimmy와는 반대로, 나는 그것이 전혀 중요한 문제라고 생각하지 않는다. 38 청중 앞에 섰을 때 나는 실질적으로 땀으로 목욕을 했다. 39 나는 개인적으로 성공을 위해 노력하는 것이 중요하다고 생각한다. 40 그녀가 유죄로 입증될 때까지는 결백하다고 믿어 주어야 한다.

EXERCISE

Unit 35

A 다음 영어는 우리말로, 우리말은 영어로 옮기시오.

01 attribute _____

02 passionate _____

03 efface _____

04 enthusiasm _____

05 induce _____

06 exert _____

07 가속시키다 _____

08 가정하다, 추정하다 _____

09 ~을 받을 가치가 있다 _____

10 책임을 져야 할 _____

11 공동으로 일하다 _____

12 실행 가능한, 그럴듯한 _____

B 다음 빈칸에 알맞은 단어를 쓰시오.

01 apt ⊜ _____

02 uphold ⊜ _____

03 affirmative ⊜ _____

04 strive ⊜ _____

05 absorbed ⊜ _____

06 intense ⇔ _____

07 selection ⓥ _____

08 flexible ⓥ _____

09 urge ⓐ _____

10 zeal ⓐ _____

11 cautious ⓝ _____

12 accessible ⓝ _____

C 다음 빈칸에 들어갈 알맞은 말을 고르시오. (필요하면 형태를 바꾸시오.)

consciousness	intensive	beware	demanding	oblige

01 Children are very _____, so adults need to care of them.

02 _____ of the neighbor's dog, as it is usually unleashed and not trained.

03 Due to the heavy smoke, several firefighters lost _____ for about ten minutes.

04 Advanced physics is one of the most _____ courses offered in college.

05 As their only grandchild, Jules felt _____ to escort his grandparents to the show.

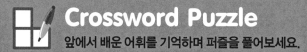

Crossword Puzzle

앞에서 배운 어휘를 기억하며 퍼즐을 풀어보세요.

1. m
2. s
3. c
4. a
5. a
6. a
7. u
8. p
9. i
10. b

Across

3 to work together with a person or group in order to achieve something

6 exactly right for a particular situation or purpose

7 to strongly suggest that someone does something

8 showing or involving very strong feelings of sexual love

9 involving a lot of activity, effort, or careful attention in a short period of time

10 to be cautious and alert to risks or dangers

Down

1 eagerness and willingness to do something without needing to be told or forced to do it

2 to make a great effort to achieve something

4 agreeing with or consenting to a statement or request

5 to regard something as being caused by

6 to increase in rate, amount or extent

Unit 36 State & Character

---

01 ☑ **hideous**
[hídiəs]

ⓐ 흉측한, 무시무시한 ⊜ horrendous   **a hideous monster** 흉측한 괴물

The car crash left a hideous scar on his face.

---

02 ☑ **blank**
[blæŋk]

ⓝ 공백 ⓐ 공백의, 백지의 ⊜ empty   **leave paper blank** 종이를 백지로 두다

★ The blank sheet of paper was quickly filled during the course of the exam.

★ I only had to fill out the blanks on the admission form.

---

03 ☑ **breathless**
[bréθlis]

ⓝ **breath** 호흡
ⓥ **breathe** [briːð] 숨 쉬다

ⓐ 숨을 못 쉴 정도의, 숨 가쁜 ⊜ out of breath

   a breathless speed 굉장한 속력

She was breathless during her brother's entire surgery.

---

04 ☑ **ceaseless**
[síːslis]

ⓥ **cease** 중단하다

ⓐ 끊임없는, 부단한 ⊜ constant, continual

   ceaseless efforts 끊임없는 노력

Not having an umbrella, I waited for the ceaseless rainfall to stop.

---

05 ☑ **competent**
[kámpətənt]

ⓝ **competence** 능력

ⓐ 유능한, 적임의 ⊜ qualified ⊜ incompetent 무능한

   a competent mechanic 유능한 기계공

We are looking for someone competent that can help us find some data we need.

---

06 ☑ **compulsory**
[kəmpʌ́lsəri]

ⓥ **compel** 강요하다

ⓐ 강제적인, 의무적인 ⊜ mandatory, obligatory

   compulsory education 의무교육

The annual medical check-up is compulsory for all employees.

---

01 차 사고로 그의 얼굴에는 흉측한 흉터가 생겼다. 02 시험을 치르는 동안 백지가 빠르게 채워졌다. / 내가 할 일은 입학 신청서의 빈칸을 채우는 것뿐이었다. 03 그녀는 남동생의 수술 내내 숨을 쉴 수 없었다. 04 나는 우산이 없었기 때문에 끊임없는 비가 멈추기를 기다렸다. 05 우리는 필요한 자료를 찾는 것을 도와줄 수 있는 유능한 사람을 찾고 있다. 06 연간 건강검진은 전 직원에게 의무다.

07 impulse
[ímpʌls]
ⓐ impulsive 충동적인

ⓝ 충동, 자극　ⓔ urge

impulse buying 충동구매

I couldn't resist a sudden impulse to hug her.

08 decent
[díːsənt]
ⓝ decency 품위, 고상함

ⓐ 고상한, 예의 바른, 알맞은　ⓔ appropriate 알맞은

decent conduct 예의 바른 행동

I'm looking for a house that is decent for a family of three.

09 definite
[défənit]
ⓐⓓ definitely 확실히

ⓐ 확정된, 한정된　ⓔ indefinite

a definite answer 확답

Some knowledge of Spanish is a definite advantage in this job.

10 delicate
[délikət]
ⓝ delicacy 고움, 섬세

ⓐ 섬세한, 우아한　ⓔ fine, elegant, exquisite

a delicate figure 우아한 자태

The ice sculpture at the wedding ceremony was delicate and beautiful.

11 devoid
[divɔ́id]

ⓐ 전혀 없는, ～이 결여된　ⓔ lacking

devoid of humor 유머가 없는

I made a vegetarian dish that was devoid of any kind of meat.

12 equivocal
[ikwívəkəl]
ⓥ equivocate 모호한 말을 쓰다

ⓐ 애매한, 확실치 않은　ⓔ ambiguous

an equivocal pronunciation 애매한 발음

She answered me in an equivocal way neither saying yes or no.

13 essential
[isénʃəl]
ⓝ essence 본질, 정수

ⓐ 필수의　ⓔ unimportant

an essential tool 필수적인 도구

Water and air are essential to all forms of life that live on the Earth.

---

07 나는 그녀를 안고 싶은 갑작스러운 충동을 누를 수 없었다.　08 나는 세 식구에게 알맞은 집을 찾고 있다.　09 스페인어에 대한 약간의 지식은 이 일에 분명히 도움이 된다.　10 결혼식에 있던 얼음조각은 우아하고 아름다웠다.　11 나는 그 어떤 종류의 고기도 들어있지 않은 채식주의자용 음식을 만들었다.　12 그녀는 나에게 긍정도 부정도 하지 않으며 애매하게 답했다.　13 물과 공기는 지구에 사는 모든 생명체에게 필수적이다.

14 everlasting
[èvərlǽstiŋ]

ⓐ 영원히 계속되는　　　　**everlasting fame** 불후의 명성

The body may decay through time, but his ideas will be everlasting.

15 exceptional
[iksépʃənəl]

ⓝ exception 예외

ⓐ 예외적인, 특별한　ⓢ extraordinary 특별한

exceptional talents 뛰어난 재능

Today, I had the most exceptional, wonderful evening of my entire life.

16 exemplary
[igzémpləri]

ⓝ exemplar 모범, 본

ⓐ 모범적인, 칭찬할만한　　　　**an exemplary official** 모범 공무원

Susan got a promotion in recognition of her exemplary conduct.

17 formal
[fɔ́:rməl]

ⓓ formally 정식으로

ⓐ 정식의, 형식적인　　　　**formal education** 정규교육

★ There is no formal agreement between the two countries.
★ I don't like wearing a formal dress.

18 gracious
[gréiʃəs]

ⓝ grace 우아, 품위

ⓐ 상냥한, 우아한　ⓢ courteous, friendly　ⓐ ungracious 무례한

gracious living 우아한 삶

The hostess greeted the guests in a most gracious manner.

19 inaccurate
[inǽkjərit]

ⓝ inaccuracy 부정확, 잘못

ⓐ 부정확한, 정밀하지 않은　ⓐ accurate, precise 정확한

inaccurate information 부정확한 정보

The old maps were usually inaccurate or incomplete.

20 inanimate
[inǽnəmit]

ⓝ inanimation 생명이 없음

ⓐ 무생물의, 생명이 없는　ⓢ lifeless　ⓐ animate 생명이 있는

an inanimate object 무생물

Some animations bring inanimate objects to life as characters.

---

14 육체는 시간이 지남에 따라 부패하지만, 그의 사상들은 영원할 것이다.　15 나는 오늘 내 인생에서 가장 특별하고 멋진 저녁을 보냈다.　16 Susan은 모범적인 행동을 인정받아 승진했다.　17 두 나라 사이에 공식적인 협약은 없다. / 나는 격식을 차린 드레스를 입는 것을 좋아하지 않는다.　18 여주인은 손님들을 매우 우아한 태도로 환영했다.　19 오래된 지도는 보통 부정확하고 완전하지 않다.　20 어떤 애니메이션들은 무생물의 물체에 캐릭터로서의 생명을 불어 넣는다.

21 incredible
[inkrédəbəl]

ⓐ 놀라운, 믿어지지 않는 ⊖ credible 믿을 만한

an incredible story 믿어지지 않는 이야기

Winning the championship was an incredible experience.

22 indispensable
[ìndispénsəbəl]

ⓐ 필수적인, 불가결의 ≒ essential ⊖ dispensable 없어도 되는

an indispensable member of staff 없어선 안 되는 직원

Meat is not indispensable for maintaining a healthy diet.

23 fierce
[fiərs]

ⓐ 사나운, 흉포한

fierce animals 맹수

Even a fierce tiger will become a house cat if it lives in a cage.

24 superficial
[sùːpərfíʃəl]

ⓐ 표면의, 피상적인

a superficial view 피상적인 관점

His analysis was too superficial to point out anything important.

25 obligatory
[əblígətɔ̀ːri]

ⓐ 필수의, 의무적인 ≒ compulsory ⊖ optional 선택의

obligatory subjects 필수 과목

ⓝ obligation 의무, 책임

It is obligatory for all competitors to wear face protectors.

26 optimal
[áptəməl]

ⓐ 최선의, 최적의

an optimal position 가장 유리한 입장

ⓝ optimum 최적 조건

Our company said its optimal level of manpower is 2,100.

27 passive
[pǽsiv]

ⓐ 수동적인, 수동의 ⊖ active 적극적인

a passive attitude 수동적인 태도

I get frustrated to witness my husband's passive nature.

21 선수권대회 우승을 한 것은 믿을 수 없는 경험이었다. 22 육류가 건강한 식사를 유지하는 데에 필수적인 것은 아니다. 23 사나운 호랑이도 우리 안에서 살게 되면 집 고양이가 되어버릴 것이다. 24 그의 분석은 중요한 점을 찾아내기에는 너무 피상적이었다. 25 모든 선수가 얼굴 보호대를 착용하는 것은 필수다. 26 우리 회사는 적정 인력수준이 2,100명이라고 한다. 27 나는 남편의 소극적인 모습을 보면 실망스럽다.

28 portable
[pɔ́ːrtəbl]

ⓐ 들고 다닐 수 있는, 휴대용의   **a portable radio** 휴대용 라디오

Many kinds of electronic devices come in portable versions.

29 pertinent
[pə́ːrtənənt]

ⓥ pertain 적합하다, 어울리다

ⓐ 타당한, 적절한   **≒** relevant, suitable   **↔** inappropriate 부적절한

a pertinent fact 타당한 사실

I couldn't think of a pertinent remark about the situation.

30 possessive
[pəzésiv]

ⓥ possess 소유하다
ⓝ possession 소유물

ⓐ 소유욕이 강한, 소유의   **possessive rights** 소유권

Children tend to be very possessive over their favorite toys.

31 prestigious
[prestídʒiəs]

ⓝ prestige 위신, 신망

ⓐ 명성 있는, 유명한   **≒** celebrated   **↔** unknown 알려지지 않은

a prestigious school 명문학교

He was prestigious for his wealth and his good heart as well.

32 priceless
[práislis]

ⓐ 아주 귀중한, 값을 매길 수 없는   **≒** invaluable, precious

↔ worthless 가치 없는   **a priceless treasure** 귀중한 보물

They have in their possession many priceless antiques.

33 prominent
[prámənənt]

ⓝ prominence 두드러짐, 현저함

ⓐ 저명한, 현저한   **≒** notable, well-known 저명한, outstanding 현저한

a prominent scholar 저명한 학자

Not every great artist was prominent in the days of his or her own.

34 prospective
[prəspéktiv]

ⓐ 앞으로의, 기대되는   **a prospective husband** 장래의 남편감

I met with a prospective investor who's interested in my business.

---

28 온갖 종류의 전자기기들이 휴대 가능한 형태로 출시된다. 29 나는 현 상황에 대한 적절한 말을 생각하지 못했다. 30 아이들은 자기가 좋아하는 장난감에 강한 소유욕을 보이는 경향이 있다. 31 그는 재력과 착한 마음씨 때문에 명성이 자자했다. 32 그들은 값진 골동품을 많이 소유하고 있다. 33 모든 위대한 예술가들이 자신이 살던 시대에 저명했던 것은 아니다. 34 나는 내 사업에 관심이 있는 예비 투자자를 만났다.

35 ☑ ready-made
[rédiméid]

ⓐ 기성품의, 이미 만들어져 있는   **ready-made clothes** 기성복

I was so busy that I had to have ready-made dinners for a week.

36 ☑ relativity
[rèlətívəti]

ⓐ relative 비교상의, 상대적인

ⓝ 상대성, 관련성   **cultural relativity** 문화적 상대성

I think it's important to respect the relativity of culture.

37 ☑ reserved
[rizə́:rvd]

ⓝ reservation 예약
ⓥ reserve 남겨두다, 예약해 두다

ⓐ 예약한, 보류한   ⊜ booked   **a reserved seat** 예약석

Some seats on the subway are reserved for senior citizens.

38 ☑ separation
[sèpəréiʃən]

ⓥ separate 분리하다

ⓝ 분리, 이별   ⊜ detachment, split-up, disconnection
     separation of powers 권력의 분리

The man and woman accepted the inevitable separation as their fate.

39 ☑ slender
[sléndər]

ⓐ 날씬한, 가느다란, 호리호리한   ⊜ slim, thin   ⊖ chubby, plump 통통한
     a slender body 날씬한 몸

The man works out everyday to keep his figure slender and fit.

40 ☑ stale
[steil]

ⓐ 상한, 김빠진   ⊖ fresh   **stale beer** 김빠진 맥주

Put the biscuits back in the tin, or they'll go stale.

---

35 나는 하도 바빠서 일주일간 미리 만들어져 있는 저녁을 먹어야 했다. 36 나는 문화의 상대성을 존중하는 것이 중요하다고 생각한다. 37 지하철에 있는 일부 자리는 노약자를 위한 자리들이다. 38 그 남자와 여자는 피할 수 없는 이별을 운명으로 받아들였다. 39 남자는 몸매를 호리호리하고 건강하게 유지하기 위해 매일 운동을 한다. 40 비스킷을 깡통에 넣어두지 않으면 눅눅해질 거야.

EXERCISE

A 다음 영어는 우리말로, 우리말은 영어로 옮기시오.

01 decent _____
02 exemplary _____
03 inanimate _____
04 pertinent _____
05 optimal _____
06 everlasting _____

07 사나운, 흉포한 _____
08 휴대용의 _____
09 상한, 김빠진 _____
10 유능한, 적임의 _____
11 전혀 없는, ~이 결여된 _____
12 섬세한, 우아한 _____

B 다음 빈칸에 알맞은 단어를 쓰시오.

01 compulsory ⊜ _____
02 indispensable ⊜ _____
03 ceaseless ⊜ _____
04 prestigious ⊜ _____
05 passive ⇔ _____
06 priceless ⇔ _____

07 equivocal ⓥ _____
08 possessive ⓥ _____
09 relativity ⓐ _____
10 impulse ⓐ _____
11 prominent ⓝ _____
12 inaccurate ⓝ _____

C 다음 빈칸에 들어갈 알맞은 말을 고르시오. (필요하면 형태를 바꾸시오.)

| exceptional | prospective | separation | superficial | hideous |

01 The toad is _____ both to the touch and sight.

02 The twins were _____ math students, achieving a perfect score on every exam.

03 The young teenagers were _____ and paid little attention to their studies.

04 Due to the _____ of his parents, Charles was not doing well in school.

05 The university offered a special open house session for _____ students and their parents.

Across

1 happening for a long time without stopping

3 expected or expecting to be the specified thing in the future

5 the action or state of moving or being moved apart

9 required by a legal, moral, or other rule

10 of a good enough standard or quality

Down

2 unusual and likely not to happen often

4 wanting someone to have feelings of love or friendship for you and no one else

6 extremely unpleasant or ugly

7 able to be carried or moved easily

8 having enough skill or knowledge to do something to a satisfactory standard

Unit 37 Shape & Appearance

---

01 ☑ **appearance**
[əpíərəns]

ⓥ **appear** 나타나다

ⓝ 외모, 출현, 출연   ⊜ look 외모   **personal appearance** 외모, 용모

★ The model's appearance was very important to the success of her career.

★ I was surprised by my father's sudden appearance at the party.

---

02 ☑ **parcel**
[páːrsəl]

ⓝ 꾸러미, 소포   **send a parcel** 소포를 보내다

My parents sent me a parcel for my birthday by post.

---

03 ☑ **blunt**
[blʌnt]

ⓐ 무딘   **a blunt pencil** 심이 뭉뚝해진 연필

I bought new kitchen knives and disposed of the old blunt ones.

---

04 ☑ **bold**
[bould]

ⓝ **boldness** 대담

ⓐ 대담한, 뻔뻔한   **a bold adventure** 대담한 모험

Every classmate thought it was very bold of you to stand up to those bullies.

---

05 ☑ **character**
[kǽriktər]

ⓐ **characteristic**
특질 있는, 독특한

ⓝ 배역, 성격, 특성   **a main character** 주인공

★ The actor does his best to make the character look alive.

★ Our goal is to let the children develop good character.

---

06 ☑ **chunk**
[tʃʌŋk]

ⓐ **chunky** (음식 등이) 덩어리진

ⓝ 큰 덩어리, 상당한 양   ⊜ mass, lump   **a chunk of ice** 얼음 덩어리

Cut the potatoes into chunks and boil them in water for fifteen minutes.

---

01 그 모델의 외모는 그녀가 자신의 직업에서 성공하는 데 대단히 중요했다. / 나의 아버지가 파티에 갑자기 나타나서 매우 놀랐다. 02 부모님은 내 생일을 맞이하여 우편으로 소포를 보내주셨다. 03 나는 새로운 부엌칼을 사고, 예전에 쓰던 무딘 것들은 버렸다. 04 모든 반 친구들은 네가 못된 애들에게 대항한 것이 매우 대담하다고 생각했다. 05 그 배우는 배역이 살아있는 것처럼 보이도록 최선을 다한다. / 우리의 목적은 아이들이 올바른 품성을 발달시킬 수 있게 하는 것이다. 06 감자를 큰 덩어리로 잘라서 15분 동안 물에 삶아라.

---

07 ☑ **coarse**
[kɔːrs]

ⓐ 조잡한, 거친   ⑤ crude, rough   ⑩ delicate 섬세한   **coarse sand** 거친 모래

Sandy's skin became much coarser and drier lately as she often worked overtime.

---

08 ☑ **convertible**
[kənvə́ːrtəbəl]

ⓥ convert 전환하다, 바꾸다

ⓐ 바꿀 수 있는, 개조할 수 있는   **a convertible car** 지붕이 열리는 차, 오픈카

Mileage is meant for discounts only and isn't convertible to cash.

---

09 ☑ **coordinate**
[kouɔ́ːrdənit]

ⓝ coordination 동등, 협조

ⓥ 조정하다, 조화시키다   ⑤ adjust 조정하다, harmonize 조화시키다

coordinate our operations 작전을 조정하다

You should coordinate your curtains and cushions.

---

10 ☑ **crooked**
[krúkid]

ⓥ crook 구부리다

ⓐ 구부러진, 기형의   ⑤ bent, curved 구부러진   ⑩ straight 곧은

a crooked line 굽은 선

It is dangerous to drive on the crooked road on a rainy night.

---

11 ☑ **dimple**
[dímpəl]

ⓝ 보조개

We love Jacob's smile because of the dimples on his cheeks.

---

12 ☑ **distinctive**
[distíŋktiv]

ⓝ distinction 구별, 차이

ⓐ 독특한, 구별이 분명한   ⑤ characteristic, unique

⑩ ordinary, common 평범한   **a distinctive feature** 두드러진 특징

The new building had distinctive features compared to the others nearby.

---

13 ☑ **distinguished**
[distíŋgwiʃt]

ⓥ distinguish 구별하다

ⓐ 눈에 띄는, 현저한, 유명한   ⑤ outstanding, eminent

distinguished services 혁혁한 공훈

She has a distinguished record as a public official.

---

07 Sandy는 종종 야근을 해서 최근에 피부가 더 거칠고, 건조해졌다. 08 적립금은 할인에만 사용할 수 있으며 현금으로 바꿀 수 없습니다. 09 당신은 커튼과 쿠션을 잘 조화시켜야 한다. 10 비 오는 밤에 구불구불한 길에서 운전하는 것은 위험하다. 11 우리는 Jacob의 볼에 생기는 보조개 때문에 그의 미소를 좋아한다. 12 새로 지은 건물은 주변에 있는 나머지와 비교하여 구별되는 특징들이 있었다. 13 그녀는 공무원으로서 뛰어난 경력을 가지고 있다

14 drowsy
[dráuzi]

n drowsiness 졸음

a 졸리는, 활기 없는 **=** sleepy, dozy 졸린 **↔** awake 잠이 깬, lively 활발한

a drowsy village 활기 없는 마을

Buses at rush hour are crowded by a bunch of drowsy people.

15 wrinkle
[ríŋkəl]

n 주름, 잔주름 **smooth out wrinkles** 주름을 펴다

You have to iron out the wrinkles in the pants.

16 feeble
[fí:bəl]

a 허약한, 연약한 **=** weak, frail **↔** strong 강한

a feeble old man 허약한 노인

The old man seems feeble in body, but his mind remained unrivaled.

17 fluffy
[flʌ́fi]

n fluff 보풀, 면모

a 보풀의, 솜털의 **a fluffy towel** 폭신폭신한 수건

There would be dozens of fluffy little chicks hatching soon.

18 fuzzy
[fʌ́zi]

n fuzz 솜털, 잔털

a 흐린, 솜털 있는 **=** blurred 흐린 **a fuzzy picture** 흐릿한 사진

There is a fuzzy line between the figures and the background in the picture.

19 gorgeous
[gɔ́:rdʒəs]

a 화려한, 수려한, 호화스러운 **=** beautiful **↔** shabby 비루한, 허름한

a gorgeous blonde 멋진 금발을 가진 여성 (비격식)

Everybody thought Helen's wedding dress looked gorgeous.

20 grand
[grænd]

n grandeur 웅장

a 웅장한, 화려한 **=** magnificent, splendid **a grand finale** 웅장한 피날레

I was overwhelmed by the grand scale of the medieval palace.

---

14 출퇴근 혼잡 시간의 버스에는 잠이 덜 깬 사람들이 잔뜩 있다. 15 너는 바지 주름을 펴야 한다. 16 그 노인은 육체적으로 연약해 보이지만, 그의 정신은 적수가 없었다. 17 곧 수십 마리의 솜털 달린 병아리들이 부화할 것이다. 18 그림에서 인물과 배경 사이의 경계선이 흐리다. 19 모두 Helen의 웨딩드레스가 매우 아름답다고 생각했다. 20 나는 중세 궁전의 웅장한 크기에 압도당했다.

---

21 ☑ **lump**
[lʌmp]

ⓐ **lumpy** 덩어리진

ⓝ 덩어리 　　　　　　　　　　　　**a lump of clay** 흙 한 덩어리

I felt a lump in my throat when I was at my daughter's wedding.

---

22 ☑ **luxurious**
[lʌɡʒúəriəs]

ⓝ **luxury** 사치

ⓐ 호화로운, 사치스러운　ⓢ deluxe　ⓐ frugal 검소한

a luxurious hotel 호화로운 호텔

The exhibits were neither luxurious nor brilliant.

---

23 ☑ **obscure**
[əbskjúər]

ⓝ **obscurity** 불분명

ⓐ 분명하지 않은, 어두운　ⓢ ambiguous　ⓐ apparent, obvious 분명한

an obscure word 애매한 단어

The room was obscure, and it was hard for me to see where she was.

---

24 ☑ **ornament**
[ɔ́ːrnəmənt]

ⓐ **ornamental** 장식적인

ⓝ 장식, 장신구　　　　　　　　　**china ornaments** 도자기 장식품

The woman looked beautiful with her silver ornaments.

---

25 ☑ **outfit**
[áutfit]

ⓝ 장비, 의복　　　　　　　　　　　**a ski outfit** 스키 용품(한 벌)

For Christmas, I put on a Santa outfit and gave presents.

---

26 ☑ **outstanding**
[àutstǽndiŋ]

ⓐ 두드러진, 뛰어난　ⓢ prominent, notable 두드러진, excellent 뛰어난

an outstanding figure 두드러진 인물

I thought that my wife was outstanding on stage.

---

27 ☑ **plump**
[plʌmp]

ⓐ 포동포동한, 통통한　ⓢ chubby　ⓐ skinny 마른　　**a plump pig** 통통한 돼지

I kissed my baby son's plump cheeks and slowly put him to bed.

---

21 나는 딸의 결혼식에 가슴이 벅차서 목이 메었다. 22 그 전시회는 사치스럽지도 않고 화려하지도 않았다. 23 방은 어두웠고 나는 그녀가 어디에 있는지 잘 보이지 않았다. 24 은빛 장신구를 입은 그녀는 아름다웠다. 25 크리스마스를 맞이해서 나는 산타 옷을 입고 선물을 나눠줬다. 26 나는 아내가 무대에서 훌륭했다고 생각했다. 27 난 갓 태어난 아들의 포동포동한 양 볼에 입을 맞추고 천천히 침대에 눕혔다.

28 **scar**

[skɑ:r]

ⓐ scarred 흉터가 있는

ⓝ 흉터, 상처　　　　　　　　　**leave a scar** 흉터를 남기다

Jenny visited a plastic surgeon to remove the scar on her face.

---

29 **seal**

[si:l]

ⓥ 봉인하다 ⓝ 인장　　　　　　**seal an envelope** 봉투를 봉하다

★ The terrorists sealed the door and stopped the police from entering.

★ Since the seal on the medication was not broken, it could be trusted that it was safe to take.

---

30 **skinny**

[skíni]

ⓐ 바싹 여윈, 피골이 상접한　　　**a skinny figure** 가냘픈 몸매

She said she had to lose weight even though I thought she was skinny.

---

31 **skyscraper**

[skaiskréipər]

ⓝ 마천루, 고층건물 ⊜ high-rise　　**a tall skyscraper** 고층 건물

The 63 Building was Asia's highest skyscraper when it was built.

---

32 **slim**

[slim]

ⓐ 호리호리한, 아주 적은 ⊜ thin, slender　**a slim waist** 가냘픈 허리

Jasmine keeps her slim figure through a balanced diet and regular exercise.

---

33 **solid**

[sάlid]

ⓝ solidity 굳음, 고체성

ⓐ 고체의, 견고한, 견실한　　　**solid reasons** 근거가 확실한 이유

Bullets can pierce thick layers of solid steel.

---

34 **verge**

[və:rdʒ]

ⓝ 가장자리, 변두리 ⊜ edge, brink　**the verge of a cliff** 벼랑 끝
on the verge of ~에 직면한

I lived a quiet life, not knowing I was on the verge of danger.

---

28 Jenny는 얼굴에 있는 흉터를 없애기 위해 성형외과를 방문했다. 29 테러리스트들은 문을 막고 경찰이 들어오는 것을 저지했다. / 약품의 봉인이 뜯기지 않았기 때문에 그것을 복용해도 안전하다는 것을 알 수 있었다. 30 그녀는 살을 빼야 한다고 했지만, 내가 보이게는 너무 말라 보였다. 31 63빌딩은 건축 당시 아시아에서 가장 높은 고층건물이었다. 32 Jasmine은 균형 잡힌 식사와 규칙적인 운동으로 날씬한 몸매를 유지한다. 33 총알은 두꺼운 층의 견고한 철을 관통할 수 있다. 34 나는 위험이 닥쳐올 것을 모른 채, 조용히 살고 있었다.

35 ☑ **sturdy**
[stə́ːrdi]

ⓐ 견고한, 튼튼한 **⊜** firm, durable, solid **a sturdy structure** 견고한 구조물

The tent seemed sturdy enough to hold up to the stormy night.

---

36 ☑ **sun-baked**
[sʌ́nbèikt]

ⓐ 햇볕에 말린, 뜨거운 햇볕을 받는 **sun-baked skin** 햇볕에 뜨거워진 피부

I smelt the salty wind and saw the sun-baked beach.

---

37 ☑ **winding**
[wáindiŋ]

ⓥ wind 굽이치다, 휘감기다

ⓐ 나선형의, 구불구불한 **⊜** spiral 나선형의 **a winding staircase** 나선식 계단

I walked through the dark, winding hallway of a castle.

---

38 ☑ **tilt**
[tilt]

ⓥ 기울다, 경사지다 **⊜** slope, slant **tilt to the right** 오른쪽으로 기울다

It is common to see young people wearing a tilted cap.

---

39 ☑ **tremendous**
[triméndəs]

ⓐ 거대한, 굉장한, 무서운 **⊜** enormous

a tremendous explosion 굉장한 폭발

★ The size of the dinosaur bones at the museum is tremendous.

★ My baby brother kept crying during the tremendous storm.

---

40 ☑ **stain**
[stein]

ⓐ stainless
얼룩이 없는, 때가 묻지 않은

ⓝ 얼룩 **ⓥ** 더럽히다 **⊜** dirty, taint 더럽히다 **a coffee stain** 커피 얼룩

★ The coat was taken to the dry cleaner so that the stain could be removed.

★ After I got home, I saw my shirt was stained with some ketchup.

---

35 텐트는 폭풍이 치는 밤을 견딜 수 있을 만큼 튼튼해 보였다. 36 나는 소금기 있는 바람 냄새를 맡고 햇살이 내리쬐는 해변을 보았다. 37 나는 성의 어둡고 구불구불한 복도를 따라 걸어갔다. 38 젊은 사람들이 모자를 기울여서 쓴 것을 흔히 볼 수 있다. 39 박물관에 있는 공룡 뼈의 크기는 거대하다. / 내 어린 남동생은 무시무시한 폭풍이 치는 동안 계속 울었다. 40 그 코트는 얼룩을 제거하기 위해 세탁소에 맡겨졌다. / 나는 집에 돌아가고 나서 셔츠에 케첩이 묻어서 얼룩져 있는 것을 보았다.

EXERCISE

A 다음 영어는 우리말로, 우리말은 영어로 옮기시오.

01 distinguished   _____

02 skinny   _____

03 fuzzy   _____

04 outstanding   _____

05 verge   _____

06 bold   _____

07 무딘   _____

08 장비, 의복   _____

09 조정하다, 조화시키다   _____

10 화려한, 수려한   _____

11 마천루, 고층건물   _____

12 졸리는, 활기 없는   _____

B 다음 빈칸에 알맞은 단어를 쓰시오.

01 obscure   ⊜ _____

02 coarse   ⊜ _____

03 winding   ⊜ _____

04 plump   ⊜ _____

05 luxurious   ⊜ _____

06 crooked   ⇔ _____

07 convertible   ⓥ _____

08 appearance   ⓥ _____

09 chunk   ⓐ _____

10 character   ⓐ _____

11 solid   ⓝ _____

12 grand   ⓝ _____

C 다음 빈칸에 들어갈 알맞은 말을 고르시오. (필요하면 형태를 바꾸시오.)

distinctive	ornament	feeble	tilt	tremendous

01 The tea from India has a(n) _____ taste and is recognized for its spiciness.

02 In his old age, my once athletic grandfather became _____ in his joints and walked very slowly.

03 The Christmas tree _____ are kept in a safe box in the attic, and taken out in December.

04 In science experiments, even a small margin of error could make a(n) _____ difference.

05 When modeling, the supermodel was asked to _____ her head to the side to appear more mysterious.

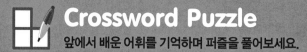

Crossword Puzzle

앞에서 배운 어휘를 기억하며 퍼즐을 풀어보세요.

정답

Across

1 tired and almost asleep

4 (of a person or their body) strongly and solidly built

6 having a rough surface that feels slightly hard

8 able to be changed in form, function, or character

9 not sharp or pointed

10 to close an entrance or a container with something that stops air, water, etc. from coming in or out of it

Down

1 having a special quality, character, or appearance that is different and easy to recognize

2 extremely beautiful or attractive

3 very big, fast, powerful, etc.

5 not well known and usually not very important

6 to organize an activity so that the people involved in it work well together and achieve a good result

7 the edge of a road, path, etc.

Mind & Feeling

---

01 acute
[əkjúːt]

ⓐ 날카로운, 민감한 ⊜ sharp 날카로운, sensitive 민감한

acute hearing 예민한 청각

I went through acute pain when I had my heart surgery.

---

02 queer
[kwiər]

ⓐ 이상한, 기묘한 ⊜ eccentric, odd   **a queer behavior** 이상한 행동

His attitude was a bit queer, as if he was hiding something from me.

---

03 glitter
[glítər]

ⓥ 반짝반짝 빛나다 ⊜ shine, glare, glisten

glitter with jewels 보석으로 반짝이다

ⓐ glittering
반짝반짝 빛나는, 번쩍이는

I was speechless before the glittering wonder of the palace.

---

04 consistent
[kənsístənt]

ⓐ 일관된, 일치하는 ⊜ steady, constant 일관된

a consistent policy 일관된 정책

ⓝ consistency 일관성

I try to make my words consistent with my actions at all times.

---

05 console
[kənsóul]

ⓥ 위로하다, 달래다 ⊜ comfort, soothe ⊖ distress 괴롭히다

console one's grief 슬픔을 달래다

ⓝ consolation 위로

My wife always stands by me and consoles me.

---

06 cowardly
[káuərdli]

ⓐ 겁이 많은, 비겁한, 비열한 ⊜ fainthearted 겁이 많은 ⊖ brave 용감한

a cowardly lie 비열한 거짓말

ⓝⓐ coward 겁쟁이; 소심한
ⓝ cowardice 겁, 소심함

Police have been too cowardly in facing physical violence.

---

01 심장수술을 받았을 때 나는 극심한 고통을 느꼈다. 02 그는 내게 무언가를 숨기는 것처럼, 태도가 약간 이상했다. 03 나는 궁전의 빛나는 장관 앞에서 할 말을 잃었다. 04 난 항상 말과 행동이 일관되도록 노력한다. 05 아내는 항상 내 옆에서 위로해준다. 06 경찰은 물리적 폭력에 대해 너무 비겁한 모습을 보여 왔다.

07 curse
[kəːrs]

ⓐ cursed 저주받은, 저주할

ⓝ 저주 **ⓥ** 저주하다 ● swear ● praise 칭찬, compliment 찬사

curse and swear 악담을 퍼붓다

★ Being very angry, he could not stop the curse words from coming out of his mouth.

★ He cursed the pickpocket who had stolen his wallet on the bus.

08 discomfort
[diskʌmfərt]

ⓝ 불쾌, 불편 ● annoyance, unpleasure **a discomfort index** 불쾌지수

My boss showed his discomfort when I was late for the meeting.

09 fragrant
[fréigrənt]

ⓝ fragrance 향기

ⓐ 향기로운 ● aromatic, perfumed ● stinking 악취를 풍기는

a fragrant rose 향기로운 장미

I recall she wore the most fragrant perfume I had ever smelt.

10 fright
[frait]

ⓥ frighten 놀라게 하다

ⓝ 공포, 두려움 ● fear, horror, panic ● courage 용기

stage fright 무대 공포증

He began to tremble with fright when the robber pointed a gun at him.

11 frigid
[frídʒid]

ⓐ 몹시 추운, 냉랭한 ● freezing **a frigid climate** 추운 기후

I only had a thin coat to protect me from the frigid night.

12 high-pitched
[haipítʃt]

ⓐ 음조가 높은 **high-pitched voice** 고음의 목소리

Dolphins can hear extremely high-pitched sounds that humans cannot.

07 그는 매우 화가 났기 때문에 입 밖으로 욕을 내뱉지 않을 수 없었다. / 그는 버스에서 자신의 지갑을 훔쳐간 소매치기를 저주했다. 08 내가 회의에 늦었을 때, 내 직장상사는 불쾌감을 보였다. 09 그녀는 내가 맡은 것 중 가장 향기로운 향수를 사용했던 것으로 기억한다. 10 그는 강도가 자신에게 총을 겨누자 두려움에 떨기 시작했다. 11 추운 밤 동안 나를 보호해 줄 것은 얇은 코트밖에 없었다. 12 돌고래들은 인간이 듣지 못하는, 극단적으로 높은 소리를 들을 수 있다.

13 humble
[hʌ́mbəl]

ⓐ 겸손한, 비천한　ⓢ modest 겸손한, lowly 비천한　ⓐ proud 자만하는

a humble request 겸손한 요구

I felt I should be humble before the great monk of the temple.

14 humiliate
[hjuːmílièit]

ⓝ **humiliation** 창피, 굴욕

ⓥ 창피를 주다　ⓢ embarrass, shame　ⓐ honor 명예를 주다

be humiliated by ~을 통해 창피를 당하다

I've never been so humiliated in my whole life.

15 glow
[glou]

ⓐ **glowing** 빛나는, 열렬한

ⓥ 빨갛게 타다, 백열하다 ⓝ 백열　**glow-in-the-dark** 야광의

We all sat side by side in the warm glow of the campfire.

16 keen
[kiːn]

ⓐ 날카로운, 예리한　ⓐ dull 무딘, 분명치 않은　**a keen edge** 예리한 모서리

His blunt skills of boxing were no match for the keen champion.

17 malodorous
[mælóudərəs]

ⓝ **malodor** 악취

ⓐ 악취를 풍기는　ⓢ smelly, stinking　ⓐ fragrant **malodorous smell** 악취

I heard skunks repel attackers with a malodorous spray.

18 mourn
[mɔːrn]

ⓐ **mournful** 슬픔에 잠긴

ⓥ 슬퍼하다, 애도하다　ⓢ grieve, lament　**mourn the death** 죽음을 애도하다

We all gathered to mourn the death of a brilliant young musician.

19 mute
[mjuːt]

ⓐ 무언의, 말이 없는　ⓢ silent, dumb, speechless

stand mute 묵비권을 행사하다

The man remained mute to the questions about his accusations.

---

13 나는 사찰의 큰스님 앞에서 겸손해야겠다는 생각이 들었다. 14 나는 평생 이렇게 창피를 당한 적이 한 번도 없다. 15 우리는 모닥불의 온기 주위로 나란히 둘러앉았다. 16 그의 무딘 복싱 솜씨는 예리한 챔피언의 적수가 되지 못했다. 17 나는 스컹크가 악취로 공격자를 물리친다고 들었다. 18 우리는 모두 뛰어난 음악가의 요절을 애도하기 위해 모였다. 19 남자는 자신의 기소에 대한 질문에 말이 없었다.

20 numb
[nʌm]

ⓐ 감각을 잃은, 마비된 ⓔ paralyzed, insensitive

numb with grief 슬픔에 빠져 멍한

I stopped playing with snow as my fingers started to get numb.

21 sniff
[snif]

ⓥ 코를 킁킁거리다 ⓝ 코를 킁킁거림 **get a sniff** 코를 킁킁거리며 맡다

★ There was smoke in the hallways, so we sniffed the air to figure out where the source of the fire was.

★ To find out the ingredients, I took a few sniffs before eating it.

22 manifest
[mǽnəfèst]

ⓐ 명백한, 분명한 ⓔ obvious, apparent ⓔ unclear 불확실한

a manifest error 명백한 잘못

ⓝ manifestation 명시, 표명

I suddenly felt confused and nothing seemed manifest anymore.

23 profile
[próufail]

ⓝ 옆얼굴, 윤곽, 태도 ⓔ outline, contour 윤곽

a low profile 눈에 띄지 않으려는 태도

Sitting next to the boy, she admired his handsome profile.

24 considering
[kənsídəriŋ]

ⓟⓡⓔⓟ ~을 고려하면 **considering his age** 그의 나이를 고려하면

Considering his time in Korea, Bill picked up Korean very quickly.

25 reluctant
[rilʌ́ktənt]

ⓐ 마음 내키지 않는, 마지못해 하는 ⓔ unwilling, disinclined

be reluctant to ~하기 꺼리다

ⓝ reluctance 싫음, 꺼려함

Some of the older staff were reluctant to use the new equipment.

26 resolute
[rézəlù:t]

ⓐ 결심이 굳은, 단호한 ⓔ determined, strong-willed
ⓔ irresolute 우유부단한

take a resolute stand 단호한 태도를 취하다

ⓥ resolve 결심하다, 결의하다

His resolute actions were quite persuasive to the crowd.

20 손가락에 감각이 없어지기 시작하자 눈을 가지고 노는 것을 그만두었다. 21 복도에 연기가 차 있어서 우리는 연기가 어디서 나는지 알아내려고 킁킁거리면서 냄새를 맡았다. / 나는 재료가 무엇인지 알아내려고 그것을 먹기 전에 코로 몇 번 킁킁거렸다. 22 나는 갑자기 혼란스러워졌고, 아무것도 더 이상 명백해 보이지 않았다. 23 그녀는 남자 아이 옆에 앉아서, 그의 잘생긴 옆얼굴을 흠모했다. 24 한국에서 지낸 시간을 고려하면, Bill은 한국말을 매우 빠르게 배웠다. 25 나이 든 직원 몇몇은 새로운 장비를 사용하기 꺼렸다. 26 그의 단호한 행동은 군중에게 제법 설득력이 있었다.

27 sane
[sein]

ⓝ sanity 제정신

ⓐ 제정신의   ⊖ insane, crazy 제정신이 아닌

a sane judgment 분별 있는 판단

As I listened to his argument, I started to wonder if he was sane or not.

28 scent
[sent]

ⓐ scentless 냄새가 없는

ⓝ 냄새, 향내   ⊜ fragrance, odor   **follow a scent** 냄새를 추적하다

The dogs followed the fox's scent to the edge of the forest.

29 odor
[óudər]

ⓝ 냄새, 향기   **an unpleasant odor** 불쾌한 냄새

He complained bitterly about the odor and the mess.

30 snore
[snɔːr]

ⓥ 코를 골다   **a terrible sound of snoring** 심한 코고는 소리

★ My brother started to snore as soon as he went to bed.

★ When she is very tired, she snores very loudly while sleeping.

31 spiritual
[spírit∫uəl]

ⓝ spirit 정신, 영혼

ⓐ 정신의, 영적인, 영혼의   ⊖ physical 육체의, unspiritual 영적이 아닌, 현세적인

spiritual guidance 정신적인 지도

Meditating at the temple was a good spiritual experience for me.

32 stillness
[stílnis]

ⓐ still 고요한

ⓝ 고요, 평온   ⊜ silence, calmness   **stillness of night** 밤의 고요함

The sound of footsteps on the path broke the stillness.

33 stimulus
[stímjələs]

ⓥ stimulate 자극하다

ⓝ 고무, 자극   ⊜ incitement 고무, spur 자극

a powerful stimulus 강력한 자극제

The discovery of oil acted as a stimulus to industrial development.

---

27 그의 주장을 들으면서, 그가 제정신인지 아닌지 궁금해지기 시작했다.   28 그 개는 숲의 가장자리까지 여우의 냄새를 따라갔다.   29 그는 냄새와 어질러 놓은 것에 대해서 심하게 불평했다.   30 내 동생은 잠자리에 들자마자 코를 골기 시작했다. / 그녀는 정말 피곤할 때면 잘 때 코를 시끄럽게 곤다.   31 절에서 참선하는 것은 매우 멋진 정신적 체험이었다.   32 길가의 발걸음 소리가 정적을 깼다.   33 석유의 발견은 산업 발달의 자극제 역할을 했다.

34 strain
[strein]

ⓝ 긴장, 피로　　　　　　　　　　　**under a strain** 긴장 상태에서

Peter couldn't stand the strain of his work and finally quit his job yesterday.

35 temptation
[temptéiʃən]

ⓥ temp 유혹하다

ⓝ 유혹　**ⓔ** lure, attraction　　**irresistible temptation** 뿌리치기 힘든 유혹

Christine fought off the temptation to give up on the project.

36 willing
[wíliŋ]

ⓝ will 의지

ⓐ 기꺼이 ~하는　　　　　　　　**willing hands** 자진하여 돕는 손길

I'm willing to help Martha if she asks for my assistance.

37 yearn
[jəːrn]

ⓝ yearning 갈망, 동경

ⓥ 동경하다, 그리워하다　**ⓔ** long　　**yearn for city life** 도시 생활을 동경하다

I yearn for a quiet, peaceful life without anything to bother me.

38 crack
[kræk]

ⓥ 깨지다, 부수다 **ⓝ** 갈라진 틈　**ⓔ** fracture

crack a walnut open 호두를 까다

★ After the child dropped the vase, it cracked in half.

★ I found a crack on the ceiling where rain kept coming through.

39 slap
[slæp]

ⓥ 찰싹 때리다　　　　　　　　　**slap one's cheek** ~의 빰을 때리다

He stood confused, rubbing the cheek that she had slapped.

40 adorable
[ədɔ́ːrəbəl]

ⓥ adore 숭배하다, 존경하다

ⓐ 귀여운, 숭배할 만한　　　　　　**an adorable baby** 귀여운 아기

The newborn puppy was the most adorable thing I've ever seen.

---

34 Peter는 힘든 업무를 견디지 못하고 결국 어제 회사를 그만두었다.　35 Christine은 프로젝트를 중도에 포기하려는 유혹을 뿌리쳤다.　36 Martha 가 내 도움이 필요하다고 하면, 나는 그녀를 기꺼이 도울 의향이 있다.　37 나는 나를 괴롭히는 일 없는 조용하고 평화로운 생활을 하고 싶다.　38 아이가 꽃병을 떨어뜨리자, 절반으로 깨졌다. / 나는 빗물이 계속 들어오는 천장의 틈새를 발견했다.　39 그는 어리둥절한 채, 그녀가 때린 빰을 문지르며 서 있었 다.　40 새로 태어난 강아지는 내가 본 것 중 가장 사랑스러웠다.

EXERCISE

Unit 38

A 다음 영어는 우리말로, 우리말은 영어로 옮기시오.

01 manifest _____ 07 불쾌, 불편 _____

02 acute _____ 08 유혹 _____

03 odor _____ 09 창피를 주다 _____

04 malodorous _____ 10 무언의, 말이 없는 _____

05 yearn _____ 11 긴장, 피로 _____

06 numb _____ 12 겁이 많은, 비겁한 _____

B 다음 빈칸에 알맞은 단어를 쓰시오.

01 reluctant ⊜ _____ 07 fright Ⓥ _____

02 stillness ⊜ _____ 08 resolute Ⓥ _____

03 consistent ⊜ _____ 09 curse Ⓐ _____

04 spiritual ⇔ _____ 10 glitter Ⓐ _____

05 fragrant ⇔ _____ 11 sane Ⓝ _____

06 humble ⇔ _____ 12 console Ⓝ _____

C 다음 빈칸에 들어갈 알맞은 말을 고르시오. (필요하면 형태를 바꾸시오.)

| frigid | queer | scent | stimulus | mourn |

01 The meat section of the supermarket is indeed very _____.

02 People still _____ the death of the famous actor.

03 The garden is full of the _____ of beautiful, blooming flowers.

04 The _____ behavior of the child will be examined by the psychologist.

05 The president of the United States offered a _____ package to aid in the recovery of the economy.

Crossword Puzzle

앞에서 배운 어휘를 기억하며 퍼즐을 풀어보세요.

정답

Across

1 a feeling of slight pain or of being physically uncomfortable

3 the desire to do something, especially something wrong or unwise

5 present or experienced to a severe or intense degree

8 to feel very sad and to miss someone after they have died

9 a thing or event that evokes a specific functional reaction in an organ or tissue

10 inspiring great affection or delight

11 slow and unwilling

Down

2 a sudden feeling of fear

4 (of a part of the body) deprived of the power of physical sensation

6 always behaving in the same way or having the same attitudes, standards, etc.

7 to make someone feel ashamed or stupid, especially when other people are present

Unit 39 Tone & Atmosphere

01 vigorous
[vígərəs]
ⓝ **vigor** 활기, 생기

ⓐ 활기찬, 박력 있는 ⓢ energetic　**a vigorous argument** 활발한 토론

Professor McFarland opened a vigorous debate about the War on Terror.

02 skeptical
[sképtikəl]
ⓝ **skeptic** 회의론자

ⓐ 회의적인, 의심 많은 ⓢ doubtful　**a skeptical eye** 회의적 시각

She was skeptical about the official report.

03 confessional
[kənféʃənəl]
ⓥ **confess** 고백하다, 자백하다

ⓐ 고백의　**confessional writing** 고백적인 글

The audience at the hall was touched by his confessional speech.

04 cordial
[kɔ́ːrdʒəl]
ⓝ **cordiality** 진심
ⓐⓓ **cordially** 진심으로

ⓐ 진심의, 따뜻한 ⓐ hostile 적대적인, 냉담한　**a cordial welcome** 따뜻한 환영

★ We try to keep a cordial relationship with our neighbors.
★ Our company held a cordial reception party for the new employees.

05 cozy
[kóuzi]

ⓐ 아늑한, 기분 좋은 ⓢ comfortable　**a cozy room** 아늑한 방

My father drowsed off near the cozy fireplace.

06 lucid
[lúːsid]

ⓐ 명확한, 맑은 ⓢ clear　**lucid explanation** 명확한 설명

Nobody thinks the river can be lucid ever again.

01 McFarland 교수님은 '테러와의 전쟁'에 대한 활발한 토의를 시작했다. 02 그녀는 공식발표에 대해 의구심이 들었다. 03 강당에 모인 청중들은 그의 고백적인 연설에 감동하였다. 04 우리는 이웃과 우호적인 관계를 유지하려고 노력한다. / 우리 회사는 신입사원들을 위해 따뜻한 환영회를 열었다. 05 아버지는 아늑한 벽난로 옆에서 잠드셨다. 06 아무도 강이 다시 맑아질 수 있다고 생각하지 않는다.

07 magnificent
[mægnífəsənt]

n magnificence 굉장함

a 웅장한, 훌륭한 **=** splendid

a magnificent view 웅장한 경치

The magnificent fireworks brought joy to the cheering spectators.

08 despairing
[dispɛ́əriŋ]

n v despair 절망; 절망하다

a 자포자기의, 절망적인

a despairing look 절망적인 표정

He worked hard to overcome the despairing situation.

09 uninterested
[ʌníntərəstid]

n v interest
관심, 흥미; 관심을 갖게 하다

a 관계가 없는, 무관심한

uninterested in politics 정치에 무관심한

Their attention wandered, and they soon seemed uninterested.

10 apologetic
[əpὰlədʒétik]

n apology 사과
v apologize 사과하다

a 사과하는, 사죄의

an apologetic tone 사과하는 어조

She forgave Tom after reading his apologetic letter.

11 argumentative
[ὰːrɡjuméntətiv]

v argue 논쟁하다, 주장하다
n argument 논쟁, 토론

a 논쟁적인 **=** quarrelsome

an argumentative essay 논쟁적인 글

It's rude to be argumentative with everything.

12 compelling
[kəmpéliŋ]

v compel 강제하다

a 강제적인, 강력한 **=** forceful

a compelling need 강한 필요성

He was absent from the meeting due to compelling circumstances.

13 elegant
[éləgənt]

n elegance 고상함

a 고상한, 품위 있는 **=** noble

an elegant dress 품위 있는 드레스

I took my wife to an elegant restaurant for her birthday.

---

07 찬란한 불꽃쇼가 환호하는 관람객들에 기쁨을 안겨주었다. 08 그는 절망적인 상황을 극복하기 위해 열심히 노력했다. 09 그들은 관심을 다른 곳에 두었고, 곧 무관심해 보였다. 10 그녀는 Tom이 보낸 사과 편지를 읽고 그를 용서했다. 11 모든 것에 대해 사사건건 따지는 것은 무례하다. 12 그는 부득이한 사정으로 회의에 참석하지 못했다. 13 나는 아내의 생일을 맞아 그녀를 우아한 식당에 데려갔다.

14 eloquent
[éləkwənt]

ⓝ eloquence 유창한 화술

ⓐ 설득력 있는, 웅변의 ⓢ persuasive **an eloquent speech** 설득력 있는 말

The people were persuaded by his eloquent words.

---

15 gloomy
[glúːmi]

ⓝ gloom 어둠, 우울함

ⓐ 암울한, 울적한 ⓢ depressing **a gloomy prospect** 암울한 전망

My grandfather's funeral day was very gloomy.

---

16 hesitant
[hézətənt]

ⓥ hesitate 머뭇거리다

ⓐ 머뭇거리는, 주저하는 **a hesitant manner** 머뭇거리는 태도

The committee was hesitant about making the decision.

---

17 cynical
[sínikəl]

ⓝ cynic 비꼬는 사람

ⓐ 냉소적인 ⓢ pessimistic **a cynical remark** 냉소적인 말

Why do you have to be so cynical all the time?

---

18 definitive
[difínətiv]

ⓐⓓ definitely 명확히

ⓐ 결정적인, 확고한 ⓢ decisive, conclusive **a definitive statement** 확고한 진술

The professor found a definitive solution to the problem.

---

19 monotonous
[mənátənəs]

ⓝ monotony 단조로움

ⓐ 단조로운, 변화 없는 ⓢ repetitive **a monotonous life** 단조로운 생활

I am sick and tired of the same monotonous work every day.

---

20 vivid
[vívid]

ⓐⓓ vividly 생생하게, 선명하게

ⓐ 생생한, 생기 있는 ⓢ vague, dull 희미한, 흐린 **vivid memories** 생생한 기억

My dream was so vivid and felt so real.

---

14 사람들은 그의 유창한 말에 설득되었다. 15 할아버지의 장례식 날은 매우 우울했다. 16 위원회는 결정을 내리는 것을 주저했다. 17 너는 왜 항상 그렇게 냉소적이니? 18 교수님이 문제에 대한 확실한 해답을 발견했다. 19 나는 매일 하는 똑같고 단조로운 일이 지겹다. 20 꿈이 너무 생생했고, 꼭 진짜처럼 느껴졌다.

21 horrific
[hɔ:rífik]

ⓥ horrify 무섭게 하다
ⓝ horror 공포, 혐오

ⓐ 무서운, 대단한 ⊜ dreadful   **a horrific accident** 끔찍한 사고

The flood caused horrific damage to the city.

---

22 logical
[ládʒikəl]

ⓝ logic 논리

ⓐ 논리적인 ⊜ rational   **a logical explanation** 논리적인 설명

This was the only logical conclusion I could come up with.

---

23 majestic
[mədʒéstik]

ⓝ majesty 위엄, 왕

ⓐ 웅장한, 장엄한 ⊜ magnificent   **a majestic mountain** 웅장한 산

We stood in awe as we looked at the majestic palace.

---

24 melancholy
[mélənkàli]

ⓐ 우울한, 생각에 잠긴 ⓝ 우울 ⊜ depressed 우울한, depression 우울

a melancholy mood

★ The orchestra played music that was melancholy and caused the audience to feel sad.

★ I was lost in melancholy after my wife's death.

---

25 mellow
[mélou]

ⓐⓓ mellowly 부드럽게

ⓐ 부드러운, 감미로운   **a mellow tone** 부드러운 말투

She often called me in a sweet, mellow voice.

---

26 hospitable
[háspitəbəl]

ⓝ hospitality 환대

ⓐ 잘 대접하는, 환대하는   **hospitable to visitors** 방문객을 잘 대접하는

Mr. Jefferson is always hospitable when we visit him.

---

27 tragic
[trǽdʒik]

ⓝ tragedy 비극

ⓐ 비극의, 비참한 ⊜ disastrous   **a tragic ending** 비극적인 결말

People were shocked by the tragic news of the accident.

---

21 홍수는 도시에 끔찍한 피해를 입혔다. 22 내가 생각해낼 수 있는 논리적인 결론은 이것뿐이었다. 23 우리는 웅장한 궁전을 보며 경외심을 가지고 서 있었다. 24 오케스트라는 우울한 곡을 연주했고, 관객들은 슬픔을 느꼈다. / 아내가 죽은 후, 나는 우울함에 빠져 있었다. 25 그녀는 종종 달콤하고 부드러운 목소리로 나를 부르곤 했다. 26 Jefferson 씨는 우리가 찾아갈 때마다 환대해 주신다. 27 사람들은 사고에 대한 비참한 뉴스를 듣고 충격에 휩싸였다.

28 mocking
[mάkiŋ]

ⓥ mock 조롱하다

ⓐ 조롱하는, 흉내 내는　ⓢ sarcastic　　**a mocking behavior** 조롱하는 행동

The long silence was broken only by a single mocking laugh.

29 objective
[əbdʒéktiv]

ⓝ objectivity 객관성

ⓐ 객관적인　ⓐ subjective 주관적인　　**objective reality** 객관적 실재

You should try to maintain an objective view about the issue.

30 persuasive
[pərswéisiv]

ⓥ persuade 설득하다

ⓐ 설득력 있는　ⓢ convincing　　**a persuasive argument** 설득력 있는 주장

Daniel's boss found his report quite persuasive.

31 reproachful
[ripróutʃfəl]

ⓥ reproach 꾸짖다

ⓐ 꾸짖는, 비난하는　　**reproachful words** 비난하는 말

My mother looked at me in a reproachful manner.

32 ridiculous
[ridíkjələs]

ⓥ ⓝ ridicule 비웃다; 비웃음

ⓐ 우스운, 어리석은　ⓢ absurd, silly　　**a ridiculous scene** 우스운 광경

It would be ridiculous to compare two movies that are from different genres.

33 sarcastic
[sɑːrkǽstik]

ⓝ sarcasm 풍자, 빈정거림

ⓐ 비꼬는, 빈정거리는　　**a sarcastic attitude** 비꼬는 태도

He made a sarcastic comment on Beck's argument.

34 satirical
[sətírikəl]

ⓝ satire 풍자

ⓐ 풍자적인, 비꼬는　ⓢ satiric　　**a satirical poem** 풍자시

Many satirical sketches on the show make fun of politicians.

---

28 긴 침묵은 단 한 번의 비웃음 소리로 깨지고 말았다.　29 사안에 대해 객관적인 입장을 유지하려고 노력해야 해.　30 Daniel의 상사는 Daniel의 보고서가 제법 설득력 있다고 생각했다.　31 어머니는 비난하는 식으로 나를 바라보셨다.　32 장르가 서로 다른 두 영화를 비교하는 것은 우스운 짓이다. 33 그는 Beck의 주장에 대해 빈정거리는 말을 했다.　34 그 프로그램의 많은 풍자적인 토막극에서 정치인들을 조롱한다.

35 **tranquil**
[trǽŋkwil]
n tranquility 평온함

ⓐ 평온한, 조용한　ⓢ calm, peaceful　　　**a tranquil life** 평온한 삶

I took a walk on a tranquil country road.

---

36 **urgent**
[ə́:rdʒənt]
v urge 재촉하다, 서두르게 하다
n urgency 긴급, 절박

ⓐ 긴급한, 절박한　ⓢ pressing　　　**an urgent message** 긴급한 메시지

He left early because of some urgent business.

---

37 **scary**
[skɛ́əri]
v scare 두렵게 하다

ⓐ 무서운, 두려운　ⓢ terrifying　　　**a scary movie** 공포영화

I was worried as a scary thought crossed my mind.

---

38 **scornful**
[skɔ́:rnfəl]
n v scorn 경멸; 경멸하다

ⓐ 경멸하는, 조소적인　ⓢ contemptuous　　　**a scornful smile** 조소

Mary gave him a scornful look, which made him tremble.

---

39 **serene**
[sirí:n]
n serenity 고요함

ⓐ 고요한, 잔잔한　ⓢ calm, quiet　　　**a serene lake** 잔잔한 호수

A serene atmosphere makes it an ideal place for a settlement.

---

40 **sinister**
[sínistər]

ⓐ 불길한, 사악한　ⓢ evil　　　**a sinister face** 험악한 얼굴

The hero stopped the villain's sinister plans.

---

35 나는 조용한 시골길에서 산책했다.　36 그는 급한 용무 때문에 일찍 떠났다.　37 무서운 생각이 들자 걱정되기 시작했다.　38 Mary는 그를 경멸적인 눈초리로 보았으며, 이것이 그를 떨게 했다.　39 그곳은 고요한 분위기 때문에 정착하기에 이상적인 장소다.　40 영웅이 악당의 사악한 계획을 저지했다.

EXERCISE

A 다음 영어는 우리말로, 우리말은 영어로 옮기시오.

01 cozy _____

02 reproachful _____

03 elegant _____

04 definitive _____

05 sarcastic _____

06 despairing _____

07 냉소적인 _____

08 논리적인 _____

09 회의적인, 의심 많은 _____

10 풍자적인 _____

11 관계가 없는, 무관심한 _____

12 잘 대접하는, 환대하는 _____

B 다음 빈칸에 알맞은 단어를 쓰시오.

01 tranquil ⊜ _____

02 vigorous ⊜ _____

03 persuasive ⊜ _____

04 magnificent ⊜ _____

05 cordial ⊜ _____

06 objective ⊜ _____

07 scornful ⓥ _____

08 hesitant ⓥ _____

09 mocking ⓥ _____

10 majestic ⓝ _____

11 monotonous ⓝ _____

12 serene ⓝ _____

C 다음 빈칸에 들어갈 알맞은 말을 고르시오. (필요하면 형태를 바꾸시오.)

mellow	sinister	compelling	lucid	apologetic

01 Even the detectives were afraid to interview the _____ criminal.

02 Please do not be _____ about the incident, as it was only an accident.

03 The lawyer failed to present _____ evidence to support his client's innocence.

04 I was sitting on the bench, looking at the swaying leaves in the _____ breeze.

05 Our favorite professor is popular because she always presents her lecture in a very _____ manner.

Crossword Puzzle

앞에서 배운 어휘를 기억하며 퍼즐을 풀어보세요.

Across

1 very silly or unreasonable

3 evoking interest, attention, or admiration

4 friendly, welcoming and generous

5 saying things that are opposite of what you mean, in order to make unkind joke

7 very clear and easy to understand

9 using a lot of strength or determination

10 causing extreme distress or sorrow

11 very good or beautiful, and very impressive

Down

2 very important and needing to be dealt with immediately

4 extremely bad, in a way that is frightening or upsetting

6 doubtful about something

8 uncertain about what to do or say because you are nervous or unwilling

Unit 40 Personality & Attitude

---

01 absent-minded
[金bsəntmàindid]

ⓐ 방심 상태의, 잘 잊어버리는 **an absent-minded person** 건망증이 심한 사람

I'm sometimes absent-minded, and leave my things behind.

---

02 clumsy
[klʌ́mzi]

ⓐ⃝ **clumsily** 서투르게

ⓐ 솜씨 없는, 서투른 ⓢ awkward **a clumsy hand** 투박한 솜씨

How could you be so clumsy and make such a mistake?

---

03 cruel
[krú:əl]

ⓝ **cruelty** 잔혹함

ⓐ 잔인한, 잔혹한 ⓢ ruthless **a cruel heart** 잔인한 기질

It was cruel of you to say those things to Helen.

---

04 cunning
[kʌ́niŋ]

ⓐ 교활한, 간사한 ⓢ sly ⓐ naive 순진한 **a cunning spy** 교활한 스파이

The fox is often depicted as a cunning animal in fables.

---

05 discreet
[diskrí:t]

ⓝ **discretion** 행동의 자유, 분별
ⓐ⃝ **discreetly**
조심스럽게, 신중하게

ⓐ 분별 있는, 생각이 깊은 ⓢ careful, considerate

a discreet inquiry 신중한 조사
be discreet in speech 언사를 조심하다

★ The man was discreet in words during the inspection.

★ I deeply regretted not being discreet in what I said to her.

---

06 earnest
[ə́:rnist]

ⓐ 성실한, 진지한 ⓢ sincere **an earnest worker** 성실히 일하는 사람

John was promoted for his earnest deeds.

---

01 가끔 나는 생각 없이 내 물건을 어디에 두고 오곤 한다. 02 어떻게 그렇게 서툴게 행동해서 그런 실수를 할 수 있어? 03 네가 Helen에게 그런 말을 한 것은 잔인했어. 04 우화에서 여우는 흔히 교활한 동물로 묘사된다. 05 남자는 조사를 받을 때 말을 조심스럽게 했다. / 나는 그녀에게 생각 없이 했던 말에 대해 깊게 후회했다. 06 John은 성실히 일한 대가로 승진하였다.

07 arrogant
[ǽrəgənt]

ⓝ arrogance 거만함

ⓐ 거만한　ⓞ modest, humble 겸손한

be arrogant towards others 사람들에게 건방지게 행동하다

People don't like Mark's arrogant attitude.

08 ruthless
[rúːθlis]

ⓝ ruth 연민, 동정

ⓐ 무자비한　ⓞ merciless, pitiless

a ruthless businessman 비정한 사업가

The people will never tolerate a ruthless dictator.

09 frantic
[frǽntik]

ⓐ 미친 듯 날뛰는, 광란의　**make a frantic search for** 혈안이 되어 찾다

★ She was very frantic with the grief of losing her dog.

★ Korean passengers on my flight were frantic with anger about the delay.

10 harsh
[haːrʃ]

ⓐⓓ harshly 거칠게, 사납게

ⓐ 거친, 사나운　ⓞ severe, rough　**the harsh realities** 냉혹한 현실

The trip to the island was cancelled due to harsh weather.

11 sincere
[sinsíər]

ⓝ sincerity 성실, 진실
ⓐⓓ sincerely 성실하게, 진정으로

ⓐ 성실한, 진실한　ⓞ genuine　**sincere in one's beliefs** 믿음이 진실된

The soldiers fought for their country as sincere patriots.

12 instinctive
[instíŋktiv]

ⓝ instinct 본능

ⓐ 본능적인, 천성의　ⓞ inborn, natural

an instinctive reaction 본능적인 반응

Dogs are known to have instinctive knowledge of direction.

13 easygoing
[íːzigóuiŋ]

ⓐ 태평한, 느긋한　ⓞ carefree

enjoy easygoing life 태평한 생활을 즐기다

You are admired for your confidence and easygoing attitude.

07 사람들은 Mark의 거만한 태도를 좋아하지 않는다.　08 사람들은 무자비한 독재자를 절대 용인하지 않을 것이다.　09 그녀는 자신의 개를 잃어버린 슬픔으로 제정신이 아니었다. / 내가 탄 비행기의 한국인 승객들은 비행 지연에 화가 나서 미친 듯했다.　10 기상악화로 섬으로 가는 여행이 취소되었다. 11 병사들은 진정한 애국자로서, 조국을 위해 싸웠다.　12 개들은 본능적으로 방향을 구별하는 능력이 있는 것으로 알려졌다.　13 사람들은 너의 자신감과 태평한 생활 태도에 대해 감탄한다.

14 feverish
[fíːvəriʃ]

ⓝ fever 열, 열중, 열광

ⓐ 열광적인, 열띤　ⓢ frantic　　**a feverish activity** 열광적인 활동

★ The singer aroused feverish excitement in the audience.

★ It was the most feverish experience I'd ever had.

15 malevolent
[məlévələnt]

ⓝ malevolence 악의

ⓐ 악의 있는, 심술궂은　ⓐ benevolent 선의의, 호의적인

for malevolent purposes 악의적인 용도로

The thief approached her with malevolent intentions.

16 temper
[témpər]

ⓝ 성질, 기질, 기분　ⓢ temperament　　**control one's temper** 화를 참다

My father used to have an ill temper when I was little.

17 stern
[stə́ːrn]

ⓐ 엄격한, 단호한　ⓢ strict　　**a stern discipline** 엄격한 훈련

The drill sergeant is very stern towards the trainees.

18 conservative
[kənsə́ːrvətiv]

ⓥ conserve 보존하다

ⓐ 보수적인, 전통적인　ⓐ radical 급진적인, 혁명적인, progressive 진보적인

conservative views 보수적인 시각

The conservative parties proposed to reduce the income tax.

19 considerate
[kənsídərit]

ⓝ consideration 배려, 이해
ⓥ consider 잘 생각하다

ⓐ 인정이 있는, 사려 깊은　ⓢ thoughtful　ⓐ inconsiderate 인정 없는, 무관심한

a considerate husband 인정이 많은 남편

It was considerate of Sam to send me those flowers.

20 malicious
[məlíʃəs]

ⓝ malice [mǽlis] 악의

ⓐ 악의적인, 심술궂은　ⓢ malevolent　　**malicious rumors** 악의적인 유언비어

Hackers used a malicious program to attack the servers.

---

14 가수는 청중에게서 열광적인 흥분을 이끌어냈다. / 그것은 내가 겪었던 일 중에 가장 열광적인 경험이었다. 15 도둑은 악의를 가지고 그녀에게 접근했다. 16 내가 어렸을 때 아버지는 성미가 매우 급하셨다. 17 훈련교관은 훈련병들에게 매우 엄격하다. 18 보수정당에서 소득세 인하를 제안했다. 19 Sam이 내게 저 꽃을 보내준 것은 매우 사려 깊었다. 20 해커들은 서버를 공격하기 위해 악성 프로그램을 사용했다.

21 merciful
[mə́:rsifəl]

n mercy 자비

ⓐ 자비로운, 인정 많은　ⓢ compassionate

merciful to one's foe 적에게 관대한

The merciful king gave the order to spare the traitor's life.

---

22 modest
[mɑ́dist]

n modesty 겸손함

ⓐ 겸손한, 조심성 있는　ⓐ boastful 자랑하는

modest about one's role 자신의 역할에 대해 겸손한

He is a very modest man for what he has done as the president.

---

23 moody
[mú:di]

n mood 기분, 마음가짐

ⓐ 언짢은, 변덕스러운　ⓐ stable 동요하지 않는

moody and unpredictable 변덕스럽고 예측 불가능한

Jenny often becomes moody and changes her mind.

---

24 naive
[nɑːíːv]

n naivety 소박, 순진한

ⓐ 천진난만한, 순진한, 잘 믿는　ⓢ gullible 잘 속는

a naive simple creature 순진하고 단순한 존재

The naive sheep was tricked by the cunning fox.

---

25 naughty
[nɔ́:ti]

ⓐ 버릇없는, 개구쟁이인　ⓐ good 착한 well-behaved 예의 바른

naughty children 버릇없는 아이들

Santa Claus has a list of who's been naughty or nice.

---

26 negligible
[néglidʒəbəl]

v neglect
무시하다, 방치하다

ⓐ 하찮은, 무시해도 좋은　ⓐ important 중요한

a negligible amount 무시해도 좋을 만큼의 양

Sometimes, we can see negligible things play a critical role in our lives.

---

27 irritable
[írətəbəl]

n irritability 화를 잘 냄
v irritate 초조하게 하다

ⓐ 화를 잘 내는　ⓢ bad-tempered

an irritable disposition 화를 잘 내는 성질

People tend to be irritable when they have a lack of sleep.

---

21 자비로운 왕은 반역자의 목숨을 살려주라는 명령을 내렸다. 22 그는 대통령으로서 자신이 해온 일에 비해서 매우 겸손한 사람이다. 23 Jenny는 종종 변덕을 부리고, 마음을 바꾼다. 24 순진한 양이 교활한 여우에게 속았다. 25 산타 할아버지는 착한 사람과 나쁜 사람의 명단이 있다. 26 가끔 우리는 인생에서 보잘것없는 것이 중요한 역할을 하고 있음을 목격하게 된다. 27 사람들은 수면이 부족하면 짜증을 내기 쉽다.

28 ☑ liberal
[líbərəl]

ⓝ liberty 자유

ⓐ 관대한, 자유주의의, 진보적인　ⓢ tolerant, generous

a liberal politician 진보적인 정치인

★ They showed a liberal attitude to divorce and remarriage.

★ College students are more liberal than the people in general.

29 ☑ optimistic
[àptəmístik]

ⓝ optimism 낙관주의

ⓐ 낙관적인　ⓐ pessimistic 비관적인

maintain an optimistic view 낙관적인 견해를 유지하다

Despite the recent economic crisis, some economic analysts are optimistic about the future economy.

30 ☑ stubborn
[stʌ́bərn]

ⓐ 완고한, 고집 센　ⓢ obstinate　　**a stubborn resistance** 완고한 저항

My stubborn husband never changes his mind.

31 ☑ personality
[pə̀:rsənǽləti]

ⓝ 성격, 개성　ⓢ character　　**a unique personality** 특이한 성격

My new partner seems to have a strong personality.

32 ☑ progressive
[prəgrésiv]

ⓝ progress 전진, 진행

ⓐ 진보적인　ⓐ conservative 보수적인　　**progressive ideas** 진보적인 사상

The progressive party was against the new law.

33 ☑ prudent
[prú:dənt]

ⓝ prudence 신중

ⓐ 신중한, 현명한　ⓢ careful　ⓐ careless 부주의한

prudent financial investment 현명한 투자

Translators should be prudent about their choice of words to prevent any possible misunderstanding.

34 ☑ rational
[rǽʃənl]

ⓐ 이성적인, 합리적인　ⓢ logical, sensible

a rational decision 이성적인 결정

We need to calm down and be rational about the situation.

---

28 그들은 이혼과 재혼에 대해 개방적인 태도를 보였다. / 대학생들은 일반 사람들보다 더 진보적이다. 29 최근의 경제 위기에도, 몇몇 경제 분석가들은 미래 경제에 대해 낙관적이다. 30 고집 센 내 남편은 절대 자기 생각을 굽히지 않는다. 31 내 새로운 동료는 개성이 매우 강해 보인다. 32 진보당은 새로운 법에 반대했다. 33 번역가들은 오해의 소지를 예방하기 위해 단어 선택에 신중을 기해야 한다. 34 우리는 흥분을 가라앉히고 상황을 이성적으로 생각해야 한다.

35 ☑ **restless**
[réstlis]

① rest 휴식

ⓐ 불안한, 침착하지 못한　**ⓔ** relaxed 침착한, 안정된　**a restless mood** 들뜬 기분

Most residents spent a restless night due to the earthquake.

36 ☑ **rigid**
[rídʒid]

① rigidity 엄격, 강직

ⓐ 완고한, 엄격한　**ⓔ** flexible 융통성 있는, 유연한　**rigid rules** 엄격한 규칙

The officials adapted a more rigid standard for safety.

37 ☑ **rigorous**
[rígərəs]

① rigor 엄함, 엄격

ⓐ 가혹한, 엄격한　**ⓔ** tough, harsh, strict

a rigorous inspection 철두철미한 검사

The government decided to carry out the rigorous control on imported goods.

38 ☑ **notorious**
[noutɔ́:riəs]

① notoriety 악명, 악평

ⓐ 소문난, 유명한, 악명 높은　**ⓔ** infamous　**a notorious robber** 악명 높은 강도

The murderer is notorious for being cruel and merciless.

39 ☑ **sociable**
[sóuʃəbəl]

① sociability 사교성

ⓐ 사교적인　　**sociable to everyone** 모든 사람에게 붙임성 있는

My sister is a sociable person who has a lot of friends.

40 ☑ **offensive**
[əfénsiv]

ⓥ offend 성나게 하다

① offense 무례, 모욕

ⓐ 불쾌한, 무례한　**ⓔ** rude　　**offensive to the ear** 귀에 거슬리는

I apologized for the offensive words I chose to use during that speech.

---

35 대부분 주민들은 지진 때문에 잠 못 이루는 밤을 보냈다. 36 당국자들은 안전을 위해 더욱 엄격한 기준을 채택했다. 37 정부는 수입 물품을 엄격히 규제하기로 했다. 38 그 살인자는 잔인하고 인정사정없기로 악명이 높다. 39 우리 언니는 친구가 많은 사교적인 사람이다. 40 나는 연설을 하는 동안 사용했던 무례한 말에 대해 사과했다.

EXERCISE

A 다음 영어는 우리말로, 우리말은 영어로 옮기시오.

01 frantic _____

02 malicious _____

03 considerate _____

04 optimistic _____

05 rational _____

06 discreet _____

07 무자비한 _____

08 가혹한, 엄격한 _____

09 본능적인, 천성의 _____

10 버릇없는, 개구쟁이인 _____

11 관대한, 자유주의의 _____

12 악의 있는, 심술궂은 _____

B 다음 빈칸에 알맞은 단어를 쓰시오.

01 merciful ⊜ _____

02 prudent ⊜ _____

03 stubborn ⊜ _____

04 notorious ⊜ _____

05 progressive ⊜ _____

06 arrogant ⊜ _____

07 irritable Ⓥ _____

08 offensive Ⓥ _____

09 conservative Ⓥ _____

10 sociable Ⓝ _____

11 feverish Ⓝ _____

12 cruel Ⓝ _____

C 다음 빈칸에 들어갈 알맞은 말을 고르시오. (필요하면 형태를 바꾸시오.)

clumsy	temper	rigid	earnest	negligible

01 She pleaded in _____ for her husband's release from jail.

02 When learning to walk for the first time, toddlers tend to be _____ and fall.

03 At the community meeting, _____ flared as people disagreed about how to spend their tax dollars.

04 The small scratch on the car was so _____ that the insurance company would not cover it.

05 While my leg was in the cast, the muscles became so _____ that I had to learn to walk again.

Crossword Puzzle

앞에서 배운 어휘를 기억하며 퍼즐을 풀어보세요.

정답

Across

1 always thinking of what other people need or want and being careful not to upset them

4 careful, thorough, and exact

6 done without conscious thought

7 getting annoyed quickly or easily

9 free from pretense or deceit; proceeding from genuine feelings

10 very rude or insulting and likely to upset people

Down

2 believing that good things will happen in the future

3 too slight or unimportant to have any effect

5 so determined to get what you want that you do not care if you have to hurt other people in order to do it

8 making someone suffer or feel unhappy

_____ 주의를 끌다

_____ 잠재의식의

_____ 공격적인

_____ 실망시키다

_____ 따르다, 응하다

_____ 황폐화하다

_____ 버리다, 포기하다

_____ 경감하다, 안도하게 하다

Description of Emotions
감정의 묘사

Movement & Motion
동작과 움직임

Explanation and Description
설명과 묘사

Tone & Atmosphere
어조와 분위기

_____ 회의적인, 의심 많은

_____ 설득력 있는

_____ 비꼬는, 빈정거리는

_____ 활기찬, 박력 있는

Appearance & Personality
외모와 성격

Mind & Feeling
마음과 감각

_____ 눈에 띄는, 현저한, 유명한

_____ 조심성 있는

_____ 강제적인, 의무적인

_____ 낙관적인

_____ 고무, 자극

_____ 일관된, 일치하는

_____ 마음 내키지 않는

_____ 창피를 주다

Chapter
08

High-Level Words

High-Level Words 1

---

01 anonymous
[ənɑ́nəməs]

ⓝ **anonym** 가명, 익명

ⓐ 익명의, 신원 불명의 ⊜ unknown, nameless ⊛ identified 신원이 확인된

an anonymous author 익명의 작가

The police received decisive information from an anonymous source.

---

02 appraise
[əpréiz]

ⓝ **appraisal** 평가, 감정

ⓥ 평가하다, 감정하다 ⊜ estimate

appraise the real estate 부동산 가치를 평가하다

I asked an expert to appraise the value of a family treasure.

---

03 belittle
[bilítl]

ⓥ 과소평가하다, 얕보다 ⊜ underestimate 과소평가하다

belittle the effort 노력을 과소평가하다

I will not tolerate it if anyone belittles the work I put in this report.

---

04 coherent
[kouhíərənt]

ⓝ **coherence** 일관성, 긴밀성

ⓐ 일관된, 조리 있는 ⊜ consistent 일관된 ⊛ incoherent 모순된

a coherent argument 논리적인 논쟁

I'm looking for a sofa that is coherent with the patterns of my wallpaper.

---

05 commemorate
[kəmémərèit]

ⓝ **commemoration** 기념(식)

ⓥ 기념하다, 축하하다 ⊜ celebrate

commemorate the victory 승리를 기념하다

The family sat at the Christmas table to commemorate the holy night.

---

06 conceal
[kənsíːl]

ⓝ **concealment** 은폐

ⓥ 숨기다, 비밀로 하다 ⊛ reveal 드러내다, 밝히다

conceal the truth 진실을 감추다

The real motives of his crimes were concealed forever in his grave.

---

01 경찰은 익명의 제보자로부터 결정적인 정보를 입수했다. 02 나는 전문가에게 가보의 가치를 감정해달라고 부탁했다. 03 나는 이 보고서에 들인 노력을 깔보는 사람은 그 누구라도 용납하지 않겠다. 04 나는 벽지 무늬와 어울리는 소파를 찾고 있다. 05 가족은 거룩한 밤을 기념하기 위해 성탄절 식탁에 앉았다. 06 그의 진짜 범행 동기는 그가 죽어서 영원한 비밀이 되었다.

07 depreciate
[dipríːʃièit]

ⓝ depreciation 가치 저하

ⓥ (가치를) 떨어뜨리다, (가치가) 떨어지다

depreciate the value of the dollar 달러의 가치를 떨어뜨리다

Laura was very disappointed when her boss depreciated her work.

08 discern
[disə́ːrn]

ⓥ 알다, 식별하다   ⊜ perceive 알아차리다   **the discerning eye** 감식안

After spending a lot of time with the twins, I can discern between the two.

09 disparity
[dispǽrəti]

ⓝ 불균형, 차이   ⊜ difference   **an income disparity** 소득 불균형

The disparity between the rich and the poor widened over the years.

10 dissent
[disént]

ⓐ dissentient 이의를 제기하는

ⓝ 이의 **ⓥ** 이의를 갖다   ⊜ assent 동의(하다)   **political dissent** 정치적 이견

The NGO gathered signatures from people who dissent the policy.

11 eccentric
[ikséntrik]

ⓝ eccentricity 별남, 기발함

ⓐ 유별난, 괴상한   ⊜ odd, weird   **an eccentric habit** 유별난 취미

The restaurant serves eccentric dishes that can't be found elsewhere.

12 ecstasy
[ékstəsi]

ⓐ ecstatic 황홀한

ⓝ 황홀, 환희   ⊜ delight, joy   **be in ecstasies over** ~에 넋을 잃다

The news made her filled with a sense of ecstasy and excitement.

13 eminent
[émənənt]

ⓝ eminence 고귀, 명성

ⓐ 유명한, 탁월한   ⊜ noted, well-known   **an eminent scholar** 저명한 학자

Eminent artists from around the world performed at the music festival.

---

07 Laura는 직장 상사가 그녀의 업무 성과를 낮게 평가하자 크게 낙담했다. 08 쌍둥이와 많은 시간을 보내고 나니 둘을 구분할 수 있게 되었다. 09 부자와 가난한 사람의 차이는 여러 해 지나면서 커졌다. 10 시민단체는 그 정책에 반대하는 사람들의 서명을 모았다. 11 그 식당은 다른 곳에서는 볼 수 없는 유별난 요리를 판매한다. 12 뉴스가 그녀를 황홀감과 흥분으로 가득하게 했다. 13 세계 각지에서 온 유명한 음악가들이 음악 축제에서 공연을 펼쳤다.

14 feign
[fein]

ⓥ feint 시늉, 가장

ⓥ ~인 체하다, ~을 가장하다　●pretend　**feign illness** 꾀병을 부리다

I know that she's only feigning to be indifferent to me.

15 inscription
[inskrípʃən]

ⓥ inscribe 새기다

ⓝ 새겨진 글, 비문　**an inscription on the gravestone** 묘비의 비문

Archaeologists are studying the inscriptions on the walls of Pyramids.

16 intricate
[íntrəkit]

ⓝ intricacy 복잡

ⓐ 복잡한, 뒤얽힌　●complicated　**an intricate plot** 복잡한 줄거리

Sometimes, attempts to mediate a fight can make it more intricate.

17 lateral
[lǽtərəl]

ⓐ 옆의, 측면의　●sideways　**lateral thinking** 수평적 사고

Motion in games has developed from being lateral to three-dimensional.

18 marginal
[má:rdʒənəl]

ⓝ margin 가장자리, 마진

ⓐ 가장자리의, 중요하지 않은
●borderline 가장자리의, insignificant 중요하지 않은
a marginal culture 주변 문화

There is often conflict between marginal opinions and the mainstream.

19 conspicuous
[kənspíkjuəs]

ⓐ 눈에 잘 띄는　●noticeable
make oneself conspicuous 돋보이게 행동하다

Jessica played a conspicuous role in making the project a success.

20 outlive
[àutlív]

ⓥ ~보다 더 오래 살다　**outlive one's child** 자식을 앞세우다(= 자식보다 오래 살다)

Artists wish for their reputation to outlive the days of their own.

---

14 나는 그녀가 내게 무관심한 척하고 있다는 것을 안다.　15 고고학자들은 피라미드 벽에 새겨진 글자들을 연구 중이다.　16 때로는 싸움을 중재하려는 시도가 싸움을 더 복잡하게 만들 수도 있다.　17 게임에서의 움직임은 옆으로 움직이는 것에서 3차원적인 것으로 발전했다.　18 종종 소수 의견과 주류 사이에 갈등이 있다.　19 Jessica는 이 프로젝트를 성공하게 하는 데 눈에 띄는 역할을 했다.　20 예술가들은 자신의 명성이 자신의 생애보다 더 오래가길 바란다.

21 premise
[prémis]

n 전제 = assumption **a major premise** 대전제

Your argument will be reasonable as long as your premises are true.

22 dubious
[djúːbiəs]

a 모호한, 의심스러운 = sure 확실한 **a dubious answer** 애매한 답변

★ He made a dubious statement about the issue to stay out of trouble.

★ People started to get suspicious about his dubious attitude.

23 fabulous
[fǽbjələs]

a 굉장한, 멋진 = spectacular **a fabulous wedding** 굉장한 결혼식

The actresses walked down the red carpet wearing fabulous dresses.

24 scanty
[skǽnti]

a 부족한, 빈약한 = insufficient **scanty evidence** 부족한 증거

We weren't able to make any conclusions with the scanty data.

25 superfluous
[suːpə́rfluəs]

a 여분의, 필요 없는 = necessary 필요한

superfluous information 여분의 (불필요한) 정보

n superfluity 여분

Adding superfluous remarks to your argument often ends up ruining it.

26 fragile
[frǽdʒəl]

a 부서지기 쉬운, 연약한 = weak, brittle **fragile bones** 부러지기 쉬운 뼈

n fragility 부서지기 쉬움

The movers treated the boxes that say "fragile" with extreme care.

27 uneven
[ʌníːvən]

a 불공평한, 평평하지 않은 **an uneven distribution** 불공평한 분배

★ The workers were mad at the uneven treatment they got.

★ The car was shaking violently as it drove on the uneven road.

---

21 당신의 주장은 전제가 참인 한 타당할 것이다. 22 그는 문제를 피하기 위해 그 사안에 대해 모호한 말을 했다. / 사람들은 그의 수상한 태도를 의심하기 시작했다. 23 여배우들이 멋진 드레스를 입고 레드카펫 위를 걸어갔다. 24 우리는 부족한 자료로 어떤 결론도 내릴 수 없었다. 25 여러분의 주장에 불필요한 말을 덧붙이는 것은 종종 주장을 망친다. 26 이삿짐센터 사람들은 '깨지기 쉬움'이라고 쓰인 상자들을 조심스럽게 다뤘다. 27 노동자들은 자신들이 받는 불공평한 대우에 화가 났다. / 차는 울퉁불퉁한 길을 달리면서 심하게 흔들렸다.

28 versatile
[və́:rsətl]

n versatility 다재다능

a 다재다능한, 다용도의   **s** all-around   **a versatile actor** 다재다능한 배우

Trying to be versatile may lead to not being good at anything.

29 affix
[əfíks]

v 붙이다, 첨부하다   **s** stick, attach   **affix a label to** ~에 라벨을 붙이다

I could tell the letter was unread by the affixed seal on the envelope.

30 boost
[buːst]

n booster 상승시키는 것, 촉진제

v 밀어 올리다, 상승시키다   **s** raise, increase

boost the economy 경기를 부양하다

The rocket was boosted up in the air with enormous energy.

31 shabby
[ʃǽbi]

a 초라한, 누추한

shabby clothes 누추한 옷

not too shabby 나쁘지 않은

The prince walked among the commoners, disguised in shabby clothes.

32 shatter
[ʃǽtər]

v 산산이 부수다, 파괴하다   **s** destroy, smash

a shattered dream 산산 조각난 꿈

The windows were shattered in pieces by a fierce gas explosion.

33 splash
[splæʃ]

a splashy 물이 튀는, 첨벙거리는

v (물 등을) 튀기다, 첨벙거리다   **splash water about** 물을 주위에 튀기다

The children were having fun splashing around in the swimming pool.

34 wretched
[rétʃid]

n wretch 가엾은 사람

a 불쌍한, 가엾은   **a wretched old man** 불쌍한 노인

I was shocked to see their wretched living conditions.

---

28 전부 잘하려다가 아무것도 제대로 할 수 없게 될 수도 있다. 29 봉투에 붙은 봉인을 보고 아직 편지를 읽지 않았다는 것을 알 수 있었다. 30 로켓은 엄청난 에너지와 함께 공중으로 떠올랐다. 31 왕자는 초라한 옷차림으로 변장하여, 평민들 사이를 거닐었다. 32 강력한 가스 폭발로 창문들이 모두 산 산조각이 나버렸다. 33 아이들은 수영장에서 물장구치며 재미있게 놀고 있었다. 34 나는 그들의 불쌍한 생활환경을 보고 놀랐다.

35 acclaim
[əkléim]

ⓥ 환호하다 **ⓝ** 환호, 절찬 ⊜ praise 칭찬(하다) **critical acclaim** 비평가들의 호평

★ She was acclaimed wildly by the audience for her beautiful voice.

★ The show has received wide acclaim for its unique approach to journalism.

36 amicable
[æmikəbəl]

ⓝ amicability 우호, 친선

ⓐ 우호적인   **an amicable attitude** 우호적인 태도

The two parties resolved their conflict in an amicable settlement.

37 arbitrary
[á:rbitrèri]

ad arbitrarily 독단으로, 마음대로
ⓝ arbitrariness 자의성, 임의성

ⓐ 자의적인, 임의의 ⊜ random 임의의 **an arbitrary decision** 독단적인 결정

My boss often makes arbitrary decisions, which makes him quite difficult to work with.

38 bizarre
[bizá:r]

ⓐ 기묘한, 이상한 ⊜ grotesque **a bizarre behavior** 기묘한 행동

There were bizarre rumors about the old abandoned house on the hill.

39 brittle
[brítl]

ⓐ 깨지기 쉬운, 약한 ⊜ fragile **brittle bone disease** 골다공증

I told the decorators to be careful with the brittle glass ornaments.

40 cognitive
[kágnətiv]

ⓐ 인식의, 인식력이 있는 **cognitive development** 인지발달

Psychologists are interested in the cognitive process of human minds.

---

35 관객들은 그녀의 아름다운 목소리에 크게 환호했다. / 그 프로그램은 언론에 대한 독특한 접근에 대해 폭넓은 갈채를 받았다. 36 두 단체는 서로의 갈등을 원만하게 해결했다. 37 나의 상사는 자주 임의적인 결정을 내려서 함께 일하기 힘들다. 38 언덕 위에 있는 오래된 흉가에 대한 기괴한 소문이 무성했다. 39 나는 장식가에게 깨지기 쉬운 유리 장식을 조심하라고 일렀다. 40 심리학자들은 인간의 마음에서 일어나는 인지과정에 관심이 많다.

EXERCISE

A 다음 영어는 우리말로, 우리말은 영어로 옮기시오.

01 depreciate _____

02 versatile _____

03 conspicuous _____

04 arbitrary _____

05 acclaim _____

06 feign _____

07 ~보다 더 오래 살다 _____

08 불균형, 차이 _____

09 초라한, 누추한 _____

10 기묘한, 이상한 _____

11 모호한, 의심스러운 _____

12 기념하다, 축하하다 _____

B 다음 빈칸에 알맞은 단어를 쓰시오.

01 belittle ⊜ _____

02 intricate ⊜ _____

03 coherent ⊜ _____

04 superfluous ⊜ _____

05 anonymous ⊜ _____

06 conceal ⊜ _____

07 inscription ⓥ _____

08 ecstasy ⓐ _____

09 dissent ⓐ _____

10 fragile ⓝ _____

11 eminent ⓝ _____

12 appraise ⓝ _____

C 다음 빈칸에 들어갈 알맞은 말을 고르시오. (필요하면 형태를 바꾸시오.)

| eccentric | boost | lateral | discern | premise |

01 Color-blind people cannot _____ between the various colors.

02 The company will sell its products on Chinese online retailers in an attempt to _____ sales.

03 Many historians believe that Albert Einstein was a(n) _____ but brilliant scientist.

04 Gymnasts must learn how to perform many _____ moves using various equipments.

05 The _____ of the essay was her strong belief that the poor have the right to affordable healthcare.

Across

2 unknown by name

5 to break suddenly into very small pieces, or to make something break in this way

8 easily broken or damaged

10 (of a person) famous and respected within a particular sphere

11 minor and not important; not central

Down

1 to do something to show that you remember and respect someone important or an important event in the past

3 very unusual or strange

4 related to the process of knowing, understanding, and learning something

6 characterized by friendliness and absence of discord

7 an idea that you accept as true and use as a base for developing other ideas

9 containing many small parts or details that all work or fit together

High-Level Words 2

---

01 ☑ demeanor
[dimí:nər]

ⓝ 행동, 태도   **straight-ahead demeanor** 거짓 없는 행동

I believe he has a warm heart under his cold demeanor.

---

02 ☑ downturn
[dáuntə̀:rn]

ⓝ 하락, 내림세   **a business downturn** 경기 하락

We need to revise our methods to overcome this downturn.

---

03 ☑ influx
[ínflʌks]

ⓝ 유입, 밀어닥침   **⊜ efflux** 유출   **influx of refugees** 피난민들의 유입

The influx of foreign cultures has changed our lives in many ways.

---

04 ☑ sneak
[sni:k]

ⓐ sneaky 몰래 하는

ⓥ 몰래 움직이다   **sneak into a building** 건물에 살금살금 들어가다

The kids were caught trying to sneak a comic book into class.

---

05 ☑ snatch
[snætʃ]

ⓥ 잡아채다   **⊜ grab, steal**

snatch at every opportunity 모든 기회를 움켜잡다

The thief quickly ran away after he snatched the lady's purse.

---

06 ☑ agitate
[ǽdʒətèit]

ⓝ agitation 선동, 운동

ⓥ 동요시키다, 일으키다   **⊜ calm** 가라앉히다   **an agitated crowd** 흥분한 군중

Some people are agitated by the excessive violence on television.

---

01 그의 냉정한 태도 이면에는 따뜻한 마음이 있을 거라 믿는다. 02 우리는 이 내림세를 극복하기 위해 우리의 방법론을 혁신해야 한다. 03 외국 문물의 유입으로 우리의 생활은 여러모로 변화를 겪었다. 04 아이들은 교실에 만화책을 몰래 가지고 들어가려다 들켰다. 05 도둑은 여자의 가방을 낚아채고서 재빠르게 도망쳤다. 06 몇몇 사람들은 TV의 지나친 폭력성에 동요한다.

07 **alienate**
[éiljənèit]
ⓐ **alien** 이질적인, 다른

Ⓥ 멀리하다, 딴 데로 돌리다　　　**the alienated class** 소외 계층

I felt lonely and alienated after transferring to a new school.

---

08 **aspire**
[əspáiər]
ⓝ **aspiration** 열망

Ⓥ 열망하다, 간절히 바라다　ⓢ desire　　**aspire to fame** 명예를 열망하다

He aspired to be the greatest classical musician in the world.

---

09 **avert**
[əvə́:rt]
ⓐ **avertible** 막을 수 있는

Ⓥ 막다, 외면하다　ⓢ prevent 막다, turn away 외면하다

avert a crisis 위기를 막다

★ Several good friends of mine helped me avert great danger.

★ He vowed never to avert from the sufferings of the unfortunate.

---

10 **collide**
[kəláid]
ⓝ **collision** 충돌

Ⓥ 충돌하다, 상충하다　ⓢ crash 충돌하다, conflict 상충하다

collide head-on 정면으로 충돌하다

The driver turned the wheel to avoid colliding with another car.

---

11 **stalk**
[stɔ:k]
ⓝ **stalker** 스토커

Ⓥ 조용히 뒤쫓다　ⓢ track　　　**stalk the prey** 먹이를 뒤쫓다

The woman reported to the police that someone was stalking her.

---

12 **condemn**
[kəndém]
ⓝ **condemnation** 비난, 유죄 선고

Ⓥ 비난하다, (유죄를) 선고하다　ⓢ criticize 비난하다, sentence 선고하다

condemned to ten years in prison 10년 형을 선고받다

★ People condemned the man bitterly for his vile crimes.

★ The murderer was condemned to death.

---

13 **contrive**
[kəntráiv]
ⓝ **contrivance** 계획, 발명품

Ⓥ 꾀하다, 고안하다　ⓢ devise　　**contrive a plan** 계획을 꾸미다

Researchers contrived a new engine that is more fuel-efficient.

---

07 나는 새 학교로 전학하고 나서 외롭고 고립되었다는 느낌이 들었다.　08 그는 세상에서 가장 위대한 클래식 음악가가 되기를 간절히 바랐다.　09 나의 절친한 친구 여러 명이 내가 위험으로부터 피하도록 도와주었다. / 그는 불행한 자들의 고통을 절대 외면하지 않겠다고 다짐했다.　10 운전사는 다른 차와 충돌하는 것을 피하려고 운전대를 돌렸다.　11 여자는 누군가가 자신을 스토킹 한다고 경찰에 신고했다.　12 사람들은 그 남자의 비열한 범죄를 신랄하게 비난했다. / 그 살인자는 사형선고를 받았다.　13 연구원들은 연비가 더 좋은 새로운 엔진을 고안했다.

14 crawl
[krɔːl]

ⓥ 기어가다, 서행하다 **ⓢ** creep

crawl about on all fours 네 발로 기어 다니다, 포복하다

The spy crawled through the bushes to avoid being detected.

---

15 submerge
[səbmə́ːrdʒ]

ⓝ submergence 잠수, 침수

ⓥ 물속에 넣다, 잠수하다, 몰두시키다 **ⓢ** sink, plunge, immerse

submerge oneself in one's work 일에 몰두하다

The diver submerged into the sea to explore marine life.

---

16 deform
[difɔ́ːrm]

ⓝ deformation 변형, 기형

ⓥ 변형시키다, 기형으로 만들다

be born deformed 기형으로 태어나다

Experts point out that high heels can deform your feet.

---

17 degenerate
[didʒénərèit]

ⓝ degeneration 퇴보

ⓥ 나빠지다, 퇴보하다 **ⓢ** worsen

degenerate with age 노화되다

The new action plan resulted in degenerating the current status.

---

18 demolish
[dimáliʃ]

ⓝ demolition 해체, 파괴, 폭파

ⓥ 파괴하다, 폐지하디 **ⓢ** tear down

demolish a forest 숲을 파괴하다

The city hired a team of experts to demolish the old apartment.

---

19 disperse
[dispə́ːrs]

ⓝ dispersion 흩뜨림, 분산

ⓥ 흩뜨리다, 해산하다 **ⓢ** break up 해산하다

disperse demonstrators 시위자들을 해산하다

The nation has a system that disperses power into three entities.

---

20 divert
[divə́ːrt]

ⓝ diversion 전환, (시선을) 돌림

ⓥ 전환하다, 돌리다 **ⓢ** distract **divert public attention** 대중의 관심을 돌리다

I needed something to divert my thoughts from my failure.

---

14 첩보원은 들키지 않으려고 수풀 사이를 기어갔다. 15 잠수부는 해양생물을 탐사하기 위해 바다 속으로 잠수했다. 16 전문가들은 하이힐이 발을 변형시킬 수 있다고 지적한다. 17 새로운 사업 계획은 현 상태를 악화시키는 결과를 가져왔다. 18 시 당국은 낡은 아파트를 헐기 위해 전문가들을 고용했다. 19 그 국가는 삼권분립 체계가 있다. 20 나는 나의 실패로부터 생각을 돌릴만한 것이 필요했다.

21 ☑ divulge
[dívʌldʒ]
ⓝ divulgence 누설, 폭로

ⓥ (비밀 등을) 누설하다 **ⓔ** reveal, disclose
divulge private information 개인 정보를 누설하다

The prisoner refused to divulge the whereabouts of his comrades.

---

22 ☑ engender
[endʒéndər]
ⓝ engenderment 초래, 야기

ⓥ 생기게 하다, 일으키다   **engender growth** 성장을 일으키다

Love was engendered as the man held the woman.

---

23 ☑ evoke
[ivóuk]

ⓥ (기억, 감정을) 불러일으키다 **ⓔ** arouse
evoke sympathy 동정심을 불러일으키다

The happy ending evoked a warm feeling among the audience.

---

24 ☑ falter
[fɔ́:ltər]

ⓥ 머뭇거리다, 주춤하다 **ⓔ** hesitate   **a faltering economy** 주춤하는 경제

He faltered for a moment to gather the courage to apologize.

---

25 ☑ flatter
[flǽtər]
ⓝ flattery 아첨

ⓥ 아첨하다, 기쁘게 하다   **flatter oneself** 우쭐해 하다

★ He flattered his boss frequently, hoping to get a promotion.
★ I was flattered with the flowers my husband bought on his way home.

---

26 ☑ summon
[sʌ́mən]
ⓝⓥ summons 호출, 소환;
(종종 수동태) 출두를 명하다

ⓥ 호출하다, 소환하다   **summon a waiter** 웨이터를 부르다

The prosecutors summoned the politician to investigate a crime.

---

27 ☑ forfeit
[fɔ́:rfit]

ⓥ 몰수되다, 박탈당하다 **ⓝ** 박탈, 몰수   **forfeit the right to** ~할 권리를 박탈당하다

She was fined $3,000 and ordered to forfeit her car.

---

21 포로는 동료의 소재를 폭로하기를 거부했다. 22 남자가 여자를 안았을 때 사랑이 싹트기 시작했다. 23 해피엔딩은 관객에게 따뜻한 감정을 불러일으켰다. 24 그는 사과할 용기를 내려고 잠시 머뭇거렸다. 25 그는 승진하기를 바라면서 상사에게 자주 아첨했다. / 남편이 집에 오는 길에 사온 꽃이 나를 기쁘게 했다. 26 검사들이 범죄를 수사하기 위해 정치인을 소환했다. 27 그녀는 3,000달러의 벌금을 물고, 차를 압수한다는 명령을 받았다.

28 suspend
[səspénd]

ⓝ suspension 정지, 매달기

ⓥ 연기하다, 정학시키다　ⓢ postpone 연기하다

suspend from school 정학시키다

The decision has been suspended until the next meeting.

---

29 hurl
[həːrl]

ⓥ 세게 던지다, 퍼붓다　ⓢ throw, fling　　**hurl a ball** 공을 세게 던지다

The demonstrators who hurled stones at the police were arrested.

---

30 immerse
[imə́ːrs]

ⓝ immersion 몰두, 담금

ⓥ 빠져들게 하다, 담그다　ⓢ involve, absorb 열중시키다

immerse one's feet in water 물에 발을 담그다

The young musician was immersed deeply in his music.

---

31 throb
[θrɑb]

ⓥ 고동치다, 맥박이 뛰다　ⓢ pound, beat　**a throbbing heart** 두근거리는 심장

My heart always starts to throb greatly if I try to tell a lie.

---

32 trigger
[trígər]

ⓥ 방아쇠를 당기다, (일련의 사건을) 일으키다 ⓝ 방아쇠, 계기

pull a trigger 방아쇠를 당기다

★ The death of an innocent student triggered a huge protest.

★ The hijacking became a trigger point for military action.

---

33 provoke
[prəvóuk]

ⓝ provocation 성나게 함

ⓥ 일으키다, 성나게 하다　ⓢ cause 일으키다, enrage 성나게 하다

provoke a laughter 웃음을 유발하다

You will be attacked by the wild animals if you provoke them.

---

34 rebuke
[ribjúːk]

ⓥ 꾸짖다, 비난하다　ⓢ scold, reprimand

rebuke an employee 종업원을 꾸짖다

The teacher rebuked the students for not working hard enough.

---

28 결정은 다음 회의까지 연기되었다.　29 경찰에게 돌을 던진 시위자들이 체포되었다.　30 젊은 음악가는 자신의 음악에 깊이 빠져들었다.　31 나는 거짓말을 하려고 하면 항상 심장이 심하게 고동치기 시작한다.　32 무고한 학생의 죽음이 대규모 시위를 촉발시켰다. / 공중납치가 군사적 행동의 계기가 되었다.　33 야생동물을 자극하면 당신은 공격을 받을 것이다.　34 선생님은 학생들이 충분히 노력하지 않는다며 꾸짖었다.

35 recede
[riːsíːd]

ⓐ recessive 퇴행의
ⓝ recession 후퇴, 경기후퇴

ⓥ 물러나다, 철회하다 **≋** withdraw
recede into the horizon 지평선 너머로 사라지다

We had to recede from the contract due to financial reasons.

36 relinquish
[rilíŋkwiʃ]

ⓥ 포기하다, 양도하다 **≋** give up 포기하다, surrender 양도하다
relinquish power to someone ~에게 권력을 넘기다

The situation was desperate and we had relinquished all hope.

37 render
[réndər]

ⓥ ~이 되게 하다, ~로 만들다, ~을 주다 **≋** make, provide
render good service 좋은 서비스를 제공하다

★ I was rendered helpless by the debts I owed to the bank.
★ I was rendered with assistance from some of my coworkers.

38 convene
[kənvíːn]

ⓝ convention 집회, 회의

ⓥ 모이다, 소집하다 **≋** congregate, assemble
convene the ministers 장관들을 소집하다

All the staff members convened for an urgent meeting.

39 retract
[ritrǽkt]

ⓝ retraction 취소, 철회

ⓥ 한 말을 취소[철회]하다 **≋** recant, take back
retract the statement 진술을 번복하다

James retracted his offer to donate his collection to the local museum.

40 defy
[difái]

ⓝ defiance 저항

ⓥ 반항하다, 도전하다 **≋** resist, challenge **defy a threat** 위협에 저항하다

Sometimes, the pupil's theory may defy that of his own teacher.

---

35 우리는 재정적 이유로 계약을 철회해야 했다. 36 상황은 매우 절망적이었고, 우리는 모든 희망을 버린 상태였다. 37 나는 은행에 빌린 빚 때문에 무력해졌다. / 나는 몇몇 동료로부터 도움을 받았다. 38 모든 실무진은 긴급회의를 소집했다. 39 James는 지역 박물관에 자신의 소장품을 기증하기로 한 제안을 철회했다. 40 때로는, 제자의 이론이 스승의 이론에 도전할 수가 있다.

EXERCISE

Unit 42

A 다음 영어는 우리말로, 우리말은 영어로 옮기시오.

01 contrive _____

02 forfeit _____

03 suspend _____

04 sneak _____

05 rebuke _____

06 disperse _____

07 비난하다, 선고하다 _____

08 일으키다, 성나게 하다 _____

09 하락, 내림세 _____

10 포기하다, 양도하다 _____

11 고동치다, 맥박이 뛰다 _____

12 변형시키다 _____

B 다음 빈칸에 알맞은 단어를 쓰시오.

01 divulge ⊜ _____

02 defy ⊜ _____

03 aspire ⊜ _____

04 falter ⊜ _____

05 agltate ⇔ _____

06 influx ⇔ _____

07 avert ⓐ _____

08 recede ⓐ _____

09 alienate ⓐ _____

10 divert ⓝ _____

11 flatter ⓝ _____

12 submerge ⓝ _____

C 다음 빈칸에 들어갈 알맞은 말을 고르시오. (필요하면 형태를 바꾸시오.)

avert	demeanor	evoke	convene	trigger

01 These pictures of snow _____ the Christmas feeling.

02 When the toy was taken away from the baby, this _____ a flood of tears.

03 The _____ of the guest speaker reflected that she had a lot of poise and grace.

04 The passenger in the car helped to _____ the accident when the driver lost control of the car.

05 According to the president of the company, we will _____ for a general meeting in the main auditorium.

Crossword Puzzle

앞에서 배운 어휘를 기억하며 빈칸을 채워보세요.

정답

Across

1   the arrival of large numbers of people or large amounts of money, goods, etc., especially suddenly

4   to go somewhere secretly and quietly in order to avoid being seen or heard

5   to hit something or someone that is moving in a different direction from you

6   to order someone to come to a place

8   to officially stop something from continuing, especially for a short time

9   to cause a reaction or feeling, especially a sudden one

Down

1   to put someone or something deep into a liquid so that they are completely covered

2   to end or ruin something completely

3   to become worse

7   to cause someone or something to be in a particular condition

01 ☑ **unanimous**
[juːnǽnəməs]
ⓝ **unanimity** 만장일치

ⓐ 만장일치의, 전원 합의의   **a unanimous rejection** 만장일치의 반대

The decision was made by a unanimous vote.

02 ☑ **authentic**
[ɔːθéntik]
ⓝ **authenticity** 신뢰성

ⓐ 진짜의, 정확한, 믿을 만한   ⓔ genuine 진짜의, reliable 믿을 만한

an authentic report 사실과 일치하는 보고

The reporters obtained information from an authentic source.

03 ☑ **verdict**
[və́ːrdikt]

ⓝ 판결, 판단   ⓔ judgment   **a verdict of guilty** 유죄 판결

The defendant waited nervously for the jury to bring in the verdict.

04 ☑ **revoke**
[rivóuk]
ⓝ **revocation** 취소, 철회

ⓥ 취소하다, 무효로 하다   ⓔ cancel, annul

revoke a permission 허가를 취소하다

His driver's license was revoked for drunk driving.

05 ☑ **warranty**
[wɔ́(ː)rənti]
ⓥ **warrant** 보증하다

ⓝ 담보, 보증(서)   ⓔ guarantee   **under warranty** 보증기간 중인

I have to pay for my car's repairs after the warranty is expired.

06 ☑ **evasion**
[ivéiʒən]
ⓥ **evade** 회피하다

ⓝ 회피, 탈세   **tax evasion** 탈세

His statement was considered as an evasion of his responsibilities.

---

01 그 결정은 만장일치 투표에 의해 결정되었다. 02 기자들은 믿을 만한 정보원으로부터 정보를 얻었다. 03 피고는 배심원이 판결을 내릴 것을 초조하게 기다렸다. 04 그의 운전면허는 음주운전 때문에 취소되었다. 05 보증기간이 만료되면 나는 자동차의 수리비를 내야 한다. 06 그의 진술은 책임 회피로 여겨졌다.

07 detest
[ditést]

n detestation 혐오, 증오

v 혐오하다 **≡** hate, abhor   **detest insects** 곤충을 혐오하다

I detest it when my boss sends me on personal errands.

---

08 scrutiny
[skrúːtəni]

v scrutinize
자세히 조사[검사]하다

n 자세한 조사[검사] **≡** examination, investigation

public scrutiny 공개 조사

The government's new policy requires close scrutiny.

---

09 extrovert
[ékstrouvə̀ːrt]

a 외향적인 **≡** introvert 내성적인 **an extrovert personality** 외향적인 성격

She is very extrovert and says whatever is on her mind.

---

10 exterminate
[ikstə́ːrmənèit]

n exterminator 해충 구제업자
n extermination
구제, 박멸, 몰살

v 박멸하다, 몰살하다 **≡** eradicate, root out

exterminate pests 해충을 박멸하다

The hotel manager hired an expert to exterminate the cockroaches.

---

11 grievous
[gríːvəs]

v grieve 몹시 슬퍼하다
n grief 슬픔

a 슬픈, 통탄할   **a grievous loss** 비통한 인명 손실

I heard the grievous news that Jane's mother recently passed away.

---

12 imperative
[impérətiv]

a 꼭 필요한, 절박한 **≡** essential, vital

an imperative conception 강박 관념

They said that my presence at the meeting was imperative.

---

13 inauguration
[inɔ̀ːgjəréiʃən]

v inaugurate
취임시키다, 발족시키다

n 취임, 개시   **Inauguration Day** 미국 대통령 취임일

Many people watched Trump's inauguration ceremony on TV or online.

---

07 나는 직장상사가 나에게 개인적인 심부름을 시키는 것이 너무 싫다. 08 정부의 새 정책은 자세한 검사가 필요하다. 09 그녀는 매우 외향적이고, 생각나는 것을 거리낌 없이 이야기한다. 10 호텔 관리인은 바퀴벌레를 박멸하려고 전문가를 고용했다. 11 나는 Jane의 어머니가 최근에 돌아가셨다는 슬픈 소식을 들었다. 12 그들은 내가 회의에 꼭 참석해야 한다고 말했다. 13 많은 사람이 트럼프의 취임식을 TV 또는 온라인으로 시청했다.

14 painstaking
[péinztèikiŋ]

ⓐ 매우 공들인

painstaking efforts 각고의 노력

Professor Wilson noticed the painstaking work I put in the project.

---

15 pathetic
[pəθétik]

ⓝ pathos 애수, 비애감

ⓐ 애처로운, 한심한, 형편없는

a pathetic plea 애처로운 간청

★ I felt so pathetic as I walked in the rainy night, all alone.
★ She was frustrated with her husband's pathetic excuses.

---

16 orthodox
[ɔ́:rθədɑ̀ks]

ⓝ orthodoxy 정설, 통설

ⓐ 〈종교〉 정통의, 전통적인 ⦿ conventional, traditional
⦿ unorthodox 정통이 아닌

an orthodox method 전통적 방법

My fiancée said she wanted to have an orthodox wedding ceremony.

---

17 tenacious
[tinéiʃəs]

ⓐ 고집스러운, 완강한

tenacious belief 집요한 믿음

I avoid getting in arguments with people who are tenacious.

---

18 vicious
[víʃəs]

ⓝ vice 악덕

ⓐ 사악한, 잔인한 ⦿ cruel, savage

a vicious cycle 악순환

I couldn't stand the vicious remarks of those who opposed me.

---

19 virtuous
[və́:rtʃuəs]

ⓝ virtue 미덕, 장점

ⓐ 덕이 높은, 고결한 ⦿ wicked 부도덕한, 사악한 **virtuous behavior** 선한 행동

I am trying to lead a virtuous life to the fullest extent.

---

20 calamity
[kəlǽməti]

ⓐ calamitous
재난의, 재난을 가져오는

ⓝ 재난, 재해 ⦿ disaster

a man-made calamity 인재

Many people argue that carbon emission can lead to calamity.

---

14 Wilson 교수님은 내가 프로젝트에 들인 공을 알아봐 주었다. 15 혼자서 비 오는 밤에 걷고 있으니 나 자신이 너무 불쌍했다. / 그녀는 남편의 한심한 변명에 화가 치밀었다. 16 내 약혼녀는 전통적인 결혼식을 올리고 싶다고 했다. 17 나는 고집이 센 사람과 논쟁하는 것을 피한다. 18 나는 나에게 반대하는 사람들의 악의 있는 말을 견딜 수 없었다. 19 나는 최대한 고결한 삶을 살려고 노력한다. 20 많은 사람이 탄소 배출이 재앙을 가져올 수도 있다고 주장한다.

21 □ catastrophe
[kətǽstrəfi]

ⓐ catastrophic
비극적인, 큰 재앙의

ⓝ 큰 재앙, 대참사　ⓢ tragedy, disaster

an environmental catastrophe 환경 재해

We are trying our best to prevent catastrophes from happening.

22 □ overdue
[òuvərdjúː]

ⓐ 기한이 지난, 밀린　ⓢ delayed, late　　**an overdue payment** 밀린 임금

Steve didn't know how he was going to pay all his overdue bills.

23 □ conspiracy
[kənspírəsi]

ⓥ conspire 공모하다, 작당하다

ⓝ 음모, 공모　ⓢ scheme　　　　**conspiracy theory** 음모이론

There are always rumors of a conspiracy behind major events.

24 □ depot
[díːpou]

ⓝ 창고, 차고, 정류소　ⓢ warehouse 창고　　　**a supply depot** 보급소

There is a beautiful girl I see every morning at the bus depot.

25 □ homicide
[háməsàid]

ⓐ homicidal 살인(범)의

ⓝ 살인　ⓢ murder　　　　**accidental homicide** 과실 치사

The clues at the crime scene indicated that it was homicide.

26 □ concession
[kənséʃən]

ⓥ concede 인정하다, 양보하다
ⓐ concessionary 양보의

ⓝ 양보, 용인, 특권　ⓢ compromise 양보, privilege 특권

mutual concessions 상호양보

Neither the union nor the company was making any concessions.

27 □ renounce
[rináuns]

ⓝ renunciation 포기, 폐기

ⓥ 포기하다, 끊다　ⓢ give up, relinquish　**renounce a title** 직함을 포기하다

The singer renounced her U.S. citizenship.

---

21 우리는 대참사가 일어나는 것을 방지하고자 온 힘을 다하고 있다. 22 Steve는 밀린 공과금을 어떻게 다 내야 할지 몰랐다. 23 중요한 사건의 배후에 음모가 있다는 소문은 늘 있다. 24 매일 아침 버스 정류장에서 내가 항상 보는 아름다운 여자가 있다. 25 범죄 현장의 단서들은 그것이 살인 사건임을 나타냈다. 26 노조와 회사 측 모두 한발도 양보하고 있지 않았다. 27 그 가수는 미국 국적을 포기했다.

28 itinerary
[aitínərèri]

ⓝ 여행 계획, 여정   **make an itinerary** 여정을 짜다

The tour guide handed me the itinerary for our trip to Japan.

29 mishap
[míshæp]

ⓝ 불상사, 불운   **ⓢ** mischance   **without mishap** 무사히

I was happy that the project went through with no such mishaps.

30 mortgage
[mɔ́:rgidʒ]

ⓝ mortgagee 저당권자

ⓝ (주택) 융자, 저당 **ⓥ** 담보로 넣다   **pay off the mortgage** 대출금을 갚다

The young couple was able to obtain a mortgage from their local bank.

31 revolt
[rivóult]

ⓐ revolting 반항[반역]하는

ⓝ 폭동, 반란 **ⓥ** 반란을 일으키다   **ⓢ** rebellion 폭동, rebel 반란을 일으키다
raise a revolt 폭동을 일으키다

★ The police tried to restrain the people who started the revolt.

★ When the new leader took office, the people revolted against the government.

32 sibling
[síbliŋ]

ⓝ 형제, 자매   **sibling rivalry** 형제간의 경쟁의식

Traditionally, the oldest son is obliged to look after his siblings.

33 stockholder
[stάkhòuldər]

ⓝ stock 주식
ⓝ holder 소유주, 보유자

ⓝ 주주   **ⓢ** shareholder   **a major stockholder** 대주주

I prepared my report for the general meeting of stockholders.

---

28 여행 가이드가 우리의 일본 여행 일정표를 건네주었다. 29 프로젝트가 불상사 없이 진행되어 기뻤다. 30 그 젊은 부부는 지역 은행에서 융자를 받을 수 있었다. 31 경찰은 폭동을 일으킨 사람들을 제지하려고 했다. / 새 지도자가 정권을 잡자, 국민들은 그 정부에 대항하여 반란을 일으켰다. 32 전통적으로, 장남은 자신의 형제를 돌볼 의무가 있다. 33 나는 주주총회를 위해 보고서를 준비했다.

34 tariff
[tǽrif]

ⓝ 관세 **⊜** duty

impose tariffs 관세를 부과하다
an import tariff 수입 관세

Two people argued whether they should maintain protective tariffs.

35 transcript
[trǽnskript]

ⓥ transcribe 베끼다, 복사하다

ⓝ 성적 증명서, 필기 **⊜** record 기록, 필기

a transcript of a speech 연설을 필기한 것

I had to submit my grade transcripts with my application form.

36 cram
[kræm]

ⓥ 밀어 넣다, 밀어닥치다 **⊜** stuff

cram oneself with food 포식하다
cram into a concert hall 콘서트 장에 빽빽이 들어차다

During rush hour, I'm always crammed on the bus among other people.

37 amnesty
[ǽmnəsti]

ⓝ 특사, 사면 **⊜** pardon

Amnesty International 국제 사면 위원회

The old man was granted amnesty for good behavior in prison.

38 recipient
[risípiənt]

ⓝ recipience 수령, 수용

ⓝ 수혜자, 수령인

welfare recipients 복지 수혜자

The new subsidy plan is meant to reach out to more recipients.

39 artifact
[ɑ́ːrtəfæ̀kt]

ⓝ 유물, 공예품

ancient artifacts 고대 유물들

Experts are trying to determine the age of historical artifacts.

40 audit
[ɔ́ːdit]

ⓥ 회계 감사하다 **ⓝ** 회계 감사

an annual audit 연례적인 감사

★ The accountant audited the company's records to find that all their practices were legal.

★ The company conducted an internal audit to prepare for an external one.

---

34 두 사람은 보호 관세를 유지해야 하는지에 대해 논의했다. 35 나는 지원서와 함께 성적 증명서를 제출해야 했다. 36 나는 출퇴근 혼잡시간에 항상 버스에 끼어 탄다. 37 노인은 감옥에서의 모범적인 행동 때문에 사면되었다. 38 새로운 보조금 계획은 더 많은 수혜자에게 돌아가도록 만들어졌다. 39 전문가들은 역사적 유물의 연대를 측정하려고 한다. 40 회계사는 그 회사의 모든 거래가 합법하다는 것을 밝히기 위해 회사 기록을 회계 감사했다. / 회사는 외부 감사를 준비하기 위해 내부 감사를 시행했다.

EXERCISE

A 다음 영어는 우리말로, 우리말은 영어로 옮기시오.

01 inauguration _____

02 orthodox _____

03 tenacious _____

04 sibling _____

05 audit _____

06 revoke _____

07 혐오하다 _____

08 음모, 공모 _____

09 융자, 저당 _____

10 진정한, 믿을 만한 _____

11 관세 _____

12 박멸하다, 몰살하다 _____

B 다음 빈칸에 알맞은 단어를 쓰시오.

01 calamity ⊜ _____

02 warranty ⊜ _____

03 revolt ⊜ _____

04 amnesty ⊜ _____

05 virtuous ⇔ _____

06 extrovert ⇔ _____

07 scrutiny ⓥ _____

08 evasion ⓥ _____

09 catastrophe ⓐ _____

10 homicide ⓐ _____

11 pathetic ⓝ _____

12 unanimous ⓝ _____

C 다음 빈칸에 들어갈 알맞은 말을 고르시오. (필요하면 형태를 바꾸시오.)

| verdict | vicious | imperative | renounce | itinerary |

01 King Henry _____ his kingship in front of the throngs of people yesterday.

02 According to our _____, we will be visiting ten cities in twelve days.

03 Even the police detectives were surprised at the _____ nature of the crime.

04 It is _____ that one seek immediate medical attention if he is experiencing unusual chest pains.

05 The court's _____ concludes that the actions of the man were criminal and he must spend years in jail.

Across

1 a plan or list of the places you will visit on a journey

3 arousing pity, especially through vulnerability or sadness

6 a secret plan made by two or more people to do something that is harmful or illegal

8 to refuse to accept someone's authority or obey rules or laws

Down

2 to kill large numbers of people or animals of a particular type so they no longer exist

3 very careful and thorough

4 violent and cruel in a way that hurts someone physically

5 a terrible event in which there is a lot of destruction, suffering, or death

7 an official decision made in a court of law, especially about whether someone is guilty of a crime or how a death happened

High-Level Words 4

01 ☑ **blade**
[bleid]

ⓝ (풀의) 잎사귀, 칼날   **a razor blade** 면도날

★ As grass consumes CO_2, water gathers on the blades as dewdrops.

★ A lawn mower uses an engine to move a set of blades in circles.

---

02 ☑ **blaze**
[bleiz]

ⓐ **ablaze** 불타는, 빛나는

ⓝ 불꽃, 폭발 ⊜ flame   **a blaze of anger** 분노의 폭발

As the blazes were fanned by the wind, it started a forest fire.

---

03 ☑ **kerosene**
[kérəsìːn]

ⓝ (난로 등에 쓰이는) 등유 ⊜ paraffin   **a kerosene lamp** 등유 램프

Kerosene oil used to be a commonly used fuel in heating homes.

---

04 ☑ **mighty**
[máiti]

ⓝ **might** 힘, 세력

ⓐ 강력한, 위대한 ⊜ powerful   **a mighty opponent** 강력한 적수

The biologist plunged into the mighty sea to explore its inhabitants.

---

05 ☑ **scrap**
[skræp]

ⓝ 파편 ⓥ 없애다, 취소하다   **scrap paper** 이면지

★ We are searching for a way to recycle scrap metal more efficiently.

★ Since the mini-volcano was successful, the remaining ideas were scrapped.

---

06 ☑ **staple**
[stéipəl]

ⓐ 주요한 ⓝ 주성분   **staple food** 주요한 음식

★ Rice is the staple grain in most countries in East Asia.

★ Protein is an important staple of the human diet.

---

01 풀이 CO_2를 흡수하면서, 잎사귀에 물이 이슬로 맺힌다. / 잔디 깎는 기계는 엔진을 이용해서 칼날이 원을 그리게 한다. 02 불길이 바람을 타고 가면서, 산불로 번졌다. 03 등유는 난방에 흔히 쓰이는 연료였다. 04 생물학자가 해양 생물들을 탐사하기 위해 거대한 바다 속으로 잠수했다. 05 우리는 고철을 더 효율적으로 재활용하는 방안을 찾고 있다. / 미니 화산 실험이 성공적이었기 때문에, 남은 아이디어는 없앴다. 06 쌀은 동아시아 많은 나라의 주식이다. / 단백질은 인간의 식단에 있어서 중요한 구성 요소다.

07 **yolk**
[jouk]

ⓝ 노른자위

egg yolk 달걀노른자

I eat a hard-boiled egg white for breakfast without the yolk.

---

08 **foliage**
[fóuliidʒ]

ⓝ 잎, 잎의 무성함

autumn foliage 가을 단풍

I go hiking with my family every fall to enjoy the beautiful foliage.

---

09 **crater**
[kréitər]

ⓝ 구멍, 분화구, (달 표면의) 크레이터

a bomb crater 폭탄이 터져 패인 곳

Craters on the moon stay sharp because there is no air to erode them.

---

10 **aggregate**
[ǽgrigət / ǽgrigèit]

ⓐ 총계의, 집합적인 ⓝ 총계, 집합 ⓥ 모으다 ⊜ collective 집합적인, sum 총계

an aggregate of 1,000 votes 총 1,000표

★ The aggregate cost of the business was greater than I thought.

★ The aggregate of crops was enough for the farmers to supply the entire village.

---

11 **amplify**
[ǽmpləfài]

ⓝ amplification 증폭, 확대

ⓥ (소리를) 크게 하다, (힘 등을) 강화하다 ⊜ magnify, enlarge

amplify sounds 소리를 크게 하다

I amplified the volume in order to make it easier for others to listen.

---

12 **insulate**
[ínsəlèit]

ⓝ insulation 격리, 절연

ⓥ 격리시키다, 단열 처리하다 ⊜ isolate 격리하다

insulate a patient 환자를 격리시키다

Glass fiber is very effective when insulating a building from cold.

---

13 **latitude**
[lǽtətjùːd]

ⓝ 위도

high latitudes 고위도 지방

The latitude of Seoul is approximately 37 degrees 34 minutes north.

---

07 나는 노른자위를 뺀 삶은 달걀 흰자위를 아침식사로 먹는다. 08 나는 가을마다 아름다운 단풍을 즐기기 위해 가족과 등산을 간다. 09 달에는 침식시킬 공기가 없어서, 분화구가 선명하게 남아있다. 10 사업의 총비용은 내가 생각한 것보다 컸다. / 곡식의 총량은 농부들이 마을 전체에 공급할 수 있을 만큼 충분했다. 11 나는 다른 사람들이 더 잘 들을 수 있도록 소리크기를 높였다. 12 유리섬유는 건물을 추위로부터 단열할 때 매우 효과적이다. 13 서울의 위도는 대략 북위 37도 34분이다.

14 compatible
[kəmpǽtəbəl]

ⓝ compatibility 호환성

ⓐ 조화하는, 호환되는   ● incompatible 조화되지 않는, 호환성이 없는

a compatible component 호환되는 부품

I couldn't find a compatible hard drive for my new laptop computer.

---

15 concave
[kɑnkéiv]

ⓐ 오목한, 옴폭한   ● convex 볼록한

concave lens 오목렌즈

Objects look smaller if you look at them through a concave lens.

---

16 breeding
[bríːdiŋ]

ⓥ breed 낳다, 기르다

ⓝ 교배, 번식

cross breeding 잡종교배

During the breeding season, a salmon swims against the current, traveling upstream.

---

17 longitude
[lándʒətjùːd]

ⓝ 경도, 경선

measure a longitude 경도를 측정하다

The nation's capital is at longitude 22 degrees east.

---

18 corrosion
[kəróuʒən]

ⓐ corrosive 부식성의
ⓥ corrode 부식하다

ⓝ 부식, 녹   ● rust 녹

prevent corrosion 부식을 방지하다

Coins are made by metals that are relatively resistant to corrosion.

---

19 demographics
[dìːməgrǽfiks]

ⓝ demography 인구 통계학
ⓐ demographic 인구 통계의

ⓝ 인구 통계

accurate demographics 정확한 인구통계

Since 2000, the demographics of the city have changed markedly.

---

20 deterrent
[ditə́ːrənt]

ⓥ deter 방해하다, 만류하다

ⓝ 억제책, 방해물   ● restraint, impediment **a nuclear deterrent** 핵 억제책

The police not only fight crime, but work as a deterrent as well.

---

14 나는 내 최신 노트북 컴퓨터에 호환되는 하드 드라이브를 찾지 못했다. 15 오목렌즈를 통해 보면 사물은 더 작게 보인다. 16 연어는 번식기에 물살을 거슬러 헤엄쳐서 상류로 이동한다. 17 그 국가의 수도는 경도 상으로 동경 21도에 있다. 18 동전은 비교적 부식에 강한 금속을 사용하여 만들어진다. 19 2000년 이후로 도시의 인구 통계가 두드러지게 변했다. 20 경찰은 범죄와 싸울 뿐 아니라, 억제 역할도 한다.

21 digit
[dídʒit]

ⓐ digital
숫자로 표시하는, 디지털의

ⓝ 한 자리 숫자　　　　　　　　　**a double-digit number** 두 자리 수

All data in a computer is comprised of two digits: zero and one.

---

22 exhaust
[igzɔ́ːst]

ⓝ 배기가스　　　　　　　　　　**exhaust fumes** 배기가스

Car exhaust is known to be one of the major sources of carbon emission.

---

23 freight
[freit]

ⓝ 화물 운송, 화물 ⓥ 운송하다　ⓔ cargo 화물, transport 운송하다
freight services 화물 운송 서비스

The rise in oil prices was followed by a rise in freight charges.

---

24 flammable
[flǽməbəl]

ⓝ flammability 연소성, 인화성

ⓐ 가연성의　ⓔ inflammable, burnable
a flammable chemical 가연성 화학물질

You must be very careful when dealing with flammable substances.

---

25 imprisonment
[imprízənmənt]

ⓥ imprison 투옥하다

ⓝ 투옥, 구속　　　　　　　　**life imprisonment** 종신형

There was no way the prisoner could escape from imprisonment.

---

26 eclipse
[iklíps]

ⓝ 일식, 월식　　　　　　**a solar [lunar] eclipse** 일식[월식]
a total eclipse 개기식

A lunar eclipse occurs when the moon enters the Earth's shadow.

---

27 liquor
[líkər]

ⓝ 독한 술　　　　　　　　　**a liquor store** 술을 파는 가게

You must reach the legal age to buy liquor and tobacco.

---

21 컴퓨터에 있는 모든 정보는 0과 1, 두 숫자로 구성된다. 22 자동차 배기가스는 탄소 배출의 한 주요 원인으로 알려져 있다. 23 기름 값이 오른 후에 곧바로 운송비용도 덩달아 올랐다. 24 가연성 물질을 다룰 때는 매우 조심해야 한다. 25 죄수가 탈옥할 방법은 없었다. 26 달이 지구의 그림자에 들어갈 때 월식이 일어난다. 27 술과 담배를 사려면 법적 나이가 되어야 한다.

28 meteorological
[mì:tiərəládʒikəl]

ⓝ meteorology 기상학

ⓐ 기상의, 기상학의

Meteorological Office 기상청

Weather reports are made using data that meteorological satellites collect.

29 crossbreed
[krɔ́:sbrì:d]

ⓥ 서로 다른 종을 교배하다, 잡종을 만들다

a crossbred dog 잡종견

Crossbreeding between two breeds of dogs is very common.

30 radiate
[réidièit]

ⓝ radiation 방사, 발광[열]

ⓐ radiant 빛[열]을 내는

ⓥ 방출하다, 발산하다 **ⓔ** emit

radiate light [heat] 빛[열]을 내다

The energy radiated from the sun is essential to all life forms.

31 avalanche
[ǽvəlæ̀ntʃ]

ⓐ avalanchine
눈사태의, 압도적인

ⓝ 눈사태, 쇄도

a sudden avalanche 갑작스러운 눈사태

A loud noise on high mountaintops may stimulate an avalanche.

32 transparent
[trænspέərənt]

ⓝ transparency 투명

ⓐ 투명한, 명백한 **ⓔ** lucid 투명한, obvious 명백한 **ⓞ** opaque 불투명한

transparent glass 투명한 유리

Transparent plastic is often used as an alternative to glass.

33 ubiquitous
[ju:bíkwətəs]

ⓐ 어디에나 존재하는, 유비쿼터스 **ⓔ** omnipresent, ever-present

a ubiquitous network 유비쿼터스 네트워크

In a ubiquitous system, all appliances will be linked to each other.

34 velocity
[vilάsəti]

ⓝ 속도, 빠르기 **ⓔ** speed

wind velocity 풍속

The velocity of an object regards the direction of its movement.

---

28 일기예보는 기상 위성들이 수집한 자료를 이용하여 만들어진다. 29 두 종류의 개를 교배하는 것은 매우 흔하다. 30 태양으로부터 방출되는 에너지는 모든 생명체에게 중요하다. 31 높은 산꼭대기에서 나는 큰 소리가 눈사태를 일으킬 수도 있다. 32 투명한 플라스틱은 종종 유리의 대체물로 쓰인다. 33 유비쿼터스 시스템에서는 모든 용품이 서로 연결되어 있을 것이다. 34 물체의 속도는 운동하는 방향과 관련이 있다.

35 combustion
[kəmbʌ́stʃən]

ⓐ combustive 연소성의

ⓝ 연소, 발화　　　　　**incomplete combustion** 불완전 연소

A combustion engine transfers energy in fuel to motion energy.

---

36 mutation
[mjuːtéiʃən]

ⓥ mutate 변화하다, 돌연변이하다
ⓝ mutant 돌연변이

ⓝ 돌연변이, 변화　　　　　**a gene mutation** 유전자 돌연변이

Geneticists study the mutation that occurs in the heredity of traits.

---

37 interstellar
[ìntərstélər]

ⓐ 행성 간의, 별과 별 사이의　　　　　**interstellar distance** 행성간 거리

★ I enjoy watching SF movies with interstellar wars and stuff.
★ Some scientists say that the universe is too big for interstellar travel to be practical.

---

38 fission
[fíʃən]

ⓐ fissionable 핵분열하는

ⓝ 분열　　　　　**nuclear fission** 핵분열

Nuclear fusion produces more energy than nuclear fission.

---

39 ventilate
[véntəlèit]

ⓝ ventilation 환기

ⓥ 환기하다, 공기를 유통시키다　　　　　**ventilate a room** 방을 환기시키다

Unfortunately, there were no windows or fans to ventilate the room.

---

40 saturate
[sǽtʃərèit]

ⓝ saturation 포화 (상태)

ⓥ 포화시키다, 적시다　⊜ overwhelm 압도하다
　　　　　saturated [unsaturated] fat 포화[불포화] 지방

The auto market is saturated with a surplus of automobiles and lessening demand.

---

35 연소기관은 연료의 에너지를 운동에너지로 전환한다. 36 유전학자들은 형질이 유전될 때 일어나는 돌연변이를 연구한다. 37 나는 행성끼리의 전쟁 같은 것이 나오는 공상 과학 영화를 즐겨본다. / 일부 과학자들은 우주가 너무 넓어서 행성 간의 여행은 실용화될 수 없다고 말한다. 38 핵융합은 핵분열보다 더 많은 에너지를 만들어낸다. 39 안타깝게도, 방을 환기시킬 창문이나 환풍기가 없었다. 40 자동차의 과잉 공급과 수요 감소로 자동차 시장은 포화 상태다.

EXERCISE

A 다음 영어는 우리말로, 우리말은 영어로 옮기시오.

01 demographics _____   07 위도 _____

02 ubiquitous _____   08 눈사태, 쇄도 _____

03 flammable _____   09 포화시키다, 적시다 _____

04 ventilate _____   10 화물, 운송하다 _____

05 aggregate _____   11 돌연변이, 변화 _____

06 fission _____   12 배기가스 _____

B 다음 빈칸에 알맞은 단어를 쓰시오.

01 deterrent ⊜ _____   07 breeding Ⓥ _____

02 radiate ⊜ _____   08 imprisonment Ⓥ _____

03 velocity ⊜ _____   09 combustion Ⓐ _____

04 mighty ⊜ _____   10 digit Ⓐ _____

05 transparent ⇔ _____   11 meteorological Ⓝ _____

06 compatible ⇔ _____   12 insulate Ⓝ _____

C 다음 빈칸에 들어갈 알맞은 말을 고르시오. (필요하면 형태를 바꾸시오.)

amplify	corrosion	compatible	transparent	eclipse

01 The _____ nature of the film allows light to pass through it.

02 The stereo system _____ the sound twice as loud as its original sound level.

03 After the blind date, Cindy concluded that she was _____ with John.

04 Due to _____, the beautiful shiny metal had turned into a dirty brown color.

05 During the _____, many people went outside to watch it take place.

Crossword Puzzle

앞에서 배운 어휘를 기억하며 빈칸을 채워보세요.

Across

3   the speed of something that is moving in a particular direction

6   a change in the genetic structure of an animal or plant that makes it different from others of the same kind

7   (of a material or article) allowing light to pass through so that objects behind can be distinctly seen

9   to emit (energy, especially light or heat) in the form of rays or waves

10   easily set on fire

Down

1   to put a lot of something into a particular place, especially so that you could not add any more

2   the process of splitting an atom to produce large amounts of energy or an explosion

4   able to exist or be used together without causing problems

5   to increase the effects or strength of something

8   a big dangerous fire

High-Level Words 5

---

01 ☑ **acupuncture**
[ǽkjupʌ̀ŋktʃər]

ⓝ acupuncturist 침술가

ⓝ 침술

hand acupuncture 수지침

A man was lying on a bed with acupuncture needles in his back.

---

02 ☑ **modify**
[mɑ́dəfài]

ⓝ modification 수정, 변경

ⓥ 수정하다, 조절하다

Genetically Modified Organism(GMO) 유전자변형식품

In hospital, patients are taught how to modify their diet.

---

03 ☑ **secretion**
[sikríːʃən]

ⓥ secrete 분비하다

ⓝ 분비, 분비물

secretion of hormones 호르몬의 분비

Many factors are involved in the secretion of gastric juices.

---

04 ☑ **ailment**
[éilmənt]

ⓝ 질환, 불쾌   ⊜ illness

throat ailments 목 질환

He has suffered from a heart ailment for more than ten years.

---

05 ☑ **alleviate**
[əlíːvièit]

ⓝ alleviation 경감, 완화

ⓥ (고통을) 완화하다, 덜다   ⊖ aggravate 악화하다

alleviate the pain 고통을 완화시키다

Matt needed to get surgery to alleviate pain in his shoulder.

---

06 ☑ **anatomy**
[ənǽtəmi]

ⓐ anatomical
해부학상의, 해부학의

ⓝ 해부학, 해부

human anatomy 인체 해부학

Medical students learn anatomy, physiology, and basic health care.

---

01 한 남자가 등에 침을 꽂고 침대에 누워 있었다. 02 병원에서 환자들은 자신들의 식이요법을 어떻게 조절하는지를 배운다. 03 위액 분비에는 많은 요인이 있다. 04 그는 10년 넘게 심장질환을 앓고 있다. 05 Matt는 어깨 통증을 덜기 위해 수술이 필요했다. 06 의과대학 학생들은 해부학, 생리학, 그리고 기본적 건강 관리를 배운다.

07 vein
[vein]
ⓐ **veinal** 정맥의, 혈관의

ⓝ 정맥, 혈관　⬤ artery 동맥

a blood vein 혈관

The nurse injected Ringer solution into the patient's veins.

---

08 autopsy
[ɔ́ːtɑpsi]

ⓝ 부검

perform an autopsy 부검하다

As a parent, I watched the entire autopsy process held in the hospital.

---

09 cardiac
[kɑ́ːrdiæk]

ⓐ 심장의

cardiac surgery 심장 수술

I wonder how a cardiac disorder affects pregnancy.

---

10 casualty
[kǽʒuəlti]

ⓝ 사상자, 피해자

fire casualties 화재 사상자

The casualties from snowfall and cold weather increased to five today.

---

11 crutch
[krʌtʃ]

ⓝ 목발

a wooden crutch 나무 목발

He broke his leg and had to walk on crutches for about two weeks.

---

12 deafen
[défən]
ⓐ **deaf** 귀가 먼, 청각장애의

ⓥ 들리지 않게 하다, 귀먹게 하다

a deafening noise 귀가 멍해지는 소음

The noise of the jets nearly deafened me.

---

13 diarrhea
[dàiəríːə]

ⓝ 설사

severe diarrhea 심한 설사

He experienced symptoms like vomiting, diarrhea, and high fever.

---

14 dizziness
[dízinis]
ⓐ **dizzy** 어지러운

ⓝ 현기증, 어지럼증

cause dizziness 현기증을 일으키다

Most causes of dizziness either cure themselves or are easily treated.

---

07 간호사는 링거액을 환자 정맥에 주입했다.　08 저는 부모로서 병원에서 한 부검의 전 과정을 지켜봤습니다.　09 나는 심장질환이 임신에 어떻게 영향을 미치는지 궁금하다.　10 폭설과 한파로 인한 사상자 수는 현재 5명으로 늘어났다.　11 그는 다리가 부러져서 약 2주 동안 목발을 짚고 걸어야 했다. 12 제트기의 소음이 나를 거의 귀먹게 했다.　13 그는 구토, 설사, 또는 고열 같은 증상을 경험했다.　14 대부분의 현기증 원인은 저절로 낫거나 쉽게 치료된다.

15 impair
[impέər]

ⓝ impairment 손상, 해침

ⓥ 손상시키다, 해치다　ⓢ worsen, harm　**impaired vision** 손상된 시력

Too much stress can seriously impair physical and mental health.

16 tumor
[tjúːmər]

ⓐ tumorous 종양의, 종양 모양의

ⓝ 종기, 종양　**a brain tumor** 뇌종양

He remained feeble because of a cancerous tumor in his lung.

17 pneumonia
[njuːmóunjə]

ⓝ 폐렴　**an acute pneumonia** 급성 폐렴
a diagnosis of pneumonia 폐렴 진단

In the past, pneumonia used to be a highly deadly disease.

18 fatality
[feitǽləti]

ⓐ fatal 치명적인

ⓝ (사고 등에 의한) 죽음, 사망자　**fatality rate** 사망률, 치사율

The fatality of cancer can be reduced by early diagnosis.

19 fetus
[fíːtəs]

ⓝ 태아　**fetus and newborn** 태아 및 신생아

An expectant mother's drinking has harmful effects on the fetus.

20 flex
[fleks]

ⓥ 관절을 구부리다, 움직이다　ⓢ bend　ⓐ straighten 곧게 하다
flex one's muscle 힘을 과시하다

Stop once an hour to flex your fingers and shake your hands.

21 fracture
[frǽktʃər]

ⓝ 골절 ⓥ 부러지다　ⓢ break　**a compound fracture** 복합 골절상

★ Seniors who suffer a fracture have a higher risk of death.
★ My arm was fractured in a bad fall, and I had to get a cast put on it.

---

15 스트레스가 너무 심하면 육체적, 정신적 건강을 심각하게 해칠 수 있다. 16 그는 폐에 있는 암 종양 때문에 몸이 연약한 상태다. 17 과거에 폐렴은 매우 치명적인 질병이었다. 18 암으로 인한 사망자는 조기진단으로 줄일 수 있다. 19 예비 엄마의 음주는 태아에게 해로운 영향을 미친다. 20 한 시간에 한 번 손가락을 구부리고 손을 흔들기 위해 멈추어라. 21 골절을 입은 노인은 사망 가능성이 더 크다. / 나는 심하게 넘어지면서 팔이 부러져서 팔에 깁스해야 했다.

22 gland
[glænd]

ⓝ 분비기관

sweat glands 땀샘

Tears are made in the tear gland, located near the upper eyelid.

23 malpractice
[mælpræktis]

ⓝ 의료 사고, 위법 행위　**⊜** misconduct 위법 행위

a malpractice suit 의료사고 소송

If a patient dies, the family can later sue for malpractice.

24 marrow
[mǽrou]

ⓝ 뼈골, 골수

bone-marrow transplant 골수 이식

If Ann gets a bone-marrow transplant operation, she will get healthy again.

25 maternity
[mətə́:rnəti]

ⓐ maternal 어머니의, 임산부의

ⓐ 출산의, 임산부의

maternity clothes 임부복

The minimum period of maternity leave is not less than twelve weeks.

26 measles
[mí:zəlz]

ⓝ 홍역

classical symptoms of measles 홍역의 전형적인 증상

When children have measles, they have a fever and small red spots on their body and face.

27 neural
[njúərəl]

ⓐ neurological 신경의, 신경학상의

ⓐ 신경의, 신경계의

neural damage 신경계 손상

The neural mechanism in human brains is not yet fully understood.

28 pimple
[pímpl]

ⓝ 여드름, 뾰루지, 작은 돌기

pop the pimple 여드름을 짜다

An adolescent boy is pointing at a pimple on his chin.

---

22 눈물은 윗눈꺼풀 근처에 있는 눈물샘에서 만들어진다. 23 환자가 죽으면 가족들은 나중에 의료사고로 소송을 걸 수 있다. 24 Ann이 골수 이식 수술을 받으면 다시 건강해질 거야. 25 출산 휴가의 최소기간은 적어도 12주다. 26 아이들이 홍역에 걸리면 열이 나고 몸과 얼굴에 빨간 반점이 생긴다. 27 인간의 두뇌 속 신경구조는 아직 완전히 파악되지는 않았다. 28 한 청소년 남자아이가 자신의 턱에 난 여드름을 가리키고 있다.

29 osteoporosis
[àstioupəróusis]

n 골다공증   **increases osteoporosis risk** 골다공증의 위험을 증가시키다

These medications can reduce fractures in patients with osteoporosis.

30 antidote
[ǽntidòut]

n 해독제   **an antidote for the poison** 독에 대한 해독제

In Thailand, the leaves are regarded as an antidote to certain poisons.

31 pediatrician
[pìːdiətríʃən]

n 소아과 의사   **consult a pediatrician** 소아과 의사에게 진찰받다

n pediatrics 소아과

Ask your baby's pediatrician for more standards about the baby's diet.

32 placebo
[pləsíːbou]

n 가짜 약, 플라시보

placebo effect 플라시보 효과 (가짜 약이 효과가 있다고 믿어 실제로 병세가 호전되는 일)

One group of patients was given a real medication, while the other group was given a placebo.

33 revitalize
[riːváitəlàiz]

v 소생시키다, 활력을 불어 넣다   **=** revive

revitalize the plants 식물들을 다시 살리다

Minerals extracted from the Dead Sea help revitalize your skin.

34 sprain
[sprein]

v 삐다 **n** 삠   **sprain one's ankle [wrist]** 발목[팔목]을 삐다

★ During the tennis match, the athlete slipped and sprained her ankle.

★ Vicky suffered a neck sprain and was taken off the field on a cart.

35 sterilize
[stérəlàiz]

v 소독하다, 살균하다   **sterilize water** 물을 소독하다

n sterilization 소독, 살균

You have to sterilize all the equipment and containers after you use them.

---

29 이러한 약물치료는 골다공증이 있는 환자들의 골절을 감소시킬 수 있다. 30 태국에서는 그 나뭇잎을 어떤 독성에 대한 해독제로 간주한다. 31 유아의 식단에 관한 기준을 더 알고 싶으면 소아과 의사에게 물어보아라. 32 한 환자 집단은 진짜 약을 받았고, 나머지 집단은 가짜 약을 받았다. 33 사해에서 캐낸 미네랄은 여러분의 피부를 소생시키도록 도와준다. 34 테니스 게임 중, 선수가 미끄러져 발목을 삐었다. / Vicky는 목이 삐었고, 들것에 실려 경기장 밖으로 나갔다. 35 당신은 모든 장비와 용기를 사용 후에 반드시 소독해야 한다.

| 36 ☑ **lethal** [líːθəl] | **ⓐ** 치사의, 치명적인 **⊜** fatal 치명적인 **a lethal weapon** 흉기 |
| | Merely touching the frog's back is enough to deliver a lethal dose of poison. |

| 37 ☑ **swell** [swel] | **ⓥ** 붓다, 커지다 **⊜** shrink 줄어들다 **swell to an enormous size** 크게 부풀다 **a swollen knee** 부은 무릎 |
| | His eyes swelled shut from allergies; he couldn't see anything. |

| 38 ☑ **syringe** [sərínʤ] | **ⓝ** 주사기 **a disposable syringe** 일회용 주사기 |
| | I used a disposable syringe to suck up the oil out of the bottle. |

| 39 ☑ **test tube** [tésttjùːb] | **ⓝ** 시험관 **a test-tube baby** 시험관 아기 |
| | Unbreakable test tubes are used for safe science experiments. |

| 40 ☑ **ward** [wɔːrd] | **ⓝ** 병실, 병동 **an emergency ward** 응급실 |
| | The children's ward was tranquil with the children still fast asleep. |

36 단지 그 개구리의 등만 만져도 독성분은 치사량에 이를 정도다. 37 그의 눈은 알레르기 때문에 부어서 감겼으며, 아무것도 볼 수가 없다. 38 나는 병에서 기름을 빨아들이려고 일회용 주사기를 사용했다. 39 깨지지 않는 시험관은 안전한 과학 실험에 사용된다. 40 어린이 병동은 아이들이 아직도 깊이 잠들어 있어서 조용했다.

EXERCISE

A 다음 영어는 우리말로, 우리말은 영어로 옮기시오.

01 pneumonia _____

02 acupuncture _____

03 antidote _____

04 measles _____

05 placebo _____

06 diarrhea _____

07 질환, 불쾌 _____

08 여드름, 뾰루지 _____

09 부검 _____

10 치사의, 치명적인 _____

11 골절, 부러지다 _____

12 사상자, 피해자 _____

B 다음 빈칸에 알맞은 단어를 쓰시오.

01 malpractice ⊜ _____

02 revitalize ⊜ _____

03 impair ⊜ _____

04 flex ⊜ _____

05 swell ⇔ _____

06 alleviate ⇔ _____

07 anatomy ⓐ _____

08 deafen ⓐ _____

09 maternity ⓐ _____

10 alleviate ⓝ _____

11 sterllize ⓝ _____

12 modify ⓝ _____

C 다음 빈칸에 들어갈 알맞은 말을 고르시오. (필요하면 형태를 바꾸시오.)

| secretion | impair | cardiac | sprain | fetus |

01 Direct contact with ultraviolet light can _____ the vision significantly.

02 The aging process is related to the reduction in growth hormone _____.

03 _____ arrest can occur without symptoms and lead to brain damage.

04 Many people believe that life starts at conception and that the _____ is a baby.

05 Be careful that you do not _____ your ankle again while playing basketball.

Across

1. to make something completely clean by killing any bacteria in it
3. a substance that stops the effects of a poison
5. a death in an accident or a violent attack
8. relating to a nerve or the nervous system
9. to make small changes to something in order to improve it and make it more suitable or effective
11. to damage something or make it not as good as it should be
12. someone who is hurt or killed in an accident or war

Down

2. causing death, or able to cause death
4. to make something less painful or difficult to deal with
6. the scientific study of the structure of human or animal bodies
7. a mass of diseased cells in your body that have divided and increased too quickly
10. the cracking or breaking of a hard object or material

_____ 익명의, 신원 불명의

_____ 인식의

_____ 숨기다, 비밀로 하다

_____ 평가하다, 감정하다

_____ 동요시키다, 일으키다

_____ 충돌하다, 상충하다

_____ 일으키다, 성나게 하다

_____ 유입

High-Level Words 1
심화어휘 1 (묘사와 설명)

High-Level Words
심화어휘

High-Level Words 2
심화어휘 2 (동작과 상태)

High-Level Words 5
심화어휘 5 (과학과 의학)

_____ (고통을) 완화하다

_____ 소독하다, 살균하다

_____ 죽음, 사망자

_____ 골절, 부러지다

High-Level Words 3
심화어휘 3 (사람과 사회)

High-Level Words 4
심화어휘 4 (자연과 물질)

_____ 만장일치의

_____ 음모, 공모

_____ 판결, 판단

_____ 유물, 공예품

_____ 격리시키다

_____ 투명한, 명백한

_____ 조화하는, 호환되는

_____ 방출하다, 발산하다

Chapter
09

Other Words

Unit 46 Multi-Meaning Words

01 affect
[əfékt]

- Ⓥ 영향을 미치다 **affect the world** 세계에 영향을 미치다
- Ⓥ 감동을 주다 **be easily affected** 쉽게 감동되다
- Ⓥ ~인 체하다, ~을 가장하다 **affect ignorance** 모르는 체하다

02 authority
[əθɔ́:riti]

- Ⓝ 권위, 권력 **supreme authority** 최고의 권위
- Ⓝ 〈보통 복수형〉 당국 **the proper authorities** 관계당국

03 capital
[kǽpitl]

- Ⓝ 자본 **flows of capital** 자본의 흐름
- Ⓝ 대문자 **in capital letters** 대문자로
- Ⓝ 수도 **the capital city of Korea** 한국의 수도

04 consist
[kənsíst]

- Ⓥ ~으로 구성되다 **consist of atoms** 원자로 구성되다
- Ⓥ 존재하다 **Happiness consists in families.** 행복은 가정 내에 있다.
- Ⓥ ~와 일치하다 **consist with one's opinion** ~의 의견과 일치하다

05 appreciate
[əprí:ʃièit]

- Ⓥ ~의 진가를 인정하다 **appreciate one's art** ~의 예술의 진가를 인정하다
- Ⓥ 감상하다 **appreciate poetry** 시를 감상하다
- Ⓥ 고맙게 여기다 **appreciate one's kindness** ~의 친절함을 고맙게 여기다

06 beat
[bi:t]

- Ⓥ 치다 **beat the drums** 북을 치다
- Ⓥ 이기다 **beat the boss** 보스를 이기다
- Ⓥ (심장, 맥박 등이) 뛰다
  My heart started to beat faster. 내 심장이 빨리 뛰기 시작했다.

07 contribute
[kəntríbjut]

- Ⓥ 기부하다 **contribute a scholarship** 장학금을 기부하다
- Ⓥ 기여하다 **contribute to our plans** 우리 계획에 기여하다
- Ⓥ 기고하다 **contribute an article** 기사를 기고하다

08 ☑ currency
[kə́ːrənsi]

- ⓝ 통화 currency exchange 환전
- ⓝ 유통, 통용 in common currency 널리 통용되는

09 ☑ due
[djuː]

- ⓐ 지급 기일이 된 become due 만기가 되다
- ⓐ ~할 예정인 due to be a father 아버지가 될 예정인
- ⓐ ~에 기인하는 be cancelled due to rain 비로 인해 취소되다

10 ☑ fair
[fɛər]

- ⓐ 공정한 a fair decision 공정한 결정
- ⓐ 꽤 많은 a fair amount of money 상당히 많은 돈
- ⓐ 살이 흰 have a fair complexion 피부가 하얗다

11 ☑ break
[breik]

- ⓥ (물건을) 부수다, 깨다 break a window 유리창을 깨다
- ⓥ (법, 질서를) 어기다, 위반하다 break a law 법을 어기다
- ⓥ (기록을) 깨다, 경신하다 break the world record 세계신기록을 깨다
- ⓥ (기계를) 고장 내다 break a watch 시계를 고장 내다
- ⓝ 휴식 during the coffee break 커피 마시는 동안에

12 ☑ cause
[kɔːz]

- ⓝ 원인 the cause of the fire 화재의 원인
- ⓝ 주장, 대의 a greater cause 더 큰 명분
- ⓝ 이유, 동기 cause for a crime 범죄 동기

13 ☑ charge
[tʃɑːrdʒ]

- ⓥ 짐을 싣다 charge a ship 배에 짐을 싣다
- ⓥ (의무 등을) 지우다 charge with duty 의무를 지우다
- ⓥ 청구하다 charge a fee 요금을 청구하다
- ⓥ 충전하다 charge a battery 배터리를 충전하다

14 ☑ conduct
[kəndʌ́kt]

- ⓥ 지휘하다 conduct a choir 성가대를 지휘하다
- ⓥ 행동하다 conduct an exercise 훈련을 시행하다
- ⓥ (열이나 전기를) 전도하다 conduct heat 열을 전도하다
- ⓥ 안내하다 conduct a person into a seat ~을 자리로 안내하다

15 ☐ **fit** [fít]

ⓐ ~하기에 적당한, 알맞은 a fit place 적당한 장소

ⓐ 건강이 좋은 physically fit 육체 건강한

ⓐ (행위, 복장 등이) 어울리는, 적절한 fit clothing 몸에 맞는 옷

16 ☐ **grave** [greiv]

ⓐ 중대한 grave responsibilities 중대한 책임

ⓐ 근엄한, 엄숙한 a grave expression 심각한 표정

ⓝ 무덤 from the cradle to the grave 요람에서 무덤까지, 평생

17 ☐ **point** [pɔint]

ⓝ 맨 끝, 뾰족한 끝 the point of a nose 코 끝

ⓝ (온도의) 도, 눈금의 점 the freezing point 어는점

ⓝ 시점, 순간 at this point 이 시점에

ⓝ 점수, 득점 three point line 〈농구〉 3점 슛 라인

ⓝ 요점, 핵심 beside the point 핵심에서 벗어난

ⓥ (무기를) 겨누다 point a gun at a person 남에게 총을 겨누다

ⓥ (손가락으로) 가리키다 point at a person 남을 손가락으로 가리키다

18 ☐ **interest** [íntərist]

ⓝ 흥미 have an interest in physics 물리학에 흥미가 있다

ⓝ 이익 national interest 국익

ⓝ 이자 annual interest 연이자

19 ☐ **item** [áitəm]

ⓝ 항목, 조항 an item of the contract 계약서 조항

ⓝ (신문 따위의) 기사 a news item 신문 기사

ⓝ 물건, 상품 a luxury item 사치품

20 ☐ **just** [dʒʌst]

ⓐ 올바른, 타당한 a just cause 올바른 목적

ad 이제, 방금 just arrived 방금 도착한

ad 다만, 단지 just once 오로지 한 번만

21 ☐ **principal** [prínsəpəl]

ⓐ 주요한 principal means of communication 주요 통신 수단

ⓝ (기관의) 장 the school principal 학교장

ⓝ 원금 principal and interest 원금과 이자

22 proof
[pru:f]

- ⓝ 증명, 증거 proof of purchase 영수증
- ⓐ (불, 총알 등을) 막는, 견디는 a bullet-proof vest 방탄조끼

23 figure
[fígjər]

- ⓝ 숫자, 수 three figures 세 자리 수
- ⓝ 모양, 형태 a four sided figure 사면체 도형
- ⓝ 모습, 외관 a handsome figure 잘생긴 모습
- ⓝ 명사, 거물, 역사상의 인물 a prominent figure 거물

24 lot
[lɑt]

- ⓝ 제비뽑기 decide by lot 제비뽑기로 결정하다
- ⓝ 땅, 토지 a parking lot 주차장
- ⓐⓓ 대단히, 크게 a lot more 아주 많은

25 margin
[máːrdʒin]

- ⓝ 여백 leave a margin 여백을 남기다
- ⓝ 차이 margin of error 오차
- ⓝ 여유 a margin of 10 minutes 10분간의 여유
- ⓝ 판매수익 profit margin 이윤 차액

26 mean
[mi:n]

- ⓥ 의미하다 What does it mean? 그것은 무슨 뜻입니까?
- ⓥ ～할 작정이다 mean no harm 해할 마음이 없다
- ⓐ 비열한 a mean guy 비열한 남자
- ⓝ 〈복수형〉 수단 nonviolent means 비폭력적인 수단

27 measure
[méʒər]

- ⓥ 재다 measure the length 길이를 재다
- ⓝ 방책, 조처 take the necessary measure 필요한 조처를 위하다
- ⓝ 치수 a small measure 작은 치수

28 moderate
[mádərət / mádəreit]

- ⓐ 절제하는 moderate drinking 절주(節酒)
- ⓐ 알맞은 a moderate plan 알맞은 계획
- ⓐ (기후가) 온화한 a moderate climate 온화한 기후
- ⓥ 알맞게 하다 moderate the settings 설정을 알맞게 하다

29 organic
[ɔːrgǽnik]

- ⓐ 유기체의 **organic food** 유기농 식품
- ⓐ 생물의 **organic evolution** 생물 진화
- ⓐ 신체기관의 **an organic disease** 장기 질환

30 fortune
[fɔ́ːrtʃən]

- ⓝ 운명 **a fortune-teller** 점쟁이
- ⓝ 행운 **good fortune** 행운
- ⓝ 재산 **make a fortune** 많은 돈을 벌다

31 general
[dʒénərəl]

- ⓐ 일반의 **the general public** 일반 대중
- ⓐ 전반에 걸치는 **a general hospital** 종합병원
- ⓝ 육군 장군 **a four-star General** 4성 장군

32 physical
[fízikəl]

- ⓐ 육체의 **physical fitness** 신체 건강
- ⓐ 물질의 **physical evidence** 물증
- ⓐ 물리학의 **a physical theory** 물리학 이론

33 plain
[plein]

- ⓐ 분명한 **in plain language** 분명한 말로
- ⓐ 꾸밈없는 **plain yogurt** (아무것도 넣지 않은) 플레인 요구르트
- ⓐ 검소한 **a plain meal** 검소한 식사
- ⓐ 평범한 **plain people** 일반 대중
- ⓝ 평지, 벌판 **a broad plain** 넓은 평야

34 plant
[plænt]

- ⓝ 식물 **an annual plant** 일년생 식물
- ⓝ 공장 **a power plant** 발전소
- ⓥ 심다 **plant a tree** 나무를 심다

35 right
[rait]

- ⓝ 권리 **the right to know** 알 권리
- ⓐ 올바른 **the right answer** 정답
- ⓐ 오른쪽의 **right handed** 오른손잡이

36 ☑ stake
[steik]

- ⓝ 내기 **play for high stake** 큰돈을 걸고 내기를 하다
- ⓝ 말뚝 **put up a stake** 말뚝을 세우다
- ⓝ 지분 **a stakeholder** 투자자

37 ☑ wear
[wɛər]

- ⓥ 입고[신고, 쓰고] 있다 **wear a watch** 시계를 차고 있다
  wear glasses 안경을 끼고 있다
- ⓥ (수염, 머리를) 기르다 **wear long hair** 머리를 길게 기르고 있다
- ⓥ ~을 닳게 하다 **wear clothes to rags** 옷을 누더기가 될 때까지 입다
- ⓝ 의복 **formal wear** 정장 **men's wear** 신사복

38 ☑ raise
[reiz]

- ⓥ (들어) 올리다 **raise one's hands** 손을 올리다
- ⓥ 건립하다 **raise a house** 집을 짓다
- ⓥ 소동을 일으키다 **raise troubles** 문제를 일으키다
- ⓥ 돈을 모으다, 모금하다 **raise funds for charity** 자선 모금을 하다
- ⓥ 기르다, 양육하다 **raise children** 아이를 기르다
- ⓥ (가격, 요금, 임금 등을) 올리다 **raise wages** 임금을 올리다
- ⓝ (임금의) 인상 **ask for a raise** 임금 인상을 요구하다

39 ☑ trunk
[trʌŋk]

- ⓝ (나무의) 줄기 **a tree trunk** 나무줄기
- ⓝ 여행 가방 **pack a trunk** 여행 가방을 싸다
- ⓝ 자동차 짐칸 **open the trunk** 자동차 트렁크를 열다
- ⓝ 코끼리 코 **An elephant has a long trunk.** 코끼리 코는 길다.

40 ☑ notice
[nóutis]

- ⓝ 통지, 통보 **without previous notice** 예고 없이
- ⓝ 게시, 고시 **put up a notice** 게시하다
- ⓝ 통지서 **give a month's notice** 한 달 후에 해고[사직]하겠다고 예고하다
- ⓥ 분간하다, 인지하다 **He didn't notice me.** 그는 나를 알아차리지 못했다.

EXERCISE

A 다음 영어는 우리말로, 우리말은 영어로 옮기시오.

01 capital _____

02 figure _____

03 plain _____

04 authority _____

05 appreciate _____

06 proof _____

07 청구하다 _____

08 재다, 치수 _____

09 물질의 _____

10 행동하다, 지휘하다 _____

11 공정한, 살이 흰 _____

12 흥미, 이자 _____

B 다음 영어는 우리말로, 우리말은 영어로 쓰시오.

01 cause for a crime _____

02 raise fund for charity _____

03 grave responsibilities _____

04 알 권리 the _____ to know

05 계약서 조항 a(n) _____ of the contract

06 오차 _____ of the error

C 다음 빈칸에 들어갈 알맞은 말을 고르시오. (필요하면 형태를 바꾸시오.)

| contribute | principal | fortune | moderate | currency |

01 Please _____ to the poor, by giving of your time and resources.

02 You can convert foreign _____ by using the monetary exchange rate.

03 Many people want to live in the area with a _____ climate all year round.

04 When my uncle died, he left behind a large _____ including a mansion and several cars.

05 The _____ reason for an increase in prices is due to the raw materials and energy cost increases.

Crossword Puzzle

앞에서 배운 어휘를 기억하며 빈칸을 채워보세요.

정답

Unit 46 Multi-Meaning Words

Across

2 clear and easy to understand or recognize

4 having opinions that are not extreme

6 to help to make something happen

8 type of money that a country uses

10 a number representing an amount

11 money that somebody invests in a company

Down

1 facts or documents proving something is true

3 the power you have because of your official position

5 a very large amount of money

6 to allow electricity or heat to travel

7 the place in the ground where a dead body is buried

9 to realize that something exists

Unit 47 Negative Meaning Words

01 □	**abnormal** [æbnɔ́ːrməl]	ⓐ 이상한, 비정상적인	**abnormal climate change** 이상 기후 변화
02 □	**contravene** [kàntrəvíːn]	ⓥ 위반하다, 모순되다, 반대하다	**contravene the law** 법을 위반하다
03 □	**counterfeit** [káuntərfìt]	ⓐ 가짜의, 위조의	**a counterfeit diamond necklace** 가짜 다이아몬드 목걸이
04 □	**discharge** [distʃáːrdʒ]	ⓥ 빚을 갚다, 방출하다	**discharge a debt** 빚을 상환하다
05 □	**unidentified** [ʌ̀naidéntəfàid]	ⓐ 미확인의, 정체불명의	**Unidentified Flying Object (U. F. O)** 미확인 비행 물체
06 □	**illegal** [ilíːgəl]	ⓐ 불법의, 비합법적인	**illegal trade** 암거래, 부정 거래
07 □	**illicit** [ilísit]	ⓐ 불법의, 부정한	**illicit drugs** 불법 약물
08 □	**immature** [ìmətʃúər] ⓝ **immaturity** 미숙, 미성숙	ⓐ 미숙한, 미완성의	**emotionally immature** 정서적으로 미숙한
09 □	**immemorial** [ìmimɔ́ːriəl]	ⓐ 기억에 남지 않은 옛적의, 태고의	**from time immemorial** 태곳적부터
10 □	**immense** [iméns]	ⓐ 막대한, 광대한	**an immense wealth** 막대한 재산

11 ☑ **immoral**
[imɔ́(ː)rəl]
ⓝ immorality 부도덕

ⓐ 부도덕한, 품행이 나쁜

an immoral man 부도덕한 사람

---

12 ☑ **immortal**
[imɔ́ːrtl]
ⓝ immortality 불멸

ⓐ 불멸의, 불사의

an immortal soul 불멸의 영혼

---

13 ☑ **impractical**
[impræktikəl]
ⓝ impracticality 실행 불가능성

ⓐ 비현실적인, 현실에 어두운

an impractical idea 비현실적인 생각

---

14 ☑ **impudent**
[ímpjədənt]
ⓝ impudence 뻔뻔스러움

ⓐ 뻔뻔스러운, 철면피의

an impudent child 건방진 아이

---

15 ☑ **inaccessible**
[ìnəksèsəbəl]
ⓝ inaccessibility 접근불가능

ⓐ 접근하기 어려운, 얻기 어려운

an inaccessible region 접근이 어려운 지역

---

16 ☑ **incessant**
[insésənt]

ⓐ 끊임없는, 그칠 새 없는
an incessant desire to succeed 성공에 대한 끊임없는 욕구

---

17 ☑ **incoherent**
[ìnkouhíərənt]

ⓐ 일관되지 않는, 모순된

an incoherent answer 두서없는 대답

---

18 ☑ **incompatible**
[ìnkəmpǽtəbl]
ⓝ incompatibility
상반, 불친화성

ⓐ 조화되지 않는, 양립할 수 없는

incompatible colors 부조화한 색깔

---

19 ☑ **incomprehensible**
[ìnkɑmprihénsəbəl]
ⓝ incomprehensibility
이해불가능

ⓐ 이해할 수 없는   **an incomprehensible question** 이해할 수 없는 질문

---

20 ☑ **inequality**
[ìnikwáləti]

ⓝ 불평등, 같지 않음

racial inequality 인종 불평등

---

21 inefficient
[ìnifíʃənt]
ⓝ inefficiency 비효율성

ⓐ 비능률적인, 효력이 없는

an inefficient system 비효율적인 체계

22 indigestion
[ìndidʒéstʃən]
ⓐ indigestive 소화 불량의

ⓝ 소화 불량

suffer from indigestion 소화불량으로 고생하다

23 infinite
[ínfənit]
ⓝ infinity 무한

ⓐ 무한한, 막대한

infinite patience 무한한 인내력

24 unemployment
[ʌnimplɔ́imənt]
ⓐ unemployed 실직한

ⓝ 실업, 실직

unemployment rate 실업률

25 inhumane
[ìnhju:méin]

ⓐ 몰인정한, 무자비한

an inhumane act 비인간적 행동

26 injustice
[indʒʌ́stis]

ⓝ 불공평, 부정

social injustice 사회적 불평등

27 nonmaterial
[nànmətíəriəl]

ⓐ 비물질적인, 영적인

nonmaterial value 정신적인 가치

28 insane
[inséin]
ⓝ insanity 광기

ⓐ 제 정신이 아닌, 미친

an insane idea 정신 나간 아이디어

29 insufficient
[ìnsəfíʃənt]
ⓝ insufficiency 부족, 결핍

ⓐ 부족한, 불충분한

insufficient exercise 운동 부족

30 malfunction
[mælfʌ́ŋkʃən]

ⓝ 오작동 **ⓥ** 오작동하다

system malfunction 시스템 오작동

31 □ **intolerance**
[intólərəns]
ⓐ **intolerant** 아량이 없는

ⓝ 편협, 참을 수 없음

religious intolerance 종교적 편협

---

32 □ **invalid**
[ínvəlid]
ⓝ **invalidity** 효력 없음, 무가치

ⓐ 실효성이 없는, 타당하지 않은

an invalid password 잘못된 비밀번호

---

33 □ **invaluable**
[invǽljuəbəl]

ⓐ 값을 헤아릴 수 없는, 매우 귀중한 an invaluable experience 매우 귀중한 경험

---

34 □ **irrational**
[irǽʃənəl]
ⓝ **irrationality** 불합리, 부조리

ⓐ 비합리적인, 이성을 잃은, 불합리한

irrational behavior 불합리적인 행동

---

35 □ **irreconcilable**
[irékənsàiləbəl]

ⓐ 화해할 수 없는

an irreconcilable difference 타협할 수 없는 차이

---

36 □ **irrelevant**
[iréləvənt]
ⓝ **irrelevance** 부적절, 무관계

ⓐ 무관한, 관계없는

an irrelevant question (논지와) 무관한 질문

---

37 □ **irresistible**
[ìrizístəbəl]

ⓐ 억누를 수 없는, 매혹적인

an irresistible desire 억누를 수 없는 욕망

---

38 □ **irresponsible**
[ìrispánsəbəl]
ⓝ **irresponsibility** 무책임

ⓐ 무책임한

irresponsible accusations 무책임한 비난들

---

39 □ **intact**
[intǽkt]
ⓝ **intactness** 온전함

ⓐ 온전한, 손상되지 않은

remain intact 온전히 남아있다

---

40 □ **malnutrition**
[mælnjuːtríʃən]

ⓝ 영양실조, 영양 부족

suffer from malnutrition 영양실조로 고통 받다

EXERCISE

A 다음 영어는 우리말로, 우리말은 영어로 옮기시오.

01 immense _____ 07 불법의, 비합법적인 _____

02 inhumane _____ 08 불평등, 같지 않음 _____

03 irreconcilable _____ 09 온전한, 손상되지 않은 _____

04 immortal _____ 10 소화 불량 _____

05 insufficient _____ 11 실효성이 없는 _____

06 incomprehensible _____ 12 위반하다, 모순되다 _____

B 다음 빈칸에 알맞은 단어를 쓰시오.

01 an inaccessible region _____

02 abnormal climate change _____

03 an irresistible desire _____

04 태곳적부터 from time _____

05 영양실조로 고통 받다 suffer from _____

06 정신적 가치 _____ value

C 다음 빈칸에 들어갈 알맞은 말을 고르시오. (필요하면 형태를 바꾸시오.)

| injustice | malfunction | infinite | immature | incoherent |

01 Parents care for their children with a(n) _____ amount of love.

02 Children are _____ and may not understand the need for everyday rules.

03 I was dumbfounded with his _____ answer.

04 Due to a technical _____, the plane was delayed for four hours.

05 In many third-world countries, there are many severe _____ against young children.

Crossword Puzzle

앞에서 배운 어휘를 기억하며 빈칸을 채워보세요.

1 i [ ] [ ] [ ] [ ] [ ] [ ] [ ] 2 c [ ]

3 i [ ] [ ] [ ] 4 i [ ] [ ]

6 i [ ] [ ] [ ] [ ]

5 i [ ]

7 i [ ] [ ] [ ] [ ]

8 i [ ] [ ] [ ] [ ]

9 i [ ]

10 i [ ] [ ] [ ]

11 i [ ] [ ] [ ] [ ]

Across

1 unwillingness to accept ways of thinking and behaving that are different from your own
3 not legally or officially acceptable
6 extremely large
7 very great in amount or degree
8 not broken, damaged, or spoiled
10 not allowed by laws or rules, or strongly disapproved of by society
11 extremely useful

Down

2 made to look exactly like something else, in order to deceive people
4 living or continuing forever
5 not based on clear thought or reason
8 not conforming to accepted standards of morality
9 not fully developed

Unit 48 Compound Words

01 ☑ breakdown
[bréikdàun]

🔵 (기계의) 고장, 파손, 붕괴, 몰락

a breakdown of a car 자동차 고장
a nervous breakdown 신경 쇠약

02 ☑ breakthrough
[bréikθrù:]

🔵 획기적 발전, 돌파구

a scientific breakthrough 획기적 과학발전

03 ☑ counterbalance
[kàuntərbǽləns]

🔵 대항 세력, 평형력

vital counterbalance 중요한 견제 수단

04 ☑ drawback
[drɔ́:bæk]

🔵 약점, 장애

a big drawback 큰 약점

05 ☑ intake
[íntèik]

🔵 섭취, 흡입

calorie intake 칼로리 섭취

06 ☑ lay-off
[leiɔ:f]

🔵 해고, 강제휴업

lay-offs of 100 employees 100명의 직원 해고

07 ☑ layout
[léiàut]

🔵 구획, 설계

an exterior layout 외부 설계

08 ☑ offspring
[ɔ́(:)fsprìŋ]

🔵 자식, 자녀, 후예

produce offspring 자손을 낳다

09 ☑ outback
[áutbæk]

🔵 (미개척의) 오지 ⓐ 오지의

visit the outback 오지를 방문하다
outback settlements 오지의 부락

10 outbreak
[áutbrèik]

ⓐ outbreaking
현재 일어나고 있는

ⓝ 발발, 급증

the outbreak of a plague 역병의 발발

---

11 outcast
[áutkæst]

ⓝ 쫓겨난 사람 **ⓐ** 쫓겨난

a social outcast 사회적 추방자
an outcast son 쫓겨난 아들

---

12 outcome
[áutkʌm]

ⓝ 결과, 과정

the total outcome 총체적 결과

---

13 outlaw
[áutlɔ̀:]

ⓥ 비합법화하다, 무법자로 선언하다 **ⓝ** 무법자, 불량배

outlaw smoking 흡연을 비합법화하다
a notorious outlaw 악명 높은 무법자

---

14 outlet
[áutlet]

ⓝ 출구, 방출구, 소매점

an outlet store 직매점

---

15 output
[áutpùt]

ⓝ 산출, 생산 **ⓥ** 산출하다, 출력하다

industrial output 산업 생산
output the data 자료를 출력하다

---

16 outrage
[áutrèidʒ]

ⓝ 난폭, 폭행, 격분

commit an outrage 무지막지한 짓을 하다
a sense of outrage 격분

---

17 outstrip
[áutstríp]

ⓥ 초과하다, 능가하다, 벗어나다

outstrip supply 공급을 초과하다

---

18 overlap
[òuvərlǽp]

ⓥ 부분적으로 ~위에 겹치다

overlap each other 서로 겹쳐 있다

---

19 overtake
[òuvərtéik]

ⓥ ~을 따라잡다, (다른 차를) 추월하다

overtake a taxi 택시를 추월하다

20 ☑	**runoff** [rʌnɔ́ːf]	**n** 흘러가 버리는 것, 결선 투표, 결승전	runoff water 흘러나오는 물 hold a runoff 결선 투표를 하다
21 ☑	**shortcoming** [ʃɔ́ːrtkʌ̀miŋ]	**n** 결점, 단점	correct one's shortcomings ~의 결점을 고치다
22 ☑	**sold-out** [sóuldàut]	**a** 매진된	a sold-out item 매진된 상품
23 ☑	**stockpile** [stákpàil]	**n** 비축량, 재고	world food stockpiles 세계 식량 비축량
24 ☑	**takeover** [téikòuvər]	**n** 인계, 탈취	a hostile takeover 적대적 인수
25 ☑	**tradeoff** [treidɔːf]	**n** 교환, 거래	a tactical tradeoff 전략적 교환
26 ☑	**turnover** [təːrnóuvər]	**n** 전도, 변경, 거래액, 이직률	a peaceful turnover of power 평화적인 권력 이양 turnover rate 이직률
27 ☑	**ultraviolet** [ʌ̀ltrəváiəlit]	**a** 자외선의, 자외선	an ultraviolet filter 자외선 필터
28 ☑	**underpaid** [ʌ̀ndərpéid] **v** underpay 저임금을 지불하다	**a** 저임금의, 박봉의	an underpaid worker 저임금 노동자
29 ☑	**undertake** [ʌ̀ndərtéik]	**v** 착수하다, 책임을 떠맡다	undertake the project 일에 착수하다

30 ☑ **upheave** [ʌphíːv]	**ⓥ** 들어 올리다, 혼란시키다	upheave the government 정부를 동요시키다
ⓝ upheaval 밀어 올림, 융기		

31 ☑ **uproot** [ʌprúːt]	**ⓥ** 뿌리 채 뽑다, 근절하다	uproot social evils 사회악을 근절하다

32 ☑ **upturn** [ʌptə́ːrn]	**ⓝ** 상승, 호전	a business upturn 경기 상승

33 ☑ **waterproof** [wɔ́tərprùːf]	**ⓐ** 방수의	a waterproof watch 방수 시계

34 ☑ **whereabouts** [hwɛ́ərəbàuts]	**ⓝ** 소재, 행방	the whereabouts of the suspect 용의자의 행방

35 ☑ **willpower** [wilpáuər]	**ⓝ** 의지력, 정신력	strong willpower 강한 의지력

36 ☑ **workout** [wə́ːrkàut]	**ⓝ** 연습, 트레이닝	get a workout 연습하다, 운동하다

37 ☑ **wrap-up** [rǽpʌ̀p]	**ⓝ** 요약, 결말	That's a wrap-up. 이것으로 일을 마쳤다.

38 ☑ **deadline** [dédlàin]	**ⓝ** 최종 기한, 마감	the deadline for applications 지원서의 최종 기한

39 ☑ **livestock** [láivstàk]	**ⓝ** 가축	livestock industry 축산업

40 ☑ **outburst** [áutbə̀ːrst]	**ⓝ** 폭발, 분출	an outburst of rage 분노의 폭발

EXERCISE

A 다음 영어는 우리말로, 우리말은 영어로 옮기시오.

01 outcast _____

02 tradeoff _____

03 uproot _____

04 breakdown _____

05 livestock _____

06 overtake _____

07 (미개척의) 오지, 오지의 _____

08 결점, 단점 _____

09 초과하다, 능가하다 _____

10 착수하다, 책임을 떠맡다 _____

11 소재, 행방 _____

12 자식, 자녀, 후예 _____

B 다음 빈칸에 알맞은 단어를 쓰시오.

01 the outbreak of a plague _____

02 upheave the government _____

03 commit an outrage _____

04 획기적 과학발전 a scientific _____

05 세계 식량 비축량 world food _____

06 칼로리 섭취 calorie _____

C 다음 빈칸에 들어갈 알맞은 말을 고르시오. (필요하면 형태를 바꾸시오.)

drawback	overlap	outburst	outlaw	underpaid

01 Buying alcohol on Sundays is _____ in certain American states.

02 It puzzled me that her smile suddenly turned into a(n) _____ of tears.

03 The _____ employees are often found working in dirty, dangerous, and demanding jobs.

04 One _____ of participating in competitive sports at an early age might be the inability to grow taller.

05 Since our weekday schedules _____, Maria and I hardly get to see each other except on weekends.

Across

2 the design or arrangement of something

5 to make something illegal

6 important discovery that happens after trying for a long time to understand

9 the place or area where someone or something is

10 to go past something by moving faster

Down

1 the result or effect of an action or event

3 a person's child

4 something that causes problems

7 to make yourself responsible for something and start doing it

8 to pull a plant and its root completely out of the ground

Word Mapping

앞에서 배운 어휘를 기억하며 빈칸을 채워 보세요.

정답

_____ 감상하다, 감사하다

_____ 지휘하다, 행동하다

_____ 재다, 방책, 치수

_____ 운명, 행운, 재산

_____ 올리다, 모금하다, 기르다

_____ 불법의, 비합법적인

_____ 비정상적인

_____ 실업, 실직

_____ 미숙의, 미완성의

_____ 오작동

Multi-Meaning Words
다의어

Negative Meaning Words
부정적 의미의 어휘

Other Words
기타 어휘

Compound Words
합성어

_____ 약점, 장애

_____ 고장, 파손, 붕괴

_____ 발발, 급증

_____ 착수하다, 책임을 떠맡다

_____ 난폭, 폭행, 격분

Appendices

Answers

Index

Answers

Chapter 1

Unit 1   p. 20

A

1 독백, 1인 극
2 승낙, 동의(하다)
3 울다, 훌쩍이다
4 구술의, 구두의
5 서로 작용하는, 대화식의
6 해석, 통역
7 demonstrate
8 mutter
9 reprimand
10 boastful
11 plead
12 bilingual

B

1 groan
2 persuasive
3 eliminate
4 understate
5 admit
6 verbal
7 glorification
8 seduction
9 proficient
10 prophesy
11 propose
12 dictate

C

1 chuckled
2 evaluate
3 contradiction
4 implored
5 prediction

Unit 2   p. 28

A

1 우화, 전설
2 은유, 상징
3 읽기 쉬운, 명료한
4 미적 감각의 있는, 미의
5 운문, 시
6 논평, 해설
7 genre
8 plot
9 postscript
10 manuscript
11 paradox
12 context

B

1 condense
2 story, tale
3 quote
4 summary
5 illiteracy
6 nonfiction
7 compose
8 criticize
9 complimentary
10 eloquent
11 theoretical
12 reference

C

1 complement
2 convey
3 literal
4 dialects
5 mediate

Unit 3   p. 36

A

1 묘사하다, 그리다
2 직관, 직감
3 단언하다, 주장하다
4 숙고하다, 사색하다
5 분석, 분해
6 모순된, 일치하지 않는
7 acknowledge
8 subliminal
9 alternative
10 criterion
11 stereotype
12 assess

B

1 infer
2 concept
3 refuse
4 complicated
5 disapproving
6 concrete
7 convince
8 meditate
9 hypothetical
10 resolute
11 clarification
12 comprehension

C

1 ambiguous
2 withhold
3 altered
4 indecisive
5 prejudice

Unit 4　　　　　　　　　　　　p. 44

A

1 공들인, 정교한	7 illustration
2 복사하다, 베끼다	8 refine
3 (영화 등의) 예고편, 미리 보기	9 adapt
4 찍다, 인쇄하다, 자국, 흔적	10 playwright
5 교묘한, 솜씨 있는	11 fantasy
6 연극의, 극장의	12 chronicle

B

1 outline	7 narrate
2 copy, mimic	8 perform
3 passage, section	9 marvelous
4 display	10 adornment
5 darken	11 theater
6 epilogue	12 entitlement

C

1 perspective
2 illiterate
3 quote
4 vulgar
5 biography

Unit 5　　　　　　　　　　　　p. 52

A

1 학장	7 admission
2 입학, 등록	8 ethics
3 인류학	9 sophomore
4 언어, 언어학	10 upbringing
5 (강의의) 계획	11 thesis
6 전문 지식	12 economics

B

1 instruct	7 certify
2 student, follower	8 coeducate
3 intellectual	9 disciplinary
4 highbrow	10 tuitionary
5 absence	11 element
6 materialism	12 extracurriculum

C

1 assignment
2 instructive
3 flunked
4 diploma
5 lowbrow

Chapter 2

Unit 6　　　　　　　　　　　　p. 62

A

1 산수, 셈의	7 equivalent
2 이중의, 두 배의	8 primary
3 (수학) 공식	9 stockpile
4 천 년간의, 천년기의	10 quotient
5 군중, 다수	11 fraction
6 4배가 되다, 4배의	12 approximate

B

1 immensity	7 equate
2 innumerable	8 notate
3 share	9 statistical
4 odd	10 massive
5 add	11 calculation
6 singular	12 abundance

C

1 Algebra
2 redundant
3 extent
4 multiply
5 reckon

A

1 양상, 모양, 점, 면
2 반원
3 정사각형, 제곱, 광장,
  정사각형의, 제곱의
4 한 조각, 일부
5 그림, 도형, 도식
6 나선형의, 소용돌이 모양의
7 erect
8 figurative
9 segment
10 scale
11 symmetry
12 dimension

B

1 superficial
2 noble
3 ratio
4 vertical
5 difference
6 increase
7 resemble
8 portray
9 analogous
10 geometric(al)
11 fluctuation
12 rectangle

C

1 comparative
2 parallel
3 phase
4 range
5 counterpart

A

1 빽빽하게 찬, 밀집한,
  압축하다
2 중간, 매개(물), 중간의
3 부분, 조각, 분해하다
4 높게 하다, 높이다
5 폭이 좁은, 부족한
6 반대의, 한쪽의, 반대로
  거꾸로
7 converse
8 location
9 cubic
10 void
11 edge
12 central

B

1 breadth
2 enlarge
3 volume
4 front
5 quality
6 sparse
7 evaluate
8 sink
9 rotate
10 broad
11 vacancy
12 space

C

1 Converse
2 layer
3 remote
4 summit
5 threshold

A

1 인접한, 즉시의, 가까운
2 말기의, 말단의,
  끝, 종점
3 주기적인, 정기적인,
  정기간행물
4 기간, 범위
5 시작, 개시, 공격
6 동시에 일어나다,
  일치하다
7 medieval
8 consecutive
9 synchronize
10 punctual
11 initial
12 preliminary

B

1 previous
2 antecede
3 coincident
4 modern
5 successor
6 diurnal
7 posterior
8 occasional
9 perenniality
10 century
11 imminence
12 priority

C

1 epoch
2 foremost
3 contemporary
4 dawn
5 posterity

414

Chapter 3

Unit 10 p. 96

A

1 경영진, 행정부
2 채용, 보충
3 지원서, 신청서, 적용
4 임대 계약
5 보증금, 예금, 예금하다, 맡기다
6 상품, 물자
7 bargain
8 donation
9 laborious
10 insurance
11 commute
12 transaction

B

1 dismiss
2 property
3 cooperation
4 combine
5 wholesale
6 boom
7 monopolize
8 afford
9 consumptive
10 bankruptcy
11 finance
12 commerce

C

1 monetary
2 receipt
3 guarantees
4 budget
5 bartering

Unit 11 p. 104

A

1 상속, 재산, 유산
2 다민족의
3 독창성, 독창력
4 귀족, 고귀함
5 왕국, 영역
6 고고학
7 advent
8 imperialism
9 privilege
10 practical
11 globalization
12 knight

B

1 traditional
2 empire
3 native
4 international
5 unstable
6 modern
7 vary
8 initiate
9 superstitious
10 revolutionary
11 feud
12 exoticism

C

1 convert
2 antecedent
3 ethnic
4 feudal
5 thrones

Unit 12 p. 112

A

1 순례자
2 도덕성, 윤리
3 금기, 금단
4 목사, 성직자들
5 악행, 비행, 범죄
6 섭리, 신
7 atheist
8 missionary
9 psychology
10 chapel
11 pastor
12 worship

B

1 ritual, rite
2 respect, honor
3 prohibition, prohibit
4 religious
5 disloyal
6 impolite
7 salvage
8 sermonize
9 dogmatic
10 charitable
11 divinity
12 benevolence

C

1 sanctuary
2 persecuted
3 pagan
4 appropriate
5 creed

Unit 13　　p. 120

A

1 강도, 빈집털이, 사기꾼
2 도망자, 탈주자, 도망하는
3 소송, 고소
4 증언, 증명
5 특허, 특허권
6 부정한, 타락한
7 apprehend
8 criminal
9 observe
10 execution
11 prosecute
12 attorney

B

1 verify
2 punishment
3 expel
4 restraint
5 illegitimate
6 genuine
7 constitute
8 validate
9 bribable
10 evident
11 judiciary
12 legality

C

1 convicted
2 smuggle
3 fraud
4 bill
5 senator

Unit 14　　p. 128

A

1 투표, 투표용지
2 군주, 왕
3 반역자, 반항자
4 (관청의) 국, 사무국, 사무소
5 거부권, 거부하다, 반대하다
6 (의무, 세금, 벌금 등을) 부과하다
7 autocracy
8 nominate
9 tyranny
10 regime
11 anarchy
12 dominate

B

1 appeal
2 congress
3 betrayer
4 representative
5 urban
6 unqualified
7 designate
8 administrate
9 autonomic
10 parliamentary
11 regulation
12 diplomacy

C

1 candidate
2 reign
3 council
4 abolished
5 Diplomatic

Unit 15　　p. 136

A

1 포장도로
2 분지, 대야
3 구역, 분야
4 쓰레기 매립지
5 교외, 근교
6 기울기, 비탈
7 congestion
8 swamp
9 geography
10 spectacle
11 monument
12 peninsula

B

1 stream
2 diversion
3 board
4 municipal
5 journey, quest
6 occidental
7 direct
8 erode
9 continental
10 eruptive
11 nomad
12 metropolis

C

1 nomadic
2 chartered
3 pedestrian
4 destination
5 expeditions

Chapter 4

Unit 16
p. 146

A

1 증발하다
2 세균, 병균
3 생명공학
4 조직
5 수소
6 염색체
7 carbohydrate
8 microbe
9 dissolve
10 fume
11 fungus
12 vapor

B

1 combine, mix
2 bud
3 sample
4 melt
5 mixture
6 rot
7 evolve
8 incubate
9 molecular
10 organic
11 biology
12 cultivation

C

1 duplicate
2 additive
3 fermented
4 genetic
5 phenomena

Unit 17
p. 154

A

1 위성
2 점성학, 점성술
3 적외선의
4 항해
5 별의, 별 같은
6 별자리, 성운
7 atmosphere
8 mercury
9 orbit
10 hemisphere
11 spacecraft
12 astronomy

B

1 disorder
2 rotate
3 scrutiny, exploration
4 uncanny
5 foreign, foreigner
6 surface
7 aviate
8 observe
9 equatorial
10 cometary
11 magnet
12 universe

C

1 supernatural
2 launch
3 gravity
4 revolve
5 earthly

Unit 18
p. 162

A

1 청동
2 중성자
3 직물
4 납
5 기압계
6 성분, 구성 요소
7 cluster
8 copper
9 nutrient
10 atomic
11 resource
12 handcraft

B

1 establish
2 appearance
3 device, equipment
4 component
5 material, stuff
6 genuine
7 rusty
8 geological
9 challenging
10 facility
11 radiation
12 hydroelectricity

C

1 leather
2 alchemy
3 facilitated
4 industrial
5 radioactive

Unit 19   p. 170

A

1 지체, 지연	7 conductor
2 기계 장치, 부품, 절차	8 transmission
3 도구, 기구	9 principle
4 기구, 설비	10 flashlight
5 순서, 절차	11 weave
6 전자의	12 manufacture

B

1 examine	7 generate
2 modify	8 censor
3 gauge	9 identical
4 immediate	10 pioneering
5 outdo	11 embroidery
6 simple	12 transformation

C

1 sophisticated
2 detector
3 implement
4 transformed
5 technical

Unit 20   p. 178

A

1 수혈하다, 주입하다	7 bruise
2 신진대사	8 symptom
3 당뇨병	9 handicapped
4 처방하다, 지시하다	10 ointment
5 구토하다	11 chronic
6 약국, 약학	12 syndrome

B

1 epidemic	7 abort
2 sanitation	8 infect
3 numb, disable	9 obese
4 suffocate	10 respiratory
5 inhale	11 diagnosis
6 mature	12 immunity

C

1 insomnia
2 antibiotic
3 contagious
4 nurture
5 sanitary

Unit 21   p. 186

A

1 눈보라	7 orchard
2 이슬비, 이슬비가 내리다	8 tropical
3 얼다, 얼리다	9 fountain
4 꽃잎	10 graze
5 유충, 모충	11 botany
6 해저의, 잠수함	12 downpour

B

1 current	7 pollinate
2 swamp	8 breezy
3 stalk	9 reptilian
4 meadow	10 torrential
5 dry	11 decomposition
6 flow	12 chill

C

1 blossom
2 frost
3 marsh
4 temperate
5 crude

Chapter 5

Unit 22 — p. 196

A
1 발표, 출판, 출판물
2 홍보, 광고, 명성
3 광고(업)
4 긴급한, 절박한
5 주의를 딴 데로 돌리다
6 한 품목, 신문기사
7 release
8 dispatch
9 correspondent
10 broadcast
11 propaganda
12 celebrity

B
1 collect, gather
2 inform, announce
3 reveal
4 excitement
5 partial, biased
6 prologue
7 inquire
8 circulate
9 voguish
10 distractive
11 transmission
12 virtuality

C
1 trend
2 editorial
3 monitor
4 classified
5 virtual

Unit 23 — p. 204

A
1 금지하다
2 고문(하다), 심한 고통
3 조화시키다, 화해시키다
4 결과적인, 결과로서 생기는
5 막다, 방해하다
6 불합리한, 어리석은
7 exclusive
8 hostage
9 negotiate
10 isolate
11 soothe
12 collapse

B
1 threaten, frighten
2 argue, argument
3 control, suppress
4 majority
5 integration
6 superior
7 discriminate
8 occupy
9 torturous
10 abusive
11 disruption
12 adversary

C
1 compromised
2 hypocrisy
3 expelled
4 abuse
5 controversial

Unit 24 — p. 212

A
1 자선을 베푸는 사람, 후원자
2 군중, 대중, 폭도
3 부서, 분할, 구분
4 반사, 반영
5 협력하다, 협동하다
6 일당, 당원, 당파심이 강한
7 confidential
8 representative
9 feminist
10 novice
11 mission
12 agenda

B
1 representative
2 protection, protect
3 crowd
4 distribute
5 swear
6 participate
7 unite
8 assimilate
9 riotous
10 reflexive
11 civilian
12 superiority

C
1 voluntary
2 correlation
3 bullying, bullied
4 flocked
5 headquarters

p. 220

A

1 야심적인, 대망을 품은
2 적수
3 해군 대장
4 넘겨주다, 항복하다, 인도
5 하사관
6 폭격하다, 퍼붓다
7 assassinate
8 colony
9 siege
10 fleet
11 warrior
12 armament

B

1 enemy
2 conquer
3 vengeance
4 boom
5 concord
6 careless
7 ally
8 confer
9 tactical
10 perilous
11 occupation
12 withdrawal

C

1 civilians
2 martial
3 treaty
4 assault
5 saluted

Unit 26 p. 228

A

1 산림 벌채, 산림 개간
2 멸종한, 활동을 멈춘
3 서식지
4 구충제, 살충제
5 피난, 피난처
6 황량한, 쓸쓸한
7 substitute
8 circumference
9 equilibrium
10 humidity
11 pollutant
12 deluge

B

1 intimidate
2 strengthen
3 pollute
4 prey
5 fertile
6 avoidable
7 emit
8 purify
9 ecological
10 filthy
11 preservation
12 evacuation

C

1 desertification
2 inevitable
3 fossilized
4 ecosystem
5 sufficient

Chapter 6

Unit 27 p. 238

A

1 굶주림, 기아
2 산, 산성의, 신맛이 나는
3 산장, 별장, 숙박하다
4 (음식이) 고급인, 값비싼, 미식가
5 굴뚝
6 거주자, 거주하는, 고유의
7 fiber
8 barn
9 texture
10 chore
11 sewage
12 grain

B

1 hallway, aisle
2 property
3 housing
4 clothes
5 nurture, feed
6 feast
7 decorate
8 leak
9 starve
10 spicy
11 seasoning
12 grease

C

1 greasy
2 litter
3 dormitory
4 domestic
5 starvation

Unit 28 — p. 246

A
1 기념일, 기념제
2 넓적다리
3 느긋한, 여유 있는
4 대, ~와 대비하여
5 임의의, 닥치는 대로의
6 소풍, 유람
7 corporal
8 mobile
9 slumber
10 posture
11 recreational
12 gamble

B
1 rest
2 bystander, onlooker
3 wander
4 essential
5 thin
6 voyage, sail
7 compete
8 attract
9 physiological
10 onlooking
11 spine
12 frailty

C
1 limbs
2 roamed / roam
3 vital
4 endurance
5 meager

Unit 29 — p. 254

A
1 성가심, 방해
2 부재자, 결석자
3 은퇴, 퇴직
4 급료, 임금
5 경비, 관리인
6 심부름, 볼일, 용무
7 frugal
8 spare
9 pension
10 property
11 allowance
12 peasant

B
1 financial
2 wasteful
3 expense, spending
4 generous
5 shortage
6 poor
7 deprive
8 thrive
9 professional
10 accumulative
11 dismissal
12 impoverishment

C
1 compensated
2 gross
3 ushering
4 vocational
5 subsidy

Unit 30 — p. 262

A
1 약속, 임명
2 일부일처
3 고아원, 보육원
4 주소 성명록, 전화번호부
5 임신
6 약속, 맹세, 약혼
7 colleague
8 descendant
9 immigration
10 marital
11 gender
12 association

B
1 endure, stand
2 inheritance
3 succeed
4 widower
5 feminine
6 deliberate
7 destine
8 form
9 hereditary
10 egoistic
11 intimacy
12 mutuality

C
1 acquaintances
2 fostered
3 spouse
4 intimate
5 relevant

Chapter 7

Unit 31 p. 272

A

1 애정, 감동	7 embrace
2 기쁘게 하다, 만족시키다	8 suspense
3 소중히 하다, 마음에 품다	9 fascinate
4 후회, 참회	10 despair
5 압도하다, 당황하게 하다	11 refrain
6 고독, 외로움	12 afflict

B

1 sadness	7 exclaim
2 comfort	8 enrage
3 surprise	9 compassionate
4 resentment	10 appealing
5 sympathy	11 affliction
6 aware, conscious	12 advocacy

C

1 apathy
2 rejoiced
3 dreadful
4 fanatic
5 resented

Unit 32 p. 280

A

1 명백한, 노골적인	7 anxious
2 자신 있는, 보증된	8 miserable
3 진심에서 우러난	9 vulnerable
4 변덕스러운, 변하기 쉬운	10 regrettable
5 비열한, 야비한	11 lamentable
6 감사의	12 dismal

B

1 perplexed, puzzled	7 deplore
2 offensive	8 oppress
3 friendly	9 nostalgic
4 optimistic	10 distressful
5 comfortable	11 shame
6 confident	12 contentment

C

1 contempt
2 agonizing
3 frustrate
4 panic
5 candid

Unit 33 p. 288

A

1 넘어지다, 비틀거리다	7 wither
2 (좋지 않은 일이) 일어나다	8 smash
3 자유롭게 하다, 해방하다	9 eradicate
4 던져 넣다, 뛰어들다	10 decline
5 뒤쫓다, 추구하다, 추격, 추구	11 extinguish
6 추진하다, 나아가게 하다	12 drain

B

1 postpone	7 receive
2 thrive, prosper	8 emerge
3 alleviate	9 explosive
4 detach	10 adherent
5 disobey	11 devastation
6 descend, decline	12 diffusion

C

1 whirled
2 fluttered
3 activate
4 elastic
5 emerging

Unit 34
p. 296

A

1 빻다, 부수다, 무너지다
2 평평하게 하다, 단조롭게 하다
3 떨다, 떨리다
4 게걸스레 먹다
5 오래 머무르다, 떠나지 못하다
6 비틀거리다
7 abandon
8 shrink
9 frown
10 relieve
11 pierce
12 extract

B

1 bestow, donate
2 comply, adjust
3 isolate, separate
4 worsen
5 shorten
6 accumulate, collect
7 yielding
8 impellent
9 perishable
10 bestowal
11 retrieval
12 forgery

C

1 subsided
2 penetrate
3 disguises
4 glimpse
5 repel

Unit 35
p. 304

A

1 ~의 탓[덕분]으로 하다
2 열렬한, 정열적인
3 지우다, 말살하다
4 열광, 열의, 열정
5 권유하다, 유도하다
6 노력하다, 발휘하다
7 accelerate
8 presume
9 deserve
10 liable
11 collaborate
12 feasible

B

1 appropriate, suitable, capable
2 support, maintain
3 positive, confirming
4 struggle, try
5 distracted
6 moderate
7 select
8 flex
9 urgent
10 zealous
11 caution
12 access

C

1 demanding
2 Beware
3 consciousness
4 intensive
5 obliged

Unit 36
p. 312

A

1 고상한, 예의 바른, 알맞은
2 모범적인, 칭찬할만한
3 무생물의, 생명이 없는
4 타당한, 적절한
5 최선의, 최적의
6 영원히 계속되는
7 fierce
8 portable
9 stale
10 competent
11 devoid
12 delicate

B

1 mandatory, obligatory
2 essential
3 constant, continual
4 celebrated
5 active
6 worthless
7 equivocate
8 possess
9 relative
10 impulsive
11 prominence
12 inaccuracy

C

1 hideous
2 exceptional
3 superficial
4 separation
5 prospective

Unit 37 p. 320

A

1 눈에 띄는, 현저한, 유명한
2 바싹 여윈, 피골이 상접한
3 흐린, 솜털 있는
4 두드러진, 뛰어난
5 가장자리, 변두리
6 대담한, 뻔뻔한
7 blunt
8 outfit
9 coordinate
10 gorgeous
11 skyscraper
12 drowsy

B

1 ambiguous
2 crude, rough
3 spiral
4 chubby
5 frugal
6 straight
7 convert
8 appear
9 chunky
10 characteristic
11 solidity
12 grandeur

C

1 distinctive
2 feeble
3 ornaments
4 tremendous
5 tilt

Unit 38 p. 328

A

1 명백한, 분명한
2 날카로운, 민감한
3 냄새, 향기
4 악취를 풍기는
5 동경하다, 그리워하다
6 감각을 잃은, 마비된
7 discomfort
8 temptation
9 humiliate
10 mute
11 strain
12 cowardly

B

1 unwilling, disinclined
2 silence, calmness
3 steady, constant
4 physical, unspiritual
5 stinking
6 proud
7 frighten
8 resolve
9 cursed
10 glittering
11 sanity
12 consolation

C

1 frigid
2 mourn
3 scent
4 queer
5 stimulus

Unit 39 p. 336

A

1 아늑한, 기분 좋은
2 꾸짖는, 비난하는
3 고상한, 품위 있는
4 결정적인, 확고한
5 비꼬는, 빈정거리는
6 자포자기의, 절망적인
7 cynical
8 logical
9 skeptical
10 satiric(al)
11 uninterested
12 hospitable

B

1 calm, peaceful
2 energetic
3 convincing
4 splendid
5 hostile
6 subjective
7 scorn
8 hesitate
9 mock
10 majesty
11 monotone
12 serenity

C

1 sinister
2 apologetic
3 compelling
4 mellow
5 lucid

Unit 40 p. 344

A

1 미친 듯 날뛰는, 광란의
2 악의적인, 심술궂은
3 인정이 있는, 사려 깊은
4 낙관적인
5 이성적인, 합리적인
6 분별 있는, 생각이 깊은
7 ruthless
8 rigorous
9 instinctive
10 naughty
11 liberal
12 malevolent

B

1 compassionate	7 irritate
2 careful	8 offend
3 obstinate	9 conserve
4 infamous	10 sociability
5 conservative	11 fever
6 modest, humble	12 cruelty

C

1 earnest
2 clumsy
3 tempers
4 negligible
5 rigid

Chapter 8

Unit 41   p. 354

A

1 (가치를) 떨어뜨리다, (가치가) 떨어지다	7 outlive
2 다재다능한, 다용도의	8 disparity
3 눈에 잘 띄는	9 shabby
4 자의적인, 임의의	10 bizarre
5 환호하다, 환호, 절찬	11 dubious
6 ~인 체하다, ~을 가장하다	12 commemorate

B

1 underestimate	7 inscribe
2 complicated	8 ecstatic
3 consistent	9 dissentient
4 necessary	10 fragility
5 identified	11 eminence
6 reveal	12 appraisal

C

1 discern
2 boosted
3 eccentric
4 lateral
5 premise

Unit 42   p. 362

A

1 꾀하다, 고안하다	7 condemn
2 잃다, 박탈당하다, 박탈, 몰수	8 provoke
3 연기하다, 정학시키다	9 downturn
4 몰래 움직이다	10 relinquish
5 꾸짖다, 비난하다	11 throb
6 흩뜨리다, 해산하다	12 deform

B

1 reveal, disclose	7 avertible
2 resist, challenge	8 recessive
3 desire	9 alien
4 hesitate	10 diversion
5 calm	11 flattery
6 efflux	12 submergence

C

1 evoke
2 triggered
3 demeanor
4 avert
5 convene

Unit 43   p. 370

A

1 취임, 개시	7 detest
2 〈종교〉 정통의, 전통적인	8 conspiracy
3 고집스러운, 완강한	9 mortgage
4 형제, 자매	10 authentic
5 회계 감사하다, 회계 감사	11 tariff
6 취소하다, 무효로 하다	12 exterminate

B

1 disaster	7 scrutinize
2 guarantee	8 evade
3 rebellion, rebel	9 catastrophic
4 pardon	10 homicidal
5 wicked	11 pathos
6 introvert	12 unanimity

C

1 renounced
2 itinerary
3 vicious
4 imperative
5 verdict

Unit 44 p. 378

A

1 인구 통계	7 latitude
2 어디에나 존재하는, 유비쿼터스	8 avalanche
3 가연성의	9 saturate
4 환기하다, 공기를 유통시키다	10 freight
5 총계의, 집합적인, 총계, 집합, 모으다	11 mutation
6 분열	12 exhaust

B

1 restraint, impediment	7 breed
2 emit	8 imprison
3 speed	9 combustive
4 powerful	10 digital
5 opaque	11 meteorology
6 incompatible	12 insulation

C

1 transparent
2 amplifies
3 compatible
4 corrosion
5 eclipse

Unit 45 p. 386

A

1 폐렴	7 ailment
2 침술	8 pimple
3 해독제	9 autopsy
4 홍역	10 lethal
5 가짜 약, 플라시보	11 fracture
6 설사	12 casualty

B

1 malconduct	7 anatomical
2 revive	8 deaf
3 worsen, harm	9 maternal
4 bend	10 alleviation
5 shrink	11 sterilization
6 aggravate	12 modification

C

1 impair
2 secretion
3 Cardiac
4 fetus
5 sprain

Chapter 9

Unit 46 p. 396

A

1 자본, 대문자, 수도	7 charge
2 숫자, 모양, 모습, 명사	8 measure
3 분명한, 꾸밈없는, 검소한, 평범한, 평지	9 physical
4 권위, 권력, 당국	10 conduct
5 ~의 진가를 인정하다, 감상하다, 고맙게 여기다	11 fair
6 증명, 증거, 막는, 견디는	12 interest

B

1 범죄 동기
2 자선 모금을 하다
3 중대한 책임

4 right
5 item
6 margin

C

1 contribute
2 currency
3 moderate
4 fortune
5 principal

Unit 47   **p. 402**

A

1 광대한, 막대한
2 몰인정한, 무자비한
3 화해할 수 없는
4 불멸의, 불사의
5 부족한, 불충분한
6 이해할 수 없는

7 illegal
8 inequality
9 intact
10 indigestion
11 invalid
12 contravene

B

1 접근이 어려운 지역
2 이상 기후 변화
3 억누를 수 없는 욕망

4 immemorial
5 malnutrition
6 nonmaterial

C

1 infinite
2 immature
3 incoherent
4 malfunction
5 injustices

Unit 48   **p. 408**

A

1 쫓겨난 사람, 쫓겨난
2 교환, 거래
3 뿌리 채 뽑다, 근절하다
4 (기계의) 고장, 파손
  붕괴, 몰락
5 가축
6 ~을 따라잡다, 추월하다

7 outback
8 shortcoming
9 outstrip
10 undertake

11 whereabouts
12 offspring

B

1 역병의 발발
2 정부를 동요시키다
3 무지막지한 짓을 하다

4 breakthrough
5 stockpiles
6 intake

C

1 outlawed
2 outburst
3 underpaid
4 drawback
5 overlap

Index

E

이것이 THIS IS 시리즈다!

THIS IS GRAMMAR 시리즈

▷ 중·고등 내신에 꼭 등장하는 어법 포인트 분석 및 총정리

강남인강
강의교재

THIS IS READING 시리즈

▷ 다양한 소재의 지문으로 내신 및 수능 완벽 대비

강남인강
강의교재

THIS IS VOCABULARY 시리즈

▷ 주제별로 분류한 교육부 권장 어휘

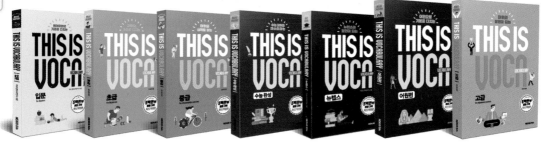

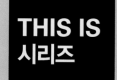

THIS IS 시리즈

무료 MP3 및 부가자료 다운로드
www.nexusbook.com
www.nexusEDU.kr

THIS IS GRAMMAR 시리즈
Starter 1~3   영어교육연구소 지음 | 205×265 | 144쪽 | 각 권 12,000원
초·중·고급 1·2   넥서스영어교육연구소 지음 | 205×265 | 250쪽 내외 | 각 권 12,000원

THIS IS READING 시리즈
Starter 1~3   김태연 지음 | 205×265 | 156쪽 | 각 권 12,000원
1·2·3·4   넥서스영어교육연구소 지음 | 205×265 | 192쪽 내외 | 각 권 10,000원

THIS IS VOCABULARY 시리즈
입문   넥서스영어교육연구소 지음 | 152×225 | 224쪽 | 10,000원
초·중·고급·어원편   권기하 지음 | 152×225 | 180×257 | 344쪽~444쪽 | 10,000원~12,000원
수능 완성   넥서스영어교육연구소 지음 | 152×225 | 280쪽 | 12,000원
뉴텝스   넥서스 TEPS연구소 지음 | 152×225 | 452쪽 | 13,800원

LEVEL CHART

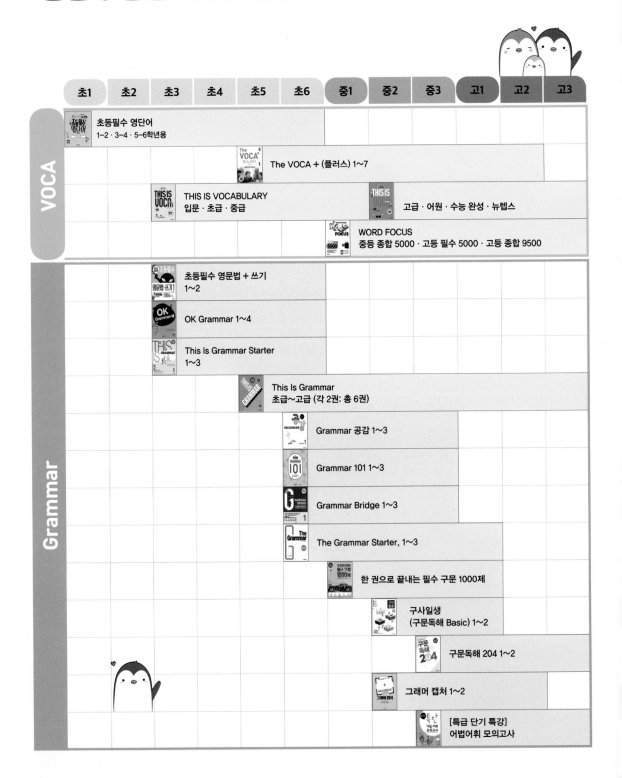

	초1	초2	초3	초4	초5	초6	중1	중2	중3	고1	고2	고3
VOCA	초등필수 영단어 1-2 · 3-4 · 5-6학년용											
				The VOCA + (플러스) 1~7								
			THIS IS VOCABULARY 입문 · 초급 · 중급				고급 · 어원 · 수능 완성 · 뉴텝스					
						WORD FOCUS 중등 종합 5000 · 고등 필수 5000 · 고등 종합 9500						
Grammar			초등필수 영문법 + 쓰기 1~2									
			OK Grammar 1~4									
			This Is Grammar Starter 1~3									
				This Is Grammar 초급~고급 (각 2권: 총 6권)								
					Grammar 공감 1~3							
					Grammar 101 1~3							
					Grammar Bridge 1~3							
					The Grammar Starter, 1~3							
						한 권으로 끝내는 필수 구문 1000제						
						구사일생 (구문독해 Basic) 1~2						
							구문독해 204 1~2					
							그래머 캡처 1~2					
							[특급 단기 특강] 어법어휘 모의고사					

초1	초2	초3	초4	초5	초6	중1	중2	중3	고1	고2	고3

Writing

공감 영문법+쓰기 1~2

도전만점 중등내신 서술형 1~4

영어일기 영작패턴 1-A, B · 2-A, B

Smart Writing 1~2

Reading

Reading 101 1~3

Reading 공감 1~3

This Is Reading Starter 1~3

This Is Reading 전면 개정판 1~4

원서 술술 읽는 Smart Reading Basic 1~2

원서 술술 읽는 Smart Reading 1~2

[특급 단기 특강] 구문독해 · 독해유형

[앱솔루트 수능대비 영어독해 기출분석] 2019~2021학년도

Listening

Listening 공감 1~3

The Listening 1~4

After School Listening 1~3

도전! 만점 중학 영어듣기 모의고사 1~3

만점 적중 수능 듣기 모의고사 20회 · 35회

TEPS

NEW TEPS 입문편 실전 250⁺ 청해 · 문법 · 독해

NEW TEPS 기본편 실전 300⁺ 청해 · 문법 · 독해

NEW TEPS 실력편 실전 400⁺ 청해 · 문법 · 독해

NEW TEPS 마스터편 실전 500⁺ 청해 · 문법 · 독해

NEW TEPS 완벽 반영

뉴텝스도 역시 넥서스!

그냥 믿고 따라와 봐!

600점 만점!!

마스터편
실전 500+

독해 정일상, 넥서스TEPS연구소 지음 | 17,500원　**문법** 테스 김 지음 | 15,000원　**청해** 라보혜, 넥서스TEPS연구소 지음 | 18,000원

500점

실력편
실전 400+

독해 정일상, 넥서스TEPS연구소 지음 | 18,000원　**문법** 넥서스TEPS연구소 지음 | 15,000원　**청해** 라보혜, 넥서스TEPS연구소 지음 | 17,000원

400점

기본편
실전 300+

독해 정일상, 넥서스TEPS연구소 지음 | 19,000원　**문법** 장보금, 써니 박 지음 | 17,500원　**청해** 이기헌 지음 | 19,800원

300점

입문편
실전 250+

독해 넥서스TEPS연구소 지음 | 18,000원　**문법** 넥서스TEPS연구소 지음 | 15,000원　**청해** 넥서스TEPS연구소 지음 | 18,000원

MP3 듣기
모바일 단어장
온라인 받아쓰기
정답 자동 채점

넥서스
NEW TEPS
시리즈

목표 점수 달성을 위한
뉴텝스 기본서 + 실전서

뉴텝스 실전 완벽 대비
Actual Test 수록

고득점의 감을 확실하게 잡아 주는
상세한 해설 제공

모바일 단어장, 어휘 테스트 등
다양한 부가자료 제공